THE HISTORICAL ESSAYS OF
OTTO HINTZE

THE HISTORICAL ESSAYS OF OTTO HINTZE

Edited with an Introduction by Felix Gilbert

With the assistance of Robert M. Berdahl

New York   OXFORD UNIVERSITY PRESS   1975

PREFACE

The writings of Otto Hintze concern not only the historical scholar working in the field of Prussian or German history but they are of interest to the general historian and the political scientist as well. They have wide applications for all scholarly endeavors in the fields of history and the social sciences. The publication of an English translation of Hintze's most important essays corresponds to a wish which has long been felt and frequently expressed.

Clearly it was not possible to publish more than a selection from the three large volumes of Otto Hintze, *Gesammelte Abhandlungen*, edited by Gerhard Oestreich, Göttingen, 1962–67. The choice was determined by two principles. All the main areas with which Hintze had been concerned—Prussian history, comparative history, and historical theory—were to be represented, and each of these sections ought to contain articles from the three periods into which Hintze's scholarly activity can be divided. Within these sections the essays are published in order of their appearance—with the exception of the article "The Hohenzollern and the Nobility," which is placed at the beginning of the section concerned with Prussian history because this article gives a survey of the entire course of Prussian history and helps the understanding of the two other, more specialized studies in this section. The choices which the Editor had to make were by no means easy. And he is aware that some reader might have given preference to articles he has not selected. But the readers ought to be aware that choices had to be made because space was limited and publication of a larger number of articles was not possible. In addition to the essay on Hintze's work and career at the beginning of the volume each article by Hintze begins with a brief explanatory introduction by the Editor which also directs attention to related work done by Hintze. Even if the volume is a selection, the reader should be able to get an impression of Hintze's entire *oeuvre*.

Hintze—not unlike Max Weber—was more concerned with finding for his complex ideas full and precise expression than with writing a simple and readable style. Translating of his essays was very difficult —much more difficult than the Editor had imagined when he undertook the task of editing Hintze's essays. Several attempts at finding a satisfactory translator failed, and at the end the translation has become the work of many hands. I want to mention Hugh West, who provided a basic English text for the most important of these essays, and Robert B. and Rita Kimber, to whom the Editor turned for a translation of Hintze's long review of Troeltsch, which because of its philosophical terminology offered particular difficulties. Robert M. Berdahl looked over all the translations and made an important contribution to their readability and precision. But the Editor must confess that he was ruthless in making changes whenever he believed that the translation did not fully reproduce Hintze's meaning. He must, therefore, accept final responsibility.

Some expressions, particularly terms of a technical character, could not be translated; they are explained by the Editor in footnotes at the bottom of the page. Hintze's original annotations are placed at the back of the volume; the advances in research have made Hintze's references to sources and literature somewhat obsolete, so that few readers will care to look at them. But they are reproduced because they have some historiographical interest since they illustrate the state of historical research in the first quarter of this century. Hintze's original footnotes usually give the titles of books in an abbreviated form and frequently without indicating year or place of publication; the footnotes in this volume have been adjusted to our scholarly standards; the titles of books are given in full and data about place and time of publication are provided.

In the course of my work on this edition I have received help and advice from many friends and colleagues. The undertaking itself is due to the initiative of Herbert Mann of the Oxford University Press. His interest in this project never flagged, and his helpful suggestions have extended to every aspect of the work, from its organization in sections to the contents of the Introduction. Throughout the entire work I could always rely on Peter Paret, whose advice was most valuable for the problem of selection, who indefatigably answered a large number of queries, and who finally gave his careful reading to

my Introduction. I would also like to mention that Robert M. Berdahl
not only examined the translations but every aspect of the work; his
collaboration improved the entire book immensely.

Among those who gave me advice in the selection of the essays I
would like to mention Gordon A. Craig, Dietrich Gerhard, and James
Sheehan, to whom I also owe useful comments on the Introduction.

F.G.

Princeton
November 1973

CONTENTS

THE HISTORICAL ESSAYS OF
OTTO HINTZE

INTRODUCTION

OTTO HINTZE
1861-1940

Those acquainted with the work of Otto Hintze are unanimous in regarding him as one of the most important, if not the most important, German historical scholar of the period of William II and the Weimar Republic. Yet the number of those to whom his writings are known is small; and his influence on historical scholarship, although profound and decisive in individual cases, has been limited. Hintze's fame has certainly not reached far beyond the German frontiers.

This neglect of one of the most important historians of the twentieth century can be explained. The foremost reason has been the inaccessibility of Hintze's writings. He published only one book of a narrative nature—*Die Hohenzollern und ihr Werk*—and even this book, although intended for the educated public, has a rather austere character. For the most part his studies were published as introductions to source publications or as articles in learned journals. A first, posthumous, incomplete collection of his essays appeared in Germany during the Second World War, and a revised and enlarged edition was published only recently.

Hintze was little concerned with the reception of his writings, and naturally this was a reflection of his temperament. Friedrich Meinecke, a close friend of his, wrote in his Memoirs that Hintze "was too proud to make his work easily accessible to the world," and added that many considered him "a knight in armor who did not open his visor and did not permit his face to be seen." Even in advanced age Hintze remained a tall, erect figure who fended off anyone whose words or behavior raised claims of familiarity. Hintze was not the type of academic who sought to impress others by his knowledge. He was cast in the mold of a high civil servant to whom distance and reserve in public contacts had become second nature. External circumstances reinforced these inclinations: illness, particularly steadily deteriorating eyesight, forced him to give up his professorship at the University of Berlin in 1920 when he was fifty-five years old. Thus his contacts with the outside world became even more restricted. His wife Hedwig Hintze, also an historian who taught as well at the University of Berlin, was eager to keep him in contact with historians of younger generations. Yet even to those who had the opportunity of meeting him, Hintze was a remote figure.

There has been a further obstacle to the recognition of Hintze's achievement. Through his training under Droysen and Treitschke in Berlin in the 1880s, and through his concern with the history of Prussia, Hintze has frequently been stamped as a prominent member of the Prussian Historical School and accordingly disposed of as representative of a historical trend that distorted history by subjecting it to a political aim: to the justification of the Prussian rule over Germany. It is indeed true that for many years Hintze was a collaborator on one of the chief enterprises of the Prussian Historical School, the *Acta Borussica;* that the chair of Constitutional and Administrative History, to which he was appointed at the University of Berlin in 1902, placed upon him the duty of teaching Prussian history; and that he was the last officially appointed Royal Prussian Historiographer. But it is misleading to deduce from this that Hintze shared the views and interests which had inspired the founders of the Prussian Historical School. When Hintze became a collaborator on the *Acta Borussica* the work of the Prussian Historical School had veered away from its original course. Moreover, Hintze had too independent a mind to accept traditional patterns of thought. He admired Prussian institutions and took great pride in the empire which Bismarck had founded. Yet its structure was for Hintze neither final nor perfect; he insisted on the need for adjusting its constitution to new social developments. Hintze never felt any sympathy for the Weimar Republic, but nothing was farther from his mind than restoration of the Hohenzollern monarchy. And there was never any doubt about his categorical rejection of the Nazi movement. His wife emigrated and then committed suicide when the Germans invaded the Netherlands, where she had found refuge. Hintze was unable to leave Berlin, but when the Prussian Academy sent him a questionnaire about his racial descent he added in his reply the blistering remark that withdrawal from an institution which asked such questions was for him a matter of course; he cut himself off from everything that happened in Germany after 1933 and in 1940 died in Berlin in loneliness and isolation.

I

When Hintze embarked on his scholarly career German historical scholarship was at its pinnacle. It was a model for historical work in most other countries, and the Prussian Historical School, although not without critics, was an essential part of the German historical establishment. Although Hintze was in many respects a product of this school, he should not be identified with it. It is in any case erroneous to consider the Prussian Historical School as possessing a fixed, unified outlook, unchanging in its political and historical ideas, interests, and methods. The leading Prussian historians were highly individualistic, and the school itself underwent numerous major developments. The historians of the middle of the nineteenth century who founded the Prussian Historical School—Droysen, Duncker, Treitschke—regarded history as an ethical process: the nations or states that prevailed were those embodying the higher morality. For the founders of the Prussian School the establishment of Prussian rule over Germany was a demand of morality; it allowed the application of all the means suitable to the desired end. Consequently in their study of Prussia these historians of the mid-nineteenth century focused on foreign policy, wars, and power politics.

But after Bismarck had united Germany by "blood and iron," an epoch of a different character followed, that of "the internal organization of political and economic life which was accompanied by party struggles and conflicts of interest."[1] Accordingly, the concern of the younger generation of historians of the Prussian School shifted from foreign policy and power politics to internal developments, to the administrative and economic history of the Hohenzollern state.

Whereas, the source publications which the older generation of Prussian historians had initiated—the *Urkunden und Aktenstücke zur Geschichte des Grossen Kurfürsten*, and the *Politische Correspondenz Friedrichs des Grossen*—were intended to throw light on the developments of the foreign policy of Brandenburg-Prussia, the *Acta Borussica*, begun in 1887, were to deal with internal administration of the Prussian state. The *Acta Borussica* owed their origin to a scholar of a younger generation, to the economist Gustav Schmoller; one of the first whom Schmoller invited to collaborate in this work was Hintze, then twenty-seven years old. When Hintze began working in Prussian history the study of administrative and economic issues had become an integral part of the problems with which the Prussian Historical School was concerned.

The shift in the direction of interest which took place in the Prussian Historical School was closely related to wider questions about the nature and aims of historical scholarship—questions that became a central point of discussion during the last decade of the nineteenth century. The triumphant emergence of historical scholarship during the nineteenth century and the pre-eminence of German historical scholarship were due to the theoretical and methodological principles which underlay the work of Leopold von Ranke, who had just died ninety-one years old, when Hintze began to work in the *Acta Borussica*.

The foundations of Ranke's historical thought were formed by his doctrine of ideas and his notion of uniqueness (individuality). Europe was for Ranke the center of history, and Europe's history was the history of the world; the intermingling and the clashes of the two racial groups that lived in Europe—the Latin and Teutonic peoples —had created a political system which consisted of a number of independent nations and states, each of them different from the other, each of them embodying an original and individual idea. The competition and the clashes among them had been the decisive factor in shaping the unique character of each of these nations and states. These assumptions suggest some of the characteristics of Ranke's historical writings and of the shape that historical scholarship took under his influence: emphasis on foreign policy as the factor determining the life of states; rejection of causality and laws in history and of the idea of progress because of the uniqueness of historical phenomena; limitation of the historian's task to description of the unique and individual so as to reveal the richness and variety of life.

Ranke's views of history reflected the romantic and idealistic trends which prevailed in the first half of the nineteenth century; they became far less compatible with the intellectual atmosphere that developed in the last quarter of the nineteenth century. The rapid and astounding advances in the natural sciences seemed to proclaim that only researches which proceeded from the observation of single cases to the formulation of valid generalizations could claim to be scientific. Areas of historical developments such as those in economics could be explained as determined by laws. And the experimental-scientific approach to psychology then arousing wide attention seemed to show the dependence of human nature on external conditions and stimuli, and to indicate the possibility of shaping and changing human nature by means of changes in surroundings. It was natural to ask whether in the face of these discoveries and developments the Rankean assumptions could be maintained, and whether it was not necessary to adjust work in history to the advances in other fields of knowledge.

In almost all European countries voices were heard that demanded a re-examination of the assumptions of historical scholarship and a reorientation of historical work. From England there came Bury's emphatic statement that "history is a science"; Henri Berr in France began to advocate *"histoire de synthèse";* and the "New History" of James Harvey Robinson and Charles Beard in the United States is a later offshoot of the same trend. The immediate impact of the historical revisionists in France, England, and other European countries was not great, although gradually and slowly they had some influence on transforming the subject matter and methods of historical scholarship.

In Germany it was different, and the dispute over methods which took place at the end of the nineteenth century and the outcome of the dispute proved to be nearly fatal for the development of German historical scholarship. The struggle was conducted with a passionate vehemence that frequently degenerated into personal abuse. It is called the *Lamprecht Streit,* because Karl Lamprecht, who had done important work in medieval economic history, was the chief protagonist in the struggle for a change in historical outlook and methods. He opened the fight in 1896 with an essay which bore the characteristic title "Old and New Trends in German Historical Scholarship," and the polemic which this treatise triggered and in which most of the better-known German historians became involved continued for several years. Lamprecht's attack on the German historical establishment ended in complete failure; and his few pupils became outsiders in the German historical profession. If German historians had always been inclined to concentrate on foreign affairs and political history, this attitude was now rigidified into a doctrine: The primary subject of history was political history. Although it was not immediately noticeable, from this time on German historical scholarship ceased to be the stimulating and leading influence it had been throughout the nineteenth century.

The categorical, contemptuous rebuff to demands for a new direction in historical scholarship may be ascribed to the fact that Lamprecht had presented these demands in the form of a pointed attack on Ranke. Lamprecht asked that Ranke's political history be replaced by a history of culture. He called Ranke's doctrine of ideas mystical; he suggested that the historian should aim at arriving at generalizations rather than merely at describing the unique, at analyzing the general intellectual atmosphere of a time rather than the thoughts or actions of individuals. And Lamprecht believed that psychology offered the possibility of revealing the evolution of the human mind, so that the study of the collective psychology in the various periods of the past would make possible discovery of a strictly logical and causal connection in the historical process. What was more, he suggested that Hegel was right, as against Ranke, in assuming the existence of a logical progress in history.

Had Lamprecht's demand for a new direction in history been presented in a less polemical and aggressive form, it might have aroused less attention but might also have been more effective. Against the attempt to disparage the work of the revered master of their profession, the German historians closed ranks.

For an appreciation of Hintze's thought and work the issues of the *Lamprecht Streit* are important because they allow a glance at Hintze's historical views and position when his apprentice years were over and he was beginning his work as a university teacher (1895). Meinecke has told us how in debates among youthful colleagues Hintze always insisted: "There are laws in history"; and his work in the *Acta Borussica*, with its emphasis on economic issues, must have made him aware of the limitations in Ranke's historical concepts. Hintze's intervention in the Lamprecht struggle—according to Meinecke "the best that was said about Lamprecht"—was remarkably moderate.[2] Hintze recognized the feasibility of going beyond Ranke and the desirability of broadening the ranges of history. "To use a geographic metaphor, we want to know not only the range and summits but also the base of the mountains, not merely the heights and depths of the surface but the entire continental mass." Hintze asserts that there is a natural tendency toward a regular pattern in the development of a nation. Nevertheless, in history general factors interact with individual factors, so that the forces which work and conflict in the historical process acquire an individual character. The unique is a basic inexplicable element in history and there is valid truth in the views which Ranke had so brilliantly set forth.

Hintze's attitude in the Lamprecht struggle reveals the problem—one might almost say dilemma—that remained crucial to his views on the theoretical questions in history. In fundamental respects Hintze adhered to the Rankean tradition. He was a political historian who placed great emphasis on foreign policy as a determining force; he regarded European history and the development of a European state system as the central event in the historical process; he upheld the role of the unique and individual as an important, unexplainable factor in history; and he did not deny that ideas influenced the course of history. But Hintze believed also in the existence of physical and psychological needs and necessities which evoked identical human reactions and whose fulfillment required a basically identical institutional structure. The action of the individual took place within a structural pattern that had its own laws. Analysis of the interaction between the necessarily evolving general pattern and the influence of individual factors and actions on shaping its particular character became the task of the historian. This task was not—or not primarily—attainment of new insights in the richness and variety of life, but improvement of the possibilities for correct action in the present by analyzing the various factors and forces that had given the present its particular character and were working in it.

II

Although this problem—the relation of individual factors and forces to general patterns of behavior and action—is at the core of all of

Hintze's historical studies and theoretical reflections, its pursuit takes different forms in the course of his life: three periods can be clearly distinguished in his intellectual production.

The first is identical with that of his active participation in the work of the *Acta Borussica* from 1888 to 1910; naturally, the research and the scholarly activities of this period were concerned with the history of Brandenburg and Prussia, and the main scholarly achievements of these years were the book-length introductions to the documentary volumes he edited for the *Acta Borussica:* on the Prussian silk industry (1892) and on the Prussian bureaucratic structure at the time of the accession of Frederick the Great (1901). In connection with the second work, Hintze also published briefer studies on the administration of Brandenburg and Prussia in the time of the Elector Joachim II and that of the first King.[3]

Although clearly an immense amount of labor, care, and thought had gone into the explanation of a rather ill-defined and rudimentary administrative structure, Hintze's studies on these subjects remained somewhat static. They appeared to be the detailed presentation of a table of organization rather than a demonstration of the effects of bureaucratic action on social life. Yet, by describing in detail what government did and could do, and by indicating to what extent its actions were dependent on and limited by communications, the structure of agriculture and trade and the availability of human resources, Hintze revealed the limits of monarchical power. In contrast to the traditional view of the "Great Hohenzollern" as creators of a new society and a new state, Hintze showed that the power which the monarchs exerted was limited by institutions created and shaped by the needs inherent in every society. The bureaucracy was the instrument of the rulers, but an instrument that followed its own rules. Only in relation to the impact which a ruler exerted on the functioning of the existing institutions was it possible to judge whether and to what extent the individual Hohenzollern prince was an innovator or reformer. However, Hintze was less interested in evaluating the achievements of the individual Hohenzollern than in readjusting the relation between change and continuity. "Below the upheavals in the court circles the basic political and social institutions preserve their coherence and advance in slow transformation; in this historical continuity becomes visible."[4] Hintze provided a demonstration of his views on the decisive importance of institutional continuity in his study "Prussian Reform Movements before 1806."[5] The study was revolutionary in that it broke with the accepted historical picture in which all light was focused on the work of the Prussian reformers and no judgment harsh enough could be found for the actions and ideas of the statesmen of the preceding period. Admittedly, Hintze's study was influenced by Tocqueville, who had demonstrated that the French Revolution continued and completed the work of the *Ancien régime;* but such a thesis had never been put forward in Prussian history. Hintze's essay has exerted great influence on all later work in this field.

Next to the issue of the relation between individual initiative and institutional continuity there was another problem which Hintze probed thoroughly during this first period of his scholarly career: that is the question of the interconnection existing among all social activities and their subordination to one central political purpose. In his introduction to the volume on administration in the *Acta Borussica,* Hintze wrote that "The cultural and welfare programs of the state yield to the requirements of power politics." Hintze did pioneering work on the economic—particularly industrial—activities in eighteenth-century Prussia, and was clearly deeply interested in these aspects of history. But it is doubtful whether he would have worked along these lines if the economic policy of the government had not been a crucial factor in making possible the maintenance of a large army and the rise of Prussia to a Great Power.

As we mentioned before, there was no doubt in Hintze's mind as to the validity of Ranke's thesis of the primacy of foreign policy, but Hintze modified and broadened it. If Ranke had meant that considerations of foreign policy must take precedence over all other political considerations and that other political interests and aims should be tackled only when and after the external security of the state was guaranteed, Hintze extended the thesis by maintaining that the government ought to aim at orienting all activities in the state—most of all, economic activities, but also education—toward strengthening the state against outside powers; concretely, the purpose toward which all governmental activities were to be directed was the maintenance of a strong military posture.

The first studies in which Hintze went beyond the Prussian sphere were devoted to an examination of the general validity and applicability of this thesis. In the essay "Military Organization and the Organization of the State"[6] he emphasized the role which the "pushing and pressing" of states against each other had in forcing each state to seek an appropriate military organization and consequently in shaping the state's internal structure. In the essay "The Formation of States and Constitutional Development"[7] Hintze tried to demonstrate the existence of a relation between the size of a state, its available means of organization, the character of its religion, the extent of its political integration, and its constitutional form. Hintze asserted that it should be possible to establish a typology of constitutional forms of which constitutions existing in the present or in the past were individually modified embodiments; and he suggested also that the particular form which the constitutional life of a state took was a modification of a general pattern underlying all constitutional development.

With these studies Hintze went far beyond his original interest in Prussian history and entered the broader field of general European history; the problems he raised in these articles occupied him throughout his life and became the center of his attention in the second period of his activity—after he had left the Acta Borussica.

This might be the place to comment on the influence of Hintze's work in Prussian history on the development of his theoretical ideas. It was very fruitful because it made him aware of the impact that administration had on the general course of politics, not only in Prussia but in all of European history. But Hintze's point of departure—Prussian history—also played a role in causing what might be regarded as limitations and weaknesses in his approach.

Prussia was for him a model, particularly a model of the absolutist state, which he regarded as a pre-formation of the modern state. Hintze therefore never asked whether the strict regimentation in eighteenth-century Prussia, particularly the organization of economic life according to the will and aim of the absolutist monarch, and its reason in the fact that the nations and states of Central and Eastern Europe were underdeveloped in comparison to the economically more advanced societies of Western Europe. Hintze's understanding of French and English history, although far-reaching and penetrating, had its blind spots. He subordinated economics to politics; in the relation between the state and its economic forces he viewed the government as the active partner which provided impetus and direction.

Hintze did not want to admit that the world of economic life had its own particular driving force and its own gravity. He was not fully aware of the complexity of the relations between the state and economic forces. This was not a serious drawback, insofar as early modern European history was concerned; and his studies of this period are his masterpieces. It is also not surprising that after the First World War he followed developments in Russia and Italy with an interest in which comprehension and criticism were finely balanced.[8] But of the development of democratic governments in the nineteenth century he had less understanding; and although all his writings show that economic developments were for him an essential part of history, we look in vain in his writings for an investigation of the rise of an industrial enterprise or a study of the development of labor. Such phenomena interested him only insofar as they came within the compass of political or governmental action. He looked upon social life from the viewpoint of government; he was above all a political historian. And in his writings up to 1920, traces may be found of a mystical belief in the state as a higher entity with a life of its own.

Hintze's notions appear highly idiosyncratic in our time, when social historians give concentrated attention to conditions and attitudes existing and developing beneath and outside the political sphere. But because there is some danger that modern social studies may come to consist of collections of factual material without meaningful results or conclusions, Hintze's approach—although perhaps overestimating what political action and governmental direction can achieve—has the merit of suggesting that studies of isolated phenomena must be complemented by investigations that show political and social life as an interconnected whole. Even if Hintze's views are no longer fully acceptable, they have value as a corrective.

III

The second period of Hintze's scholarly work begins around 1910 with his withdrawal from active participation in the *Acta Borussica,* and extended over the next ten years. The enormous amount of archival research which collaboration in the *Acta Borussica* had required collaboration had put a severe strain on his eyes from which they never fully recovered. But new, widened historical concerns rather than physical necessity provided the spur for a change in the direction of his work.

Hintze had become primarily interested in pursuing the course on which he had embarked in his essays "Military Organization and the Organization of the State" and "The Formation of States": the investigation of problems related to administration and constitutional affairs within the framework of general European history. Indeed, in 1908 and 1910 he published two articles—"The Origins of the Modern Ministerial System"[9] and "The Commissary and His Significance in General Administrative History"[10]—which may be regarded as single chapters in a history of European administration. These essays are superb pieces in raising questions that had never been asked before, in assembling and controlling an almost unending mass of source material, and in focusing this material on the solution of a specific problem.

According to Hintze these are studies of a comparative nature. But they are comparative history only in a limited sense. The essays deal with developments in different European countries which have a common root, and Hintze demonstrates the presence of such common root by examining the situation existing before the formation of different national entities in Europe. Comparisons serve to show the existence of a common element behind the institutional variations which developed in the course of time. Comparisons are illustrations; they do not form the point of departure for raising questions or indicating problems that need investigation. Hintze assumed that the situation which led to the development of an administrative structure was identical in almost all Latin-Teutonic peoples. From the same beginnings they all developed a centralized bureaucracy, and each government was composed of ministers in charge of departments with separate functions. The means, however, by which these institutional developments came about and the extent of power which bureaucracy and ministers possessed depended on circumstances in which external factors—particularly issues of security and actions of individuals—played their role. Thus, although fundamental needs were identical, led to similar patterns of development, and produced institutions resembling each other, the bureaucratic structure and the ministerial system of each European country had its peculiar aspects and features and each was a unique formation. The difference between the English system of government and those of the Continental countries was among the most striking examples of a deviation from a common pattern.

In these articles Hintze demonstrated also that changes in the methods of government are not purely nor even primarily the result of necessary technical changes or improvements, but are produced by shifts in the distribution of power within the state and by the need for adjustment to new external threats and new social forces. In this way administrative history becomes not only a mirror but also an integral part of European history, as well as a means by which the various stages of its development can be more sharply delineated. These two studies are administrative history in a new key; and it must be added that few, if any, works of similar scope and importance have been done in this field since then.

Hintze's intention of concentrating his future efforts on a "constitutional and administrative history of the modern European states" was clearly stated in his response to the address with which he had been welcomed to membership in the Prussian Academy in 1914. One might find this same intention of occupying himself with a broader area in the fact that in 1909, in four small volumes, he brought out a collection of his studies and essays mostly concerned with Prussian history, so that, taken together, they could be considered as a summary and *finis* of his works and views on Prussian history.

Although in the life of a writer or scholar different periods of activity may be distinguished, they can never be sharply separated; either because of previously entered commitments, or because of the intellectual investment he has made, he will keep up his contacts with his previous interests. In the decade following his departure from the *Acta Borussica,* Hintze continued to publish a considerable number of articles on Prussian history. Two of them deserve particular attention because they reveal his theoretical views and attitudes to the problem of Prussia. In the article "Preussens Entwicklung zum Rechtsstaat,"[11] Hintze criticizes the general view that an independent judicial power or political guarantees were sufficient to establish the rule of law in a political body; he considered the establishment of a code of administrative procedures as crucial. Clearly this study is not only an assertion of the importance of administrative issues for history and politics but also a defense of Prussia, which, though it might have lacked some of the usual features providing safety against authoritarianism, possessed a thoroughly organized and strictly regulated administrative structure.

The other article—"The Hohenzollern and the Nobility"[12]—is of a more critical nature. Hintze assails the view that Prussian tradition demanded the maintenance of a dominating influence of the East Elbian nobility. Although he does not deny that during a certain period the cooperation of monarch and nobility was crucial in establishing Prussia as a Great Power, he emphasizes the tensions and conflicts which originally characterized the relations between the Hohenzollern and the nobility, and he maintains that with the rise of a new industrial society the monopoly of power by the nobility could no longer be justified.

Some of Hintze's articles on Prussian subjects during these years may have been results of research undertaken in the course of his work on the *Acta Borussica;* others may have been by-products of the book *Die Hohenzollern und ihr Werk,* on which he worked in these years and which appeared in 1915. The article "The Hohenzollern and the Nobility" in particular was a short résumé of the basic views which he had explained in the larger work, which might be regarded as the last but also the best history of Prussia written by a member of the Prussian Historical School. Yet one might question, whether, during this period, when his interests had gone beyond the borders of Prussia, Hintze would have undertaken the task of writing a comprehensive history of Prussia had it not been his duty as Royal Prussian Historiographer to celebrate the five-hundredth anniversary of Hohenzollern rule in Brandenburg-Prussia.

Yet there was a compelling reason why it was difficult, if not impossible, for Hintze to lay aside the problems of Prussian and German history: the increasingly critical period into which German politics had entered after 1905—internally, the steady growth of the Social Democratic Party, and externally, the formation of the Entente Cordiale and the Triple Entente. Hintze's basic political attitude was not different from that of most professors at Prussian universities. They considered themselves influential civil servants who expected from the government ample support in all that concerned the conditions of their work. But they also felt it their duty to render loyal service to the monarch. They gave advice to the government; if they recommended reforms their intention was to make only the necessary adjustments to changed circumstances in order to maintain the existing system. To the outside world Prussian professors or academicians were defenders of the status quo, not its critics.

It was almost a matter of course that Hintze would write frequently on the political issues of his time and that he would take his stand on the side of the government. It must be admitted that he used his historical expertise to become a committed and persuasive advocate of the main tenets of the government in domestic and foreign policy. Hintze rejected parliamentarism in favor of the existing half-constitutional, half-authoritarian régime, and advocated the building of a navy that would permit Germany to enter upon *Weltpolitik* and become a world power.

For the Hintze of this period Prussia's importance reached beyond a particular period of history. It was not only the model of an absolutist state; its structure enjoyed features that every healthy modern state ought to possess.

Maintenance of the privileged position which the nobility possessed in eighteenth-century Prussia was no longer justifiable. In the same manner that the Hohenzollern monarchs had fought and tamed the nobility and taught them to become valuable servants of the kings of Prussia, monarchy and civil service now had the function and the duty to grant bourgeoisie and workers the position due to them and to establish the right balance among the various groups of society. Monarchy and civil service stood above parties and classes, and could and should act as arbiters among them. As Hintze explained in the article "Das Monarchische Prinzip und die konstitutionelle Verfassung" (1911),[13] the guiding and directing position of monarch and civil service had been brought about because in Prussia "in the age of absolutism the state has almost entirely absorbed society with its economic interests."[14] The reasons for the maintenance of a strong authoritarian system in Prussia-Germany were historical, which meant that the reasons for the rise of parliamentarism were historical also; thus parliamentarism should not be assumed to be a progressive step above monarchical constitutionalism. In Hintze's view it was a complex concatenation of events which resulted in the establishment of a parliamentary republic in France; under other circumstances France could have become a constitutional monarchy like Prussia. In any case, "the monarchical principle has become so intertwined with the entire political structure in Prussia and Germany that, without the complete transformation that only a revolution could bring about, it cannot be replaced by the principle of parliamentary government."[15]

As always with Hintze, however, the explanation of an individual phenomenon was complemented by a general one; and the genetic explanation was supplemented by a functional one. The existence of a competitive European state system in which the various powers "push and press" against each other required—at least on the European continent—a political organization in which military needs are of primary importance. The constitutional monarchy in Prussia-Germany epitomized this requirement: "The most essential reason for our monarchical constitutional system of government is the fact that we are surrounded by the greatest military powers of the Continent and that an enormous military-political pressure from the outside weighs upon our long frontiers which nature has given no protection,"[16] wrote Hintze in his essay "Machtpolitik und Regierungsverfassung" (1913).

These notions are a direct—and almost crude—application of the idea of the primacy of foreign policy. The same idea in a somewhat modified form made Hintze a protagonist of German *Weltpolitik*. If in previous centuries the "pushing and pressing" that controlled the formation of states and their internal life had been limited to Europe, rivalries and tensions now began to extend over the entire globe; any state that remained content with what it had in Europe would sink to the level of a second-rank power; if a state wanted to remain a Great Power it would have to take part in this race for overseas possessions.

In the essay "Imperialism und Welt-Politik"[17] (1907), Hintze distinguished twentieth-century imperialism from the imperialism of earlier times which aimed at establishment of one empire comprising the entire known world. The new imperialism of the twentieth century, according to Hintze, is a historical necessity, a step forward in the process of history. "The movement of imperialism appears to introduce a new epoch in the political balance of power. The old European system of states is to be replaced by a new world-system of states; the powers begin to arrange themselves on this new broadened base and to delimit among each other their spheres of interest."[18]

Hintze realized that overseas expansion required the creation of a strong German navy, and that a particular purpose of naval construction would be to check British power. To Hintze, Great Britain was the great obstacle to the establishment of a world-state system and a global balance of power; Great Britain sought to maintain an empire of the old style—one that exerted domination or at least control over the entire world. Thus, Britain's traditional policy was in opposition to what Hintze regarded as the desirable feature of world politics: "Not *one* world empire is the aim of modern imperialism, but a number of world empires, coexisting or equally independent, and in a balance of power similar to that which existed in the old European system of states."[19] When the first World War began, Hintze conceived of it chiefly as a struggle "to destroy the predominance of England." "The requisite of a true balance of power in the world-state system at which we aim is England's abandoning her claim to domination of the seas."[20] In Hintze's mind Germany pursued in the first World War the just aim of preventing England from establishing its rule over the world.

In all Hintze's political discussions the factors of national security and military strength played a prominent role; one is even tempted to say that his misjudgments reflect the influence which military considerations exerted on his historical and political thought; Prussian military thinking inclined to focus on land warfare and tended to underestimate or overlook the problems that arose when their plans extended beyond the Continent. Despite shrill and repellent notes, however, his political views should not be judged particularly nationalistic or militaristic; in their main political content they are those of the professional and social group to which he belonged; and it might even be said that, in contrast to the emotional chauvinism that many of his colleagues displayed, Hintze always argued coolly and rationally; and he never disparaged the historical achievements of other nations, nor did he deny their right to exist. It is important, however, to be aware that in this period of his scholarly and academic activity when Hintze began to work in a wider scholarly field, he still remained firmly tied to the problems, the traditions, and also the prejudices of the world in which he lived, that of imperial Germany; the continued existence of this bond indicates the extent of the reorientation which the collapse of this world made necessary for him.

IV

In Hintze's case the shock of defeat and revolution in Germany in 1918/1919 was aggravated by its impact on his scholarly concerns and tenets. Prussia, although it continued to exist, had lost all the features that had made it in Hintze's eyes a unique formation and in many respects a model. The outcome of the war demonstrated that the authoritarianism of a constitutional monarchy did not guarantee superior military order or strength. Nor did a constitutional monarchy, in contrast to what Hintze had believed and written, appear to be more than a transitional stage on the road to parliamentary democracy. In foreign affairs Germany's career as a world power had been terminated before it had really begun, and the influence and strength that non-European powers like the United States and Japan had acquired undermined Hintze's thesis that the European state system would be succeeded by a world-state system in which, in a widened theater, the same European powers that in the past had been the driving forces in world history would continue to have the dominating role.

The questions which the course of political events necessarily raised for Hintze's historical thinking were intensified by events in his personal life. He was pursued by illness, his eyesight further deteriorated, and he gave up his professorship at the University of Berlin, making use of his right to early retirement. These circumstances determined the form and character which his scholarly work took in the last period of his life, after his retirement from the University in 1920.

Hintze's weak eyesight made it impossible for him to undertake archival research, and he had to be economical in his reading. There was little chance of his completing the large work on European administrative and constitutional history which he had projected before the war; instead he expressed his ideas in a number of lengthy essays. One can observe that most of the material on which these essays were based—whether sources or monographic literature—had been published before or during the first World War; it was then that he had studied this material. Even the essay "Calvinism and Raison d'Etat in Early Seventeenth-Century Brandenburg" of 1931,[21] which uses archival material, is written on the basis of excerpts made in earlier years in the context of his work in the *Acta Borussica*. He returned to these notes because he had developed a special interest in the influence of Calvinism, as a result of an intensive study of the writings of Max Weber in the 1920s, and he wanted to investigate Weber's thesis in a concrete case. This procedure—examination of the historical validity of modern theories on the basis of material collected in former years—is characteristic of Hintze's working methods in this last period.

His reading focused on important contemporary works of sociological and historical theory. His reviews of the works of Sombart,[22] Troeltsch,[23] and Franz Oppenheimer[24] were full-length essays. But he wrote also extended criticisms of Max Scheler and Hans Kelsen, and the various reviews in which he discussed Max Weber's writings and studies on Weber show the importance he attributed to him. It is evident that in this last period of Hintze's scholarly activity Max Weber was the dominant intellectual figure with whose thought he felt he ought to come to terms. Theoretical interests, as we have noticed, had always been strong in Hintze, and the physical difficulties under which he labored in later years made work along such lines particularly appropriate. His main interest became the problems of historical conceptualization and of the relation between history and sociology. Nevertheless, his writings were never purely theoretical; they were saturated with facts. Only by means of facts was it possible to demonstrate the contribution that a clear conceptual system could make toward a better understanding of the past or to test the correctness and applicability of theories—whether those of others or Hintze's own. It was a fortunate coincidence that for such purposes extended research in source materials was hardly needed. Hintze re-examined—it might be more appropriate to say, he rethought—the developments that had been the object of his research in previous years in the light of recent historical and sociological theories. The essays in which he expressed his views were published in scholarly periodicals like the *Historische Zeitschrift* or among the reports of the Prussian Academy; and although they reached only a restricted audience, they made a great impression on those who read them and were appreciated as important attempts to invigorate the study of history.

Hintze's essays of this period may be divided into two groups: one is formed by studies of primarily theoretical content; the other consists of studies in which Hintze applies these theoretical insights to a reconstruction of important stages in the historical process. To the second group belong the articles "Calvinism and Raison d'Etat . . . ,"[25] "Wesen und Verbreitung des Feudalismus,"[26] the "Typologie der ständischen Verfassungen des Abendlandes,"[27] and the extended essay "The Preconditions of Representative Government in the Context of World History,"[28] which might be regarded as a summary and conclusion of the preceding studies on feudalism and on the system of Estates.

In many respects these studies continue the work which Hintze had done or planned in earlier years. Although they are concerned with the history of constitutional forms, Hintze placed them in close connection with the development of an administrative apparatus and, as in the studies "The Commissary" and "The Origins of the Modern Ministerial System," he demonstrated that the constitutional developments of the various European nations, as much as they might vary in details, originate from a common root and follow a similar pattern. But these articles show also significant modifications and changes in Hintze's views. He now considered the most striking feature in European constitutional history to be the development of representative government, which found its most recent and modern form of expression in parliamentarism. Although on various occasions Hintze suggested that parliamentarism might not be the last and final step in constitutional development, he now accepted the notion that it represented a later and higher stage than the constitutional monarchy or other forms of government; explanation of the development toward parliamentarism became his central concern.

An interesting illustration of a modification in Hintze's views is the fact that he now took a different, much more positive view toward British political developments in the eighteenth century. A more important indication is the change in his conception of the state, which he conceived no longer as an institution with a life of its own existing independently and above social groups; it had become a mere apparatus, changing in its functions and purposes according to external circumstances and alterations in the distribution of power. This re-evaluation of the role of the state was prerequisite for the most important scholarly contribution made by these essays: the description of the Estates system as a form of government, as a "state" that provided the link between feudalism and representative government. These essays show also how Hintze modified and refined his notion of the comparative method. He continued to examine and to explain why, out of common roots and similar patterns of development, institutional organizations of an individually distinctive character arose. But if, despite differences in particular aspects, the system of representative government was common to all European states, it was also a particularly European phenomenon. In order to prove and to explain this thesis, Hintze went beyond the frontiers of Europe and compared the development of European civilization with that of other civilizations. In his opinion the distinctive feature of European civilization was the separation between secular and spiritual power which stood in the way of the rise of an all-powerful despotism extending over the entire civilization. In contrast to the unified political organization characteristic of most other civilizations, this separation of ecclesiastical and political power in Europe allowed and promoted the formation of a number of different states—of a European state system. Since Europe was a relatively small geographical area, the various European states "pushed and pressed" against each other, and this led to a "consolidation and rationalization of state operations";[29] that explains the particular role of European civilization in the history of the world.

Hintze uses here the comparative method "to give a greater precision to the pecularity of a phenomenon."[30] At another place—in his discussion of the sociological views of Franz Oppenheimer—he expresses the same idea although in a somewhat different context: "You can compare in order to find something general that underlies the things that are compared, and you can compare in order to grasp more clearly the singularity (*Individualität*) of the thing that is compared, and to distinguish it from the others. The sociologist does the former; the historian, the latter."[31] It should be added that in Hintze's eyes the problem of the relation between history and sociology was more complex than this brilliant, if somewhat pat, formulation would suggest; he returns to this problem again and again in his essays of a theoretical character.

Hintze's theoretical essays are important in a twofold way: as disclosing the basis of his insights on the course of European constitutional history, and as contributing to the discussion of problems with which the historical thinking of our time is still concerned.

If these essays are read together they seem to contain a strange contradiction. Hintze admires Sombart for conceiving of capitalism as a "historical entity of singular nature" (*Historisches Individuum*); and yet has great reservations about the manner in which Troeltsch places the notion of "individuality" in the center of historicist thought.[32] What this apparent contradiction shows is that Hintze is still trying to reconcile the Rankean historiographical tradition with the less idealistic attitude which characterizes the scholarship of the twentieth century. The chief difficulty seems to him the emphasis that traditional history places on historic totalities possessing an original and unique character; they are regarded to be "individualities" and, as such considered to have a value of their own. Because of this connection between individuality and value the historian is inclined to be satisfied with an aestheticizing description of the appearance of the original and unique in history. For Hintze, who is interested in social groups or institutions rather than in persons, the uniqueness of a historical entity, its "individuality," in constituted by the fact of its being different from something else. Briefly, Hintze tries to divest Rankean ideas of their transcendental connotations.

The same tendency may be found in Hintze's observations on the role of ideas in history or in his criticisms of the use of notions of evolution by historians. Hintze came to eschew the belief that ideas are a superstructure over material conditions (this is an instance of an allusion to Marxist theories in Hintze's work: he sometimes refers to particular aspects of Marxist thought but never discusses them systematically). To Hintze ideas were important. Yet he does not accept the Rankean theory that ideas have a life of their own and possess the force to determine the character of an age and the course of its events. For Hintze ideas become a historically effective force only if they are in combination with concrete interests, with a drive for greater power or material advantage.

Hintze's objections to the use of evolution by the historian are of a similar kind; he fears that this notion can seduce the historian into assuming that historical institutions grow according to an innate tendency and that their evolution is metaphysically determined, beyond human control. For Hintze the determinants of historical development are human needs and desires that stimulate human action; these the historian must describe, explain, and understand. Movement in history can lead upward and downward; progress cannot be excluded, but it cannot be taken for granted. In all the essays of his last period Hintze's conception of history is strictly pragmatist. He fights on two fronts: against defenders of Rankean idealism he might take a strictly pragmatist line; against positivists he might defend the value of Rankean notions. His aim is to transform the traditional Rankean concepts in order to make them compatible with a pragmatist view of history. The historian, he believes, can attain this end by extended use of a comparative method and a stricter system of historical conceptualization.

If the uniqueness of a historical event or force, its "individuality," is not to be grasped intuitively but has to be demonstrated pragmatically, unavoidably comparison then becomes the appropriate method for the establishment of the particular nature of a historical entity. But comparison between two or among several phenomena requires some general element common to all of them—that is, a system of concepts into which the various phenomena of historical life can be fitted. In his search for a firmer conceptual base of historical work Hintze was decisively influenced by Max Weber's "ideal types" (Idealtypen),[33] but he did not consider them entirely satisfactory for the purposes of the historian. It was not enough to form a wide-meshed system of logical concepts into which the material of history could be organized. Historical events and entities were peculiar modifications of, and deviations from, a general pattern that itself was formed by history and historically conditioned. The concepts which the historian needed must partake of both the general and the particular, because if "they were only concrete and individual they would never lead to insights of wider significance, and if they were only abstract and general they would never have applicability to particular situations or circumstances." "From the material which the experience of political observation and historical study places at our disposal we select according to our judgment—and that means not without a certain arbitrariness—characteristic features, reduce them to their essential forms, and combine them in a creative mental act to a lively totality. . . ."; by means of such constructs "we can orient ourselves amid the disturbing abundance of phenomena and possess a criterion for scientific judgment."[34] The "ideal types" that historians could usefully employ were "visual abtractions."[35]

Hintze indicates in these sentences that the formation of such concepts presupposes a certain amount of "historical intuition"; despite his pragmatic and even rational approach, he had no reservations about trusting historical intuition. We might see a weakness in this reliance on intuition. It was deeply rooted in an approach to historical theory that began with Droysen and had been elaborated by Dilthey. Clearly this is an issue on which further work is required, but it is clear also that Hintze touches upon a point which is crucial for the distinction between sociology and history when he demands for historical works concepts which lie between the abstract and the concrete and are nourished by the material of history. Hintze could refer to the two articles of this period which we discussed before as proof of the fruitfulness of historical intuition in creating concepts that serve to illuminate the entire process of European history.

V

What is the contribution of Hintze's work to the present-day discussion on the nature and function of history? To a large extent Hintze's views are the result of personal experiences. He experienced the collapse of the Bismarckian Reich whose foundation must have been the great event of his boyhood, experienced, too, the victory of the Western democracies, the emergence of the United States and Japan. Clearly these events are reflected in the revisions and modifications that his views on the nature of the state, on the development of representative government, and on the importance of Europe underwent in the 1920s. He could gauge the importance of these events with a cool objectivity, free from traditional prejudices, because he was now no longer a participant but merely an observer of the political and academic scene.

But the 1920s, the years after the First World War, represent also the beginning of an important new chapter in historiography, and Hintze's work and views have to be seen in relation to this development. The struggle of political versus social and cultural history which had been a crucial event in the early years of Hintze's scholarly career was now renewed; but in the changed circumstances of the post-war situation, the result was different. Social and cultural historians began to dominate the scene. Even in Germany, where the political historians had triumphed and reigned more completely than in any other country, the intellectual atmosphere changed, although the period of greater intellectual openness was brief and succumbed soon to the suffocating pressure of the Nazi regime. There can be no doubt that the altered intellectual climate provided an added stimulus to Hintze's thinking and writing in his later years. Among the recognized historians in Germany he was one of the very few who had manifested constantly an interest in a beneficent relation between history and the social sciences. Because in Germany the change to new forms of history and new methods represented a radical departure, the interest in historical theory and in finding a firm theoretical foundation for the new approach was particularly strong.

Thus, Hintze's writings belong to the debate on the relation between history and the social sciences that started in the 1920s and has been going on since then. What does his work contribute to these discussions? There is no doubt that his ideas on these questions are still stimulating and deserve our attention. Despite his interest in sociology and related fields, the importance of history remained for him indisputable; he placed great value on the study of the past. Not only the content of our thinking but also the forms of social life and the character of our institutions are patterned by events of the past; the shape that they have or take cannot be deduced from scientific investigations establishing generalizations about human behavior, about the functional character of organizations and institutions, about psychological structure, and the order of economic values. All these phenomena are subject to the impact of external forces, to the accidents of history; and they continue to exist and work in history in a modified form which they have received in these clashes with historical accidents. The past cannot be removed from the world in which man lives; it has entered into man's thought, into the institutions which surround him or which he creates, and into the manner in which he looks upon the world.

The historical dimension forms an integral part of human life and action. But recognition of the existence of distinct and different entities determined in their formation by the vagaries of past events did not induce Hintze to conclude that the historian ought to focus primarily or exclusively on the particular and individual factors and forces of historical phenomena; his attention ought to be directed to the interaction between the patterns of general development and the modifications they undergo through the accidents of history. The historian must find a middle way between history as application of general laws and history as demonstration of the individuality and variety of life. This involves more, however, than acquaintance with the work in the field of social sciences which of course Hintze regarded as quite as necessary for the historian as is knowledge of history for the social scientist. It meant that the generalizing approach ought to be built into the work of the historian. Hintze suggested the creation of a conceptual framework which would bridge the gap between the abstractness of generalization and the concreteness of aesthetic description. This idea still seems valid and deserves further exploration. By means of strict concern with his conceptual apparatus the historian might be able to erect a framework which overcomes the division of history into work that analyzes long-range trends and work that focuses on factual description of events—and which again makes universal history possible.

It is true, of course, that historians will be judged according to their discoveries about the past as set down in their writings, rather than according to their theories. And in fact, as we have indicated, Hintze has written some of the most important and illuminating historical essays of the twentieth century. But their relation to his theory is significant. Historians frequently shy away from theory and leave it to philosophers who are remote from the practice of historical work; or they consider theory as a place for giving vent to private confessions of personal philosophy. It is one of the most impressive features of Hintze's work that it shows that when theory and practice go hand in hand they support and fructify each other.

FELIX GILBERT

A Note on Bibliography

The literature on Otto Hintze is not large. The article by Juergen Kocka in *Deutsche Historiker*, edited by H.-J. Wehler (3:41-64), although brief and condensed, provides an excellent analysis of Hintze's work and thought. Important contributions to our understanding of Hintze have been made by Gerhard Oestreich. He wrote the article on Hintze in the *Neue Deutsche Biographie* (vol. 9), with a list of Hintze's works and a complete bibliography; published a number of essays on particular aspects of Hintze's thought; and—most of all— edited the recent, revised edition of the three volumes of Hintze's *Gesammelte Abhandlungen,* with extensive introductions. Even if you do not entirely agree with Oestreich, who finds in Hintze's develop- ment an increasing trend toward sociology, these introductions must form the point of departure for any study of Hintze's thought. More- over, Oestreich also provides information about Hintze's personal life, about which we know very little.

The characterization of the young Hintze in Friedrich Meinecke's *Erlebtes* (Stuttgart, 1964), is almost the only existing lively description of Hintze's personality. Single aspects of Hintze's thought have been dis- cussed by Ludwig Dehio in his essay "Ranke und der Imperialismus," in which he placed Hintze's political views in the context of the po- litical attitude of the German academic community, and by Theodor Schieder, who in his *Staat und Gesellschaft in unserer Zeit* (translated by C. A. M. Sym as *State and Society in Our Times* [Camden, N.J., and London, 1962]) remarks on Hintze's definition of types. Some unpub- lished dissertations are mentioned in the bibliographies of Kocka and Oestreich.

The literature about Hintze in English is even more meager. His work is briefly discussed in Georg G. Iggers, *The German Conception of History* (Middletown, Conn., 1969), which also discusses the *Lam- precht Streit.* An article by Walter M. Simon, "Power and Responsi- bility: Otto Hintze's Place in German Historiography" in *The Respon- sibility of Power,* edited by L. Krieger and F. Stern (New York, 1967; pp. 199-219), analyzes Hintze's political views, but in isolating them from those of his contemporaries makes Hintze a more nationalistic figure than he was. Dehio's presentation of the same issue is more balanced. Dietrich Gerhard's article "Otto Hintze: His Work and Sig- nificance in Historiography" in *Central European History* (3:17-48), gives a good description of the content of Hintze's writings, so that it represents a useful guide to Hintze's work.

Notes

1. From Hintze's essay on "Gustav Schmoller," printed in *Gesammelte Abhandlungen*, 3:520.
2. See p.
3. *G.A.*, 3:204–55, 313–418.
4. *Ibid.*, 313.
5. See pp. 64ff.
6. See pp. 178ff.
7. See pp. 157ff.
8. See *G.A.*, vol. 1, the essay "Wesen und Wandlung des modernen Staats," particularly pp. 470–96.
9. See pp. 216ff.
10. See pp. 267ff.
11. See *G.A.*, vol. 3.
12. See pp. 33ff.
13. See *G.A.*, 1:359–89.
14. *Ibid.*, p. 365.
15. *Ibid.*, p. 379.
16. See *G.A.*, 1:439.
17. See *ibid.*, 457–69.
18. *Ibid.*, p. 469.
19. *Ibid.*, p. 469.
20. "Der Sinn des Krieges," in *Deutschland und der Weltkrieg*, ed. Hintze, Meinecke, Oncken, and Schumacher. But see also *ibid.*, "Deutschland und das Weltstaatensystem."
21. See pp. 88ff.
22. See pp. 422ff.
23. See pp. 368ff.
24. See *G.A.*, 2:239–312.
25. See below, pp. 88–154.
26. See *G.A.* 1:84–119.
27. See *G.A.*, 1:120–39.
28. See pp. 302ff.
29. See below, p. 313.
30. *G.A.*, 2:381.
31. See *G.A.*, 2:251.
32. See below, p. 385; *G.A.*, 2:380.
33. See Hintze, "Max Webers Sociologie," *G.A.*, 2:135–47.
34. See *G.A.*, 1:470.
35. *Ibid.*

PRUSSIAN HISTORY

1

THE HOHENZOLLERN
AND THE NOBILITY

Otto Hintze was not a personality inclined to irony; otherwise one might wonder whether he chose the titles of some of his writings with tongue-in-cheek. The title of his one extended narrative history, *Die Hohenzollern und ihr Werk* (The Hohenzollern and Their Work), suggests a treatment full of patriotic and monarchical enthusiasm; yet it is, in its sobriety, conciseness, and objectivity, almost the opposite. Likewise the present essay—a lecture published in the *Historische Zeitschrift*, Volume 112 (1914)—has a title which might arouse the expectation that Hintze will praise the alliance between the "Hohenzollern and the nobility" as the foundation of the greatness of Prussia and Germany; but again—perhaps with the exception of the concluding sentences, which reflect the essay's rhetorical origin—this essay is a very sober, critical analysis.

Admittedly, the article has a slightly defensive political content. Hintze explained that he intended to demonstrate that the attacks of the Social Democrats on the Prussian Junkers as the evil spirit of Prussian history, although they might contain a grain of truth, were exaggerated and partisan. He placed great emphasis on the role played by the nobility during the eighteenth century—when Prussia rose to become a Great Power—in the army and the civil service and in educating the rest of the population to selfless service to the state. But he shows also that during the first centuries of Hohenzollern rule in Brandenburg there was no cooperation between those rulers and the nobility, and that they fought each other bitterly; he indicates, however, that after the collapse of the *Ancien régime* there was no longer any reason for special privileges of the nobility. He had some bitter remarks for the Junker parliament of 1848 and for the Landowners' League, with their claims for an exceptional and advantageous position for the landowning nobility in the modern world. In the era of imperialism, Hintze suggested, the maintenance of Germany's position in the world depended on the middle class quite as much as, if not more than, on any other group of society.

Despite such allusions to the political problems of his time, this is primarily a historical article. Hintze discussed what he considered a central problem of Prussian history; he wrote this lecture when he was summarizing his many years of research in Prussian history in *Die Hohenzollern und ihr Werk,* a still unsurpassed, masterly survey of the entire course of Prussian history. The essay "The Hohenzollern and the Nobility" may be regarded as a brilliant résumé of the conclusions of the larger work.

The role of the nobility in Prussian history has been great, and it has given rise to many different interpretations, depending on social and political viewpoint. We may say that the general verdict of our own democratic era has been too unfavorable, that the historic services rendered by the Prussian nobility have been underestimated, since they are no longer in evidence before us: the great period of the nobility lies in the past. The social-democratic view of history in particular gives a distorted vision of the relation of the nobility to the state and to the sovereigns that created and governed the nobility—and Prussia has been the main example, criticized with bitter mordancy and demogogic zeal, as in Max Maurenbrecher's book (significantly entitled *The Hohenzollern Legend*), in which the Junkers of the provinces east of the Elbe are depicted as the evil principle of Prussian history. They are represented as directing all their energies toward exploitation of the rural population which they were given or which they had subjugated; they are supposed to have shifted all burdens onto others, all the while acquiring for themselves all kinds of economic and social privileges, and to have sought a commanding position in the state so that the state became their preserve and the sovereign himself no more than executor of their desires, in accordance with the well-known old democratic doggerel, "The King may well be absolute, providing that it does us good" (*Und der König absolut, wenn er unsern Willen tut*).

It cannot, nor should it, be claimed that this picture is false in all its features or that the interpretation does not contain some truth. As it stands, however, it is partisan and exaggerated, and distorted by hatred. In particular, the relation of the Hohenzollern sovereigns and the nobility has been presented in a slanted

and erroneous manner. I hope to put this right. I am not pleading
for or against the nobility, and seek only to show in general terms
what was the relation between the nobles and the sovereigns in
the course of the five centuries of Hohenzollern rule. Recent
scholarship has made many aspects of this more comprehensible than used to be the case; and we can easily arrange the discussion in accordance with the three great epochs of Prussian internal history.

The first epoch covers the period of the old petty territorial
state in "the Electoral Mark of Brandenburg," in the Duchy of
Prussia, in Cleves-Mark, and in all the other regions united under
the Hohenzollern scepter. This epoch marked in the main the
foundation of the economic, social, and political power of the
landowning nobility. During the second epoch, these various
regions were gradually welded together and became provinces
of a unitary state under the absolutist rule of the Great Elector and his successors in the eighteenth century. This was an
era of conflict and strife between the sovereigns, who pursued
the idea of a powerful military state, and the provincial nobility,
to whom this idea was in the beginning repugnant, but who
finally put themselves without reserve at the disposal of the new
state. The third epoch, in which we ourselves are living, is that
of the completed, unified state which, by the laws of growth in
political life, has become a constitutional state in which the privileges of the nobility are in principle eliminated, and which tries
gradually to realize the ideal of the equality of all citizens. In this
epoch the nobility still enjoys the fruits of its close connection
with the throne, which nourished its devotion to the monarchical
military and bureaucratic state; and also many advantages are
still left from its old economic and social privileged position. The
earlier exclusiveness of its position in state and society has gone,
however, and in all areas of life the middle classes have asserted
their competition with great vigor and triumphal success: even
the sovereign is no longer exclusively surrounded by noblemen,
particularly in the government of the state.

Nobility and monarchy to some extent belong together. The lesser nobility, with which we are here chiefly concerned, was indeed a creation of the prince. It was a service nobility, for nobility has always been bestowed on those who served the sovereign. The main body of the lesser nobility, particularly in the Prussian provinces, came from *ministeriales*—that is, the sovereign's horseback-riding servants who later acquired the status of knight. But this service and vassal nobility, possessing a firm basis in its landed estates, often treated the sovereign liege-lord with scant respect, especially when old traditions were interrupted with a change of dynasty, the nobility having been settled on the land a great deal longer than a new sovereign coming from abroad.

This happened with the accession of the Hohenzollern to the Mark of Brandenburg, which was accompanied by a veritable revolt of the nobles. In the fifteenth century the task of the rulers of the House of Brandenburg was to restore and permanently to strengthen the territorial state, which had been created by the rulers of the Ascanian house in the thirteenth century and which in the confusion of the fourteenth century had almost disintegrated. This was rendered all the more necessary by the interests of Germany as a whole, for the strengthened Polish Kingdom threatened to annihilate the German civilization of the colonized regions east of the Elbe. It was no accident that the Emperor Sigismund sent the Burgrave of Nuremberg as chief military commander (*oberste Hauptmann*) and vicar to the Mark one year after the Teutonic Knights had been defeated by the Poles at Tannenberg. This marked an attempt to establish an ordered territorial state in the Mark of Brandenburg, with strict enforcement of internal peace (*Landfriedensordnung*) and a powerful sovereign; but the nobility of the Mark, under the leadership of the Quitzows and their friends, resisted by making unrestricted use of their right of feud and by claiming an independence which was incompatible with an organized state. The nobility of the Mark, with this opposition, hoped to gain freedom from any princely power, and to become immediate subjects of the Emperor, on the

same lines as the knights of Swabia and Franconia, where no
strong princely ruler could emerge. Because of the weakness of
the imperial power, however, and the lawlessness in which in
these restless times the nobles indulged, the result of independence would have been anarchy and disintegration, and finally
armed invasion by the Polish neighbors. The first Elector of the
House of Hohenzollern managed to destroy the castles of the
Quitzows and their associates and to establish an internal peace
which gave security and the possibility of prosperity. But there
was no complete overthrow of the nobility. The outcome, once
this initial test of strength had been decided in favor of the Elector, was a kind of compromise: the nobility abandoned its resistance to the establishment of an effective princely rule, but otherwise retained, generally speaking, its possessions, privileges, and
a considerable amount of power.[1]

Frederick II of the Iron Tooth (Eisenzahn), the effective
founder of princely rule in Brandenburg, subdued the defiant
towns and, on the basis of Papal privilege, brought the clergy of
the land into real dependence on the sovereign. He attempted
also to draw the savage, illiterate nobility of the Mark to his
court, to instill in them loyalty to the prince, and to promote
among its members a nobler and more civilized way of life, in
accordance with the Christian ideals of the time. He pursued this
dual task by creating the Order of the Swan, just as had the
Dukes of Burgundy, with their Order of the Golden Fleece. He
succeeded to only a very limited extent, however. In 1495 the nobles' right of feud had been abolished by Imperial legislation,
and the general peace of the Empire had been proclaimed. In
Brandenburg, when a part of the lower nobility was too poor to
live off their lands, and regarded feuding and robbery as their noble privilege, massive punitive expeditions were carried out
against these noble violators of the peace. These persecutions
were the mark of the rule of Joachim I.

This persecution has been described, though not entirely correctly, as a conflict between the sovereign and the nobility. There

is a famous threatening doggerel that a Junker of Otterstedt is supposed to have written on the door of the Elector's chamber: "Watch out, little Joachim; if we get you we'll hang you" (*Joch-imke, Jochimke höde dy; Fange wy dy so hange wy dy*). The truth of this has not been impeccably attested, though no doubt the doggerel aptly expressed the mood in certain circles toward this strict and ruthless master. Study of the documents of the Diet[2] shows, however, that by no means did the entire nobility put up this resistance to the Elector: only individual, though numerous, members of the nobility provoked by their lawless conduct the harsh intervention of the Elector's sword of justice. In the assemblies of the noblemen neither knights nor prelates placed obstacles in the way of the Elector's execution of justice against their robber colleagues. Nevertheless, the whole body of the nobility was shaken by vast and violent disturbances which accompanied the persecution and execution of the numerous noble violators of peace. This must be regarded as the death agony of the old feudal nobility, bellicose and fractious, lawless and immoral, and as a concomitant of the great social transformation that turned the nobleman from warring knight to agriculturist.

This opened the way for great economic and social changes. Under the old manorial system the knights did not farm themselves to any large extent; they merely lived on the rents and levies they drew from their dependents. The manor now became a demesne (*Gutsherrschaft**), whereby the knight demolished

---

* The system of agriculture that came to be characteristic of the region of Germany east of the Elbe. Its chief feature was that the landlord himself farmed the estate, living off the revenues gained by selling its produce in distant markets, and using the services of the serfs, who were therefore bound to the soil. The estate formed a legal administrative unit (*Gutsbezirk*), and the landlord held police and judiciary powers over the peasants. As a result, the peasants were forced deeper into serfdom. *Grundherrschaft* is the system of agriculture characteristic of the southern and western portions of Germany. Its chief feature was that the landlord did not himself farm the estate but lived off the payments of cash and kind received from his peasant tenants. Because they were less under the economic control of their lord, peasants under this system enjoyed a greater degree of freedom than those under the system of *Gutsherrschaft*.

the peasants' farms and enclosed all the land into his own estates, which he managed and farmed himself. There thus arose agrarian enterprises on a great scale, though they did not reach the size or the coherence of today's estates, which emerged in the nineteenth century. Yet it was a form of economy which was very different from that formerly pursued on the estates of the nobility, and from those that have continued to exist in western Germany, where conditions were not so favorable to large-scale enterprises as they were in the east. In the east, the corn trade—and particularly corn exports—had passed from the hands of townsmen to the knights; and this in itself provided a strong impulse to agricultural expansion. Besides, in the east it was easier for landowners to burden their serfs with *corvée* obligations, which because of the lack of servants and equipment were necessary for the increased enterprise. Probably, also, the example of Poland had some effect, where at that time large estates originated, based on the labor of serfs.

Thus, the land-owning nobility to the east of the Elbe became, after the end of the fifteenth century a class of agriculturists farming on their own, claiming *corvée* from their bondsmen (*erbuntertänigen Bauern**) in place of dues. They developed, in this economic system, a capacity for business, and a habit of ruling, of commanding, and of organizing such as were not possessed to the same extent by the nobility of western or southern Germany, who lived from their ground rents. This created the type of the East Elbian Junker, who is widely different from the typical nobleman of western Germany.

Clearly, the Hohenzollern princes were interested in making their nobility give up robbing and feuding, and in turning them toward a domestic, economics-oriented life in the country. On

---

* Like the term *leibeigen*, refers to serfs bound to the soil. Although there was no qualitative difference between the two categories of servitude, *Leibeigenschaft* was considered a humiliating and inferior status, and Frederick the Great endeavored to abolish it. *Erbuntertänigkeit* (hereditary bondage), however, remained until the Emancipation Edict of October 1807.

the other hand, they were interested also in keeping the number of peasants at its existing level, and regarded it as a princely duty to prevent oppression of the peasants by the noblemen. Enclosure was sometimes forbidden, and in the Chamber court (*Kammergericht*) the Elector's councilors attempted to limit the *corvée* burdens of the peasants and to compel the knights to feed them while they were doing *corvée* duty. These efforts on the part of the rulers remained largely ineffective, however, and were not insisted upon, for the princes depended on the nobility and needed its good will on account of the taxes that the Diet (*Landtag*) had to approve. Thus matters remained very largely as they stood, and the nobles were not hindered in the formation and augmentation of their estates.

In the Diet the nobles were the leading element. The curia of the prelates had been fused with theirs since the Reformation, and in power and prestige, the towns were greatly inferior to the higher estates. It was only for the benefit of these latter that Elector Joachim II had to give assurance, in 1540, that he regarded himself as bound to seek the advice and consent of the Estates in all matters affecting the ultimate fate (*Gedeih und Verderb*) of the country, and especially not to enter upon any alliance without having secured the approval of the district councilors (*Landrat**). "District councilor" meant something different then from what it did later, for district councilors were the members of a commission composed of knights and destined to advise the sovereign. By means of these councilors, therefore, the nobility had a decisive influence on foreign policy. The district councilors must be distinguished from the court councilors, who lived at the Court of the Elector as his officials charged with the business of government. The Elector was expected to choose even these Court councilors from the ranks of the nobles and at their prompting; the knights claimed that they should be governed, in accordance

---

* The official at the head of the administration of a county. The Prussian *Landrat* was originally the representative of the Estates, but became the chief executive of the central government on the local level.

with the rights of citizenship (*Indigenatsrecht**), only by natives and equals. In general this right was recognized by the rulers, although in many individual cases they ignored it so as to employ particularly efficient and reliable councilors and chancellors.

The anger of the nobility at this was shown in drastic clarity in two documents found in the archives of the Diet of 1542, from which I should like to quote a few sentences.[3] These are suggestions and complaints that a number of "poor nobles"—as they described themselves—presented to the permanent delegation of the Estates and subsequently to the Diet, with which the Elector was discussing new taxes. The "poor nobles" were the lesser landowners in contrast to the greater ones who were chiefly represented in the delegation. Fifty had held a meeting and complained in their petition that they could not get to speak in the Diet; and they grumbled at the errors in decisions (*böser Unrat*) and the disorganization in the government, for which, in their opinion, the use of foreign councilors—that is, men from Meissen (Saxony)—by the Elector was responsible: this was a ruinous practice. On this point they said, "We wish to dismiss the evil councilors and to plough with our own oxen; in no other way can our affairs be properly conducted. Our beloved princes of old also did this, we well know, and did not suffer any man of Meissen as councilor in this land." Further, the parts of the domain lands that had been pledged to these councilors should be taken back, and no new promises of this kind be made to the Elector's favorites. "When this has happened and been decreed," the letter continues, "then we shall deal with our own affairs. We wish to see the threads in the hands of him who governs us, and he must pay due regard to what we want, for we shall make things hot for him if we cannot see where he puts our money: the whole land knows all about this, and so do we."

---

* Statute limiting officeholding to those born in the county with which the work of the office is concerned. In the case of Brandenburg, this meant that officers bearing on the affairs of the Altmark (a part of Brandenburg west of Elbe, with its own estates and estate administration) were limited to men from the Altmark, and this meant, in practice, the nobility of this area.

This strong language, somewhat reminiscent of that used by the Landowners' League (*Bund der Landwirte**) today, irritated the Elector, when he got word of it; he reprimanded the discontented for having assembled without his permission and stressed that, by the feudal law of the *Sachsenspiegel,* the councilors were parts of the liege-lord's body. Nonetheless, the dissidents' manifest was not wholly in vain: the sovereign's power was very strictly limited by the nobility and the Estates in general; they had a right not only of approving taxes but of administering them as well: and by their complaints (*Gravamina*) they exerted a certain amount of control over the princes' government, and it was customary that in legislation and politics nothing of importance was done without their advice.[4]

Thus the sovereign's power in the sixteenth and seventeenth centuries was restricted by the Estates—and principally by the nobility. It was the same in the other territories which the Hohenzollerns acquired in the seventeenth century. East Prussia turned into a veritable nobles' republic after 1566, under the weak rule of the elderly Duke Albrecht; and the nobles' power was still further increased and reinforced in the reign of his mentally defective son. Government was carried on by the four High Councilors (*Oberräte*), or Government Councilors (*Regimentsräte*), who were nominally ducal councilors but in fact acted as trusted agents of the ruling aristocratic clique. Moreover, the heads of the nobility were represented on the board of district councilors (*Landratskollegium*), and thus had powerful influence on public administration; and in the various districts into which the land was divided, these noble district heads behaved and ruled in a manner redolent of the Polish *starosty.* It was a narrow circle of old, strictly Lutheran families that exercised government—the Tettaus, Ostaus, Wallenrodts, Kreytzens, Schliebens, and a few

---

* "Landowners' League"—an association founded in 1894 for the protection of agriculture against tendencies toward free trade; it was dominated by the owners of the large estates east of the Elbe and exerted a strong, reactionary influence on German politics.

others. Even a great family like that of the Dohnas had for a long time no influence on account of their Calvinism, which excluded them from the ruling clique. Only the Great Elector changed this; he asserted the right of even Calvinists (his coreligionists), to hold office, and he rendered the prescripts of the law of citizenship—on which the nobility insisted—ineffective by according the right of citizenship even to foreigners—that is, men of Brandenburg proper—when the hour was favorable. Here, as elsewhere, he broke the Estates' power: and the nature of the means he had to use was displayed in his dealings with Christian Ludwig von Kalckstein, a figure typical of the indiscipline and fractiousness of the East Prussian nobles who conspired with Poland against the Elector and refused to recognize his sovereignty. With craftiness and violence, Kalckstein was seized in Warsaw and carried over the border; then he was tried for high treason, subjected even to torture (in violation of the privileges of the East Prussian nobility) because the Elector wished to know the names of his associates, and finally he was condemned to death and executed.[5]

Thus the Great Elector broke the resistance of the East Prussian nobility to the new military, centralizing monarchy. And yet, the words which an East Prussian—perhaps a Dohna—used in explaining to the Minister von Fuchs on the accession of Frederick III in 1689 the situation in East Prussia, show how powerful the influence of the nobility in the administration had remained.[6] He said, the ordinary knights had pushed the great lords from the board of district councilors and likewise excluded the *ordo civicus,* and "they themselves [had] taken over the entire board, all good has come to an end in the land, and the sovereign must at all times negotiate with these district councilors about his rights, even his very bread; so long as this goes on, the Elector will be ruler more *nomine* than *omine.* All the while the district councilors send the ball over to the high councilors and the High Councilors play it back to the district councilors; and anyone who does not tag along with this, even His Serene Highness, will have to pay for it. If anyone in Prussia manages to become district councilor and adminístrative chief, then his uncles and his brothers-in-law are in clover; and all the little Junkers around are expected to revere the Lord District Councilor and Lord Chief as an idol. If His Serene Highness hands over *œconomica* to the charge of these people, as it is in the hands of the Starosty in Poland, then we will have everything we want or need."

The conflict between Great Elector and Estates in the Rhenish and Westphalian territories of Cleves and Mark, was not quite so vehement as that in East Prussia. Here, too, it was principally the nobility that resisted the foundation of the new centralized military state. A nobleman of Cleves, Wylich von Winnenthal, had complained in 1653 to the Emperor and the Empire at large about the Elector's behavior; but he paid for this disrespectful conduct toward his sovereign with imprisonment. At first, however, the Elector was obliged to give way to the Estates; he had to dismiss all the non-native officials he had appointed, to make all the officials to include in their oaths obedience to the decrees of the Estates, to promise not to bring troops into the country or build fortresses without the prior agreement of the Estates. Only in 1660 and 1661, after the victorious conclusion of the Swedish-Polish war, did he get rid of these chains and was able to assert the sovereign's right of garrisoning; the Estates' privileges, and especially the privileges of the nobility, were nonetheless left by and large unimpaired.

In all these conflicts with the provincial Estates the particular point at issue was the requirements of the new standing army, for the army served as a kind of iron hoop which forced the various formerly separate territories together to form a larger centralized state. This was not a product of princely caprice and arbitrariness, but it was a European necessity from which no state could escape if, in the constant rivalry on the Continent, a state wanted to secure or preserve its independence. The notion of such military and political power was novel to the Estates, which were rooted in the apolitical goal of petty, territorial still-life: thus the nobility in particular for many years opposed the sovereign's ambitions in the realm of politics and power. The strongest resistance came from the regions most distant from the center of the monarchy and the seat of the centralizing government—in East Prussia and in Cleves Mark, where there were also disturbing foreign influences at work, from Poland and the Dutch Republic.

The nobles of the Mark of Brandenburg presented the least difficult problem to the Great Elector, and were brought around to the idea of a military and centralized state with relative ease. Even here, however, for several years, there was considerable tension, because at the end of the great war, the Estates demanded the dissolution of the army, whereas the Elector tried to introduce the *miles perpetuus*. But this tension was fairly easily resolved at the Diet of 1653, when the Estates agreed to make sufficient provision for the army (for seven years in the first instance), in return for far-reaching confirmation and extension of their privileges; thus they in effect abandoned their resistance to the army and the formation of the new political order. The chief interest of the nobility in Brandenburg was to remain undisturbed in the development of their estates and in the exercise of their authority over their serfs. The result was a compromise, the nobility renouncing its resistance to the standing army, and to the expense this would involve, and the Elector therefore agreeing to strengthen and confirm the nobility in its economic and social interests and in its local seignorial position.[7] This clearly shows that the struggle between the new princely power and the nobility was not a war of annihilation; what was at stake was rather an attempt on the Elector's part to compel this first and most important of the Estates to recognize and, as far as possible, also to serve the new political order, based on the necessities of *raison d'état*.

Subsequent to this turn of events, the role of the nobility underwent a complete change. At earlier times, in the small, separate territorial states, the nobility had prescribed how the sovereign was to behave in both internal and external affairs; in the new

military and centralized state, the Diets and the assemblies that
replaced the Diets became unimportant and powerless provincial
representations, and above them appeared the new officialdom of
the unified state, overwhelmingly superior in force and power, instruments at the command of the centralized princely authority.
The Diets in many of the provinces, especially Brandenburg and
Prussia, ceased to function, and taxation passed out of the Estates'
control to that of the sovereign's officials. The introduction of the
Excise, a special system of taxation for the towns and based
mainly on indirect taxation of consumption, divided town and
country and isolated the nobility, such that there was no further
community of interest in the question of taxes among the Estates. The countryside continued to pay the *Kontribution*, a taxation system built particularly on a land tax, which had been introduced during the great war; and in most provinces the old
custom was reinforced by which these taxes fell not on the nobility but only on the peasants. Frederick William I, who abolished
what remained of the Estates' administration of taxes, tried to
make the nobility also pay a land tax. But he encountered such
tough passive resistance in Pomerania and the New Mark that he
was obliged to drop the plan. Only in East Prussia, in introducing
a general land tax (*Generalhufenschoss**), did he carry through
a uniform system of taxation of both nobility and free and unfree
peasants—but in this case the Teutonic Knights had already made
sure that no special aristocratic tax exemption could be made. In
Silesia and West Prussia, also, the nobility was not exempted from
taxation, and here again, under Frederick the Great, the nobles
were made to pay, though not so heavily as the peasants.[8]

In the reign of Frederick William I there is still a marked strain
of antagonism and mistrust regarding the nobility, at least in
some of the provinces. This emerges, indeed sometimes dras-
tically so, in his Political Testament of 1722,[9] where for his suc-

---

* *Hufe* was originally a peasant's farm, and later a fixed amount of land, so
that the term served as a land measurement, and could be used for tax es-
timates.

cessor's benefit, he characterized briefly the nobility of the various provinces. He gave him the general advice of being obliging and gracious to the nobility as a whole in all the provinces, to distinguish the good from the bad, to reward the loyal so as to gain their attachment and respect. At that time the East Prussian great nobility seemed to Frederick William the most dangerous to the monarchy. "My successor must keep a wary eye on the Finck and Dohna families, or they will take away a good part of the government from him; both these families still hanker after the old Prussian-Polish *privilegia*, of that you may be sure."

Altogether, however, he was aware that he had brought the nobility in East Prussia under control by the reform of taxation and tax administration which accompanied the introduction of the general land tax; and it must be stressed that it was an East Prussian nobleman who put the interests of the state above his own class interests in this difficult matter, and thus helped the King's reforms toward success—Count Truchsess von Waldburg, who ended his days in Königsberg as head of the administration (*Kammer- und Kommissariatspräsident*). The reforms had not been carried through without resistance: it was then that Frederick William I wrote his famous remark, "I ruin the authority of the Junkers and build my sovereignty like a rock of bronze." The King spoke very harshly of the nobility of Cleves-Mark: "As for Cleves and the County of Mark," he said in his Political Testament, "the vassals there are dumb oxen, but malicious as the devil. They are very jealous of their privileges, but all the same they'll do as my successor desires or demands of them." In fact the King had suspended the Diets of Cleves-Mark, which had still been held annually, because the proceedings had been very disorderly, and the government had met difficulties. But then he again permitted the Diets to be held, in the expectation that these troubles would cease.

The nobility of these lands had a special interest in the convocation of regular Diets, for in the Empire only such nobility as sat and voted in Diets were granted admission to ecclesiastical

endowments, and this was of immense importance in the providing for younger sons and daughters. This factor made the nobility very pliant in politics; Frederick William I did not encounter any further strong resistance there, though he also found
there no particular inclination to, and no great capacity for,
serving the state. "These people are intriguers and false as well,"
said the King, "and they drink like beasts—they know nothing
else. If a man from Cleves leaves home at an early age and is educated in Berlin, then he turns out brave, good, and clever, and
can fitly be used by every successor." In their private affairs, however, they manage badly, and eat up more than their income.

For the rest, he judged the vassals on the lower Rhine to be more
Dutch and Imperial-minded than Prussian. In Guelders the vassals were, he said, wholly Imperial-minded, and his successor
must keep a strict watch on Marquis Hönsbröch, for he behaved
toward his prince most wickedly and awaited only the occasion
to put himself under the Emperor's jurisdiction. The King had a
low opinion also of the vassals in the Westphalian parts of the
country—Minden, Ravensberg, Tecklenburg, and Lingen. They
were, he thought, stupid and opinionated, and his successor
should not make much use of them, for they were too easygoing
to be good servants. Yet if he met them with a gracious welcome
and countenance they would do what he wanted. The nobility of
Pomerania and the Mark were a different matter: "The Pomeranian vassals are true as gold; they gripe sometimes; but if my successor says it must be so, and tells them in the right way, none of
them will give any trouble. As for the New Mark, it is in all respects similar to Pomerania; but the vassals are always grum-
bling, particularly in the Krossen district. But you must not hold
these grumblings against them, for there is no substance to them
—it is only the custom of the land. The middle and lower Mark
have the most loyal nobility of all, and they will willingly and
gladly do whatever you command."

Only the nobility of the Old Mark and Magdeburg drew his
real fire. "The vassals of the Old Mark are bad, disobedient peo-

ple, who do nothing in good part, they are always surly and mischievous in their duties to their prince. My beloved successor must keep a firm grip on them and not treat them too well, for there are many mischievous characters among them. The Schulenburgs, Alvenslebens, and Bismarcks are both the chief and the worst families of the land; the Knesebecks are also bad. The Magdeburg vassals are like these from the Old Mark, only rather worse; the Halberstadt ones are the same."

What the King particularly objected to in the behavior of the nobility of the Old Mark and Magdeburg was their resistance to a measure that was particularly characteristic of his whole relation with the nobility: the allodification of the knights' estates. These estates were traditionally fiefs: their owners were expected to do service by providing horses; but this had not been done within living memory, although it was for this that the nobility had demanded and been accorded freedom from taxation. Frederick William I desired these services to be redeemed by payment of money, and in return he loosed the feudal bond which had previously bound the estates. The estates were to become free property of the nobles in return for payment of the fief burdens, which were assessed at forty talers annually as the equivalent of one cavalry horse. The King had issued this decree on his own in 1717, and the Old Mark and Magdeburg nobility had refused to obey, maintaining that it was contrary to their privileges. They even brought action against their prince to the Imperial Court Council (*Reichs-Hofrat*), which gave the Emperor a much desired opportunity for all kinds of chicaneries against Brandenburg. The lawsuit was one of those that never ended; but for many years, the vassals of the Old Mark and Magdeburg had the King seize the disputed feudal dues by military action; the vassals would not make the payments voluntarily.[10]

It is interesting that even with the conversion of the knights' estates into free property, the personal bond of fealty did not break; the nobles still were vassals of the King, their liege and sovereign lord—and remained obligated to service and loyalty;

and in Frederick William I's reign the vassals' duties were sharply emphasized. A code of discipline for vassals was introduced. The officials in the Chambers for war and domains (*Kriegs- und Domänenkammern*) were required to keep lists of all the nobles in their district and to inform the King of their doings. Vassals were forbidden to take service abroad; they could not even go abroad without royal consent, nor could they send their sons on travels or to foreign universities. The King wished the sons of the nobility to take service with him, above all as officers in his army: vassalage was to be revived in the new form of an officer's service and loyalty relationship. This was one of the essential principles in Frederick William I's internal policy, the effects of which particularly emerged under his successor. He wished no more foreigners to be officers, replacing them by the indigenous nobility as far as possible. For this reason he founded the Cadet Schools of Berlin, Magdeburg, and Stolpe, where the sons of the nobility were to be trained for a military career; this enabled the often very poor nobles of the eastern provinces to give their sons an education that befitted their status. Often the King had to force parents to leave their children with him for this purpose—in East Prussia particularly the sons of the nobility were frequently almost kidnapped by non-commissioned officers and mounted police, and brought to the Cadet Schools—but the King consoled the parents by letting them know that their sons were in good hands, lodged in clean rooms, educated in all the useful sciences and arts, and brought up to be good Christians.[11] At that time it was not as yet a privilege of the nobility to occupy officer posts; it was rather a duty, often felt to be extremely onerous.

The effects of the close link that was gradually forged between the nobility of the land and the officer corps of the army were of vast importance in determining the spirit and character of the Prussian state. Under Frederick William I and his successor, the officer class was the first and most esteemed in the state. Even the King regarded himself as an officer—he always wore a uniform and treated the officers as his comrades—and he was able, through his example and through discipline, to instill in the officer-corps a high sense of professional duty. The recruiting of the officer corps from the indigenous nobility gave the corps a homogeneous character, increased its professional reliability, and strengthened the corporate sense of honor and comradeship as a result of the introduction of aristocratic ways of life.

Just as the officer was a nobleman, the conscripted soldier (*Kantonist**) was a peasant; and the relations between lord and peasant, the habits of command and obedience on both sides, the automatic subordination and confidence in the superior's leadership, provided a powerful psychological basis for strict military discipline. Similarly, the education of the nobility in the officer corps had important effects on the political ideas of the provinces. In the officer corps the young nobles learned reverence for the monarchy, and unconditional surrender to the service of the state; and this in turn affected the nobles in the provinces, who up till then had been imprisoned in the narrow concerns of their particular region and had regarded the idea of the state which the King represented with indifference or indeed with distaste. Thus, through the link with the officer corps, the fractious, malcontent Junkers of the eastern provinces turned into a loyal monarchist class, in which the idea of the state implanted by the King struck powerful roots. Frederick the Great said in his Political Testament of 1752[12] that he had always insisted that the officers did not describe themselves as *Marker, Magdeburger, Pomeranian,* or *East Prussian,* but became used to the common name of *Prussian.* The Prussian officer of Frederick's time was the first representative of a Prussian political consciousness; and from this officer corps the Prussian ethos passed to the nobles of the eastern

---

* A conscript soldier whose service within his regiment was limited to two months a year so that he could carry out his regular work the remaining months of the year. In practice, only younger sons of peasants (not the eldest son) and journeymen were subjected to this regulation. For purposes of carrying out this law, the country was divided in *Kantone,* and the administration was in the hands of the most prominent landowner of the Kanton. Since the landowner was frequently an officer, a regiment was usually composed of peasant sons working on his estate or living around it.

provinces. But only in the nineteenth century was this consciousness extended to include all the citizens.

The great age of the Prussian nobility, however, began only
with the reign of Frederick the Great. Under Frederick William I,
who opened the way, there was a distinct middle-class strain and
a clear feeling that the interests of state, as represented by the
King, will frequently clash with the interests of the nobility. It
was said in the Political Testament of 1722 that, if the General
War Commissaries (*Generalkriegskommissare*), who controlled
military administration, taxes, and police, wanted to be loyal
servants of the King, they must have the whole nobility against
them. Frederick William I made several of his middle-class Cabinet secretaries into ministers and ennobled them; the bureaucracy
he created was almost equally made up of nobles and non-nobles.
Moreover, he never quite overcame a certain suspicion of the district councilors, the nobles in charge of the districts in their double role of royal civil servant and trusted agent of the local nobility. In some parts of the country, particularly the Old Mark and
Magdeburg, the King broke with the custom according to which
the Estates of the district presented men of their choice for this
post by simply appointing former officers or men devoted to him
to be *Landräte*. He regarded with particular mistrust the attempts of the landowning noblemen to take over parts of the
royal domains, as had happened earlier in Poland and Sweden on
a large scale. When the domains were farmed out he was careful
to have as tenants only non-nobles, so that no mixing of noble and
royal lands should take place. He ordered investigations of those
pieces of land of the royal domain that had come into nobles'
hands in earlier times on account of some failure to insist on royal
property rights; thus fiscal lawsuits in the courts were frequent
and created a good deal of bad blood among the nobility. Frederick William I did not even shrink from buying out some of the
knights' estates so as to increase the royal domains; in this he followed the example of his friend the "Old Dessauer," who had
bought out almost all the nobles in his tiny state.

In all these respects his successor thought and acted differently. Frederick the Great remarked that a procedure like buying up knights' estates might fit the Prince of Zippel-Zerbst but not the King of Prussia. The King of Prussia must have a numerous and prosperous landowning nobility which could supply officers for the army; this he thought more important than possession of a large domain. He ordered that the fiscal lawsuits to redeem lapsed royal property be discontinued so as not to prejudice the vassals' interests: "For it is their sons that defend the land; and the breed is so good that it merits to be preserved by every means." These words were penned in 1748.[13] The King had already had the chance to perceive the excellent qualities of his noble officers in the course of two wars. In his Political Testament of 1752, also, he declared that preservation of the nobility was one of the main objects of Prussian political interest: one might be able to find richer nobles, but none more courageous and loyal.

Like his father he characterized the nobility in the single provinces, and the points on which he differed from his father are not without interest. He sustained the East Prussians against the reproach of dishonesty: they were clever, and industrious, but they should not be permitted to remain all the time in their own province. The Pomeranians were straightforward and loyal, and made the best officers and officials; only their too-open manner ill-fitted them for diplomacy. He esteemed the nobility of the Mark Brandenburg for their loyalty and commitment to the state, but they lacked the intelligence of the Prussians and the solidity of the Pomeranians; he found them too pleasure-loving, and this he ascribed to their proximity to Berlin. He had a high opinion of the Magdeburgers: they had sharp minds and had produced some remarkable men. The men of Lower Silesia were good men but a little stupid, not by nature but because of their bad education; they were vain, inclined to luxury and extravagance, very susceptible to pomp and titles, but without real perseverance in work and without appetite for the hardship and privations of military service. The Catholic Upper Silesian nobility was still wholly in sympathy with Austria. The Westphalians from the counties Mark and Minden were an able breed of men; their education made them a little clumsy, and they had no great social presence; but they did have a more valuable talent—that of making themselves useful to the state. Frederick II was as harsh as his father in his judgment on the nobles of Cleves, calling them imbecilic and muddle-headed and believing them to be a race degenerated by drink. It may be added that the Cleves nobility had almost wholly died out by the end of the eighteenth century; in the Diet of 1800 the knights numbered only two. In general, however, the King praised the nobility, calling it the basis and the pillar of his state.

So as to maintain the noble families in possession of knights' estates, Frederick reintroduced the old custom by which these estates could not be bought by non-nobles: non-noble capital was to work in trade and industry. Where these estates were in non-noble hands, the King wished to deprive their owners of the seignorial privileges bound up with such ownership, such as prayers in church for the patron, membership in the Estates of the district, and in particular the right to choose the district councilor: for Frederick the Great had restored this right and promoted in every possible way self-administration by the nobles in the districts, which indeed were chiefly associations of knightly estate-owners. To preserve the nobility in their possession of land he even suggested and favored the establishment of estates with primogeniture. The Seven Years' War increased still further his esteem for the nobility. When not enough nobles for replacements in the officer corps were available, he appointed students and other non-nobles; later, however, these commoners were sent off to hussar and garrison regiments, which did not yet count for as much as the others.

It was particularly in the Seven Years' War that the nobility made vast sacrifices in goods and life. Many noble families counted dozens of deaths in the battles of the great King, and many estates went to wrack and ruin because their owners were fighting under the King's banner. When it came to restoring the land after the war, the King gave help with considerable sums of money to the landowning nobles of particularly ravaged provinces. To relieve the need for credit he caused the landowning nobility of various provinces—first of all in Silesia—to form credit institutions for noblemen; they were called *Landschaften;* and, in order to cover the need for credit of single owners, they issued bonds for which either all or at least a good part of the owners of knightly estates stood security. At the outset these institutions were supported by government loans.

The King knew exactly how far he could go in supporting the nobility without prejudice to the common interest of the country and without injury to the principles of justice. The Pomeranian knights who demanded more than he thought appropriate, received the answer that they were like spoiled children, asking for more the more they were given. He took care of the peasants as well as of the nobles, and if he suspected oppression or injustice by the nobles, he intervened very sharply. Thus he took the miller Arnold so emphatically under his protection against his lord Count von Schmettau and his neighbor District Councilor von Gersdorff that a change in the entire judiciary system was brought about. Moreover, the King would gladly have abolished serfdom and the heavy *corvée* burden, but here he was hindered by his concern for the interests of the noble estate-owners. The servitude existed by law, and it was still believed at the time that an estate could not be cultivated without *corvée* labor. The lords would have had to be compensated if the system were ended, and the King regarded this as impossible: in this respect everything remained largely as it had been. Only in one matter did the King decisively go against the interests of the noble landowners: emphatically he insisted that no peasant farm should be enclosed in the lords' estates, and no peasant land used to expand the area of the estates: rather, any peasant farm that became vacant was to be taken over by another peasant farmer.

The King's policy also greatly restricted the nobility's use of its agrarian produce in the eighteenth century. The nobles had to resign themselves to prohibition of wool export, which lowered the price of raw materials in the interest of the native cloth industry. The King would not tolerate excessively high corn prices; the border was largely closed for import and export of corn so that the corn trade could be effectively influenced by buying and selling from the royal magazines. The King was the greatest corn merchant of his country. Since the market was essentially closed, he could dictate the prices, and what he wanted was moderate prices remaining as stable as possible—neither too low nor too high. He wanted, as he said, to hold the balance between the corn producers—in the main, landowning noblemen—and the consumers, particularly the manufacturing laborers and the soldiers.[14]

Like the officers, the ministers and presidents of the administrative boards (*Kollegien*), were taken, under Frederick the Great, exclusively from the ranks of the nobility. The middle-class Cabinet secretaries were no longer appointed ministers, as they had been under his predecessor, and Frederick appointed only one non-noble as minister—Michaelis, minister of the province of the Mark and General Postmaster (*Kurmärkischer Provinzialminister*). Frederick always took his side against his noble colleagues, but did not make him a noble. He was in general very sparing with patents of nobility. He was convinced that certain talents he demanded from presidents of the chambers (*Kammerpräsidenten*) and ministers, as from his officers, could, broadly speaking, be found only in "men of rank." Nor is this altogether surprising, considering the notion of the middle class that lies at the basis of Goethe's *Wilhelm Meister:* the hero believes he can become equal in attitude and behavior to the members of good society only by means of the theater. The King was a stout believer in Horace's maxim: *Fortes creantur fortibus et bonis,* and he was of the opinion that the noble, to whom middle-class professions were closed as much by class custom as by administrative prescriptions, would all the more go in for bravery of conduct and efficiency in service. He would always have much more capacity than non-nobles in using weapons, in commanding, representing, and in all tasks that required authority and energy.[15]

The reign of Frederick the Great marked a clear turning point in the relationship between monarch and nobility. The hostility had gone out of it, the mistrust disappeared. The nobles were drawn to serve the interests of state as represented by the King; in both army and bureaucracy they fulfilled onerous and responsible duties. Above all, they became imbued with that Prussian state ethos of which the King set an example to his country; hence the close alliance between King and nobility, which was maintained through the stress of twenty battles and has lasted until the present day. It was not the nobility as such that Frederick the Great favored, it was only the nobles who gave distinguished service to the state, above all in the army. He had neither respect nor rewards for courtiers and idlers; they were good only as furnishings for the antechambers.

It may be said that the nobility of Frederick's epoch represented the class of truly active citizens in the Prussian state, and so it largely remained until 1806. Then the great reforms carried out under Stein and Hardenberg changed all this fundamentally. The whole social structure of the state was altered: the class-privileges of the nobility, insofar as they were of a constitutional nature, came to an end. The lord-peasant relation was dissolved; serfdom disappeared; the peasants became free property-owners, though diminished in number and area, since a great part of the former peasant land passed to the nobles by the new arrangements; and only then did these estates come to acquire their modern size and cohesion. But knightly estates were no longer exclusively reserved to the nobility: non-noble capital was no longer prevented from buying them. The concepts of landowner and nobleman were no longer identical, and the nimbus of local rulership, previously attached to the hereditary lord and his judiciary authority on his estates, began to disappear after the emancipation of the serfs—though this was a slow, gradual process: patrimonial jurisdiction was abolished only in 1849, and the police power of the estate-owners only with the district organization (*Kreisordnung*) of 1872.

In place of differences according to birth, there now came differences according to profession and property. Property and education, status and standard of living, now became decisive in determining the social position of individuals and families. Even in the army the nobility lost its privileged position, for in the end the rule that only young noblemen (or *Junkers*, as they were briefly described) were admitted as officer candidates had become a privilege. In place of these Junkers, who were often put into the army at fourteen or fifteen years of age, the ensigns (*Portepeefähnriche*) appeared, and they had to be at least seventeen years old, and show a certain degree of education. Otherwise the evaluation of their personality and origin was left, as before, to the regimental commander, so that the aristocratic character of the officer corps was maintained, but it was now based on education and social status rather than purely on noble birth. If on one hand the nobility was deprived of its exclusive privilege in land-ownership and a military career, on the other, it was no longer hindered from practicing middle-class professions; so that here too the barriers of the old feudal and Estates social order were removed.

The suspension of the nobles' taxation privileges met the greatest difficulties. It was a matter of course that the nobility should pay like the other Estates the new tolls, taxes on consumption and above all the new graduated income tax (*Klassensteuer*) of 1820. Yet the exemption from land taxes that Hardenberg had wished to remove in 1810 in fact remained in force until 1861. It was realized that land taxes would be an easement likely to lessen the value of the estates, and that therefore some compensation ought to be made; but this could not be afforded in the bad financial situation of the reform era. In 1861, when the comprehensive regulation of land taxes was made to include noble estates as well, such compensation was paid; but it had to be returned to the states when, as a result of Miquel's tax reform, the land tax was no longer levied by the state but left to the communal associations.

The reforms of Stein and Hardenberg by and large have been unfavorable to the nobility. It is of course a grotesque and wholly untenable proposition to inculpate the Junkers for the catastrophe of 1806; nonetheless it is fair to say that the old social order in which the nobility took such a prominent role was not compatible with the requirements of the modern state, and that it had to be replaced by the idea of a general and equal right of citizenship if all the forces needed to restore the state and secure its freedom and independence were to be set in motion. Frederick William III, in whose reign these crucial events took place, had a certain simple, almost middle-class, strain, and his most important advisers did not come from the Junker class east of the Elbe. Stein was a Baron of the Empire, wholly West German in his views and ways of life, with a marked distaste for the Junkers east of the Elbe. Scharnhorst was son of a Hanoverian peasant. Gneisenau's father was a noble, but he had a non-noble mother and grew up in wholly non-noble circumstances, without contact with his noble relatives. Hardenberg, also Hanoverian, was a nobleman, an aristocrat from head to toe, but he was inspired by the ideas of the French Revolution and the bureaucratic system of the Bonaparte state, and expressed the quintessence of his proposed reforms in 1807 in the phrase "Democratic institutions under the monarchical government."

It was with Hardenberg that the Junkers of the Mark came into the most heated conflict. In the assembly of notables convoked in 1811, they sharply and adversely criticized his reform laws; the protest petition sent to the King by the Estates of the districts Krossen, Lebus, and Beeskow-Storkow, used such sharp and disrespectful language against the Chancellor and his plans for reform—which after all had been presented in the name of the King —that the signatories, Marwitz and Finckenstein, became involved in a trial for *lèse majesté* and were imprisoned in the fortress of Spandau.[16]

This hard clash between King and nobility clearly shows how times had changed since the days of Frederick the Great, yet it did not destroy the bonds that had united Crown and nobility since those days; and the revolution of 1848 gave the nobility a new opportunity to present itself as a support of the throne and a protecting wall for the monarchy against the flood tide of revolution. The so-called *Junker Parlament,** which opposed the agrarian legislation of the National Assembly and made the cause of the monarchy its own, the foundation of the *Kreuzzeitung* and the Prussian *Volksverein* which were led by nobles, could be presented as actions that saved the principle of monarchy; and in the years of reaction the prestige and influence of the nobles from east of the Elbe were greatly increased, particularly through the creation of the *Herrenhaus* (Upper Chamber).[17] Finally, Bismarck emerged from this environment as a giant figure of world-historical dimensions, and nothing recently has given the much-reviled east-Elbian Junkers more prestige and respect than the fact that this powerful figure came from among them and reckoned himself as one of them. But of course the interests Bismarck represented were of a different and a higher order than the class interests of the nobles and the Conservative party; the acute political antagonism that existed between him and the nobles' *Kreuzzeitung* party was revealed in the notorious declaration of 1876 by which the Junker party decisively dissociated itself from this great member of their class.[18]

By and large, however, Bismarck attached himself in both internal and external affairs to the Frederican tradition and in consequence his period of political activity raised again the prestige and importance of the nobility in all spheres of life. The personal entourage of the monarch had in general remained composed of noblemen and is still so today. In the officer corps, in the higher civil service, and especially in the diplomatic service the nobility has as prominent a role as in land-ownership, in the

* Name given by Liberals to the meeting of the landowners held in September 1848 in Berlin to protest the abolition of the tax-exempt status of knights' estates.

Herrenhaus, and in the self-administration of the districts and provinces. The old nobility has, however, been supplemented by a new nobility whose patents were given in return for meritorious service; and its importance is based on concrete facts rather than purely legal reasons. The nobility's privileges are gone, and even the old nobility can preserve its traditional prestige for any length of time only by personal achievement.

It may be said that the Prussian nobility has proved itself in the course of time better than the French, which was never drawn by the Crown into the service of the state to the same extent as happened in Prussia; rather, as a dangerous rival to the power of the King the French nobility was systematically forced into a passive, useless life that ruined it. Even as rural landowners the French nobles lived off their revenues and so did not possess the power, which managing their own estates might have given them, so that everyone naturally regarded them as superfluous and inconvenient. On the other hand, the mainly small and poor nobility of Prussia cannot compare with the great, proud aristocracy of England, though to a certain extent Germany's ruling dynasties and mediatized princes are analogous to it. Even the political role of our nobility was quite different, though it seems to me in our political circumstances, a suitable and healthy one. In England the aristocracy traditionally went hand in hand with the lower and middle classes to break the power of the Crown—as it managed to do. In Prussia the nobles were the chief champions of the Crown, and their historical importance was due to the fact that they were protagonists of a monarchical state ethos that subsequently extended among the middle and lower classes.

This process of internal development has, of course, remained incomplete. A considerable part of the lower classes did not follow this course of development, prevented from doing so by a socialist agitation inspired as much by democratic hatred of the nobility as by distaste for a strict monarchical order of state. Social Democrats regard the Prussian Junkers as the bulwark of the political and social order they combat; and this ought to induce those of the middle class feeling hostility toward the nobility to reconsider their position. There is no real antithesis nowadays between nobles and burghers; and the greater the strength and cohesion in the ranks of the parties that wish to preserve the existing state, the more we may hope to win for the Prussian and German idea of the state those members of the working classes that remain aloof. For this idea of the state signifies the will and the strength to defend our state and our way of life from the dangers involved in our geographical position in the middle of the Continent, surrounded by other great military powers. Since we cannot extend our Continental frontiers, we must be able to obtain by trade and colonization what we need to feed our growing population. This is a goal toward which nobility, middle class, and working class can and must collaborate, each in his own interest and all in the interests of the whole.

2

PRUSSIAN REFORM
MOVEMENTS BEFORE 1806

This article appeared in the *Historische Zeitschrift,* Volume 76 (1896) and is Hintze's first publication in this periodical, which printed in later years many of his most important studies. It is almost the first work in which he went beyond the field of Prussian economic history in the mercantilist period, with which, as a collaborator of Schmoller in the *Acta Borussica,* he had been concerned in the preceding years. Of course, as a look at the footnotes demonstrates, this article grew also out of intensive research in the Central Prussian Archives, the *Geheime Staatsarchiv,* and was addressed mainly to scholars working in the same field of Prussian history.

Hintze had no doubt that when he referred to Boyen's "gradual transition from old to new," the reader was aware that the first volume of a Boyen biography by Friedrich Meinecke had just appeared in which Boyen's intellectual development had been analyzed for the first time. He took acquaintance with Georg Friedrich Knapp's work on the *Bauernbefreiung* (1887) for granted and assumed that his readers knew the collection of Hans Delbrück's *Historische und politische Aufsätze* (Berlin, 1886), in which, particularly in an essay on the Prussian officer corps, Delbrück had presented the thesis that the loss of extended Polish territories possessed by Prussia before 1806 was prerequisite for a reform aimed at broadening the basis of government. Hintze considered superfluous any explanation of the term "Nassau Memorandum"—that it embodied the first detailed statement of Stein's ideas for the reform of Prussia, written in Nassau in June 1807; and he regarded no further comment needed when he mentioned "the defeat" or "the catastrophe"; this could mean only Prussia's defeat in the war with Napoleon. Nor did Hintze find it necessary to state explicitly that the two chief reformers, Hardenberg and Stein, had held important government posts before Prussia's defeat—the one as head of the administration of Ansbach-Bayreuth, and the other as State Minister for Trade. Hintze saw himself intervening in a scholarly discussion which was going on and, with this article, he aimed at the participants in this discussion.

Nevertheless, within this sanctioned area of Prussian history from the times of Frederick the Great to those of Napoleon, Hintze, already in this early article, showed his intellectual independence and his unwillingness to accept traditional views untested. Hintze's generation of historians, as Friedrich Meinecke, then Hintze's closest friend, remembered in his *Memoirs*, believed that it was time to take a new look at Prussian history and to regain critical objectivity. The historians of Hintze's generation were doubtful not only about scholars like Droysen and Sybel, the heads of the Prussian School, who had glorified the institutions of Prussia and the course of Prussian policy in order to show that Prussia was destined to leadership in Germany; but they were skeptical also of the views of the succeeding generation, who threw all light on the reformers as the protagonists of entirely new liberal ideas and who considered the institutions, actions, and men of the preceding period as utterly bad and spineless. In contrast to such painting in black and white, Hintze and his friends were concerned to demonstrate the existence of historical continuity even in this period and to show how the new grew within and out of the old. Hintze's essay was a pioneering effort in this direction, and represents a remarkable scholarly advance. It was only a few years earlier that Hans Delbrück, in his essay "Der Preussische Landrat," had categorically stated that "of the first fundamental reforms that were carried out after the defeat, almost nothing had been taken previously into consideration." Later research has very much followed Hintze's line—to find in the eighteenth century the roots for the great changes of the early nineteenth century.

Hintze's essay has another distinguishing feature: it is a study in administrative history, and may be regarded as a model of research in this field. Through widespread research in administrative papers and files it does not only study administrative measures from the point of view of the central agency but also their consequences and ramifications on the local level and the attitude of the population to them. We receive a most comprehensive picture of the complex and differentiated administrative structure in the various territories of Prussia in the old régime. One cannot quite escape the impression that the attention and care that Hintze devoted to the analysis of the Prussian administration in the *Ancien régime* has made him almost too aware of the difficulties which the government faced and, therefore, perhaps somewhat too benevolent in his evaluation of the bureaucracy. Hans Rosenberg, in his book *Bureaucracy, Aristocracy, and Autocracy* (Cambridge, Mass., 1958), which takes up many of Hintze's points, emphasizes the social rigidification that accompanied the rise of the administrative bureaucracy and intensified the resistance to change; and Reinhart Koselleck, in his book *Preussen zwischen Reform und Revolution* (Stuttgart, 1967), has observed that the concentration on administrative tasks prevented Hintze from giving due attention to the more fundamental constitutional issues. Yet the continuing discussion of the questions with which Hintze dealt shows that his essay is still a most valuable and almost the best possible introduction to the problem of Prussian history.

We usually date a new era in Prussian history from the reforms associated with the names of Stein and Hardenberg, with whom political ideas emerged that were to be of immeasurable importance in times to come. These ideas, however, were not the only significant factor in the transformation of the state's institutions, which was of course the primary concern. Some efforts went with these new ideas, others against them; and these latter efforts were unmistakably bound up with the needs and the traditions of the old Prussian state, whatever their significance as regards the new order that was to come. The past gave them justification; and so long as the basic features of Old Prussia—the army and the bureaucracy—were maintained, the continuity of Prussian history was preserved.

Contemporaries thought this was a complete breach with the past—an absolute revolution in public affairs—and the reformers were understandably reluctant to associate their activities with any past ones. Altenstein, a philosophical friend of Fichte, wished to reconstruct the state from its foundations in accordance with the highest idea of morality; and Hardenberg, always receptive to ideas, took this speculative thought, which so greatly accorded with his own liberal reforming plans, and made it his own. All in all, Stein's political ideas were in absolute antithesis to the spirit of government in Old Prussia; nonetheless, the reforms carried out after 1807 may be regarded to some extent as a continuation of the efforts that had been made since the accession of Frederick William III. The old structure of the state did not perish without making an attempt to regenerate itself from within. This attempt was, in the main, a failure; yet history must not, for all that, pass it over in silence. These efforts lacked the

energy and idealism of the later period, but they had practical
importance in that they formulated and clarified the work that
would have to be done; they needed the powerful prompting of
events to reach their goal. But the political leadership that was to
put these reforms into effect had to be favorably disposed toward
them; without such inclination, the path toward reform would
not have been taken immediately after the defeat.

These early attempts at reform have not yet been made known
in full, and I should like to expand the existing picture in some
of its essential features by using new documentary material.[1]

Frederick William III was a long way from sharing that blind-
ing optimism so common in Prussia before Jena. The reforming
mood that he showed from the beginning came from a conviction
that he often expressed, that prevailing conditions both in the
army and in the civil service would spell ruin for the state unless
something were done. As in 1807, on his accession to the throne,
two royal commissions were charged with the task of reform—
one military, which had been established in 1795 but was now
re-instituted, and one administrative, charged with examining
the governmental system from the standpoint of the new spirit of
the times (*Zeitgeist*). Von der Goltz has given an account of the
military in his work *Rossbach und Jena,* but the administrative
has received no attention.[2] It has been said of the King's proposals
for reform in the army that they hardly touched the heart of the
problem,[3] and we may say much the same of the Instruction to
the Financial Commission, which clearly bears the personal
stamp of the King. It displays sound judgment and profound
study of the basic principles of administration, but there is nothing of a systematic reform program inspired by creative political
ideas—in fact it is a written version of all sorts of reforming
tendencies held by elements in the high bureaucracy. The nature
of this document shows how greatly masters had changed since
the death of Frederick the Great: the King no longer merely ordered his servants, he required their advice.

There was not yet any talk of social reform; but this subject did have considerable importance in the years that followed. It was in fact a minister, Struensee, who in August 1799 described the plans for social reform in these terms to the French *chargé d'affaires*:

The creative revolution was made in France from below; in Prussia it will be made slowly and from above. The King is a democrat in his own way—he is working untiringly to restrict the privileges of the nobility, and will follow Joseph II's plan; only with slower means. In a few years there will be no privileged class in Prussia.[4]

This was obviously said essentially to impress the Frenchman, and we can leave aside the question of whether the King's intentions regarding reform went so far and were so decided; but, as for the idea that he took his principles from the French Revolution, this is indeed a cause for legitimate doubt. The French Revolution was the most powerful expression of a general line of thought; the idea that society and state ought to be based on the natural rights of the individual had for long been a common belief of European civilization. In Prussia, in combination with traditions of Frederick the Great, they were given a particular form of expression by the jurists who produced the draft of the General Code of Laws, especially by Suarez, through whom Frederick William himself had been introduced to the field of constitutional and administrative law. Suarez is obviously the source from which the King drew his notion of the need for equality among citizens, and his terminology appears several times in royal announcements of these days. Again, part of what Suarez has to say in his lectures foreshadows the formula by which Stein expressed the basic ideas of reform in his Political Testament.[5] Suarez wrote a maxim to the effect that the wise governor must rule and take care of his subjects not as machines but as free citizens, and that each of them should be able to use his powers and capacities as he sees fit, in his own direction and for his own happiness.

The Cabinet councilors Mencken and Beyme represented the continuing influence of Suarez' ideas in the royal entourage, and they may be thought of as the men chiefly involved in the efforts for reform. Mencken played a dominant role[6] at the beginning, though he speedily withdrew.[7] Beyme had formerly worked on the Law Code and was brought from the Chamber Court into the Cabinet[8] because of his reforming activities. He was the force behind the liberation of the serfs.[9] No more than Mencken was he a statesman on the grand scale, but he did have more industry and driving ambition, and acquired decisive influence, particularly in internal affairs. He was not lacking in concern for higher considerations, though he did lack much practical experience in administration. His method of conducting affairs was not without a strain of legislative formalism and doctrinaire overemphasis. His personal conflict with Hardenberg and his passionate battle with Stein were explicable by the unhealthy part he took in 1805 and 1806, in combination with Lombard, in foreign affairs. There was no such conflict of principle in the conduct of internal affairs.[10]

Cabinet government itself did not further the course of internal reform. It placed obstacles in the way of the responsible executive ministers without being able to replace their influence. Given the irresolute nature of the King, this had a crippling effect on all parts of the machinery of state, which was based on the assumption that there would always be a purposeful unitary impulse from above. There was a vast difference between the 1807 reform committees working under Stein's impulse and those of 1798, which were left largely to themselves. Only a strong, dictatorial will can put through great reforms; thus the government might prepare, but it could not complete.

The preparation for reform advanced most in the area of measures regarding the social structure. It would be incorrect to say that the social order on which Frederick the Great's state had rested went on existing until 1806, rigidified to a closed system; or that the legislation of 1807 transformed the Estates system at one stroke into a modern, egalitarian state. Changes had been taking place slowly for a long time. The legislation of 1807 was basically the conclusion of a process that went back many years.

The freeing of the serfs was done in Prussia in two stages. The emancipation of the privately owned serfs of which the suspension of hereditary serfdom was only the first step, was preceded by a freeing of the Domain serfs which was carried out, as Knapp has shown, largely between 1799 and 1805 in a form to serve as a model. It was a "soundless, all-pervading reform," which, in its social and political consequences, went far beyond the later regulation on the serf question.[11]

The suspension of the hereditary serfdom of the privately owned serfs was, however, more closely connected with reform efforts before 1806 than has been generally known. From 1798 onward, the King pursued the plan of abolishing hereditary serfdom for all non-adults and thus letting it gradually die out;[12] and while the Legal Commission approved, it was rejected by the *Generaldirektorium** and thus was not put into practice.[13] It is now clear from the Cabinet correspondence that the King by no means abandoned his intention, and tried to put it into effect by means of regulations for the single provinces, first in East Prussia with the help of Minister von Schroetter and Chancellor von Goldbeck, who had ratified the adverse votes. They opened negotiations with deputies of the Estates,[14] and when this did not have the desired effect,[15] they requested promulgation of a unilateral royal decree, the central point of which was that all children born after the day of homage were to be free of hereditary serfdom. The draft of this decree, dated February 6, 1803, was not executed by the King, although its contents fully accorded with his intentions; probably he was wary of provoking a conflict with the Estates at this critical juncture.[16] Schroetter, in agreement with the Cabinet, continued his attempts to win the East Prussian nobility for the King's plan. Some nobles, with the King's hearty approval, began privately to free their serfs; among these

---

* General Directory, abbreviated name for the *"General-Ober-Finanz-Kriegs-und Domänen Direktorium,"* the central authority for the *"Kriegs- und Domänen-Kammern"* in the provinces (see *Kammer,* p. 77). The General Directory developed into the highest bureaucratic authority in Prussia.

nobles were all the Dohnas, a Finckenstein (Schönberg), and Schroetter himself.

From the normal procedures indicated in the Instrument of Emancipation that Schroetter communicated to Beyme, it was obvious that the new arrangements were to be based largely on the principle of free contract. Compulsory resettlement of peasants on small farms that fell vacant was not encounraged. This compulsion had been the core of the so-called "peasant protection" against "enclosure"; but now the state could scarcely make use of compulsion against the seigneurs, when they had already abandoned their own power to force peasants to accept some form of employment at their behest. Obviously these lords could no longer be forbidden occasionally to enclose a peasant farm; and, as a result of economic changes, such an inclination was already strongly in evidence.

As we know from Knapp's researches, "peasant protection" in East Prussia was then weak and, up to 1806, control was hardly possible.[17] However, after the ordinance of May 31, 1806,[18] created a solid legal basis and safeguarded the practical execution of the prescriptions against enclosure, the estate-owners who had freed their serfs appeared to the other members of their class to enjoy a privileged position, for the strictness of the law could not easily be applied to them. Thus, the East Prussian nobility was brought to see advantages in the renunciation of serfdom, and permission to enclose was obtained in 1807 as equivalent to freeing the serfs. Stein threw his veto into the scale against this fatal clause, but he was only partly successful. Peasant protection lost a great part of its effectiveness, and the basic maxim of compensating the seigneurs by peasant land became the cornerstone of all subsequent legislation to abolish serfdom.[19]

The abolition of the nobles' privileges in the possession of manors corresponded to this freeing of peasant land; but even this was not wholly a product of 1807. Frederick the Great, by asserting the principle that only nobles could own land, attempted to slow down an irresistible social and economic process in the interests of the state rather than in the interests of a class;[20] but this principle was no longer strictly maintained after his death. With the growing need for capital and the growing indebtedness of the large estates, this benefit, in time, became a plague for the landowners themselves. Hertzberg praises Frederick William II for making a breach with the Frederican principle, and Marwitz complained bitterly that under Frederick William III royal permission for a non-noble to acquire a manor, as forbidden by the law of the land, was never again refused.[21]

The 1807 legislation merely shattered the shell within which the new system had slowly and almost unnoticeably been developing; yet neither economic developments nor the reform legislation destroyed the political and social hegemony of the great landowners in the east. The strong collective spirit of this ruling class remained unbroken, and largely managed to assimilate the non-noble invaders.

Nevertheless, the immobility of the rural property and class relations began gradually to loosen up, and this in turn affected the military organization of the Prussian state for almost a century. It had become impossible to keep the ordinary conscripted peasant soldier of the cantons in his place and to keep manorial estates free from the incalculable effects of freedom of movement; consequently it was necessary to open a new source for the recruiting of the army, the more so as the great changes in the European situation, in the Empire and in Poland, had set strict limits to the possibility of foreign recruiting. These connections were fully realized only long after the events, but similar considerations prompted, even before 1806, the plan for diminishing the number of foreigners in the army, limiting exemptions, and creating a territorial militia; even lessening of the rigidity of discipline and a general admission of members of the bourgeoisie to officers' posts were envisaged.

I cannot involve myself here in further exploration of these efforts at reform, which von der Goltz has extensively described. In the main, however, they did not achieve their aims—though they were not, historically speaking, in vain. They were products of the first phase in the great psychological process leading to the reforms; and the King himself was at the very center of this process. It was only after long, painful meditation and vacillation that he arrived at the better insights and decisions to which his proposal to the commission for military reorganization bore witness; his obstinate, uninspired nature had to be conditioned for some time before he could be reconciled with executing anything out of the ordinary.

The effect of the 1806 catastrophe consisted more in abandonment of belief in false authorities than in a conversion of the leading personalities. Before 1806 no one thought much about universal conscription; yet this innovation, by far the greatest and most pregnant for the future that the Reform era created, would have been impossible without the Prussian past, without the cantonal system and the military of the state as a whole. The historical demonstrations used by Scharnhorst as a means to persuade the King that his bold plans were correct were not merely for show (*Blendwerk*); it was just this miraculous blending of old and new that was characteristic of the military reform. The new Prussian army created by Scharnhorst and Boyen still bore, unmistakably, the basic character of the Frederican era; it certainly was a long way from such doctrinaire projects as the election of officers. The old aristocratic Prussian character of the officer corps was maintained even after non-nobles were admitted to the corps. As before, the officer felt bound to the King by a special personal loyalty; and this was more than a mere citizen loyalty, but reached back to the feudal age of military history.

There is one little-mentioned point in these deliberations on the effect of military conditions on the social and financial field, which emerges with particular clarity. This point was the one that, characteristically, the King most appreciated: the improvement of the soldiers' economic position.

Wages had remained the same since Frederick William II's time, although the basic cost of living had doubled. The King

wanted to raise the soldiers' wages by 25 per cent, and this was
finally done. Even so, the soldiers were urgently in need of civil
employment as a supplementary source of income. This obtained
not only for the volunteer guardsmen but also for soldiers in
full service. But the exclusive privileges of the guilds frequently
worked against this. Thus, maintenance of the army not only
became a burning question of finance, it also presented a social
problem, since the old military arrangements turned out to be
incompatible with the civilian manufacturing system. It was in
this context that the radical demand for total abolition of the
guild obligations was raised—to my knowledge, for the first
time in Prussia—in the deliberations of the Financial Commission.[22] The demand did not of course pass without opposition.
Its opponents feared that such a sudden change would lead to
dangerous ferment among the manufacturing population. It
was agreed to postpone execution of the plan until quieter
times and to come to some agreement with neighboring states in
the matter. But in order to initiate and facilitate transition to
freedom of trade one member of the committee proposed that
military personnel[23] should be immediately freed of guild and
occupational restrictions—although soldiers who wished to carry
on a business of their own should be subject to the usual civil
burdens. There was no general ordinance on this, yet it would
seem from the decision in a litigation that this was the procedure
followed in practice.[24]

This was an important transformation in the position of the soldiers regarding civil society. Subsequent legislation made the
soldier into a citizen; the aim of these efforts was to provide the
soldier with means for existence in civil life. These two tendencies, both extremely different in their point of departure and their
military effect, were at one in their social purpose: abolition of
the gap between civil and military, and fusion of soldier with the
citizen.

In financial terms, only a relatively trivial sum was involved
in the wage increases, which for a long time occupied the center

of the commission's deliberations—not more than a half-million talers annually.[25] But in discussing them, important considerations regarding financial reform in general emerged. A Cabinet order of October 13, 1798, told the Financial Commission to consider the possibility of making the nobility liable to the land tax. The nobles' payments made in lieu of feudal service (*Lehnpferdgeld*) were no adequate replacement of the burdens of feudal service; altogether, it was said, the intention of the King was to bring the exempted classes to take their share of public burden.

It was probably General Courbière[26] who suggested this idea and thus touched upon a point in the Prussian tax system where reform was most needed. Though not a farmer himself, to forestall the reproaches of his peers, should the plan be executed, he had gone so far as to put his own wealth into land.

The Cabinet order to the Financial Commission was revealed by a breach of official secrets[27] to a Hamburg newspaper,[28] and provoked concern in the country. A number of noble corporations, particularly in the Electoral Mark,* approached the King with arguments that opposed these intentions, citing the written rights of the Estates.[29] But the Financial Commission itself raised grave doubts, referring partly to the rent-like character of the tax, and partly to the unquestionably antithetical rights of the nobility;[30] for the moment there could be no question of the state's paying compensation. Finally, in place of the land-tax reform the Commission recommended, in the main, a proportionate increase in purchase-taxes on goods used by the propertied classes; and simultaneously a total abolition of all the various freedoms from excise and customs possessed by the privileged classes.[31] The King resigned himself without much difficulty to these proposals, and thus came about the Edict of January 25, 1799, formally drawn up by Struensee, giving legislative expression to the idea.[32]

* Actually means the Mark Brandenburg, i.e., the electorate of Brandenburg. It comprised different territories with their own administration and their own Estates, particularly the Old Mark (Altmark) west of the Elbe, and the New Mark (Neumark) east of the Oder.

The suspension of nobles' privileges provoked attempts at resistance. The Estates, not only in the Rhenish and Westphalian territories but in the Electoral Mark as well, demanded to be heard before the Edict took effect.[33] The Crown asserted its sovereign rights in matters of finance and reaffirmed the principle which it had enunciated that no one class of citizens should continuously suffer from preferences given to another class. When the Mark nobility would not be satisfied with this, further representations in the matter were simply forbidden.[34] This was a preliminary version of the conflict that Hardenberg had to fight in 1811.

Other reforms achieved during the period up to 1806 in the field of financial administration were intimately bound up with the discussions of the Financial Commission. The simplification of the important salt monopoly, with which Stein began his activities as directing minister of the General Directory; the abolition of inland tolls, which he soon afterward undertook; the setting-up of the statistical office, through which important data were to be gained as a basis for future policies in commerce and manufacturing; and the combining of the Excise administration with the Boards of War and Domains (*Kriegs- und Domänen-Kammern**) which was largely carried out before 1806—all these reforms, of which Stein is usually regarded as the originator, were merely the execution of plans the Financial Commission had recommended after careful examination,[35] and in part they stemmed from royal suggestions, particularly the abolition of inland tolls—

---

* *Kammer* has a number of different meanings, so that it has to be translated in various ways. Sometimes the word "chamber" will be appropriate, though the most frequent occurrence in the context of Prussian history is *Kriegs- und Domänen-Kammer* (sometimes referred to merely as *Kammern*), a collegiate administrative board that administered the princely domains in the various provinces and collected the tax levied on the rural population for military purposes, the so-called *Kontribution*. Briefly, the *Kriegs- und Domänen-Kammer* (probably best called "Boards of War and Domains"), had chiefly financial tasks but exercised also some judiciary functions (*Kammerjustiz*). The officials on the Boards of War and Domains were *Kammerräte*, which might be translated as "Chamber councilors." *Kammergericht* (Chamber Court) has nothing to do with the judiciary authorities of the Board of War and Domains, but was the highest court of appeals in Brandenburg.

on this point the King had expressed a firm will in his Instruction.[36]

That all these plans remained unfulfilled for so many years was largely the fault of Struensee. There was something tragic about this often misjudged statesman. He should not be judged merely on the basis of the few frivolous-sounding sarcasms he is reported to have uttered, such as the famous phrase "We have still a bit of time before the building collapses" (*Eine Zeitlang werde die Pastete wohl noch halten*). He was the most significant representative of the old Frederican system in an era struggling toward new forms; he was a cool, clear, mathematical man, one who, for all his recognition that existing circumstances could not be maintained, deeply doubted the value of every reform, for he was unable to include the *imponderabilia* of political life in his calculations. He had none of the blissful, unthinking quality by which so many of the senior officials managed to deceive themselves as to the real state of affairs; but as a Cassandra, he could see only the signs of collapse, not the stirrings of new life. It is understandable that he impressed many people, particularly the younger ones; but how Schoen could have seen him as the greatest of the Prussian ministers, the saviour, is incomprehensible. This skeptic lacked every quality necessary in a reformer, both the easy confidence and the faith that moves mountains. Unperturbed by the popular movements of his day, he systematically developed the Frederican system to its logical conclusion. He maintained the tariff system—not without justification—against the King's vague inclination toward free trade; and indeed perfected it because of the financial crisis of 1799;[37] and likewise he simply did nothing, as member of the Financial Commission, to reform the Excise* system, as the King had suggested in the Instruction he gave. As he declared to the Commission that, had he been aware of any means of improving things, he would, as minister, have proposed it long ago to the King.

---

* *Akzise* (= excise). A tax on foodstuffs and other goods to which the inhabitants of towns were subjected and which was originally raised at the town gates.

Nonetheless even at this time far-ranging ideas of reform were expressed and discussed. The essential principles from which the later transformation of indirect taxation in Prussia was drawn emerged in the papers of the Financial Commission for the first time, though not of course as a systematic whole[38]—they mention a division between frontier tolls and consumption taxes; limitation of the latter to a few main items that could easily bear them, whereas the great number of other items was left untaxed; extension of the simplified taxes on consumption to the countryside by including rural brewing and distilling. These were all ideas on which, if they were suitably combined—a comprehensive reform of the Excise system could be based, but which Struensee, despite occasional admonitions from the King, failed to carry out.[39]

Here again it was only Stein who undertook the reform, at least on one important point. On October 9, 1805, in context with his plan for issuing Treasury Bills, he proposed to the King that to cover payments of interest a uniform tax on the manufacture of alcoholic beverages, on slaughtering, and on the baking of white bread should be introduced for the countryside. The obvious intention behind this was to remove the sharp separation of town and country which had for many years been proved to hinder economic progress. As his Memorandum declared,

On an increased uniformity (*Gleichheit*) of town and country rests the possibility of placing on the land some of the enterprises now wholly confined to the towns and thereby providing the economy on the one hand and manufacturing on the other with cheap labor.[40]

This very part of Stein's requests met with the King's wholehearted approval; a Cabinet order of October 15[41] instructed the minister to take the necessary measures at once. But there is no evidence in the documents that this happened. Stein, in a Memorandum of October 26,[42] requested that this innovation, which might encounter many difficulties, be represented in an official pamphlet as a patriotic sacrifice required by the present emergency; his Memorandum breathed both patriotic pride and warlike ardor. The general political tendency of the proposal was obvious; it was not accepted: the fateful turn of foreign affairs prevented the execution of the already decided measures concerning reform of the Excise. At all events the decision in principle regarding this important matter made a breach in the old Excise system: the direction toward reform was no longer in doubt.

The civil service in Prussia had grown step by step with the fiscal system, and if the one needed reform, it was matched by the other. Nowhere was this relation more strikingly evidenced than in the establishment of the General Office of Control (*Generalkontrolle*), where data concerning the entire financial administration were to be collected so as to give a general picture of the economy, for such a general picture had been in abeyance since the death of Frederick the Great. As in the case of the foundation of the Supreme Military Council (*Oberkriegs Kollegium**) in 1787, the establishment of the General Office of Control separated one of the most important tasks of royal absolutism from the person of the monarch. But even the organization of the fiscal "authorities" no longer corresponded to their tasks, which had grown in scope and volume: the most important aspect of the King's own program for reform anticipated a change in the procedural methods of the General Directory in step with the new times. The provisional Instruction of March 19, 1798, marked the first step in this path: it broke with the now unworkable principle of an entirely collegiate organization, and accorded the departmental heads a certain degree of legitimate independence and exclusive responsibility;[43] but the weekly plenary discussions for general affairs which were then reintroduced did not suffice, considering the complicated bureaucratic structure, to give unity and consistency to the administration.

More was done in the Financial Commission: one of the brightest of the junior officials, Privy Councilor Borgstede,[44] cham-

---

* Created only at the end of the eighteenth century as the central authority for military affairs. "Supreme Military Council" seems an appropriate rendering, so long as it is understood that this agency was concerned with administration, not military strategy.

pioned wholly modern ideas of reform. He demanded that provincial departments should no longer exist in the central authority but that affairs ought to be divided on technical lines among four specialist ministers who were to form a collegiate commission, while the single ministries would be organized on hierarchical lines (*Bürosystem*). He placed particular importance on the organization of a powerful collegiate provincial administrative authority, which was to be created by extending the competence and responsibility of the Chambers, in which all branches of administration should be concentrated.[45]

It is characteristic of the then prevailing tendency in the Cabinet that, on the close of the Commission's work, Borgstede was entrusted with making more detailed proposals regarding the reform of the administration. On giving a further extensive version of his plan,[46] he admitted that great difficulties would result from introducing them in this form, and he proposed a transitory stage. He clung to the basic idea of lightening the burden of the central authorities, of strengthening the provincial authorities, and of giving the ministers greater freedom of action in their own spheres; but he also wished to preserve the two great provincial departments—one for the former Polish provinces, including East Prussia, and one for the Imperial areas (*Reichslande*), including Silesia. There were also to be three specialist ministries—for Finance, War, and Excise and Trade. In the college of ministers the general controller (*Generalkontrolleur*),[47] whose position was to be linked with that of the finance minister, was to take the chief post, and after him the most senior of the ministers.

Hardenberg, whose right hand in the Franconian department was Borgstede, went still further in the proposals he added to the Memorandum.[48] He recommended the formation of a unified council of ministers beyond the framework of the General Directory, on the basis of the old Council of State. And the five ministers of the General Directory would be supplemented by another three—for Justice, Foreign Affairs, and the Interior, who would also take charge of religious affairs, feudal matters, and the royal household.

Clearly, ideas were taking shape that later formed the basis for the reorganized central authorities. Only one point—the most important one—was not touched upon: the position of the Cabinet councilors between the King and the ministers. Their abolition was to become later the cardinal point of the reform. Evidently Hardenberg then still believed that a ministerial council could work successfully and effectively even with the existing Cabinet: the antithesis between Cabinet councilors and ministers had not yet developed in its later acuteness. Hardenberg, like most of the other ministers, had particularly harmonious relations with Beyme; it is possible that an opportune strengthening and consolidating of the ministerial authority might have prevented the full development of Cabinet government that took place during the next few years. The general controller, who had one foot in the Cabinet and the other in the General Directory, was of course a rudimentary version of a Prime Minister—a man like Stein could have done almost anything in such a position. But the plans of reform were not realized in this form.

It was principally Minister von Voss[49] who gave a different twist to the plans of Borgstede and Hardenberg. Voss seems to have taken umbrage at the idea of being subordinated to a directing minister.[50] He did not want any great changes in the composition of the central authority—although the ministers were to acquire a freer hand in their departments.[51] He placed the main importance wholly on the organization of the provincial authorities; he accepted the idea of greater efficiency, greater independence, and greater responsibility on the part of the Chambers, into which he wished to concentrate all the various branches of provincial administration. Like Hardenberg, he sought to abolish the judicial powers of the Chambers (Kammerjustiz*), and then to transfer the administration of Church, schools, and paupers to the bureaucratic agencies. This would both raise the authority of these provincial agencies and free the General Directory from the plague of detail. The idea behind

* See note on *Kammer* above.

all this was decentralization of administration on bureaucratic lines, and this he expected to simplify and revivify the conduct of affairs and replace paperwork by real action.[52]

The Voss plan[53] was accepted by the King on July 10, 1800, and was to be put into effect by stages—at first in the department of Voss himself, which at the time embraced the Mark, Pomerania, and Southern Prussia.[54] After a year Voss was able to tell the King that the new arrangements had succeeded as he had expected, and to propose that they be extended over the whole monarchy.[55] Schroetter[56] gave his consent for the Old Prussian department, and Heinitz, in agreement with Provincial Governor (*Oberpräsident*) Stein,[57] for the Westphalian department. The alteration in the position of the Boards for War and Domains[58] (*Kriegs- und Domänen-Kammern*) thus took place as early as 1801 in Prussia, a year later[59] in Westphalia. In connection with this development, unification of the Excise administration with the Chambers[60] and abolition of the juridical powers of the Boards,[61] were undertaken gradually in single province.[62] The new system had not yet been wholly introduced when war broke out.

The aim of these reforms was twofold: to transform the Boards for War and Domains largely into a provincial administrative agency such as was later to be displayed in the provincial governments (*Regierungen*),[63] and also to raise the departmental heads in the General Directory to the status of directing ministers.

The position of the ministers had been changing for some time, both toward above and below. The ministers strove for greater freedom in directing and controlling their area of administration against the collegiate restrictions of the old system. With regard to the King, they now had a more strictly defined responsibility and greater awareness of their proper functions than had been true in the reign of Frederick the Great and Frederick William II. "Servants of the King" had been transformed into "servants of the state."

We are considering a great, slow but steady metamorphosis in

the old system of the Prussian bureaucratic state. The old autocratic system was gradually disintegrating, and a new bureaucratic system was developing. In proportion to the increasing
weakness and uncertainty of the workings of the royal Cabinet,
the position of the higher and middle civil service became freer
and more independent. Sooner or later this change had to reach the
goal which it did not reach then—the creation of a Ministry of
State, equipped with all the powers then accorded to the King.
That vast transformation of the Prussian system of government
was completed in the conflict over the elimination of the Cabinet
government that went on in 1806/1807. With its elimination one
factor that had paralyzed the state in its moment of crisis was removed—the uncertainty of the supreme direction.

There was another factor, which continued to exist for a long
time: the Prussian state was not rotten within, but it had not
completed its evolution, impeded in its development because it
lacked strong roots in the masses; it had no national basis. It was
the unforgettable service of Stein and his companions to call
forth the moral power that would make up this void, and the
powerful impulse to which those days gave birth has been affecting and shaping our political system even in most recent times.
Both the national idea, however, and the principle of a general
participation in government were more a program for the future
than the substance of what was realized in the reform period. It
was largely the civil service—which Stein so often berated—that,
cooperating closely with the King and without the intervention
of any popular movement, produced a transformation in the structure of the state.

Again, at the existing level of social development in most of
the Prussian territories, the bureaucracy alone was capable of
effecting this progress. The rural masses would exist for many years
to come in economic dependence, while the populace of the towns
could only gradually become equal to the tasks required by local
self-government and general military service. At the beginning
of the nineteenth century, Prussia lacked a compact, responsible,

politically active middle class that could stand on an equal footing with the landowning aristocracy. The social forces that could take the part of the Third Estate in Prussia were armed by their education rather than by their wealth, and these forces found their natural center in the organized civil service. This was the bridge between the Prussia of Frederick the Great and the Prussia of Stein and Hardenberg. Here the sober rationalism of the Enlightenment, the radical demands of the new idealism, and the historical conservatism of a feudal element that had never quite disappeared combined on a middle line and the doctrinaire contrasts between them receded before the demands of practical politics.

The civil service of the Reform era could acquire this importance only because its younger elements, imbued with the new culture, had already, before Jena, championed contemporary ideas of reform. To appreciate the significance of this development the historian must examine the pre-Jena activities of the higher civil service and army officers more carefully than has hitherto been the case. As has been shown recently, Boyen's development shows in a striking manner this gradual transition from old to new. Something of the same might be done, for instance, in Schroetter's case. Frederick William III's attempts at reform were in large measure a mere reflection of the changes in the general temper of the civil service, though these attempts in turn unquestionably furthered the process. A movement of this kind offered great possibilities for an individual reformer to emerge; reform would not have come about had there been no individual reformer of this kind: Frederick William III's attempts at reform failed because they were not yet promoted by a ruthless and resolute will. Indeed, insofar as they spread doubt and confusion in government circles, they themselves may even be indirectly responsible for the collapse of 1806.

The policy of neutrality and the mood of reform are connected; both came from a feeling of inadequacy. Prussia's need for peace stemmed from the exhaustion of the state's finances; but the

peaceful atmosphere created by this policy prevented the execution of reforms on a grand scale, particularly in the field of military organization. Again, it was in the nature of the Prussian state
that military requirements shaped the whole of internal government: without a solution of the problem of military reform, no
comprehensive change could take place in the political sphere.
After 1807 all the internal reforms were inspired mainly under
Stein's influence, by the idea of liberating the state from foreign
rule; but before 1806 the essential political driving force was
lacking—the vital connection with the great issues of political
existence and power.

Reform before 1806 encountered the greatest difficulty in the
social sphere. Delbrück in particular has always stressed that no
reform could have been imaginable before the loss of the Polish
provinces. This was of course important, but it does not seem to
me to have been the decisive factor. Stein, in the Nassau Memorandum, showed the way in which the Polish obstacle could be
skirted—at the time he was thinking in terms of a separate administration in accordance with the principle of nationality. At
the Congress of Vienna Hardenberg insisted on claiming a large
part of Prussia's former Polish possessions even after the promulgation of the conscription decree (*Wehrgesetz*). More important
than the loss of the Polish provinces, to my mind, was the elimination of royal autocracy; the irresolution of the monarch, the
subordinate position of the royal assistants, the atrophy in ministerial energy and in responsibility, must be regarded as the real
seat of the political weakness of the Prussian state.

This political weakness was fatal for Prussia and not any moral
decline, of which there are currently many exaggerated notions.
The undeniable moral ills of the time were in reality merely the
obverse side of great cultural progress, concomitants of a movement that replaced the moribund patriarchal order of the past
by the ideal of individualistic, aesthetic education. Besides, in
Prussia herself, the aesthetic idealism was beginning to turn into
an ethical and political idealism, Fichte sought refuge in Berlin,

and this cosmopolitan radical had become a patriot already before the catastrophe. Schleiermacher's thought, too, turned to
political and national ethics before the defeat of Prussia. In the
younger generation of officials and officers an abundance of talent was maturing, inspired by ideas of German education, by the
doctrines of Kant and Smith. The spiritual and moral forces that
were to regenerate the state were ready; the defeat of 1806 did
not produce them, though it gave them a powerful impulse and
opened to them the path toward a productive activity. It is unquestionably correct that without the collapse of Jena no basic and
all-pervading reforms like those of 1807 could have been made
in Prussia; but it is equally certain that the defeat itself would
have produced a general mental paralysis instead of a general
stimulus had the government of the state not already been affected by a change in mood that could in an emergency be translated into terms of political resolution and deeds. The transformation of the Prussian state after 1807 proceeded not by a harsh
breach with its own past, a precipitate aping of foreign models;
it happened in close connection with earlier developments. This
transformation marks a watershed between two areas: while it
concluded the great monarchical reforms of the eighteenth century, it also ushered in a new era in the life of the state.

3

CALVINISM AND RAISON D'ETAT IN EARLY SEVENTEENTH-CENTURY BRANDENBURG

This study, which appeared in 1931, was the last article Hintze published in the *Historische Zeitschrift* and actually his last long historical
investigation. Appropriately it combines his early concern with Brandenburg-Prussian history and his more recent interest in the sociology
of Max Weber and in the questions Weber and Troeltsch had raised
about the influence of Protestantism on the development of the
modern world. Hintze's study might be divided into two parts. First
he investigates and demolishes the story that the conversion of the
Elector Johann Sigismund to Calvinism in 1613 infused a new, more
ambitious spirit into Prussian politics. Then, in the longer second part,
he tries to indicate the true channels through which Calvinist energy
permeated into the sleepy life of Brandenburg. For this second part,
Hintze made extensive use of Volume I of the *Acta Brandenburgica*,
which had come out in 1927 and dealt with the years 1604-1606. To a
certain extent, Hintze's study is a review of this volume; he quotes
at length from the documentation of this work (such passages are
given here without quotation marks, since modern English can hardly
be regarded as a precise reproduction of early seventeenth-century
German; and understanding of Hintze's essay is facilitated if it is read
with the first volume of *Acta Brandenburgica* at hand. Hintze's article

is somewhat uneven: it moves between insights that illuminate the entire institutional developments in modern Europe, and detailed, almost minute discussions of the problems that Brandenburg faced in the early seventeenth century. Because today's reader, who has not been taught history at a Prussian *Gymnasium* before the First World War, may not be entirely familiar with developments of Hohenzollern history, a brief factual explanation may be appropriate.

The Electors of Brandenburg in the period under discussion were Johann Georg (1571–98), Joachim Friedrich (1598–1608), and Johann Sigismund (1608–19). But, in addition to Brandenburg, members of the house of Hohenzollern ruled in other states, too: they were Margraves of Ansbach and Kulmbach, and of Bayreuth in Franconia, and Dukes of Jägerndorf in Silesia; and one of the members of the Ansbach line had become Duke of Prussia as a vassal of the King of Poland. His only son, Albrecht Friedrich, was mentally ill, so that government was carried on under the guardianship (*Kuratel*) of his nearest relative, the Margrave George Friedrich of Ansbach-Kulmbach. When Georg Friedrich died in 1603, the Hohenzollern rulers of Brandenburg attested their claims to guardianship of the mentally ill duke Albrecht Friedrich and, after his death, to his succession. These claims were reinforced by the marriage of Johann Sigismund, then presumptive heir, later Elector of Brandenburg, to the sister of the Duke Albrecht Friedrich.

This marriage, however, had yet another aspect. The Duchess Marie Eleanore of Prussia, the mother of Duke Albrecht Friedrich of Prussia and of Johann Sigismund's wife, was the oldest daughter of the Duke of Jülich-Cleves, and since her only brother was mentally ill and had no children, she could claim for her descendants—i.e., for Johann Sigismund's wife and their children—succession in the dukedom of Jülich-Cleves. Similar claims, however, were also made by her three younger sisters, who were married to the Count of Pfalz-Neuburg, to the Duke of Pfalz-Zweibrücken, and to the Margrave of Burgau. Wolfgang Wilhelm, Count of Pfalz-Neuburg (Count Palatine), converted to Roman Catholicism to secure the support of the Emperor and the Catholic German princes for his claims to Jülich-Cleves. The struggle for succession in Jülich-Cleves became a struggle between Catholics and Protestants.

One further historical explanation might be helpful. Margrave

Georg Friedrich of Ansbach, who died in 1603, had succeeded in combining under his rule all the Hohenzollern possessions in Franconia and Silesia, i.e., Ansbach, Kulmbach-Bayreuth, and Jägerndorf. After his death they came into the hands of the Brandenburg-Elector Joachim Friedrich, who gave Ansbach to his brother Joachim Ernst, Bayreuth to his brother Christian, and Jägerndorf to his second son Johann Georg, younger brother of Johann Sigismund.

Prolegomena

The combination of the appearance of the first three volumes of the *Acta Brandenburgica* covering the years 1603–1608, and the likelihood that the death of their deserving editor, Archive Director Klinkenborg, will bring about a prolonged interruption in the series,[1] has caused me to re-examine in the light of the new documents a problem I devoted my attention to many years ago; and I should like to present the results of this re-examination here.

The question is whether and in what way the nature and direction of politics in Brandenburg were influenced by the infiltration of Calvinistic ideas into governing circles, and whether we may attach any epoch-making significance to this turn of events for the history of Brandenburg-Prussia. As we know, this question has already been raised, and decisively answered in the affirmative by J. G. Droysen. But his thesis has been rather generally rejected, mainly because he tried to make the primary bearer of this Calvinist influence the Elector* Johann Sigismund himself, whom he regarded as an Evangelical and political figure of the same class, although not of the same caliber, as the Great Elector —a view that has proved untenable. The question arises, however, whether another bearer of this influence cannot be established. In and of itself the thesis of an affinity between Calvinism and modern *raison d'état* is thoroughly worth considering, and it has received a broader and profounder dimension through recent sociological research.

In this regard I am thinking particularly of the assessment, which emanated some twenty years ago from the Heidelberg

---

* The English word for *Kurfürst* is used here by Hintze when he means the Elector of Brandenburg; there were six other Electors (*Kurfürsten*) in Germany.

school of sociologists, of Calvinism as midwife in the establishment of the modern political and social order. Georg Jellinek chose to regard the Puritan Independents' demand for a guarantee by the state of freedom in religion and conscience as basic for the development of the so-called Rights of Man, the legal foundation of individual rights in modern constitutions. Max Weber has shown how, particularly in England and Scotland, capitalism, the modern form of economic enterprise, received a strong boost from the ethics and economic convictions of Puritan Calvinism. Troeltsch has generalized this thesis and evaluated the general significance of the Protestant ethic for the modern notion of profession and its application. May we not, then, establish something similar regarding the influence of Calvinism and the stricter, more ascetic forms of Protestantism in general on the modern *raison d'état* of the seventeenth century?

Raison d'état and capitalism are after all closely allied sociologically. What else is capitalism than modern *raison d'économie?* *Raison d'état* and *raison d'économie* stem from the same root. The increase in activity of the economic and political entrepreneurs (as one may refer to the founders of modern states), the heightened intensity and rationality of economic operations and state administration and policy, the subordination of the individual arbitrariness of leaders in politics and economics to the interests of the "firm" or the "state" in its new character: all these fit together. Even the new view of the office of the prince and of political action as a responsible, methodically and steadily exercised vocation made headway just as did its equivalent in the business activities of the bourgeoisie. This ethic of vocation and the heightened intensity and rationality of operations are apparently tied to the strict Protestant ethic, particularly as Calvinism developed it in the fearful earnestness of its doctrines of predestination and the justification of the elect.

We must of course be careful to avoid giving the erroneous impression that we claim that Calvinism gave birth to modern *raison d'état*. Nor was this Max Weber's view regarding the emergence of capitalism. He intended only to show that under certain conditions, like those in England and Scotland in the seventeenth and eighteenth centuries, Calvinism promoted and reinforced the socio-economic process in which capitalism was formed. Likewise, our hypothesis claims only that *raison d'état* was promoted by capitalism.

Modern *raison d'état* developed in this period in the context of the great struggle between France and the Austrian and Spanish Habsburgs, which was decided by the Thirty Years' War. This struggle, whose first phase had already been played out in the sixteenth century in the wars between Francis I and Charles V, reached its most deadly form in the Netherlands' struggle for freedom from Spain, which was at the same time a religious war between Calvinism and the new Tridentine Roman Catholicism. Throughout the world, and especially in Germany, Calvinism and the related trends in Protestantism became the champions in the struggle against the Catholic-Jesuit attempt to restore the old order. The politically most developed peoples professed this form of Protestantism, which was far more energetic and daring than German Lutheranism. Even if France, with Henry IV's conversion to Catholicism, no longer stood in the Calvinist camp, she still remained far removed from the Roman and Spanish form of Catholicism. She rejected the political consequences of Trent, and systematically and successfully developed, on the basis of the Concordat of Bologna (1516), her Gallicanism, a monarchical French state church, which could grant toleration even to the Huguenots. The French remained the sworn enemy of the Spaniards, who, through their operations along France's eastern frontier, tried to cut the French off from Europe, the better to defeat the Dutch. Thus, France and the Netherlands were welded into a political community of interest for more than a half-century, and to this anti-Roman, anti-Spanish community those German Protestants attached themselves who inclined toward the Reformed* persuasion, and for whom the Peace of Augsburg

---

* Used by Hintze as synonymous with Calvinist.

had failed to guarantee the necessary security for their confession. In this way the great world-historical struggle at the beginning of the seventeenth century shook even the German Protestant world, which had sought in vain to protect itself with the Formula of Concord.* Out of this situation arose the political impetus that Calvinism exercised on Brandenburg.

The question arises whether religious motives were at work in this impetus, or whether it was more a matter of external political pressure. It seems to me that this question is historically more important than the one that used to be commonly debated—whether Johann Sigismund adopted the Calvinist faith from religious or from political motives.

All human activity, political and religious, stems from an undivided root. As a rule, the first impulse for human beings' social action comes from tangible interests, political or economic (which were closely allied for the German princes of the sixteenth and seventeenth centuries). Ideal interests elevate and animate these tangible interests and lend them justification. Man does not live by bread alone; he wants to have a good conscience when he pursues his vital interests; and in pursuing them he develops his powers fully only if he is conscious of simultaneously serving purposes higher than purely egotistical ones. Interests without such spiritual elevation are lame; on the other hand, ideas can succeed in history only when and to the extent that they attach themselves to tangible interests.

The Marxist model of substructure and superstructure seems to me not a happy way of expressing this peculiar connection between interests and ideas. Quite apart from the fact that this simply deprives the "ideology" of any reality of its own, it suffers from the defect of being conceived in a static spirit, whereas it is intended to illustrate the dynamic of revolution. Where the substructure undergoes convulsion, the superstructure does not

---

* Formula of Concord (*Konkordienformel*) of 1577, a religious statement accepted, among others, by Brandenburg, Saxony, and the Palatinate, which tried to bridge differences between Lutheranism and Calvinism.

follow suit with a corresponding change but collapses with the whole. I find more satisfactory the model of a polar system of interest and ideas. In the historical sense, neither can live over the long haul without the other. Each needs the other as its complement. Where interests are energetically pursued, an ideology develops to give them inspiration, strength, and justification. This ideology is, as an indispensable part of the life process that produces action, as real as the "real" interests themselves. Conversely, where ideas want to conquer the world, they need to be drawn by tangible interests, which in turn may often divert the ideas from their original goal or even alter and falsify them.

Research in the sociology of religion like that of Max Weber has shown that the substance of religion, the real religious experience, is a primary phenomenon that cannot be derived from external circumstances, particularly from economic circumstances. Such research has shown also, however, that the modalities of its operation in the world—the cult, dogma, ideal of piety, and organization of the Church—are at every turn dependent on certain social prerequisites that in large part are rooted in economic interests. Where the religious interest asserts itself unconditionally we find a flight from the world, the life of solitude or monkish asceticism. Where it attempts to participate in the world as it is it must submit to many refractions and, by making concessions to them in one degree or another, ally itself with *raison d'état* or *raison d'économie*, which will carry it forward. In return it endows these interests with spiritual qualities that strengthen them and make them capable of greater success.

Viewed from this perspective, the question of the motivation of a conversion of a politician loses a great deal of its significance, particularly in an age like the sixteenth and seventeenth centuries, when matters of religious faith were the strongest means of binding and dividing mankind, similar to the way nationality does today. At that time religious faith was for politicians often only the powerful ideal exponent of a comprehensive complex of interests, not only for politicians of Henry IV's breed but also for types like the great Prince of Orange. We can see in this complex of interests the rudimentary beginnings of the formation of national states. This was not nearly so evident in Germany as it was in France or the Netherlands, because here the way toward the national state was blocked by the overgrowth of petty princely dynastic interests. German Lutheranism, however, was not suitable to justify the course on which the dynastic policy of the Hohenzollern was then embarking—namely, the formation of a large state composed of a number of separate territories.

This is already clear from Droysen's presentation, which incidentally is among the most brilliant that this historian of Prussian politics, rich in ideas and for a long time unduly underrated, ever wrote. Even today it can still be usefully read, even though it has been factually far superseded, thanks to the growing completeness and accuracy of the documentary research of M. Ritter and R. Koser. But Droysen has a richness of historical vision (*Fülle der Gesichte*) that escapes his successors, inclined to see history in terms of *Realpolitik*. He even had some sense of the deeper sociological dimension of historical research, which is one of its main preoccupations in the present day. His basic methodological principle that the historian's task is to "understand by research" (*forschend zu verstehen*) comes close to the aims of today's so-called "understanding sociology" as it has been applied to historical studies, especially to economic history. Droysen's portrayal of the political significance of Lutheranism and Calvinism is a descriptive abstraction, similar to that which the modern sociological school employs under the rubric "ideal types." Following this portrayal and sometimes elaborating on its suggestions, we can characterize the difference between the two confessions in their significance for political life in the seventeenth century in something like the following fashion.

Lutheranism corresponded in general more to a patriarchal, or even to a manorial-patrimonial, spirit of social and political institutions, Calvinism more to a freer, cooperative, and corporative spirit. Lutheranism clung more to the tradition-bound, antiquated

forms of life of the waning Middle Ages, but Calvinism possessed a decided affinity for the spirit of the modern political and
social order. Individual awareness of the self, and the realm of
the personal rights of the individual, were more strongly developed in the social institutions of the Calvinist states than in
those of the Lutheran states. The church congregation for the
Lutherans was very largely a mere community of believers, based
more on religious custom than on ecclesiastical law; whereas for
the Calvinists it was imbued with a corporative spirit fortified
and standardized by law and with a powerful organization that
enabled it to exercise church discipline throughout all areas of life.

The Calvinist congregational system, the principle of cooperative self-government of the church through a system of presby-
teries and synods, in princely states as well as in city republics,
presumed a social and political structure of the state which could
be found during the sixteenth and seventeenth centuries in
France (if only partially) and (even more) in the Netherlands,
Switzerland, Scotland, and England, but in Germany only in the
territories of the extreme northwest bordering on the Netherlands
and France. Thus when we speak of "Calvinism" we must always
keep in mind that we are using a catchword that was often felt
in Germany at the time, in the sixteenth and seventeenth centuries, to be improper and odious. People would much rather be
called "Evangelical and Reformed" than "Calvinist." In fact the
Reformed Church of Zwingli in Switzerland was not to be glibly
equated with the Calvinist Church. In Germany men of the Reformed persuasion avoided this designation because they were
willing to accept the Augsburg Confession as basis although they
did not want it to be recognized as entirely "invariable." In this
way they could claim that their denomination was included in
the terms of the religious Peace of Augsburg in 1555—a claim
that was naturally contested by both Catholics and many Lutherans and, as is well-known, was not really established until
the Peace of Westphalia.

The contrast between Catholic and Calvinist was always more

acute than that between Catholic and Lutheran, and the Lutherans' hostility toward the Calvinists, the "sacramentalists,"
was in Germany often greater than their hostility to the "Papists."
On the Calvinist side, particularly in the Reformed Church in
Germany, there was more readiness for toleration than on the
other side. This can be explained not merely by the intertwining
of religious with political antagonisms but also by the different
mentality of Calvinism on the one hand and of the Lutherans
and Catholics on the other. "You have a different spirit," said
Luther to Zwingli after the vain attempt to come to an agreement
with Zwingli on the Eucharist. This difference in spirit, however,
rested on a stronger rational ingredient, which distinguished the
Reformed doctrine from the Lutheran as well as the Catholic.
The Reformed doctrine—"Calvinism," as it is generally called for
short—tried to clear away everything magical and mythical from
the religious mysteries. It put into practice, we could say, the
law of Identity and Contradiction, which for the primitive, naïve,
miracle-believing way of thought, to which not only the Catholic
Church but also Luther clung, by no means yet possessed undis-
puted authority. This most clearly illustrates the progressive and,
we could almost say, enlightened character of Calvinism. We
can therefore understand that those who had remained on an
inferior intellectual level disliked the progressive way of thought
of their opponents and that this rejection took on that stupidly
malicious character that so easily sets in when there is complete
lack of reciprocal understanding, particularly when practical conflicts of interest get involved.

For such conflicts were by no means lacking. They were well
provided for in the *reservatum ecclesiasticum* of the Peace of
Augsburg, and in the advancing policy of restoration of Catholicism, renewed and strengthened by the Council of Trent. It was
a policy abetted by the Jesuits and championed, in league with
the Curia, by the related and soon allied ruling houses of Spain
and Austria. This great world-conflict, which forms the world-
historical background to the present publication of our Branden-

burg archives, had its focus in the Netherlands, from where Calvinist propaganda sought to arouse general armed resistance to the *iugum Romano-Hispanicum*, particularly with regard to the Jülich succession, a question deeply implicating the House of Brandenburg. In this struggle, as elsewhere throughout the world, Calvinism advocated political and social principles and interests that were frequently opposed not only to Catholic tradition but also to the traditional order in the Lutheran states.

Calvinism strove for—or presupposed—a political and social order no longer based predominantly on agrarian foundations, and one that in the rural setting favored free peasant communities more than feudal manorial rule. This social order, however, had grown far beyond the agrarian base, and had seen a highly developed urban life with flourishing industry, trade, and shipping. In opposition to the old monarchical and seignorial ties, it strove toward political liberty, be it in the form of the autonomy of the Estates or even in that of republican independence. To be sure, this republican independence was not really democratic but rather was patrician and in some circumstances even "baronial," as in parts of France and in Scotland. It carried with it a certain strain of democratic leveling, however, though at the outset only among the petty-bourgeois stratum of the towns. Here and there the new social order was even allied with monarchist tendencies, as in the Netherlands, where the Gomarist party cooperated with the Orange party against those of the freer Arminian orientation, which got its main support from among the merchant patricians.

This political and social order had a natural affinity for Calvinism, but stood in express opposition to the universalist imperialistic aspirations that Spain and the House of Habsburg represented. It rested entirely on local autonomy and inclined toward federative combinations. In the Swiss Confederation and the Republic of the United Netherlands in particular, this kind of combination had generated viable political entities of a wholly new type. In larger political bodies this easily led to confederacies, and these were then confronted by a Catholic League, as first happened in France and then in Germany. In these instances the conflicts of interest, which were tied to the religious conflict, developed easily into civil war. The great advantage France had over Germany in this period was to have already undergone and surmounted this crisis. The religious wars in France, tied as they were to opposition to the national enemy, Spain, had become an advanced school of *raison d'état*, and in particular Henry IV himself had learned in this school. Even after his conversion to Catholicism—which was unquestionably the prevailing national religion—Henry remained the virtual head of the resistance to the Spanish universalist monarchy and protector of the German Protestants, who had once supported him as a fellow believer in his war for the Crown and who still regarded this Catholic king who guaranteed a far-reaching tolerance and security to Protestants, as a natural ally against oppression under the *iugum Romano-Hispanicum*.

Recognition of a kind of moral and political protectorate by the King of France is an integral part of the Calvinist political picture. Everyone knew, of course, that France did nothing without profit, and remembered suspiciously the concessions that Maurice of Saxony and the German Protestants had had to make for French help in the reign of Henry II. And yet, the German Protestants could no more do without the alliance of France in the struggle against the world domination of Spain and Austria than the Dutch could earlier. William of Orange himself had come close to making a French prince—the Duke of Anjou—or even King Henry III himself, protector of the Netherlands. If one reads the published letters and documents on the foundation of the Union* of German Protestants one has sometimes the impression that we are observing the beginnings of the French policy in favor of a Rhineland Confederation. It was Henry IV

---

* League of Protestant princes and seventeen Imperial towns concluded in 1608, in order to strengthen the Protestant position in the German Empire.

who time and again insisted on the necessity for such a Union;
and he wished thereby to gain help for France against Spain—a
policy that had its dangers for the interests of the German Empire.

German Lutheranism ineradicably bears the stamp of the mal-
formed political life in which it grew up. It is indissolubly tied
to the territorial petty princes and feudal Estates constitution.
Both were permeated by an apolitical, patrimonial spirit, which
was still further strengthened by the secularization of church
lands in the Reformation. This attitude was particularly evident
in the northeastern lands of Germany, the regions of manorial
rule such as Brandenburg and Prussia. The local sovereign, to
whom the government of the Church was accorded as *membrum
praecipuum ecclesiae*, was at the same time the greatest landowner in the country and had patronage over the church parishes
in his domain. The government of the Church was basically exercised through this sovereign's consistory—that is, from the top
down, by the sovereign and a clergy largely dependent on him,
without any significant participation by the congregations and
lay representatives. This accorded with the undeveloped or
atrophied condition of the constitution of the rural community,
with its preponderance of the manorial lords who were also the
patrons of the churches in their districts and exercised a strong
influence in filling the parishes. These manorial lords, the nucleus
of the assemblies of the Estates, had not only an ideal but also a
strong material interest in maintaining the Lutheran church order—first, at least in some places, as partners in the secularization
of monastic property, but primarily, because of the Lutheran in-
junction of obedience to authority: the local landowner saw in
the Lutheran church order a useful instrument for the domestica-
tion of hereditarily subjugated peasants. This was an essential feature, and it became a church for Junkers and pastors.

Urban life was underdeveloped in these overwhelmingly agricultural regions, and had sometimes even been stunted, commerce
and business having everywhere fallen off since the middle of the

sixteenth century. There was room here neither for a self-confident guild democracy nor for a proud patriciate. Lutheranism could teach people to put up with bad times with pious forbearance, but in its contemplative religious inwardness it did not have the capability of awakening economic energies or stimulating the entrepreneurial spirit or strengthening the backbone of the oppressed townsmen against the arrogance of the neighboring landed nobility with whom their interest conflicted in many areas.

In one matter, however, the Lutheran Estates of town and country were at one: both wanted to remain what they were, coveting nothing more than a more or less comfortable, static life in a petty state, under a government to be carried on by natives of the region and in agreement with the Estates. They wanted to make no sacrifices for the expensive dynastic ambitions of the sovereigns and dreaded the prospect of religious strife in the Empire, as in the time of the Schmalkaldic War. They wished to enjoy the blessings of the religious peace and to keep away from the errors of the Calvinists, who were not included in the terms of the Peace and were considered to be a source of political unrest. They wanted to adhere to the Formula of Concord in order not to come into conflict with the Emperor and the Empire on the side of the Dutch rebels. They wished to escape the "bustling machinations" (*geschwindenden Praktiken*) of the world rivalries and lead a restful, quiet life in peace with God and in honesty but also comfortably enjoy life's simple, natural pleasures. The sovereigns themselves, though they desired as great an increase as possible in territory and subjects, thought of this more in a patrimonial than in a political sense. When they ran into trouble, it suited their Lutheran temperament, as Joachim Friedrich expressed it, to try all amicable means and counsels, and commend the rest to God.

Heroic decisions, display of power, and Machiavellian politics had no place in this context. The policies of a Maurice of Saxony were not typical of German Lutherans, but a very rare exception which, like his tie with France, gave his attitude a Calvinist aspect, although his basic Machiavellian attitude in turn separated him from Calvinism. In contrast, the genuine type of German Lutheranism was represented in Joachim II of Brandenburg, who steered clear of the Schmalkaldic War and who as loyal Elector of the Empire did not want to fall out with the Emperor. When in 1562 he made his confession of faith in the cathedral after surviving a dangerous illness, he let his smooth court preacher Agricola dispute with the more rigid-minded Provost Georg Buchholzer on the thesis that faith alone, and not good works, was sufficient for blessedness. He then cavalierly closed the disputation of the earnestly declaiming theologians with a jocular and frivolous jest: "Now I'm off to eat—that's better than doing good works because you have to. With this I commend myself to God —and you, Georg, to the devil." "Upon this," says the commentator, "some answered 'Amen.'" This was the same Joachim II who, through a judicious policy of dynastic marriages, envisaged the extension of his dynasty's rule to far-distant territories but also had to promise his Estates not to enter upon any alliances involving the prosperity or ruin of the land without their consent. It was also in his reign that "poor nobles" complained in distinctly undeferential fashion about the employment of "foreign" councilors— i.e., from Meissen—making it very clear that they wanted to hold the reins in their own hands, that only their own men should govern.

The inner logic of this religious-secular system of government rested on the deliberate isolation of the country within an apolitical, patrimonial sphere, in which it was impossible to imagine that the state was power. The marriage policy, with its prospects and expectations of new territorial acquisitions, did not really contradict this, insofar as it dealt primarily with the increase of dynastic income and there was no question for the time being of fusing the widely disparate territories into a powerful state. Only when the dynasty encountered difficulties in realizing its hereditary claims at the beginning of the seventeenth century did it recognize the impossibility of asserting its claims with the spirit and means of a petty Lutheran principality.

What this Lutheran system of petty German princes completely lacked was the idea of expansion by power, and application of armed force to enforce legal claims. The age of the feudal system was past for them, and the age of political warfare had not yet come. The feudal levy and the urban militia were nowhere militarily effective. Here and there, an attempt was made to organize a "defense force," by gathering the peasants of the prince's domains together for training in arms—as, for instance, in East Prussia, where the war veteran Fabian von Dohna, leader of the German auxiliaries in the Huguenot wars, took matters in hand. It was typical of the times, however, that nothing substantial came of this, because the nobility disliked arming the rural population—even when it was not their own—and soon managed to bring the system to an end. It was the same everywhere. Yet to take on mercenaries would have meant regular taxes, and this the Estates were still less willing to undertake. The Lutheran spirit was pacific and apolitical. It did not produce bold warriors or wily diplomats. That was more the business of the Calvinists.

Brandenburg, with her interests in the successions in Prussia and on the Rhine, was now faced with the fateful question whether to orient herself toward the east or toward the west. In the east, Lutheranism was more beneficial to her cause; in the west, Calvinism. At first she chose a middle course, one that suited her political traditions. She emphasized what was common to the two faiths and sought to maintain good relations with the Elector of Saxony and the Emperor, on the one hand, and with the Elector Palatine, the Netherlands, and France on the other. Crypto-Calvinism sprouted at the court of Joachim Friedrich, while the official religion remained Lutheran.

That is the characteristic feature of the years on which we are concentrating. Even Johann Sigismund himself can be designated at this time as a crypto-Calvinist. After his visit to Heidelberg in 1605 he inclined increasingly toward the Calvinist doctrine, without making the decision of a public conversion. The question that used to be much discussed—whether his conversion was caused by political motives—has been wrongly framed. The question that ought to be asked is whether political motives restrained him for years from making a public confession of his religious conviction; and this question must doubtless be answered in the affirmative. What held him back was, first, regard for the reigning Elector, his father, who, as the documents show (Nr. 2179), as late as a year before his death had the Superintendent-General, Pelargus, write a tract against the Calvinists. Then he was held back by concern for the succession in East Prussia and also, doubtless, he feared an open breach with Saxony and the Emperor and dreaded the threatened Imperial ban that Saxony—his rival in the question of the succession in Jülich—was ready to execute by invading the Mark. There was in addition his Lutheran spouse's distaste for Calvinism, a distaste that constantly increased until it became a passion. These considerations and concerns did not disappear or recede until after 1613, when both the personal entourage of Johann Sigismund and also the political situation at large were radically transformed. The public conversion to the Reformed Church was primarily fulfillment of a duty of religious conscience. That this also had ancillary political significance, it seems to me, cannot be excluded. But what that meaning was, and above all what consequences the step had on the politics in Brandenburg, is an open question and is not easy to answer.

Johann Sigismund

Although the effect of the Calvinistic spirit on the politics of Brandenburg must be regarded as problematical for the beginning of the seventeenth century, it was no longer so by the middle of that century. Whoever reads the so-called "Political Testament" of the Great Elector, with its close interweaving of Reformed religiosity and modern *raison d'état*, and keeps in mind his actual political deeds, will abandon any doubt that by this time the Reformed persuasion, in a strongly religious mind, was a power that exerted substantial influence on politics. Moreover, it influenced not only the responsible, professional, steady and methodical political method of proceeding but also the nature and shape of political goals.

Of course the inner connection between religion and politics appears in this context to be rather different from Max Weber's view, in his investigation, in the sociology of religion, concerning the connection between Calvinism and capitalism. One does not really find here the belief, based on the doctrine of Predestination, that the proof of election is reflected in the success of worldly undertakings directed to the glory of God. One finds, rather, the simpler, naïve belief, flowing apparently from Old Testament sources, that religious conviction establishes a covenant between man and God, almost a relation of trust and service which guarantees the loyal servant, besides salvation, prosperity in his earthly concerns—provided of course that these too are conducted in the spirit of that service relation—that is, to the glory of God. This conception was peculiar also to the later German Pietists of A. H. Francke's stamp, as well as to the Moravians (*Herrenhuter**) and other Protestant sects concerned with promoting success in solid business activities.

As we know, methodical instructions for the successor, like these initiated by the Great Elector, remained a custom in the ruling house of Brandenburg for more than a century afterward. In Frederick I's unpublished Testament, whose political content is less significant, the connection of the Reformed religion with politics stands out prominently. Frederick William I's instructions to his successor emanate from a religious conviction that admittedly bears no longer specifically Calvinist but Pietist traits; it is permeated, however, by an ascetic Protestant ethic that is regarded as the basis for the exercise of political rulership. If Frederick the Great in his Political Testament replaced this reli-

---

* A group of the Moravian sect, who called themselves *Herrenhuter* because *Herrenhut* was the name of the settlement on the estates of Count Zinzendorf where they had found protection from persecution.

gious posture with a purely secular, politically realistic one, a closer examination reveals that this enlightened ruler's categorical imperative of duty and ascetic devotion to his vocation, as well as his transcendental conception of the state as standing above the ruler, cannot be derived, or explained, purely from the rationalism of the Enlightenment, but have their origin in emotional depths, so that the religious motives of his predecessors were, so to speak, secularized, transformed into a worldly form.

But of particular interest is that at the beginning of Frederick William I's instructions we find a passage—strangely enough unnoticed until now—which, in a survey of the history of the Hohenzollerns, ties the connection between Reformed religion and successful politics to Johann Sigismund and his epoch. Perhaps Droysen had this remark in mind when he characterized this first Reformed ruler of the House of Brandenburg as an exemplary Evangelical personality and tried to have him establish the bond between Brandenburg politics and the Reformed spirit, which became evident with the Great Elector.

Frederick William I warned his successor against the life of luxury that was then in vogue at other German courts, with "mistresses, comedies, operas, ballets, masquerades, balls, gorging and guzzling, which lead to a debauched life." He should lead a pious life, give good example to his people and his army, repress those "scandalous pleasures" and dreadful sins which established Satan in God's place, and not tolerate them in his lands. Above all, he himself should not embark on an ungodly life, which was "never tolerated in our House; none of these sins have been practiced in the House of Brandenburg since the time of Johann Sigismund." "Read the history of our House," the King continued, "and you will find that this is the truth, and therefore God has steadfastly blessed our House. Be sure that the blessings that are still given us come from our pious ancestors." His son ought to follow his father's example: he had always begun with God, and God had never abandoned him, but had stood by him with might and strength.

Thus, Frederick William I was of the opinion that the reason for the divine blessings that had so far graced the politics of the House of Brandenburg was the moral and religious life of his predecessors, their Puritan strictness and simplicity. And he believed that the chain of these pious predecessors began with Johann Sigismund—that is, with the first ruler to profess the Calvinist faith.

This is of course by no means a full and valid historical proof for the epoch-making political importance of Calvinism in the House of Brandenburg, but it is still testimony that has to be taken seriously and whose origin and foundation have to be investigated. How did Frederick William I come to this opinion? Where did his assessment of Johann Sigismund, for which he appeals to "the history" of his House, come from?

However simple this question appears, it is difficult to answer. The official histories of the House of Brandenburg, which the Great Elector had suggested and supported, produced in fact only one great complete work, Samuel Pufendorf's *History of the Reign of the Great Elector*. Everything else, particularly all that concerns the earlier history of Brandenburg, remained stuck in preliminary sketches and in fragments that never have been printed and whose hidden presence in the royal archives has become hardly known. Pufendorf's monumental work deals only with the Great Elector's reign itself, not with those of his predecessors. It goes back to the earlier period only in several excursus —as, for instance, that on the question of the Jülich succession in the fourth book. It occasionally deals with Johann Sigismund, but only in a documentary, pragmatic way, as was the wont of this political-propagandistic historian. It gives no over-all estimate of Johann Sigismund's character and no judgment of the historical significance of his conversion. The work was certainly never read in the original either by Frederick William I or his successor—it was written in a difficult Latin and was really directed only to scholars. Certainly, translation into French was entrusted to Antoine Teissier, a Reformed exile who later became Councilor of

Legation and Historiographer, and a German edition existed in print after 1710. But these were abridgments of this vast work and they generally left out those very excursus into the earlier history of Brandenburg.

With regard to the earlier rulers of the Hohenzollern family, a supplement to Pufendorf exists in the French translation of a Latin work by the Electoral Archivist Cernitius, a stepbrother of the Electoral Chamberlain Antonius Freytag, in whose house Johann Sigismund died. It was undertaken by order of King Frederick I, by Historiographer Teissier, and appeared in Berlin in 1707. It goes to the end of George William's reign. Two years before, in 1705, the same Teissier had already published an *Abrégé de l'histoire des Electeurs de Brandenbourg*, which in question and answer form—apparently for the classroom—dealt with the whole history of the House of Brandenburg, including the Great Elector. In neither of these works, however, is the personality of Johann Sigismund as a ruler assessed in a manner which permits us to regard them as the sources for Frederick William I's view. All that is reported of Johann Sigismund is that he introduced the Reformed religion, and the translation of Cernitius adds a defense against the reproach of Sleidani's *Continuator* that this implied inadmissible Calvinist innovations. In contrast, the personal piety of Joachim Friedrich is particularly in the small compendium. Neither of these books, however, is a "history" of the House of Brandenburg in Frederick William I's sense: the Cernitius translation ends with George William and could not therefore shed much light on the rise of the House of Hohenzollern; the small catechism of the history of Brandenburg nor can even be designated as a "historical narration."

The only printed work which takes in the whole history of Brandenburg, including the history of the Great Elector, but still without the reign of the first King, and which Frederick William I could have known, if only in abridgment, is that of Gregorio Leti, an Italian who wrote historical *belles lettres* on a grand scale for use in court circles. Leti wrote, among other works, a history

of the House of Brandenburg in Italian in two folios, the first dealing with the earlier history of Brandenburg and dedicated to the
Elector of Saxony Johann Georg III, the second containing the
history of the Great Elector and dedicated to him (*Ritratti his-
torici della casa elettorale Brandenburgo,* Amsterdam, 1687). The
treatment of Johann Sigismund in the first volume is superficial,
however, and says little. It corresponds in no way to the picture
Frederick William had in mind. Moreover, it is unlikely that the
King was acquainted with the Italian original. He would more
probably have known the smaller French edition dedicated to his
mother, Queen Sophie Charlotte, who had literary interests (*Abrégé de l'histoire de la Maison Sérénissime et Electorale de Bran-
debourg, écrite par Grégoire Leti,* Amsterdam, 1687). It was still
more superficial and even less consonant with Frederick William I's idea. In any case both books abounded to such a degree
in exaggerated and inflated flattery that it would be strange if
Frederick William had recommended them to his successor as
character-building, since he urgently warned the same successor
to "beware of flatterers and of sycophants."

Now our first question, naturally, ought to be about the education in history that Frederick William I received in his youth, and
about the books that formed the basis of this education. It is on
this particular point that we learn very little from the very thorough and illuminating essay by Heinrich Borkowski,[2] which has
exhaustively studied the available archival material. The first
mentor (*Ephorus*) of the young, intractable, unstudious prince,
Johann Friederich Cramer, who was soon dismissed because of
his pedagogical shortcomings, had published a Latin translation
of Pufendorf's introduction to the history of the European states
(1688). He probably used this as basis of instruction. But we do
not know on what text instruction in the history of Brandenburg
was founded. Under his able successor Rebeur, the offspring of a
French refugee family, a compendium of world history was prepared for instruction in history; but once again, we hear nothing
about the history of Brandenburg. We may perhaps fill this gap

by referring to the above-mentioned *Abrégé* of Antoine Teissier
of 1705, but we have already indicated the role Johann Sigismund
plays in that.

Much more important was the personal character of the teachers and the spirit in which they worked. About that we are well
informed. The man in charge of education and instruction was
Count Alexander Dohna, from the East Prussian branch of that
widely ramified family which since the end of the sixteenth century had created a sensation by its adoption of Calvinism and
cultivation of a Western European outlook, and which had made
for itself a unique position that the thoroughly Lutheran and less
educated landed nobility in East Prussia found difficult to tolerate.[3] This Dohna was the eldest son of that Count Friedrich whose
memoirs (edited by Borkowski) are an extremely important
source of cultural history. Friedrich Dohna started out in the service of Frederick V, Elector Palatine and Winter King of Bohemia;
and then had been Governor of the Principality of Orange, because of a marriage connection with that House; and finally
entered the service of the Great Elector of Brandenburg as a diplomat, a career he guided his sons into. This Count Friedrich
Dohna had acquired the barony of Coppet on Lake Geneva, which
became later the seat of Necker and Madame de Staël, and set up
there a kind of court of the Muses from which all luxury was
banned but where virtue and wisdom were nurtured. Count Alexander's mother was a French marquise from the House of Dupuy-
Montbrun, and one of his brothers succeeded her in her French
possessions as Marquis de Ferrassières. The tutor to Count Friedrich's sons was Bayle, the famous author of the *Dictionnaire*,
much read at Queen Sophie Charlotte's court (in fact it seems
that on Bayle's recommendation the Italian Leti made his way to
Berlin).

The education of Crown Prince Frederick William was conducted by Dohna thoroughly in tune with Reformed religiosity,
though in a way in which the difference between the Lutheran
and Calvinist confessions was not sharply emphasized. Cramer,

the first tutor, had been converted to the Reformed faith before
he occupied the post. Rebeur, who succeeded him, was by birth
a Calvinist, for he came from a family of French refugees in Berlin and had made the acquaintance of Count Alexander Dohna in
Switzerland. He was appointed by Dohna and worked in the
same spirit. How strongly this moral and religious instruction
affected the otherwise recalcitrant and unteachable pupil emerges,
among other places, from the fact that his strongly emphasized distaste for opera, comedies, masquerades, and balls in his
1722 instruction to his successor apparently stems from this
source. In the Instruction to Dohna, which Dohna probably
influenced if he did not draft it himself, this theme had already
played a role: the Crown Prince was to gain disgust and dislike
for such frivolous pleasures—an aim we see that was completely
achieved. Just those things that had to do with religious and moral
principles fell on good soil with this unruly pupil. This attitude
makes it comprehensible that what he learned in his history lessons about the exemplary Evangelical personality of Johann Sigismund and his political significance remained vividly in his mind.
It is an easy step to assume that Frederick William's instruction
in the history of Brandenburg was influenced by certain traditions
of the Dohna family.

The recently published state papers of Brandenburg demonstrate that Johann Sigismund's confidants—who like himself were
Calvinists or close to Calvinism—were in intimate contact with
the Dohnas in East Prussia and attempted to raise the able
veteran Fabian von Dohna to the position of *Oberhauptmann** and
Oberstburggraf† against the intrigues and opposition of the Lutheran landed nobility which dominated in the Estates. Leader
of the German auxiliary troops of Henry of Navarre and of the
French Huguenots, and diplomat of the Elector Palatine,‡ Fabian

---

* Officer; the rank of general did not yet exist, and the prefix *ober-* or
oberst- indicates an officer of the rank of general.
† Officer at the head of the many fortified castles that the Order of Teutonic
Knights had built in Prussia; consequently the *Oberstburggraf* was in reality
the commander of the military forces in Prussia.
‡ *Kurfürst* of the Pfalz, residing in Heidelburg; Count Palatine was the ruler
of Pfalz-Neuburg.

von Dohna was a frequent adviser of Johann Sigismund since the latter's Prussian marriage (1594) and was one of the most devoted adherents to the cause of Brandenburg in Prussia. Until then the Calvinist faith of the Dohnas had been an almost insuperable obstacle to them in East Prussia, where they were not allowed to succeed to a position that corresponded to their possessions and their military and political talents and achievements. This changed when East Prussia passed into the hands of the Reformed Hohenzollern. The Dohnas remained the most reliable supporters of the House of Brandenburg in Prussia, and in the service of this House they attained, as generals and as diplomats, high honors and influential positions at court and throughout the country at large.

The first of this series was Abraham von Dohna,[4] a nephew of old Fabian, who had studied at Heidelberg under the famous Reformed theologian Scultetus and had been schooled in warfare under Prince Maurice of Orange in the Netherlands. He served the Elector without salary for seven years and helped him particularly in the acquisition and administration of the guardianship over Prussia; Johann Sigismund then brought him to Berlin as military commander and councilor. In Berlin, Abraham von Dohna, though occupied in inspecting fortresses and military installations, became by force of circumstances and by his lively religious interests the chief assistant to Johann Sigismund in the matter of his conversion and in establishing the new service of worship at court. Thus the Dohnas were intimately involved with Johann Sigismund and with the new Reformed era of the House of Brandenburg. Naturally they regarded Johann Sigismund, the first Reformed Elector of Brandenburg and Duke, as an epoch-making figure, who ushered in a new and better age.[5] Moreover, the fact that during his reign Hohenzollern authority was permanently established not only in Prussia but on the Rhine as well, allowed this first Reformed ruler to be regarded as the founder of the greatness of the House of Brandenburg from still another point of view.

It is unmistakable that for the Dohnas themselves the Reformed faith and the related Western European, especially

French, culture had been important factors in the rise of their house to power, honor, and prosperity, despite all the difficulties that initially attended it and that the spiritual attitude they inherited or acquired through education endowed them with solid ability. They probably assumed the same to be true of the Reformed Hohenzollern house, and so it is very likely that the historical education Rebeur gave the young Crown Prince was in harmony with this outlook. Above all, the Lord Chamberlain (*Oberhofmeister*), Alexander Dohna himself, probably shaped the historical outlook of the unruly Crown Prince in a completely different way from that of his actual teachers, by commanding his respect as a high-ranking officer and cultivated man of the world. In any case he exercised an enduring political influence on his pupil. The preference for East Prussia that became evident from the moment the Crown Prince ascended the throne can certainly be ascribed in large part to his East Prussian mentor, who was also, until his death in 1728, one of the King's main assistants in the so-called *Retablissement** of East Prussia.

On Frederick William I's accession and in the years that followed, the Dohnas generally played a great part at the court of Berlin and in the government of the state. A glance at the *Acta Borussica* of this time gives ample documentary proof of this. Count Christoph von Dohna, a minister and general who, at that time, was regarded as a kind of Prime Minister, was the younger brother of Count Alexander, the Court Chamberlain and tutor of Frederick William I. Alexander himself was promoted to field marshal and took part with the King in the siege of Stralsund in 1715. There in the line of battle, Frederick William made the acquaintance of Jacques Egide Duhan de Jandun, "governor" to the field marshal's son; he had already chosen him as the teacher of his own son when he wrote the Instruction of 1722. This was the man to whom Frederick the Great owed his knowledge of history, particularly that of his own House. For his primary education he had another instructor, a German Calvinist, the teaching assist-

---

* Resettlement of peasants for better use of the land.

ant Hilmar Curas, who had also taught two of his sisters, later the Princesses of Bayreuth and Ansbach. He had written and published textbooks on universal history and the history of Brandenburg (1723) which, as the dedication shows, were particularly the basis of the lessons given to the princesses. But their content was directed to a child's intelligence and was so concise that this outline of the history of Brandenburg, in which the conversion of Johann Sigismund is not given epoch-making political significance, can hardly be what the King had in mind.

When Frederick the Great himself embarked on writing the history of his House, he recalled that his teacher Duhan de Jandun had prepared a written sketch of it which he had used in his lessons. Frederick instituted inquiries about this manuscript of his teacher, who by then was dead. It was found still in the possession of the writer's mother, and was used by Frederick. Apparently it was then returned to the mother and has been lost without a trace.[6] This, I believe, is the "history of our House" that Frederick William I alludes to in his Instruction. Even though he could scarcely have read the manuscript himself, he surely would have known something of its spirit and of the author's views on important points. The author himself would have been strongly influenced in his conception of Johann Sigismund by the Reformed tradition of the Dohna family to which he had attached himself. That Frederick the Great did not himself share this conception is easy to understand because of the purely secular, "enlightened," politically realistic character of his historical writings. He had little more to say of Luther and Calvin than that one had married a nun and the other had put a personal enemy to the stake. He reckoned neither of them among the great minds that have furthered the progress of mankind.

In contrast to his great pupil, however, Duhan de Jandun, who had come to Berlin at a very early age as a Reformed religious refugee from France and had been taught by the famous La Croze, was and remained a pious Calvinist. This was stressed in the *éloge* of the Berlin Academy—which by the way was not written, as we sometimes read, by the King. It was in fact his works on the history of Brandenburg—which unfortunately have not been published—that opened the gates of the Academy to him.

To put all this in a concise formula: Frederick William's views on Johann Sigismund and his importance in the history of the House of Brandenburg are based on a pious Reformed legend planted by the Dohna family in the Prussian royal house through their influence on the education of Crown Prince Frederick William. Psychologically this meant that a generation strongly convinced of the beneficial effect of its Reformed religion upon its worldly aspirations and accomplishments ascribed this miraculous working of grace to the prince and his government who had first assumed this faith and granted its adherents in his lands protection from persecution and discrimination and assistance in their private and political aims.

Even though this is an indication of the natural affinity between modern *raison d'état* and Calvinism, it still is not proof of the correctness of the thesis that such an affinity showed itself in the person and politics of Johann Sigismund and that therefore this Prince really opened the era whose strongest representative was the Great Elector. For Johann Sigismund we have no document containing the kind of evidence the Great Elector's so-called Political Testament presents. The *Confessio Sigismundi* published in 1614 is a learned theological tract without a real personal touch or moral and political application. It is probably the work of his spiritual advisor, Martinius Fuessel, court preacher of Zerbst. Droysen, who maintained this thesis, relied mainly on two passages in letters of Johann Sigismund to his wife Anna from the period shortly after his accession to the throne.

Droysen did not really quote these remarks nor did he give their date, but fitted the words, somewhat altered, into his own narrative. Their basic thrust was that Johann Sigismund stressed his religious conscientiousness in the conduct of governmental affairs, and in his office as prince felt and acknowledged himself

to be the responsible servant of God. These statements therefore
are wholly in the spirit of the Reformed concept of the prince's
vocation. Whether they are sufficient to justify the concept of the
Elector as a personality who proves his Evangelical character also
in political life, is another question, which I do not dare answer
in the affirmative, for expressions like these were in vogue at the
time and are possibly mere formulas. In any case, the letters have
not yet been printed in the present collection. When I mentioned this to the editor, he told me that the very voluminous correspondence of the princely couple would not be dealt with until
the later volumes. From his own study he did not have the impression that Johann Sigismund was the model Evangelical character that Frederick William I and Droysen thought him to have
been. He particularly stressed Johann Sigismund's extensive life-
long dependence on his confidential secretary, Reichard Beyer,
even in his correspondence with his wife. Yet, even Beyer, whose
busy pen we often meet in these volumes, does not seem to have
been an independent political personality in his own right, with
power and aims of his own.

Beyer was from Holstein, which is to say from the Danish
sphere, at that time of great importance in Brandenburg politics
because of blood relations and the decided Protestantism of the
Danes. He appears until 1608 as an adherent of Rheydt and his
patroness, Duchess Marie Eleonore of Prussia, and as an intermediary between them and his lord, Johann Sigismund. After these
two died (1608), however, Beyer seems to have become increasingly dependent on the Electress Anna, who in the course of time
had become ever more hostile to Calvinism and ever stricter in
her East Prussian Lutheran orthodoxy—and this shattered her
initially close relations with her husband. Primarily, Beyer, as
long as he lived, seems to have kept Johann Sigismund from making open confession of Calvinism, because of the Prussian situation and in agreement with the Electress. His death probably
had something to do with the great changes in the Court of Berlin at Easter 1613 which culminated in the reorganization of the

disunited Privy Council. The Council was henceforth to be headed by Margrave Johann Georg of Jägerndorf, as representative of his brother the Elector.[7] This was an unmistakable strengthening of the Calvinist element. Abraham von Dohna replaced Adam Putlitz, a Calvinist but believed to be also a free-thinker, who became the most influential adviser of the Elector in the next years. Abraham von Dohna initiated the measures of the Calvinist church reform and watched over their execution.[8]

Meanwhile the political situation had radically altered since Johann Sigismund's accession. In 1609 the Netherlands had concluded their twelve-year armistice with Spain which at least the state party—in contrast to the Orange party—sought to maintain if possible; the dangerous crisis in 1610, which threatened to end in a great European war, dissolved, after the assassination of Henry IV, without such catastrophe. Since then Brandenburg's link with the Reformed party and the Western powers no longer meant an immediate danger of war. At the same time the Western powers' inclination to champion Brandenburg's interests on the Lower Rhine was substantially diminished, whereas the Jülich question—which now with the settlement of the Prussian question had come again to the forefront of Brandenburg interests—assumed an increasingly dangerous form. A whole series of political changes had made the outlook for the peaceful resolution of the succession struggle more and more remote. An attempt had been made to come to an agreement with Saxony in the convention of Jüterbog of 1611—on the basis of Saxony's participation in the preliminary occupation of the Jülich lands, and under the condition of a legal decision of the succession by the Emperor and a court of princes to be appointed by both the pretenders. This attempt, which even the Electress protested against, had run aground on the opposition of the Count of Pfalz-Neuburg; and over this issue the earlier good relations between Brandenburg and Neuburg had turned into hostile rivalry. The young Count, Wolfgang Wilhelm, had taken the side of his Bavarian brother-in-law, and his open conversion to Catholicism was now only a matter of time. The Union which Johann Sigismund had finally joined in 1610—without being able to pay his membership dues—totally failed in the Jülich question. What had been a question of law within the Empire had become a question of power among the European states—that is to say, primarily between Spain and the Netherlands, which despite their twelve-year armistice, continued to exploit for their own purposes the party struggles on the neutral soil of the Empire. Thus military help for the Elector of Brandenburg from the Netherlands was now more necessary than ever before. On the same day as Johann Sigismund announced his impending solemn conversion to the Reformed faith to the clergy and councilors of his Court, he appointed a legation to the States General to ask for help from the Netherlands.[9]

Under these circumstances one will have to admit that political motives exerted a direct influence on Johann Sigismund's decision finally to make a public confession of faith to the Reformed doctrine. This instance confirms our general interpretation that it would be an all too crude application of the principle of causality if, in the question of a conversion, we would only ask whether faith determined policy, or policy determined faith. We are rather dealing with a basic change in direction that concerns all spheres of life. Although the religious interest might be at one end and the political interest at the opposite end, they are interdependent and, after often violent see-sawing, they reach the equilibrium necessary for living.

Ranke, too, was of the opinion that in emphasizing Johann Sigismund's inner religious convictions one need not exclude the contributory factor of political motives. Of course he did not know the tensions of the political situation in 1613 as exactly as we know them today, and therefore thought more in terms of motives of domestic politics, of the Elector's desire for a freer hand against the Lutheran Estates when he withdrew from community of faith with them. The actual effect of the conversion does accord with this interpretation. A Reformed prince who ruled the Church of his princedom no longer as *membrum prae-*

cipuum ecclesiae but by virtue of his political sovereignty, had a stronger position vis-à-vis the Lutheran Estates; and he freed himself from being bound to the narrow limits of a territorial Church—a bondage difficult to square with his intention of creating a larger territorial complex with several confessions. In spite of this it may be doubted whether this effect of the change of conversion was a conscious motive. The parallel events cited by Ranke in East Prussia (the Osiander affair*) and in Saxony (the case of Chancellor Crell) must have had a deterring effect rather than that of inviting emulation. Johann Sigismund's position was not strong enough to provoke the resistance that could be expected. He foresaw it and tried to blunt it by repudiating religious coercion from the outset. Indeed, it would have been impossible to proceed in Brandenburg, let alone East Prussia, like the Reformed rulers in Cassel or Heidelberg. The economic and social structure of the East Elbian lands and their manorial economy precluded this: Lutheranism suited them well, Calvinism not in the slightest.

From this point of view, Calvinism emerges as a principle reinforcing monarchical power, in contrast to the function it otherwise often had in history—that of animating the resistance of the Estates to heterodox princes. Of course, this function was not entirely lacking either, as we recognize when we regard the other side of the power of a territorial ruler—its relation to the imperial power. In Germany, too, Calvinism inspired and directed the resistance of the Estates of the Empire to the Catholic Emperor. The Emperor Matthias was of course the choice of the Elector Palatine and the Elector of Brandenburg; but the mood of the sharply divided Diet of 1613 shows the vehemence of the Protestant opposition led by the Reformed Estates.

The significance of Johann Sigismund's formal conversion to the Reformed party lay, broadly speaking, principally in that it

---

* Andreas Osiander was a Lutheran theologian whose views on the doctrine of the justification through faith involved him in bitter fights with other Lutherans and with the Calvinists.

established the faith of the House of Brandenburg for the future, and thus established as a basis of policy the orientation toward the West, even though this orientation was beset by many fluctuations until the time of the Great Elector; especially Johann Sigismund himself did not stick to it firmly and resolutely. If we consider his political behavior in the following years, particularly his withdrawal from the Union against Dohna's advice, we will not be able to characterize him as an exemplary Evangelical personality. The assessment that Koser allotted his personality seems to me correct: he was a man inclined to religion but he had no head for politics and no strength or independence of character. His dependence on the leading figures of his entourage is striking. "He rides in the same position you sit him in" was a contemporary observation that might be applied to his political activity as well. It must also be mentioned that his health broke down early. He suffered his first stroke in 1616, at the age of forty-four, and it obviously robbed him of much of his political energy. In 1618 he had a second stroke, which wholly crippled him and made him unfit to govern. He was not made to be the pioneer of a new direction.

Rheydt

We can hardly regard Johann Sigismund as having been the protagonist of Calvinist influence on the policy of Brandenburg. Evidently the man who fulfilled this historical role was Rheydt, whom we have already mentioned. His significance in the history of Brandenburg can be seen in its proper light on the basis of the recent publication. Editor Melle Klinkenborg has drawn appropriate attention to this important individual in a special essay that deals particularly with Rheydt's part in issuing the Privy Council Order of 1604.[10] I cannot accept all the details of his discussion, and on the whole I have a different interpretation of Rheydt's historical role.

With more sight than Lampert Distelmeier, whose vision did

not go beyond the world of a small territorial state, Rheydt deserves to be called the first modern statesman in Brandenburg
history. To my mind, his significance emerges in its proper light
only if he is regarded as the apostle of political Calvinism and
of the *raison d'état* of France and the Netherlands against the
principles represented by Spain and Rome. He must be evaluated not only as a loyal, more or less skillful, prudent, and successful servant of the House of Brandenburg but also as an exponent of one of the great tendencies governing the European
situation at that time. He must be seen as a statesman of high
caliber who did not get absorbed by the trivial ambitions of petty
princes and states but whose primary concern was to integrate
Brandenburg, with her expectations and claims, as an active
power factor in the Franco-Dutch front for the great world struggle against the Roman-Spanish-Austrian reaction.

I would like—*si parva licet componere magnis*—to compare
him with Baron vom Stein, for whom also the dynastic interests
of Prussia meant very little beside the idea of the German nation and of the world struggle against the Napoleonic universal
monarchy. Like Stein, Rheydt flashed like a meteor through the
history of Brandenburg-Prussia, and like Stein he has beamed
light on an idea that only later came to strength and effectiveness. Stein's legacy was the national idea in a revived Prussia.
What Rheydt injected into the House of Brandenburg for the entire future, at the very moment when it was about to extend its
rule far beyond the sphere of a petty principality, was the unprecedented idea of a powerful, unified, centralized state, which
as the leader of the Protestant cause and as the disciple of French
and Dutch statecraft, regarded as the aim of its existence an
independent position in the world.

Ott-Heinrich von Bylandt, Lord of Rheydt and Prembt, came
from an old noble family in the Duchy of Cleves. His family had
not been able to maintain its immediate subjection to the
Emperor but it still held a higher and more independent position in the territories under Jülich rule than the landholding

nobility in the German territories were used to. Rheydt was a pious Calvinist and, along with Count Wirich von Daun, the most influential man of the Protestant opposition in the Estates who called themselves—apparently on the Dutch model—the party of "patriots" and who, in agreement with the Protestant pretenders (Brandenburg, Neuburg, Zweibrücken) and the States General, put up stubborn opposition to the policy of Catholic Restoration, which the government pursued in the interests of Spain and Austria.[11]

Already in the lifetime of the old Duke Wilhelm the government had been in the hands of a kind of regency when it became known that the hereditary prince, Johann Wilhelm, was mentally ill; after his death (1592) its power had been confirmed and reinforced. It consisted of several Catholic court and local officials, under the supervision and direction of Imperial commissaries, charged with taking care of the Spanish and Austrian interests and also the general Catholic interests. The government had been formed at the exclusion of the Protestant pretenders, who had urged in vain to be represented. It pursued the goal of preparing the establishment by force of an Imperial administration of the contested lands, in view of the imminent opening of the succession question, in order to preclude from the outset that in these regions—so important in the European politics of the time—a Protestant dynasty cooperating with the States General against Spain would get installed. Instead, they sought to smooth the way for cooperation between Spain and Austria in the interests of the restoration of Catholicism. The government then already attempted to suppress so far as possible Evangelical and Reformed religious services in the Jülich lands, but it could not prevent the extension of the Spanish-Dutch war to these lands, even though they belonged to the neutral German Empire; and the war wrought great damage.

A particularly crass and brutal violation of the Empire's neutrality and of Protestant interests was the invasion, early in 1598, by the Duke of Mendoza and his twenty thousand Spanish mercenaries, who were quartered on the Jülich lands for a long time and were expected to make up for their unpaid wages by robbing and plundering. At this time Count Wirich von Daun, who had tried to mount the most forcible resistance to the invaders from his castle of Broich, was murdered by the undisciplined troops despite a promise of safe-conduct. The Spanish soldiers were told that when they marched through Rheydt's lands or were billeted on them, they were on property particularly fit for exploitation and spoliation. Rheydt, in order to avoid Daun's fate, found himself forced to abandon the land of his fathers and seek employment and livelihood in a court sympathetic to his outlook and willing to support resistance to the *iugum Romanico-Hispanicum.* He turned to Ansbach, to the Hohenzollern Margrave Georg Friedrich, who was well known as one of the heads of the party of Protestant princes and also as one of the most energetic advocates of the Protestant claimants to the Jülich succession. Although Georg Friedrich worked above all in the interests of the House of Brandenburg, he did not conceive of this task narrowly: in agreement with him the three Protestant princely houses had already united in 1593 to pursue their claims jointly.

Perhaps Rheydt harbored the hope of taking a position at the Court of Ansbach similar to that which Christian of Anhalt, the younger brother of the reigning prince and an outstanding military and diplomatic agent of the Protestant activists, had created for himself as an official at the Court of the Elector Palatine. It must also be realized that right at this time when all Protestant Germany was in uproar at the Spanish breach of peace, Georg Friedrich sounded the battle cry: this was the moment for the Protestant claimants to act in order to give their claims a strong moral and political basis. They must chase the invading Spanish mercenaries from the country; this was the best way to prepare its acquisition. Otherwise they would lose all credence in the country. He began himself to arm in his own military district, Franconia; and in agreement with like-minded Protestant princes such as the Landgrave Moriz of Hesse and Duke Heinrich Julius of Brunswick, the military chiefs of the Upper Rhenish and Lower Saxon districts, embarked on an armed intervention on the Lower Rhine. In the following year, however, shortly before the Spaniards left the land on their own, this enterprise collapsed rather pitiably because the willingness to sacrifice and the energy of the Protestant allies was in general too small.

At this moment of rebellion against the Roman-Spanish yoke Rheydt entered the service of Margrave Georg Friedrich as, characteristically, *Kriegsoberst*. But as a councilor, which he remained until Georg Friedrich's death on April 26, 1603, he was also Georg Friedrich's assistant in general political affairs and was later regarded in the House of Brandenburg as a kind of executor of the political testament of this ruler, whom Koser has called the one statesman among the Hohenzollern of that time. Rheydt, like this ruler, combined the dynastic interest of the Hohenzollern house in the matter of the succession with the general political principle of active Protestantism; except that for Rheydt, in contrast with the Margrave, Protestantism was always in the foreground, while in special circumstances dynastic interests receded into the background. His patroness, the Duchess Marie Eleonore of Prussia, a woman of political acumen and great prestige at the court of Brandenburg, who had recommended him to the Elector for employment and position, misjudged him when she emphasized only his devotion to Brandenburg's dynastic interests. He was and remained primarily a Calvinist statesman to whom the great idea of a general war against Spain, for the salvation of Protestantism, was the dominant concern of his life.

To be sure, this ideal was considerably dampened at first by the fiasco of 1599. In particular the Elector Joachim Friedrich was merely confirmed in his faint-heartedness. As early as 1601 he considered as good as lost the Strassburg cause of his younger son, Margrave Johann Georg, who had been elected Bishop by the Protestant canons but then encountered a superior competitor in Cardinal Charles of Lorraine. In February 1603, in a message to the convention of the associated Protestant princes in

Heidelberg, he refused outright to join the Union that had been proposed in the light of this very question of Strassburg. Soon thereafter in the Diet of Regensburg of 1603 his opposition defeated the projected Protestant policy of obstruction, and this attitude was interpreted by the Protestant activists as a formal desertion, and did much damage to the reputation of the House of Brandenburg in these circles.

This happened shortly before Georg Friedrich's death and not long before Rheydt's entry into the service of the Electoral House of Brandenburg. Nevertheless, despite this faint-hearted turn in the old Elector's policy, he could hope to find fertile soil here for his political plans because with the death of Georg Friedrich (who as custodian to the mentally deranged Duke of Prussia had also been regent of that land) the questions of the succession of the Brandenburg Elector to that position and of the recognition of his son's right of succession, which was based upon his marriage to Anna, daughter of Marie Eleonore, had become pressing so that a new effort became unavoidable. A closer understanding with the Protestant activists was required also because of the Jülich succession to which again Anna could make claim. Moreover, Rheydt could count on the support of the Prince-heir (*Kurprinz**), Johann Sigismund, son-in-law of his protectress Marie Eleonore; he was far removed from his father's timidity and had been allowed to participate in some business, particularly the succession problems, which concerned him particularly. Reichard Beyer, Johann Sigismund's confidential secretary, nurtured the understanding between Rheydt and the prince. Thus it was possible that immediately after the old Elector's faint-hearted disavowal a revival of the Brandenburg policy of *rapprochement* with Calvinism and Western European *raison d'état* came to pass under Rheydt's far-reaching influence.

When Johann Sigismund—already thirty-one years old—made ready in April 1603 to visit his "Lord Cousin" Georg Friedrich in Ansbach, he expressed in a letter to Rheydt of April 14 the hope

* Heir presumptive to the Elector.

that this would be his school of military and political affairs, for until then he had occupied himself with scholarly, particularly legal, studies. This is the earliest documentary evidence we have of a close tie between them. This hope was not fulfilled: ten days later Georg Friedrich died. In his place, however, Rheydt himself became confidential advisor to the young prince in military and political affairs, without yet receiving a formal appointment to the Elector's service. Probably it was also Rheydt who encouraged Johann Sigismund, in his own behalf and without consulting the Elector, to restore ties with the Elector Palatine Frederick IV in the interest of the Jülich succession. This conformed thoroughly to the tradition of Georg Friedrich. On February 14, 1604, the Elector Palatine gave a very encouraging answer to a letter from Johann Sigismund in which, among other things, he called attention to the role of Denmark. Now a great struggle began at the court of Berlin between Johann Sigismund and his adherents on one side and, on the other, Chancellor von Löben and the other councilors who regarded the Union with distaste in order to influence the Elector's decision. Johann Sigismund won out. On March 23 his confidential secretary Reichard Beyer reported triumphantly to Rheydt, who was staying at the time at Königsberg with Marie Eleonore, *Cecidit Babylon* ("Babylon has fallen"). The Elector had decided to go himself with his son to Christian IV of Denmark, while Rheydt was entrusted with the important mission to the Court of the Elector Palatine. The instruction Rheydt received, signed by Johann Sigismund but based on a draft by Chancellor von Löben—doubting, cautious, and discreet —is the opening document in the publication under discussion.

Rheydt's mission succeeded beyond all expectations. One has the impression that the person of the Ambassador, well known as a decided champion of political Calvinism, awakened in the Court of the Elector Palatine a new confidence in Brandenburg and aroused hopes of fruitful collaboration. The prevailing method of concerted action by the three claimants was now abandoned because it was seen that it did not lead to the goal, particularly because of the attitude of Neuburg. Instead, a closer tie between the House of Brandenburg and the Palatinate was projected, to be strengthened eventually by the usual dynastic means, a marriage between Johann Sigismund's son Georg Wilhelm, then twelve years of age, and one of the Princesses of the Palatinate (Charlotte was the one later chosen). With regard to the religious difference (since one side was Lutheran and the other Calvinist), they relied on the "famous moderation in religious affairs" that prevailed at the Court of Brandenburg. In place of the previous plan of joint action in the Jülich succession with Neuburg and Zweibrücken—whose rulers were related to the House of the Elector Palatine—a fair consideration by Brandenburg of the claims of these two Houses was envisaged—which meant that Brandenburg would consult them as a matter of course on any kind of partition when it took possession of the contested lands.

It was of great importance that the link between the Palatinate and Brandenburg should be extended also to the States General, because it was recognized that monetary aid from them was absolutely necessary. The most interesting thing from our point of view, however, seems to me to be the emphasis placed on the necessity of connecting the general interest of Calvinist politics with the particular interest of the Brandenburg succession—an emphasis that suited Rheydt's personal intentions as much as those of the Palatine court, and yet represented an admonition to Brandenburg that was not entirely inappropriate.[12]

A special Memorandum called attention to the fact that few people were taking "the common cause" seriously, each one "looking to his own private interests without considering what this meant for the common cause." Thus the affairs of the Pope and Spain were constantly on the increase and were pursued sometimes with force and sometimes under the façade of law by means of proceedings before the Imperial court. Whenever there were Diets of any kind the "Papists" closed ranks, whereas there was no end to Protestant divisions; indeed, some Protestants even applauded this development. If this were to continue, the necessary outcome would be nothing less than total repression of all the Protestant Estates, and total domination by the Pope and the Spaniards, to the eternal shame and ridicule of the Protestants, who would earn the contempt of posterity, and to the irreparable disadvantage of the dear fatherland, the German nation. Then all particular agreements would be in vain.

Rheydt is told to bear this in mind, and to feel obliged after his return to arrange things with the House of Brandenburg in such a way that the impending confidential correspondence and consultation might serve the common interest. Brandenburg, too, ought to do as the Palatinate had already done, and bring to the attention of the other Protestant Estates the vicious intrigues of the Pope and his adherents and the dangers of proceedings before the Imperial court. The other Estates should be provided with the necessary information, so that the Protestants might hold together at Imperial, District, and other Diets no less than the "Papists," vote as a bloc, and put into effect by joint action what had been unanimously resolved. In this way, the Memorandum concluded, Almighty God would bestow all the more benefits and blessings on the attainment and preservation of private interests.

This program of a decided political Protestantism, as matters then stood, was identical with Calvinism and, in its characteristic linking of general and particular interests, set the tone for Rheydt's political activity in the service of Brandenburg. All the conflicts in which he became involved and which ultimately crippled his effectiveness originated in his invariably placing the general interests of Calvinism higher than the particular dynastic interests of Brandenburg. At first this meant considerable political stimulus and led to the promulgation of the Privy Council Order of 1604 in which something of the spirit of Calvinist *raison d'état* can be detected.

The establishment of the Privy Council of 1604 presents in itself a problem that has not yet been satisfactorily solved. On one hand it appears as a continuation and reorganization of the old

Council Chamber (*Ratsstube*) already organized by Joachim II.
The "Privy Chamber councilors" appointed since that time—that
is, councilors who were used not in the litigations of the court of
appeals (*Kammergericht*) but rather in the Elector's own "private and secret" affairs, in financial (*Amtskammersachen*) and
political business—were not entirely separated from the old Council Chamber. The establishment of the Privy Council of 1604,
considered in its own terms, appears merely as the final, though
not yet complete, separation of general political business from
the business of the court of appeals and from the offices for financial administration, which emerged at that time as special agencies, particularly for the domains and princely revenue. On the
other hand, the document of 1604 that established the Privy
Council reveals such a clear consciousness of an epoch-making
new foundation that we should not give too much weight to these
morphological connections. The solution to this difficulty will be
found in the fact that after 1604 we are dealing with political life
on a new, higher plane, one to which constitutional developments
had just then become adapted. It was an ascent from the low
lands of territorial still-life that was mainly limited by the horizon
of the Empire, to the higher regions of European politics, with
its wider horizon and harder tasks.

The political environment had radically altered. There was a
feeling in backward Brandenburg that one ought to adjust to the
altered situation. Hence the appeal to "the example of other well-
ordered polities and governments." No one uses or knows the
term and concept "modern state," but these events announce the
transition to it. We might say that Calvinism, which entered upon
the scene together with the Palatinate, was the midwife that
brought modern *raison d'état* into the world of Brandenburg politics. The document itself says as much. Although it maintains
that it was primarily the "high and difficult matters"—in particular the question of the Prussian and Jülich successions—that led
to the change in governmental structure, the document mentions
also the religious conflicts which have created a general political

situation that made the realization of Brandenburg's claims difficult. "Above all," the document runs, "since the dangerous machinations of the Papists and the persecution of our true religion can be felt increasingly and are being asserted by force, it is all the more necessary for us to meet all the evil we encounter with good counsel."[13] This is the same tone that dominated Rheydt's negotiations with the Elector Palatine in the summer of 1604; it is the expression of a resolute Protestant policy as was then proclaimed only in the Calvinist camp. The orthodox Lutheran party at the Court of Brandenburg understood this theme in all its ramifications, and attempted immediately to tone it down.

There are two versions of the document establishing the Privy Council, both dated December 13, 1604, both signed and sealed by the Elector. One was later amended and, with its corrections and additions, used as the model for the other, apparently final, version. The most important of these additions followed the sentence just cited, and ran as follows:[14]

In so far as discord occurs in religious matters or in matters of that kind and comes before the Privy Council, our Privy Council should not presume to deal with them itself but should refer them to our ecclesiastical consistory (*unser geistlich Consistorium*), and matters of this kind should be decided and discussed on the basis of our ecclesiastical order, which is founded on our true Augsburg Confession presented to the Emperor Charles V in the year 1530.

This was a precautionary measure carried out probably at the instigation of the Lutheran Consistory (General Superintendent Pelargus) and the Lutheran Chancellor von Löben, in order to restrict the Calvinist spirit speaking from these pages and also to tack on a veiled reference to the Formula of Concord,* which it was not thought feasible to mention openly.

The chief representative of this Calvinist spirit who aroused

* A religious statement drawn up in 1577 for the purpose of bridging differences between Lutheranism and Calvinism and accepted by Brandenburg, Saxony, and the Palatinate among others.

the Lutheran opposition was obviously the Lord of Rheydt, although he was not the only Calvinist sympathizer among the councilors. His contrast to the Brandenburg-Lutheran party at court was clear from the beginning. Klinkenborg has brought to light a previously unnoticed document of considerable significance regarding Rheydt's place among the councilors and his part in the transformation of the council. I interpret it differently from Klinkenborg and believe that he overestimates its significance when he calls it directly a first draft of the Privy Council Order of 1604. It was written by August Hildesheimer, the confidential secretary, and calls itself "Appointment of Our Chamber and Privy Councilors who constitute from now on our Privy Council Chamber and what they should do in it." Specifically,

In our Privy Council Chamber the following should sit as councilors: the Lord of Reeth, our Chancellor J. v. L. (Löben), C. v. W. (Waldenfels), Chr. Benkend. (Benckendorf), our Vice Chancellor, Heironymus v. Dieskau, Dr. Friedrich Pruckmann, and our C. (Councilor) Joachim Hübner so long as he remains here in the capacity of councilor.

The Elector wanted to add a secretary to keep minutes so that the Elector would always be able to have, on request, a report on what happened in the council. Those Privy Councilors not prevented by diplomatic or other service were to gather daily in the Council Chamber to confer on political issues related to the claims to succession and to Imperial and border questions, and also to give their attention to the Elector's domains and his revenue, its maintenance and recovery. Everything dispatched by the council was to be signed by the Chancellor or one of the councilors.

This draft lacks everything that lends the Order of 1604 its real historical significance. It lacks consciousness of the need to meet the demands of a new era in politics. It lacks any hint of a new spirit in the policies of Brandenburg. It lacks also the stricter separation of political affairs from the domain and financial administration—which was fundamental to the new order—and likewise lacks the severe and firm regulation of the chairmanship, of inquiry, of the recording of votes, of rules of procedure in general. The document is obviously governed by the intention of letting business continue to proceed as it always had in the Council Chamber. Even the old ordinance of Joachim II had prescribed a daily gathering of the councilors in the Council Chamber, and the Elector was to be given a report on their deliberations during the hours for audiences. All this remained as it was. The only departure from Joachim's ordinance was the secretary who kept the minutes; but a model for such an office had surely already been established in practice in the meantime.

Obviously the reason for this draft was the addition of several new councilors to those already holding office. That fact in itself was occasioned by the death of Margrave Georg Friedrich of Ansbach (1603), then Regent of East Prussia. It increased the administrative burdens and led to enlarging the number of councilors, in that both men who dealt primarily with Prussian and Jülich affairs under Georg Friedrich—Waldenfels and Rheydt—were taken into the service of the Elector of Brandenburg. Apart from these two, who came from the court of Ansbach, we find two other new councilors: Dieskau, whose family came from the privileged (*schriftsässigen*) nobility of the Magdeburg Stift,* and was close to the Margrave Johann Sigismund, and Hübner, son of the old teacher of the Elector Joachim Friedrich, who because of his ties with the Danish court was particularly useful just then. The personnel of the council was not yet complete, as is shown by one of the later-eliminated notations, "Other councilors. . . ." In fact, of all the councilors enumerated in the Ordinance of December 13, 1604—if we omit Count Schlick, who was a special case—it lacks only Pistoris. Pistoris had been in the service of Brandenburg since 1600 as councilor of the court of appeals, and had belonged to the delegation in Regensburg in

---

* The Archbishop of Magdeburg (by then a Protestant Prince or administrator), in contrast to the town of Magdeburg (which had its own government), ruled over extended territories around Magdeburg, in which some families of the landed nobility enjoyed particular privileges that made them almost independent.

1603. He was—and perhaps this gave grounds for some concern—decidedly of the Reformed persuasion, as was Dieskau, although in Dieskau's case this conviction was assuredly less pronounced.

I cannot go along with Klinkenborg's view that this draft represents Rheydt's original plan for the organization of the Privy Council and that the plan entailed placing all business in the hands of the councilors to the exclusion of the Elector's power of initiative (as happened in the Palatinate under Friedrich IV), and that Rheydt himself was to be chairman and director of the council. I believe, on the contrary, that this meager sketch corresponds more to the original intention of the Elector and his Chancellor of changing as little as possible the existing business routine and of leaving the conduct of affairs as before, in the custody of the Chancellor. That Rheydt should be named first among the councilors can be explained simply by his higher rank, which is emphasized here as elsewhere in official documents by the otherwise unused designation of "Lord" (*Herr*). The chairmanship or a leading position in the council in no way is attached to this. He was not even entitled to substitute for the Chancellor. Documents were supposed to be signed by the Chancellor or anyone of the councilors. Next in line was the Vice Chancellor. Yet this order of rank in the council, which gave Rheydt precedence over Chancellor Löben, was retained in the final document and can have aroused the Chancellor's jealousy, since he had formerly been preceded in rank at court only by Count von Schlick, the Lord Chamberlain.

As for Schlick himself, the absence of his name from the list is explained by the fact that as a personal advisor and associate of the Elector he was not generally counted among the councilors and in any case took no part in the regular sessions in the Council Chamber. If, despite this, the final decree on the organization of the council named him chairman, this was—as the remark about the obstacle his personal attendance on the Elector might create indicates and as the subsequent documents show without doubt—a purely formal position of honor and a temporary expedient to palliate the sensibilities of the two rivals Rheydt and Löben. Rheydt could have claimed his higher birth as entitling him to the chairmanship of the Privy Council; Löben could have pointed to his many years as Chancellor. Rheydt, to be sure, once declared—and we may as well take his word for it—that he had always regarded "pre-eminence" as a foolery he did not want to be burdened with; but Löben placed all the more weight on the preferential position he had acquired among the councilors. That Rheydt should be named second, and he himself third, chairman (even though the Chancellor received a number of concessions) reinforced their professional antagonism by personal jealousy.

In my opinion, therefore, Rheydt had nothing to do with this so-called first draft of the council ordinance. It was really a preliminary and wholly inadequate proposition to do nothing. On the other hand, it seems to me that the real Ordinance of December 13, 1604, particularly in its original wording, is thoroughly imbued with his spirit. In other words, I would like to stand on its head Klinkenborg's view that Rheydt suffered a first heavy defeat with the establishment of the Privy Council: the tendencies pursued by Rheydt found epoch-making expression in the Ordinance of 1604, in contrast to the antiquated habits of the old Brandenburg Chancellery government as represented particularly by Löben. These tendencies, moreover, sprang from the spirit and political experience of Western European Calvinism, which had had nowhere in Germany greater influence than in the Electorate Palatine.[15]

Klinkenborg has rightly shown that the allusion to "the example of other well-ordered polities and governments" in the Ordinance refers primarily to the Electorate Palatine, whose Superior Council (*Oberrat*) Moriz Ritter has described and evaluated.[16] The connection between them should not, however, lead us to expect the Brandenburg ordinance to be a mere copy of the Palatine's. The Court and Chancellery ordinance of Elector Palatine Ott-Heinrich in 1557 corresponded to the Brandenburg Court ordinance (*Hofordnung*) of Joachim II which was some twenty years older, and contains prescriptions about the activities of the councilors and the Chancellery. The Palatine ordinance is a great deal more modern than Brandenburg's and could serve as a model for the new Brandenburg Ordinance by its detailed prescriptions for eliciting opinions and for the seating arrangement, wholly absent in the old Brandenburg Court ordinance. Still there is no question of a word-for-word agreement. The limiting of the council sessions on political affairs to two days of the week—Tuesdays and Thursdays—could also have been taken from the Palatine model, but I would not suggest that Rheydt had actual knowledge of the expert opinions of the Palatine councilors of 1603 but used what he had seen of the actual conduct of business at the Palatine court. In general the practical application and the political principles underlying these ordinances are significant rather than the formulations. That the Superior Council of the Palatinate under Friedrich IV carried the total burden of business to the exclusion of the Elector's initiative is a fact established by Ritter from his documentary studies of government practice in the Palatinate. This can be explained by the Elector's lack of political talent and energy, but it was by no means foreseen in the Court and Chancellery ordinance of 1557 or in any other organizational prescriptions. In principle the Elector's participation in the deliberations of the council was envisaged, and a decision of the council was not automatically binding on him. The daily assembly of the councilors, as projected in the so-called first sketch of the Brandenburg ordinance, does not permit us to conclude that there was any intention of depriving the Elector of his initiative in the conduct of affairs. The question of where this initiative is to be found is certainly crucial in evaluating the system of government, but to answer it the procedure for dealing with correspondence to the sovereign, especially from abroad, is decisive. In the old system, it was the Chancellor who was authorized to open all such letters and to deal with them as he saw fit. It also depended on his judgment which were to be passed on to the Elector for his cognizance and further action. This was the cardinal point in the old form of Chancellery government. In the new Order of 1604 it was supplanted by a new method of procedure. Now all these letters were to be delivered to the Elector's confidential secretary (*Kammersekretär*) by the head messenger, and he was to present them immediately unopened to the Elector, who read them himself and determined how to cope with them further. Either he himself gave an immediate decision on what was to be done about them and how to answer them; or he called in the councilors and discussed the matter with them before making a decision; or, finally, he referred the matter to the Privy Council for joint consideration (*Kollegialische Behandlung*), and as a rule he will have adhered to their decision.

Such was the new method of government. It could be called a personal government of the sovereign from his "Chamber," but in conjunction with his councilors or the Privy Council as a whole. The new institution of Chamber Secretary was characteristic of this system of government—"chamber" here meaning what was later, after the French model, called "Cabinet." It was the workroom of the sovereign—a new meaning for the ambiguous word "chamber," and a new phenomenon in court and government operation of the petty territorial states of Germany. In the greater states of Europe this way of governing was already generally in force in the sixteenth century, just as was the institution known as the "Council of State."[17] Whether it had already been introduced into the Palatinate before 1604 I am unable to say from the sources I know. Ritter's account makes no argument for it. Its introduction into Brandenburg, however, can be traced directly to the French example, which a man as worldly-wise as Rheydt would certainly have known, whether from his Rhenish homeland and the neighboring Netherlands or from the multiplicity of relations between France and the Court of Ansbach.

We have a detailed *Règlement* from the times of Henry III in France dealing with the procedures of a primitive Cabinet government; in detail it may differ from the arrangements in Brandenburg, but as a whole it foreshadows them.[18] Here, too, the

King is presented early in the morning with the incoming mail, unopened, in a violet velvet case. He opens the letters and distributes them with directions to the four secretaries, according to their department. If the King makes a decision at once, the secretary presents the document to him on the following day for his signature. These *secrétaries des commandements du Roi et des finances*, the later "Secretaries of State," are the link between King and council. The arrangements can be found elsewhere as well—e.g., in England and in Spain. They may well have come from the Papal Court, where the Cardinal Secretary of State even today represents this office in a form almost wholly unchanged since its inception in the fifteenth century. For Brandenburg, however, France was the immediate model.

Even the limiting of council sessions in important affairs of state to two days of the week (as we find in the Palatinate and Brandenburg) might be traced to the French model. In France a *Règlement* of February 18, 1566, undertook for the first time a distribution of the different business of the council among the various days of the week so that two days—Wednesday and Friday—were reserved for judiciary matters, and on the remaining four days *conseils d'état et des finances* were held. By the end of Henry IV's reign, further specialization led to the division of the Council of State into four departments, among them the *Conseil des affaires étrangères*, also called the *Conseil d'en haut*, because here the King himself usually presided.[19]

The seating order was less important in French council ordinances than they were Germany, since in France the great lords, up to the princes of the blood, and the high clergy up to the Cardinals, played the major role in the Council. The bureaucratic element that prevailed in Germany and indeed usually composed the entire council was represented in France only by the *maîtres des requêtes* who were employed mostly on judiciary questions, and by the above-mentioned *secrétaires des commandements du Roi et des finances* (corresponding to the German Chamber secretaries). For this reason these secretaries, who after the mid-sixteenth century were also called Secretaries of State, advanced in France to the position of the leading ministers of the *Ancien régime;* whereas in the German states, particularly in Brandenburg-Prussia, such positions were occupied by Privy Councilors.

This is perhaps the profoundest difference between the council and governmental systems of French and German absolutism. It is also an important reason why the "government in council" as conducted in Brandenburg by the Great Elector after Louis XIV's example, later changed to a "Cabinet government" that became much more autocratic in character than it ever was in France. In the beginnings, however, the autocratic type of government in Brandenburg obviously followed the French model. This important turn of events—the departure from the medieval Chancellery government as signified by the Privy Council Ordinance of 1604—must be regarded as the work of that statesman who had received his political training in Western Europe and who seems to us to be the main exponent of political Calvinism in Brandenburg.

The Ordinance of 1604, which established the Privy Council, provided not only a new system of government but also a new program of government, which likewise can be traced to the Western European, French, and Dutch *raison d'état* that only Rheydt could have transmitted. Here, for the first time in the history of Brandenburg, the dominating interests of modern *raison d'état*—the financial and the military—in full recognition of their usefulness to further economic prosperity and productive capability—appeared alongside the religious interest as the main aims of the Elector's policy. This energetic concentration of the financial, economic, and military forces of the country in the service of high policy—reminding us of Frederick the Great's image of the *Quadriga**—was of course the great secret of modern statecraft as then practiced by the House of Orange and Henry IV. It shows that the Ordinance of 1604 establishing the Privy Council was not

---

* Frederick II the Great stated in his Political Testament that a ruler must direct military affairs, administration, foreign policy, and finances in the same unified manner in which the driver of a *quadriga* guides his four horses.

the work of the Chancellery but of a statesman who wished to make out of Brandenburg, with her aspirations in Prussia and on the Rhine, a real state of European character, one that could play an independent role in the future great world struggle as the Reformed Netherlands did. Of course, the impact of modern *raison d'état* was frequently broken and deflected by the dense medium of the patrimonial, petty-state system of Estates, which then was still in full force in Brandenburg.

With regard to finance all that was discussed was the domains (*Kammergut*), not yet any system of regular taxes. But the domains served no longer merely as a means to maintain the sovereign's honor and dignity, but were also considered as the foundation (*Vorlage*) for political enterprises. The expression *nervus rerum gerendarum* made its appearance; later, Frederick William I liked to use this phrase, and he might well have remembered it from this very ordinance. "Economic policy," to which here a clear meaning is given, appears for the first time in a Brandenburg state paper, refers only to trade and not yet to manufactures, and the main items of this trade are the export goods—grain and wool. Nonetheless, the open recognition that trade is badly managed, that it is almost extinguished, the acknowledgment of the necessity to terminate the stoppage of navigation on the Elbe and the Oder to Hamburg and Stettin; the intention of bringing interested parties from town and country together for consultation on trade measures—all this shows a liberal, modern conception of a task which fitted a man who knew Holland and France, where the rudiments of mercantilism had emerged, but which could not be expected from the men of the old Chancellery government in Brandenburg.

The military measures envisaged still follow traditional lines: mustering of urban and rural militias (*Lehnsmilizen*) and maintenance of fortresses. But there is already talk of a defense organization (*Defensionwerk*) and of employing colonels and military experts like Rheydt himself, to whose care military affairs had been particularly entrusted. The phrase *tempore pacis de bello cogitandum* sounds like a fanfare in the still-life of the territorial state and shows that the new idea of political power was coming into existence, even though preservation of the religious and political peace was proclaimed to be the supreme aim of the Elector's policy.

The new political spirit that this governmental program reveals cannot have been instilled into the Brandenburg Court by anyone but Rheydt. It came with Calvinism from Western Europe. Of course, at that time Calvinism was still regarded with suspicion at Joachim Friedrich's court: in these very years, the Elector had General Superintendent Pelargus preach and write against the Calvinists, while he himself, by a remarkable irony of fate, was decried throughout Germany as a Calvinist, because of certain architectural changes in his cathedral. Nevertheless, the court gladly fell in with and made use of the stimulus to political enterprise that the adherents of the Reformed faith brought with them from Western Europe; the new political era that began with the organization of the Privy Council in 1604 cannot disavow the influence of Calvinist *raison d'état*.

The political stimulus at the Berlin Court marked by the promulgation of the Ordinance of 1604, produced in 1605 two important actions. In the West, a close alliance was made on February 7 with the Elector Palatine, after negotiations conducted by Rheydt whereby the marriage discussions between the Elector of Brandenburg's grandson Georg Wilhelm and the Palatine Princess Charlotte were formally settled. On April 25 both Electors made an alliance with the States-General, which in return for the payment of three hundred thousand guilders promised military help to protect the rights of Brandenburg in the Jülich lands for the next three years, in case the Duke died or the Spaniards invaded the country. In the East in negotiations with Poland and the Prussian Estates, which issued in April in the Treaty of Cracow concluded by Löben and Waldenfels, Brandenburg secured the investiture and, if the case arose, the succession as well as the transfer of the guardianship and administration of the country.

The conditions were harsh. Among other things, three hundred thousand guilders were to be paid, and in certain circumstances Brandenburg was pledged to give aid to the Catholic liege-lord Sigismund III of Poland against Protestant Sweden, which this Jesuit-inspired renegade from the House of Wasa hoped to win back to the Catholic Church.

These were apparently great successes for Brandenburg policy, but the price had been high. The heavy payments exceeded the financial capacity of the Brandenburg court, and closer scrutiny casts doubt particularly on the value of the agreement with the Netherlands. In Prussia the guardianship and administration placed at Brandenburg's disposal the revenues of the country which Margrave Georg Friedrich had received. This was a palpable advantage. In the Jülich lands, however, everything depended on further events, and the worth of Dutch military help seemed to become more questionable as time went on.

Thus this first attempt at an energetic pursuit of the claims of succession led to a complete political turnover at the Court of Brandenburg. A first sign of this was the dismissal of Privy Councilor Hübner, who had been chosen to conduct the negotiations with Poland together with Vice Chancellor Benckendorf and the Calvinist Wedigo von Putlitz. Immediately before the departure of this delegation in January 1605 there was a bitter altercation between Hübner and Löben in the Privy Council, in the course of which Hübner, an adherent of Johann Sigismund's party, and long since irritated by the "intrigues and despicable ways" of the Chancellor, let loose his pent-up "just and honorable resentment and anger."

The substance of the argument was apparently Löben's rejection of a proposal of Hübner's for the instructions to the legation. Presumably, therefore, it was in connection with this quarrel that shortly after the departure of the legation another mission with more extensive powers was sent after it, consisting of Chancellor von Löben himself and Privy Councilor von Waldenfels, a former adviser to Margrave Georg Friedrich of Ansbach on Prus-

sian affairs, who, in contrast to Rheydt, had attached himself to
the Chancellor's party. These new envoys did not cooperate with
the others in Warsaw and studiously kept them away from their
secret negotiations with the Poles—of which Hübner greatly
complained in a report. Initially he refused at the end of the
Warsaw Diet to which he had been sent—his colleague Benckendorf became ill and died there—to go with Löben to Cracow,
where Löben and Waldenfels concluded the treaty with King
Sigismund. He pretended that he had promised to go to the King
of Denmark immediately after the Warsaw Diet to talk over an
appointment in the Danish service. In Berlin this was regarded
as a request for dismissal, and he was therefore dismissed before
the end of the five-year term to which he had been appointed in
1603. Apparently he was saddled with responsibility for the unfavorable conditions of the treaty, and he desperately defended
himself against it. With regard to the salary demands he raised,
he was paid off in a way that seemed appropriate.

The Chancellor was now rid of this disquieting colleague,[20]
and he now took up his cudgels with his main opponent, Lord
von Rheydt. He reproached Rheydt for acting contrary to his
instructions in the Treaty with the States-General and for not se-
curing sufficiently the interests of the House of Brandenburg.
It must be admitted that this reproach was not wholly unfounded.
One of the main points was that the Elector himself was entered
as the main party to the Dutch treaty, whereas his son, Margrave
Johann Sigismund, was mentioned in the second line only. According to the instructions, it should have been the other way
around: Johann Sigismund, as the Elector and his adviser Löben
saw it, was the one primarily interested in the Jülich inheritance
and should therefore have appeared as the primary ally of the
States-General. The Elector wished only to impart his paternal
approval in an "addendum" in which he "consented" to the arrangement without committing himself in any way to the States-
General, whose military help would hardly be of use to him.

A more evident demonstration of the patrimonial, private-law conception of the Elector and his Chancellor, characteristic of the old territorial Chancellory system, can hardly be imagined. Naturally the representatives of the States-General, accustomed to thinking politically, would not have agreed to this; and Rheydt, who also thought politically, did not even present it to them. The States-General were chiefly interested in getting their hands on great sums of money as soon as possible for their increasingly difficult war of liberation. How could they have expected such sums from Johann Sigismund, who at that very moment was complaining to his father that his income was not sufficient to bring up his numerous children in accordance with their rank? The Elector, however, thought he could assure his house of Dutch military help for the acquisition of the Jülich inheritance in future years without himself assuming any financial obligation in his own lifetime, and without drawing upon himself the displeasure of the Emperor and the risk of the ban of the Empire by his son's military pacts with the States-General. The placing of his name before that of his son in the treaty was all the more distasteful to him because the payments to the Netherlands now coincided with those to Poland—three thousand guilders—and the Estates of the Electorate evinced no great desire to finance the dynastic policy of expansion of their ruling house. Fifty thousand was raised with great difficulty to pay the first installment of the Dutch aid, after the Palatinate had already paid the same sum. It was feared that this would "purchase" war and not the Jülich inheritance, especially since just at this time the military situation of the Netherlands became unfavorable. While Rheydt and Johann Sigismund emphatically demanded that all strength should now be exerted to assist the Netherlands, on whose fate the Jülich inheritance depended, the inclination emerged ever more strongly at Court and in the Privy Council to be freed from this dangerous treaty.

Even apart from dragging in the person of the Elector, the councilors found in the treaty with the States-General questionable violations of the aims and interests of the House of Brandenburg. The military help of the States-General, which was to be given on the death of the mentally ill Duke or in the case of an enemy assault on the rights of Brandenburg, was called in the treaty merely "assistance," and thus would be canceled—so the councilors' argument ran—if Brandenburg were not in a position to appear with forces of her own. Besides, this help had been spelled out only in general terms, without any exact prescription for the number of troops or special mention of artillery and munitions. Finally, the negotiators had made the help contingent upon the United Provinces' being in a condition of "prosperity" that would make their support possible and practicable.

Rheydt replied to the distrust of the councilors toward the Netherlands with arguments betraying his rocklike confidence that the States-General would do everything in their power to achieve the common goal—that the Jülich lands would fall to their rightful Brandenburg heir and not to the "Papists." He said that the Orange family and the other honorable and God-fearing men with whom he had had to deal were beyond any suspicion of double-dealing. God had, to the astonishment of the whole world, chosen these men as an instrument to resist the Baal and Anti-Christ in Rome, and to preserve and to erect His true Church. He hotly protested against the charge of having acted contrary to his instructions. One might say, however, that he interpreted them in a different way from that intended by Lutheran councilors like Löben and Waldenfels. Primarily, indeed exclusively, these men had the particular dynastic interest of Brandenburg in mind. But Rheydt regarded this interest as indissolubly linked with the interests of "the commonweal," the *res publica Christiana,* whose head and center were, for him, the Reformed United Netherlands. Wholly confident of their absolute devotion to the common cause—the struggle against the Catholic Restoration—he had negotiated with the Dutch in Brandenburg's name and concluded the treaty. He expected and demanded the same devotion from Brandenburg. Rheydt liked to present himself as an "unlettered trooper" (*ungelehrter Lands-knecht*), although he was by no means lacking in classical education. He put no particular stock in precise minutes or in the observance of diplomatic precautions. He explained that he could not always drag along paper, pens, and ink on his travels and negotiations; and what he had in mind was something more like a "gentleman's agreement."

This was the germ of the conflict, in the course of which all the councilors were finally to oppose him—even Pruckmann and Pistoris, both adherents of the Calvinist cause. They still remained in the tradition of dynastic territorial particularism, while Rheydt had a European horizon. "Where are the scornful in the Europe of today?" he once asked the Elector in a memorandum, making a play on the "seat of the scornful" mentioned in the Psalm. "Are they not the enemies of the Gospel: the Pope, the Emperor, Spain, and their adherents?" This Calvinist politician always thought in terms of the great world contest between the religious parties. He wished to draw his political wisdom not "from the Machiavello" but rather from the Book that all must revere and accept; and it was primarily the Old Testament that provided him with examples and axioms. He well knew that the forces of Brandenburg which he wished to inject into the great world struggle were in themselves limited and inadequate. But, as he once declared to Margrave Johann Sigismund, "God can and wants to help, with lesser as with greater means, if only the right goal, that is, the glory of God, is being sought" (No. 1991). The Elector and his councilors were afraid that armed intervention in the Jülich question would violate the constitution of the Empire and could bring about the ban of the Empire for breach of peace (*Landfriedensbruch*). Rheydt opposed this idea with the interpretation that this would not be a question of breach of peace but of defense of the frontiers of the Empire against a non-German aggressor—namely, Spain. Thus an intervention to uphold one's own rights would also be a patriotic act for the Empire, and it was therefore both a right and duty for the Elector.

As for the Emperor, the same principle held that Rheydt had
laid down for Brandenburg regarding her Polish liege-lord: "The
axiom that God's will is submission to the ruler must be refined
and understood to mean only a government that promotes the
glory of God and His word and administers equal justice. These
conditions I cannot find in the King of Poland, but exactly the
opposite." He harbored a deep distrust of Sigismund III. Sigismund was to him a Swede who had renounced his Evangelical
faith and was now making war, with Jesuit help, on his native
land and on the true Evangelical Church. The Treaty of Cracow,
which obliged the Elector in certain circumstances to defend
Prussia from a Swedish attack, was certainly not to Rheydt's
taste. In his mission to Prussia (1607) his Calvinism did not buy
him success. A great part of the knights there had come out in
opposition to the treaty, but for different reasons than his—because their rights had not been sufficiently respected in the
question of the guardianship and succession, and they feared for
their privileges and for the exclusive rule of Lutheranism.

Nor could Rheydt's ties with Fabian von Dohna help much.
It was said in Berlin that the attitude of the councilors in the Prussian government (*Regimentsräte*) had become more difficult during Rheydt's presence, and it was suspected that Rheydt, who
always had Johann Sigismund's interests first in mind, was working
against the Elector. That is what the Margravine Ann had told him
in confidence. It contributed to making his position in Berlin and in
the Privy Council untenable. He had concerned himself little, or
even not at all, with his office as Court Marshal, which had after all
been intended merely as a sinecure. He was rarely visible at court.
He was no courtier, and the daily "attendance" on Their High-
nesses—without which, as Reichard Beyer anxiously warned him,
a councilor's influence easily disappears—was not to his liking.
When not traveling, he usually resided at his fief in Caputh near
Potsdam, where also he occasionally received delegates from the
patriots of the Jülich lands. In 1605, after his first appointment,
there had been talk of his wanting to marry, and the fief of Neu-

enhof was assigned to him for his wife in her widowhood. But this was later withdrawn, and nothing seems to have come of the marriage. He never enjoyed a settled existence. In the Privy Council he became assailed, isolated, was regarded as impossible. He once (1607) spoke bitterly of his having been driven out of the Privy Council by insults and mockery.

When in March 1607 he realized that it was impossible to make available any more subsidies to the Dutch, he became resigned enough to retiring into private life, and his faithful assistant Reichard Beyer did the same, adding that henceforth he felt ashamed to go outside the country. But despite Rheydt's being for a long time in the disfavor of the Elector, it did not come to this. The clever and energetic Duchess Marie Eleonore took his part with her usual determination, and it was to her influence that Rheydt owed a new appointment (his third) in 1607; and this freed him from attendance at court and permanent residence in Berlin, and permitted him to serve the interests of the Elector in his own country.

At this moment the general situation in the world underwent a significant change, in that peace negotiations opened between Spain and the Netherlands. They were conducted in the Hague, and gave Brandenburg occasion to be represented for the first time at a European peace conference. It was a dual representation: the Elector empowered Privy Councilor von Dieskau to be his plenipotentiary, and Rheydt was appointed as the special representative of Johann Sigismund. The Elector had just then decided to turn Jülich affairs entirely over to the Electoral Prince, but gave him an allowance of only ten thousand guilders a year for the purpose. After long hesitation, the Electoral Prince took over direction of these affairs, but, as could be foreseen, this led to constant friction with Chancellor von Löben, who held the tiller in Berlin. The immediate point at issue was whether, and in what way, the succession of the House of Brandenburg not only in Jülich but also in Prussia should be treated in the peace negotiations. For a long time Dieskau did not receive the instructions necessary to proceed in the issue. Johann Sigismund grew impatient. Probably he shared the opinion of his Chamber Secretary, Beyer, that the Chancellor was counteracting them in every possible way, all the while pretending to be the most loyal of all; and he now allowed himself to be carried away into including accusations of this kind against the Chancellor in his increasingly frequent correspondence with his father. The charges were immediately rejected by the Elector on the significant grounds that the Chancellor and the councilors were obligated to look out for the Elector's interests alone and no others. But the Chancellor must have received word of these accusations and decided on a counterstroke. Löben seized this opportunity to ask the Elector to permit his resignation, after twenty-one years of service, citing as reasons the weakening of his strength by the increasing burden of work, and the inadequate staff of the Privy Council (April 24, 1608). The Elector, as Löben had foreseen, rejected it immediately (April 25). He told the Chancellor that he had his full confidence, that he would protect him against all calumny, and he held out the prospect of the appointment of two new councilors and a secretary, whom Löben was to propose. Thus the Chancellor's position was strengthened anew, and he used his victory to check the emerging Calvinist co-government.

At this very time the Regensburg Diet was dissolved without recess. From the beginning its meetings stood under the impact of the Donauwörth affair and the advancing Catholic Restoration and were marked by strong religious tension. The delegates of the Protestant princes, with the exception of Saxony, who took a mediating attitude, left Regensburg and met in the Ansbach village of Anhausen to discuss a new Evangelical Union. The Brandenburg delegate, Pruckmann, who, it seems, had proposed this meeting, was not represented at it. He had hurried to Berlin and handed in a report on May 1 in which he pointed to the example of Switzerland and the Netherlands and, despite the attitude of Saxony, emphatically—indeed enthusiastically—recommended this Union as the only means of saving the Protestant

faith and German liberties. That this appeal found no response in
the Elector can certainly be ascribed to Löben's work against it,
for he had always been an opponent of the Protestant Union.
Brandenburg like Saxony stayed away from the preliminary
Union, which was discussed and settled between May 2 and May
4 of 1608, by the delegates of most of the other Protestant princes
gathered at Anhausen.

Meanwhile a similar attempt, which wanted to establish a new
alliance with the Netherlands, was thwarted. Rheydt was carrying on the negotiations in the Hague in behalf of Johann Sigismund, and it was probably not without his involvement that the
Dutch suggested to Dieskau, the official representative of the
Elector of Brandenburg in the Hague, that the Protestant princes
of Germany should enter into an alliance with the States-General
in order to strengthen the Protestant cause in the peace negotiations with Spain; it might be particularly effective and impressive
if the princes established beforehand a Union among themselves.
The Dutch did not want to make the alliance directly dependent
upon such a Union, but were eager to join with individual German
princes—primarily with the Elector Palatinate and Elector of
Brandenburg—in order to strengthen their existing ties with
France, England, and Denmark. They hoped that then the other
princes would gradually join in.

Johann Sigismund in Berlin gave his most ardent support to
this plan, and it seems that Pruckmann continued to advocate at
least the Protestant Union in the Privy Council. In these circumstances Löben had recourse to the Estates to frustrate the plan.
Joachim II's old promise that no alliance would be made without
the consent of the Estates was dusted off and put into practice.
On June 7 a committee of Electoral Estates of the Mark was
asked, among other questions, how the offer of a Dutch alliance
should be dealt with. All reasons for it and against it were extensively discussed in the proposition. This probably reflected
the discussions in the Privy Council, Pruckmann representing
the *pro*, Löben the *contra*. The speed with which the Estates

gave their reply—their Memorandum was in the hands of the
government by June 8—shows that the meeting had been well
prepared and skillfully managed. The Estates' opinion amounted
to this: The Protestant princes, particularly of Brandenburg,
should negotiate the alliance with the States-General not singly
but in concert and, like the Estates of the Kurmark, the Estates
of all the other lands ought first to be asked for consent.

This was a resolution after the Chancellor's heart, and the
Elector accepted it and gave notice to his son to this effect. Negotiations among the princes at Hof were envisaged, but from
the beginning Saxony refused to participate. Thus the plan was
shelved and the irruption of Calvinist politics into the quiet territorial still-life was once again fended off. But Löben did not
keep power in his hands for much longer. On July 17, 1608, the
Elector Joachim Friedrich died, and Johann Sigismund, then on
a journey to Prussia that he could not interrupt, sent his confi-
dant, the Calvinist-minded Adam von Putlitz, to Berlin as his
governor (*Statthalter*). Putlitz caused first Count Schlick and
then, after some time (1609), Löben, to resign. The Chancellorship remained unoccupied for a long time; it lost its political
importance forever. This turn of events was characteristic of the
transition to the modern state. The direction of affairs in the
Marks was transferred to the Governor. This office, which then
first appeared in Brandenburg, was modeled on the French *lieu-
tenants du roi*—the *gouverneurs*. Such viceroys existed later in
other provinces as well. Johann Sigismund's brother, Margrave
Ernst, was appointed Governor in the Jülich lands after the
House of Brandenburg seized possession of them in 1609; and
on Ernst's death in 1613 his son Georg Wilhelm replaced him. In
the Mark, after Putlitz was relieved of this post in 1613, another
brother of the Elector, Johann Georg of Jägerndorf, was appointed. The direction of the Privy Council, and the position of
the link between Elector and Council, seem to have also been
transferred to Johann Georg:[21] it was he who received all incoming correspondence and reported on its contents to the Elector.

This change, as we have said, coincided with the death of Reichard Beyer, the old friend and collaborator of Rheydt's, who had been *Kammersekretär* for a number of years. Even after Johann Sigismund's accession to the throne Beyer had remained his real guide and adviser, but he had adjusted long before to the changed state of affairs, particularly after he was no longer under the influence of Rheydt's moral and political power.

Rheydt himself was no longer at the new Elector's side. In June 1608, in the course of one of his frequent journeys, he had fallen gravely ill in Delft—of pleurisy, it seems—and after an apparently incomplete recovery, returned to his post at the Hague. This is our last trace of him in the documents. On October 9, 1608, Governor Putlitz announced his death to the Elector, after a report from Dieskau, the Electoral Ambassador at the Hague, at whose side Rheydt had represented Johann Sigismund. He had no longer seen the conclusion of the armistice between Spain and the Netherlands, which represented a fatal turning point for Calvinist world politics. Nor did he see the opening of the Jülich succession through the death of the mentally ill duke. He was the mentor of Johann Sigismund at the time when Johann Sigismund as Electoral Prince advocated an active Protestant policy, linked to Brandenburg's dynastic interests. But Johann's policy as Elector was shaped by other advisers.

Conclusion

This is as far as I shall take events, for it is at this point that the recently published documents come to an end. I wanted only to show how the reception of modern *raison d'état* in Brandenburg was tied to the effective work of this statesman, which was dominated completely by the aims of Calvinist world policy; short-lived and often obstructed as it was, it was of crucial significance. His model for the policies and structure of the greater Brandenburg-Prussian state of the future was primarily the Republic of the United Netherlands under the Orange dynasty, but another model also was their most powerful ally, the France of Henry IV. These two models, however, could have their full effect in the state of Brandenburg-Prussia only after the Spanish-Austrian hegemony had been defeated by the superior French policy in the Thirty Years' War. But it is important to recognize that this was the aim of the leading statesman already when the Privy Council was founded in 1604. It can be said that Calvinism formed the bridge by which Western European *raison d'état* made its entry into Brandenburg. And the more the power of the House of Orange in the Netherlands faded into the background in the face of the republican constitution the more the model of monarchical France had its influence on Brandenburg.

This is not so much a matter of single political institutions and administrative instruments as of the fundamental nature of political life and its attainments. The endeavor to become an independent political power in Europe; the harnessing of all the military and financial power of the country toward this end by means of a strong monarchical government; the well-planned overcoming of the resistance, with which the various Estates opposed this goal in a state composed of relatively independent territories; the absolutism that emerged from this, and relied on a monarchical, bureaucratic civil service and later on a standing army—the tight concentration of the provinces into a centralized, governable, productive, single state—these features of Brandenburg-Prussia had found their model in France. By contrast, Imperial Austria, in pursuing similar aspirations, followed the Spanish and Burgundian pattern, which relied on a looser association of territories and on less rigid military and bureaucratic structure. Hence the striking parallels in French and Prussian administrative history in the seventeenth and eighteenth centuries, parallels that owe less to direct borrowing than to the efforts of similar basic political tendencies. If, in spite of this, Prussia's system of government had its own peculiar character, different from that of France, the reason, besides the different historical origins of the constitution of the German Empire and its states, was to a large extent Prussia's Protestant spirit, particularly the basically Calvinistic ascetic dedication to their profession of her three great rulers in the seventeenth and eighteenth centuries. At the time of the Seven Years' War the French saw with astonishment what had become of their pupils in Brandenburg. Out of a sense of their own superiority they had completely neglected to notice "*que les Hohenzollern fabriquassent leur Prusse imprévue*," as Lavisse has expressed it.[22] The structure that the Hohenzollern built rises from the ground only after the reign of the Great Elector. But its foundations lay deeper; and the help of the Calvinistic spirit animating the Great Elector in the laying of the early foundations of the edifice of Brandenburg-Prussia should not be underestimated.

COMPARATIVE AND
ADMINISTRATIVE HISTORY

4

THE FORMATION OF STATES AND CONSTITUTIONAL DEVELOPMENT: A STUDY IN HISTORY AND POLITICS

This essay was published in the *Historische Zeitschrift*, Volume 88 (1902); it belongs, therefore, to an early period of Hintze's scholarly activity. Indeed, it is of particular interest to those studying Hintze's intellectual development because some of the theses with which Hintze remained concerned throughout the remainder of his career initially appear here.

Hintze continued to consider the influence which foreign affairs exerted on the shaping of domestic politics in a number of articles—for instance, in the essay "Military Organization and the Organization of the State." The views on the nature of feudalism which Hintze presented in this article are explained and discussed at greater length in the systematic investigations of European constitutional and administrative developments which he published in the 1920s (see the Introduction to the article "The Preconditions of Representative Government," on p. 302). This article is not yet a study in comparative history; Hintze calls it rightly a "study in history and politics." The comparative approach is only to a limited extent used as an instrument that might lead to new interpretations and explanations; the many allusions to events and institutions in other areas and countries are primarily exemplifications of the theses Hintze propounds. Yet the great, world-embracing variety of these illustrations certainly suggests the beginnings of an interest in a "comparative historical method."

In later years Hintze treated all these issues—the relation of foreign policy to internal politics, the problem of feudalism, the validity and the limits of a comparative historical method—in a more penetrating and elaborate manner; nevertheless, this early article has a particular value because it states there various theses and views in a particularly simple and clear manner.

Moreover, this essay—as, for instance, in the critical remarks on Treitschke's work on *Politics*—shows Hintze's discontent with the lack of theoretical foundation in the historical work of his time; from the outset Hintze was convinced that the study of history ought to lead beyond the description of individual phenomena to insights of a general character.

It is often held that the growth and change of a political constitution are dependent on the social developments within society: it is conditioned by the changing power relations among the different social classes, which succeed each other in dominating the character of the régime or at least influencing the government. Karl Marx regarded the class struggle as the great driving force behind all historical events; and many observers, even if in general they would shrink from such a one-sided approach, have felt unable to deny that a people's political constitution is in effect shaped by its social structure. There is of course a germ of truth in this; but one point is overlooked—namely, the development of the state in relation to its neighbors.

The formation and the demarcation of the state's territory within which the social developments take place—briefly, alterations in the external existence of a state—have their bearing on its internal structure. Basically, the external existence of state and people is regarded as a fixed and immutable quality. Interest has tended to center on the social changes that occur within this set framework, changes that are then deemed responsible for the alteration of the political institutions. This is, in effect, to wrench each single state from the context in which it was formed; the state is seen in isolation, exclusive in itself, without raising the question whether its peculiar character is co-determined by its relation to its surroundings.

The adoption of this point of view seems to me to explain why most modern historians distrust and dislike political theories. In history, the predominant factor is the foreign policy of states—and foreign policy is not much discussed in political theory. Even Treitschke treated international relations (*Beziehungen der Staa-*

ten untereinander) at the end of his system, and nowhere did he discuss the decisive influence that they have had on the structure and constitution of each single state. On the other hand, Ranke, with his remarkable instinct, sensed that not only the existence of states but also their constitution is often shaped by foreign policy.

The objection might be made that foreign affairs cannot be brought into a scientific system; no theory can cover the events of world history, the power struggles of states and nations. This, however, is not the essential point; what is at stake is whether, and to what extent, the external form of a state, which is conditioned by factors of foreign policy, has had an influence also on its internal structure, i.e., on its constitution. Further, we must establish whether the cases of which this is true are isolated and exceptional, or whether they can be organized in groups and presented as evidence of a typical regular pattern.

In essence, class struggles and social tensions are not very different from external power conflicts and international rivalries, for these internal conflicts, in their detail, are by their nature no object for a general theory of the state. Obviously, however, they affect the state's internal politics: the growth and change of a constitution result from alterations in power relations, from the increased or diminished importance of the various classes for the political whole. External conflicts between states form the shape of the state. I am assuming this "shape" to mean—by contrast with internal social development—the external configuration, the size of a state, its contiguity (whether strict or loose), and even its ethnic composition. You cannot evaluate a constitution without taking into account whether you are dealing with Rome as city-state or as Empire, whether you analyze a national, unitary state like France or a multinational conglomerate like Austria, a medieval feudal state, a sixteenth-century territorial state, or a modern Great Power. Only when the state has received a firmly delineated shape can its political life and its pattern of government develop.

As I see it, states appear in history in a number of typical shapes, each one related to some form of internal organization. The form of Oriental despotism is common to the universal empires of ancient times and to non-European civilizations.[1] The city-states of both ancient and modern times all share an essentially similar organization, whatever the variations in detail; the territorial states, both in Germany and in France, are characterized by the existence of an Estates system: composite territorial states which turned into unitary states regularly undergo an era of absolutism. The fully fledged unitary national state, finally, tends toward a representative system as its appropriate constitutional form.

These strange connections, which have struck me in comparative studies of constitutional forms, deserve a closer look. The problems they present are legion, and no solution can here be attempted. The explanation I shall propose here in a few brief indications is based on the idea that the formation of states contains causal factors which determine the state's constitution. States are created by war, colonization, conquest and peaceful settlement, through amalgamation of different parts and through their separating from each other; and all this is bound up with an alternating process of intermingling and separation of races and civilizations, tribes and languages. The European peoples have only gradually developed their nationalities; they are not a simple product of nature but are themselves a product of the creation of states. Thus, reference to national custom or character cannot sufficiently explain constitutional forms, however important such factors may be in shaping their ethos. I shall consciously refrain from discussing questions of national customs and character; they can be investigated only through descriptions of the life of individual nations. A comparative study like the present one must seek a comprehensive stress on the morphological side of the matter. And however important the national spirit may be for institutions, other factors must be considered in explaining the various forms of states. The life of the internal constitution adjusts itself to the conditions of the external political existence, and the external shape of the state is a reflection of the situation prevailing at the time of its formation and is the consequence not only of power struggles but also of the geographical situation and the then existing means of communication.

It used to be thought that everything could be explained in terms of individual will power, planning, and calculation; and nowadays it is equally widely held that the driving forces of history are to be found in the natural conditions of each country or in the relations of economic production; yet there is also an abiding and fruitful truth in the basic notion of the Historical School of Law (*Historische Rechtsschule*)—that laws and constitution are a product of the *Volksgeist*. In the ultimate analysis it is always spiritual forces and events that create or destroy social institutions. The impact of the outside world must pass through an intellectual medium; and the only question is how strong is its refraction, to what extent it possesses independent vigor and can exert a counterweight. With this reservation we can—indeed, must—stress that in the life of peoples external events and conditions exercise a decisive influence upon the internal constitution. History does not permit progressive spiritual development, following its own laws, as was supposed by Hegel; there is rather a constant collaboration and interaction of the inner and the outer world.

This may suggest how the causal relation between the shape of a state and its constitutional development ought to be viewed. This is a matter not of some inanimate mechanism, by which the one affects the other, but rather of living forces and movements at work. The process in which a state is shaped produces aims, habits, needs, and views, and they create among leaders and masses a distinct intellectual disposition that favors a particular type of constitutional structure. Analysis of this process of psychological mediation must be regarded as the main task if we want to explain these phenomena; we cannot solve these problems here, we can only make suggestions. It is not necessary that those who are active in creating a constitution—whether they are individuals, or groups, or peoples—are conscious of the connection between the internal structure and the external formation of the state, and that this connection can be documented. Those involved in action usually are aware only of immediate needs but not of the more remote basic facts which have produced these needs. Moreover, historical changes usually have a great variety of causes.

The following remarks are intended to be understood in this sense. I begin with a few observations on the city-state. This was the only form of political life that Aristotle had before his eyes. For him the various forms of city-state constitutions were the forms of states in general; this explains why he neglects monarchy, which he treats as a vanished form, and also why he has a special interest in democracy, which appears as the form proper to a city-state, the πολιτεία κατ᾽ ἐξοχήν. What is common to ancient and modern constitutions of city-states is based, it seems to me, on the peculiar character of this political organization. Even where the foundation of a city-state was the work of a monarchical rulership, after it had come into existence it soon emancipated itself from monarchical authority; for close union simply in terms of space and intense communication among the inhabitants produced a vigorous, unified, collective political consciousness. In larger forms of state, this consciousness emerged only at a much later stage, if at all. This communal spirit is responsible for the inclination toward a republican form of government common to all city states: the associative principle of organization prevails over the authoritarian. The state consists of the community of citizens. When the city-state is fully developed, monarchical rule is abnormal and at best transitory, brought about by internal factionalism and outside assistance.

All city-states share the characteristic governmental institutions of elders, of a wider and a smaller council, citizenry, and representatives of the citizenry. The democracy of the Athenian city-

state is entirely different from the democracy of the United States
of America. In Athens a wholly unified community of citizens
was constituted as state, and acted directly as its executive organ;
in America there is a highly complicated composite structure,
with strict separation of the political functions, with representative institutions, and strongly developed executive power. By all
experience to date, direct democracy would seem possible only
in very small states with a communal character—existing, apart
from the city-states, in rural district communities like the old
Swiss Cantons.

As πολιτεία belongs to πόλις, *imperator* belongs to *imperium*.
When Rome developed into a great empire, it also turned from
a republican form of state to an imperial one. It is easy to see
that the process of constitutional development was influenced by
the territorial extension. The need for permanent military occupation of Spain made untenable the old military system of citizen
militia and annually changing commanders. Standing armies and
prolonged commands emerged as harbingers of a new monarchical constitution; and the conquest of Gaul by Caesar accelerated
developments in this direction. The outcome of three centuries of
change was the establishment of an Oriental despotism with
Diocletian. It may be said that the entire constitutional development of ancient times varied between the extremes of city-state
and universal empire.

All the great empires of ancient times and of the non-European
world were despotic in their form of government. So far as historical experience goes, free constitutions emerged only where
a number of states existed next to each other on equal terms, the
independence of each one being recognized by the others. Today
we are inclined to consider this the normal and natural condition
in the life of states; but this is not the case. Such a society of
states has always been the exception, if we look at the past of
the human race; it is a phenomenon that emerges only once on a
large scale—namely, in the European system of states, which
owes its rise to a wholly individual historical process. In the

Greek world of states, in the Italian states of the *Cinquecento*, a similar system of balance of power existed, but within a comparatively narrow, merely national framework; and the states of the Diadochis, which might be presumed to fit into this scheme, existed barely for two centuries—they were remnants of a disintegrated empire, not viable new formations. Outside this circle, wherever in the world something of a higher civilization and extended communications existed, we find the tendency to form world empires which sought to rule the entire civilized world as they knew it, and which refused to recognize other states as equal or independent.

The description "world empire" must be understood as relative, being defined in territorial terms by the horizon of civilization and communications. Egypt had an area only of four-fifths that of the German Empire—400,000 square kilometers; the Assyrian and Babylonian Empire covered 1.5 million square kilometers, three times as much as modern Germany. But these isolated civilizations, surrounded by desert, probably had required many centuries to become politically unified and, at their height, were a world unto themselves; and the inhabitants were scarcely aware of the existence of a world outside their empire. A gigantic step forward in the political organization was made when the Persian Empire was created—with its 5 million square kilometers it was equal in size to European Russia. Alexander's empire embraced 4 million; the Roman Empire at Augustus' death 3.3 million.[2] These great areas, which become less extended when the center of history moved from the continental spaces of Asia to the geographically more compact Europe represent the οἰκουμένη, the *orbis terrarum* of those days. The Inca Empire of Peru and the Aztec Empire in Mexico are similar phenomena. Even Turkey, with 2 million square kilometers, India, and China proper, equal in size to Alexander's Empire (4 million square kilometers), were for centuries worlds of their own in civilization and politics. These were all parts of the world's population that had been organized as closed units, that imagined themselves to be the whole, and did not know the notion of a society of equal states.

The characteristic form of government of all these empires is what we call Oriental despotism, the essence of which, it seems to me, is the union of secular and spiritual power in the person of the head of state. The Egyptian Pharaohs were gods on earth; the Emperors of China were "Sons of Heaven"; they were also the chief sacrificial priests of their realms, and they alone could approach the Lord of Heaven. The Turkish Sultans were also Caliphs, spiritual heads of the faithful *Moslemin*. The Great Kings of Persia consciously carried out a religious policy through which they changed from patriarchal heads of a tribe into theocratic despots, finally enjoying divine honors on the same lines as the divinity to which, in their day, Alexander and the Roman *imperatores* laid claim. After the introduction of Christianity into the Roman Empire a strongly marked caesaropapism emerged, replacing the old form of the cult of the emperor. The same system prevails even today in Russia, where it was taken over from Byzantium; the Russian government has constantly remained a kind of Oriental despotism, despite the facts that many of its institutions have undergone Western influence and that it has become part of the European state system, so that the idea of a world-empire in the old sense has paled.

Originally, theocratic despotism and world empire went together. The idea that the ruler has no equal in the world and occupies a super-human position, similar to a god's, was closely bound up with the universalist nature of the state itself. It would appear that the position of the head of tribe, which had evolved in analogy with that of a patriarchal family, was the pattern for the development of unlimited monarchical power (the Roman *princeps* was a singular phenomenon); but with the extension of their authority over many tribes and peoples this original patriarchal spirit evaporated. The formation of the role of the Great Kings of Persia affords a classic example.

The imperial form of state was the political legacy left by the ancient world to the modern Latin-Teutonic peoples of the West. The universalist idea lived on not only in German political formations, but also, and most importantly, in the organization of the Roman Catholic Church. This led to a split of vital significance between temporal and spiritual power; in place of caesaropapism there came a dualism of Church and State, of *imperium* and *sacerdotium*. The main cause of this change lay in the moral and political power acquired by the Roman Church upon the collapse of the Empire. The Merovingians had taken over the old system of caesaropapism; but it could no longer be upheld by the Carolingians. As usurpers, they lacked the divine sanctification which, in the eyes of the people, the Merovingian dynasty enjoyed, and they sought a substitute for this in the link with the Church. Thus, after Charlemagne the Church was able to maintain, and even to extend, the unity of its organization, while the secular counterpart, the universalist state, broke up during the second half of the ninth century. Thus the Church succeeded in emancipating itself from the power of the state. Roman capacity for organization and Roman art of government survived through language and writing, and not only preserved the Church's independence but made the Church for centuries the only effective representative of the notion of a Western universalist state.

The struggle of Empire and Papacy, a characteristic feature of the entire Middle Ages, provided the possibility for the creation of a European system of states. Neither of the two forces— neither the spiritual nor the secular—was able to realize the idea of a universal Christian empire, for the other constantly stood in the way. In consequence, a group of coordinated and independent states could develop between Emperor and Pope. The concept of sovereignty, as it emerged in France at the end of the sixteenth century, expresses not solely but primarily the notion of independence from both Emperor and Pope.[3]

Thus, the basic pattern of European politics is the coexistence of a number of sovereign states, which, despite all their antagonisms, have roots in a common civilization, and despite friction and wars, recognize each other's existence; this situation has not only produced modern international law but has exerted a significant influence on public law as well. The system of balance of power—often upset but always restored—has prevented any ruler from possessing permanently unlimited power. At earlier times the rivalry of states with each other had been bound up with the antagonism between Church and State. In almost every case, the Estates of Empire showed signs of these conflicts: in Germany the power of the princes was reinforced in the most patent way by the conflict of Emperor and Pope; in England King John's defeat at Bouvines at the hands of the French and Papal party created the situation from which the Magna Charta resulted: without the opposition to a victorious Church, with which the barons had initially been allied, the Crown would not have been forced into these concessions, even though King John's subjection to the Pope at the last moment altered the situation. In France the political significance of the Estates-General dates from the role they took in 1302 in the conflict between Philip the Fair and Pope Boniface VIII.

The discord between Church and State during the Middle Ages gave social forces their full importance in public affairs. It is significant that the juristic doctrine of corporation was founded by the medieval Romanists and Canonists.[4] State and society to some extent became separate, whereas in the ancient world they had remained undivided; social forces organized themselves in various forms and achieved political significance as guilds and corporations, as leagues of towns and knights, as unions for maintaining public peace, as associations of territorial Estates and the like. All Estate systems and representative constitutions can be regarded as a reunion of the separate elements of state and society.[5]

I suggest, therefore, that the peculiar relations through which states were formed in the Middle Ages (the dualism of spiritual and secular power, the emergence of a group of competing states) created the conditions for the development of Estates.

Neither Russia nor Turkey nor China produced such constitutions, and therefore none of these countries possessed a real political aristocracy. If Japan is an exception among these Eastern states, it must be borne in mind that she witnessed a similar division between spiritual and secular power to that which took place in the West[6] because the Shogun acquired a powerful position as Major Domus of a Mikado who steadily diminished in importance.

In the West the real basis on which aristocratic power and Estates systems arose was feudalism, which itself can be explained in terms of the particularities of the political process, in which states were formed. A distinction must be drawn between the fief system as an essentially military institution developed in the peculiar circumstances of the Frankish Empire, and the feudal system in general, which was a form of political organization opposite to government characterized by offices and officeholders. A feudal constitution in this sense can be found elsewhere as well —for instance, in Turkey and Japan. It would seem that in the Ottoman Empire the system rested on preservation of old patriarchal and military institutions by a warlike, nomadic tribe that had occupied and established itself permanently in large cultivated regions; they used their own traditional institutions for the establishment of a new political order.[7] In Japan feudalism proceeded from an attempt to imitate the great centralized Chinese state which—in view of the weakness of the central power —produced a system of the semi-sovereign powers, vaguely dependent on the center.[8] This was a process very similar to that at work in the Frankish Empire.[9] It would appear that the feudal system commonly represents an attempt to create a political organization over relatively large spaces with the means of a still incompletely developed civilization. Natural economy was the rule, communications were inadequate, and there was none of the intellectual discipline or technique of centralized administration; hence the peculiar type of decentralization whereby officials were granted land and were bound in personal fealty to a lord

—a process that led, after a few generations, to the creation of independent local power formations. This organization rested on the mentality and the customs of a patriarchal family structure; liegemen were household followers higher in status and separated from the other members of the retinue. The psychological bonds holding together the members of a feudal state were products of a family-like domestic order, and not those of a fully developed political order.

I regard as the main cause of the rise of feudalism the discrepancy between the size of the space to be controlled, and the available means of control, whether such means were of a material or psychological nature. In general, the political organization of settled tribes gradually spreads from smaller to larger areas; sometimes in world history, however, primitive forms of political organization are transferred directly to a geographically extended political area and this process involves the legacy or imitation of a more ancient, higher civilization. Thus the Franks pushed their way into the Roman *imperium*, and Charlemagne's empire was an attempt to restore a world empire by means of a primitive civilization. It was, as it were, an extensive kind of political formation in which there was an obvious discrepancy between the extent of the area to be governed and the available means of intellectual and political control. Roman tax systems, the military discipline of a standing army, a full-fledged bureaucratic apparatus—all this was absent.

This state was not a product of the innate needs of the Germanic tribes and was not appropriate to their capacity for civilization. It arose from an act of imitation, from the still influential notion of great political spaces.[10] The effectiveness of this notion can be seen in the moves of the states situated around the Carolingian Empire: everywhere during the next centuries the isolated tribes and small states joined in larger political formations, which in turn were imitations of the Western European great state: hence the great Moravian empire of Svatopluk in the ninth century, the great Polish state of Boleslaw Chrabri in the tenth century, and the Anglo-Saxon state of Alfred the Great in the ninth century. The Slavonic states, extensive political formations of the purest type, soon disintegrated; but England managed to organize herself as a unitary state. There were elements of a fief system in the Anglo-Saxon state, but as a whole it was not, properly speaking, a feudal state. The introduction of full-fledged feudal institutions by the Norman conquerors had the opposite effect to that which feudalism had on the Continent.

Despite feudalism, which was not an indigenous element in England, perhaps even because of feudalism, which in England was transformed into a military and absolutist bureaucratic regime under William the Conqueror, England became the first centralized, unified state in Europe; whereas on the Continent the feudal system spread unchecked, and led to the disintegration of the large states. Old England had an area of some 15,000 square kilometers; in the conditions of the eleventh century such an area could be organized. France and Germany were between four and five times as large; in areas of this size, organization could not succeed. The type of state that corresponded to the political capacity and requirements of the population emerged when these states broke up into duchies, and when in France in the tenth and eleventh centuries, and in Germany in the thirteenth and fourteenth, new territorial states grew up. They were effectively organized and capable of developing a competent administrative apparatus, since the area involved matched the means for political and intellectual control. These territorial states did rest in many respects on the feudal system; but they overcame it in their political organization, as England did, because feudalism was no longer needed. They produced the beginnings of a permanent bureaucratic organization, and an effective administration.

Otherwise the characteristic of the typical territorial state was its peculiar Estates system, both in France and Germany. The French provincial Estates were initially much like the German Diets. This peculiar system cannot be fully explained as an outgrowth of feudalism: in Germany the independent knights (*minis-teriales*) were more important than the vassals. The court of the ruler formed the nucleus, though the local lordship and the relative autonomy of Estate members were factors of significance. In Germany it was not by chance that the term *Landschaft* (area of land) was used for the territorial Estates. As a whole they represented the area which had been consolidated into a state. The formation and association of the Estates was generally based not on an arbitrarily forced union but on a gradual coalescence of one single territory out of its original parts. The development of the Estates system was an automatic concomitant of the formation of these territorial states.

Such are the main conclusions of modern research regarding these aspects of administrative history.[11] Moreover, the peculiar dualism of the Estates system, the lack of any theoretical basis for a unitary state, the theoretical and practical antithesis of prince and country, which developed to its full extent only in the territorial states of Germany, were all produced by the conditions under which the territorial states had come into being. It was chiefly the patrimonial interpretation of princely rule that impelled the country to make itself into a second ruling power beside the prince, such that it was not merely an object of the prince's rule, which at the time to a certain extent was still regarded as a private right. The clear-cut concept of a truly public power was absent, and this lack can be traced to the fact that the princes still felt themselves to be subordinate members of a higher political organization, that the pre-eminent public power was still seen as being vested in the Emperor and the Empire as a whole, that the territorial states lacked the criterion of sovereignty. Once they acquired this, once the territorial princes regarded themselves as embodying true public power, the dualism of the Estates systems was overcome.

The way this happened was for the prince to suppress the Estates and to establish absolute rule. The Republic of the United Netherlands—where, in reverse, the Estates removed the monarchical head—was a singular case in Europe, unless we include the Swiss confederation, which did not in fact involve the formation of proper territorial states.[12] In America the United States offers the example of a similar development. Federal state and confederation appear as products of a process of political formation shaped by history; they are not a league of states based on international law and formed by free choice. Monarchical power began the political organization of a group of territories, but could not achieve the goal of complete political unity. The state of association in which these countries found themselves on the disappearance of monarchical authority was perpetuated in federative forms of constitution, which at first altered little in the internal structure of the separate states.[13]

Federative states preserve the old system of government, unitary states destroy it. The classic example of this is the Continental absolutist state of the seventeenth and eighteenth centuries. Absolutism, as established in France with Richelieu and in Prussia with the Great Elector, can be regarded as a concomitant of that process of political organization in which a conglomerate of separate territories becomes fused into a unitary political structure. The French provinces, with their particularist Estates and autonomous *Gouverneurs,* were, like East Prussia and Cleves, not provinces in the modern sense—i.e., identically ruled parts of a monarchical unitary state; they were small states on their own, and the links which tied them together were not much more than a mere personal union; in economy, law, and system of government they were to some degree left on their own and strictly separate from each other. The efforts of the monarchical authority to fuse these parts into a whole which was administratively, financially, and militarily unified, produced modern absolutism. This unity could not be created in cooperation with Estates-General; in France, after bad experiences, at a decisive moment, the attempt was abandoned; in Prussia such an attempt was not even made. The particularism of the counties, and their resistance to the idea of fusion into a larger state—which would make greater demands upon them than the existing life in a petty-state did—everywhere produced a conflict in which the power of the Estates was destroyed.

Over a period of time the idea of a larger state resided alone in the monarchy, and an absolutist bureaucracy was the natural constitutional form in this period of transition. It was the situation of the European state system that made the formation of greater states historically necessary. France was forced in this direction by her struggle with the Habsburgs; and once France had set the example, it became a necessity for the other European states to follow her example if they wished to preserve their independence. The development of military and political power and constant military preparedness were possible only on the basis of a larger, centrally ruled and administrative territory. The militarist system, with all that it entailed in political terms, proceeded from the power struggles and rivalries of the Continental states after the close of the Middle Ages.

England, in her isolated, relatively secure position, with a prevailing interest in maritime and commercial activities, did not need this kind of militarism; this is an important factor in explaining her diverging constitutional development. After the accession of the Stuarts, however, we find even in England efforts to unify, by means of the predominant authority of the Crown, Scotland and England, which then were joined only in personal union. The Stuarts felt that monarchical control of the Anglican Church might offer the requisite means. They attempted, therefore, to extend the constitution of the Anglican Church to Scotland so that they would have an effective instrument for the establishment of an absolutistically ruled unitary state. The attempt failed in England, not only because of the strength of English political institutions but also because of the country's geographical-political situation, which spared England the necessity of a strong military apparatus.

Subsequently on the Continent absolutism made itself superfluous by its own success: it had fulfilled its historic function, that of the creation of great national unitary states. With further progress in this process of political formation, forces emerged that worked toward a new order of affairs. Absolutism suppressed what Montesquieu called the intermediary forces; it did not by any means abolish the differences between the Estates; on the contrary, it purposely sought to maintain the Estates' social order as useful basis of the absolutist system of government. The preferential position which the nobility and the privileged classes enjoyed, however, was legal and social rather than political. The idea of a general citizenship began to penetrate into the political sphere, by virtue of the regime's absolutist nature and the unitary character of the state; to this idea the notion of general citizen rights was soon added. The population accustomed itself to fixed duties laid down by the state, to taxation and military service, to daily contacts with the civil servants of a centralized state, and, in consequence, acquired a sense of political cohesion, the rudiments of a common political interest. The idea of a unified political order—for which absolutism had created the needed external forms—became now an innermost concern of the population itself. A latent consciousness of nation and state originated, and it needed only a special occasion to emerge in all its strength. The individuals became conscious of being a people (*Volk in subjektiver Qualität*);[14] previously there had been no more than a populace divided up by region and class—a mere object of government.

It cannot be denied that this process, finally leading as it did to representative government, contained among many other factors a social factor of immense significance; for there emerged an educated and propertied middle class. It would, however, be wrong to stamp the representative system merely as a creation of the bourgeoisie. There was a vigorous middle class (*Bürgertum*) in the states of the Continent long before anyone thought of a representative constitution—the small units into which the political world was splintered offered no foundation. Besides, the representative system in England in the classical age of parliamentarism was based not on the trading and manufacturing classes in the large towns but rather on the various strata of rural aristocracy. The momentum ushered in by the formation of a unitary state and the consciousness of general citizenship acquired by the people were more important in the development of this form of government than was the particular stage of economic and social development; indeed, this stage was to some extent itself a product or concomitant of the growth of a centralized policy. It has been known for many years that mercantilist economic policy, which had created the basis for the development of modern national economy, was part of the formation of the absolutist state.[15] It prevailed over local organizations, it founded a free market extending over the whole state, marked it off against the outside world, and in economic life replaced local divisions of labor by national ones. Obviously, this meant extraordinary progress in industrial development: without this era of economic promotion through the state, the development of the bourgeoisie would have been impossible.

This is particularly true of England, where this class came to power with the Parliamentary Reform of 1832, precisely at the end of a grandiose mercantilist era. But England had a representative constitution ever since she had been a self-sufficient, consolidated, national unitary state—that is, since the reign of the first three Edwards and still more since the Tudor period. So long as the English kingdom had a foot on French soil, the system of government was more on the lines of Estates system in the Continental sense, because of the vehement alterations in the power relations between Crown and magnates that were connected with foreign policy. Only after England had permanently limited herself to her insular sphere, and still more after her emancipation from Rome, was the notion of a unitary state fully realized. The real modern representative factor of Parliament—the House of Commons—only then acquired its determinative influence as against the House of Lords, which was a medieval Estates body. This representative constitution was monarchical in tone until the Revolution, aristocratic from 1688 to 1832, and democratic after the reforms of the nineteenth century.

These changes reflect general features of European development and probably are based essentially on social changes in the population. Nonetheless, the tendencies to which they gave rise could become embodied in the constitution only by means of the rivalries between the two great parties: they needed popular support, and, ultimately from the viewpoint of *raison d'état*, made concessions to the democratic trends. If Disraeli forced the Conservative Party to make the electoral reform act of 1867, he probably had similar considerations at the back of his mind such as those that led Bismarck in the same year to introduce universal suffrage as a popular basis for the future Empire. Modern imperialism has an elective affinity to democratic principles.

I shall conclude my remarks here, fully aware that I am far from having exhausted the theme; this has not been possible in so limited a scope. I wanted to explain what I envisage as the causal connection between certain types of political bodies and certain constitutional forms of government. In conclusion I should like to stress that I do not regard the conditions under which a state develops to be the only reason for its constitutional form; I have set forth merely a general rule that can be strengthened or modified by many other causal factors. My morphological approach was directed only toward drawing up an outline within which the colorful and multifarious life of historical reality which defies formulae evolves.

5

MILITARY ORGANIZATION AND THE ORGANIZATION OF THE STATE

Hintze delivered the following lecture before the Gehe Stiftung in Dresden on February 17, 1906. The Gehe Stiftung was established by Franz Gehe, a leading German industrialist, in order to stimulate interest in careers in public life and to provide training for such careers. Accordingly, Hintze selected a broad historical topic that would throw light on the present. Several times he alludes to political events of the recent past and to the contemporary situation. He mentions the revolt of the Hereros in German Southwest Africa, a struggle that had dragged on since 1904. He refers to the conflict between Emperor Franz Josef and Hungary over the demand for use of the Magyar language in the Hungarian *Honveds*—a conflict that led to new elections and the establishment of a non-parliamentary government in Hungary. Hintze's views on France reflect the tension, aroused by the Dreyfus Affair, between the political leadership of the Republic and the military leadership; the Dreyfus Affair ended officially only in 1906 when the Court de Cassation declared the earlier condemnation of Dreyfus as "wrongful and erroneous." Finally, when Hintze says that "events of the recent past have once again clearly demonstrated that the world is not yet ready for perpetual peace," his audience will have understood this as an allusion to the Morocco crisis which had brought Europe to the brink of war during the preceding summer.

These allusions to the contemporary scene are but illustrations of a broad topic that was central in Hintze's historical thinking. In discussing the relation of military and political organization he combined the scholarly traditions in which he had grown up—the ideas of the Prussian Historical School and of Ranke's "primacy of foreign policy"—with notions developed in the younger science of sociology.

When I received the flattering invitation to speak to you on military organization and the organization of the state, it was clear to me from the outset that I could not deal with the subject by means of general arguments and by reference to examples drawn from all epochs and societies, but rather that my task was to present the changes in the relations between state organization and military organization and their interaction as a continuous historical process. I do not want to deny that the first mode of procedure—if it is handled in the way that Herbert Spencer, say, used it in his *Principles of Sociology*—can lead to important results. But for the historically schooled sensibility there is always a certain intolerable brute force in the method. Almost as though it is scarcely possible to avoid it, individual institutions are brutally wrenched from their contexts in the past, to such a degree that history and ethnology are merely plundered for evidence for theses that are basically just derived from general reflections. Even disregarding that: how intangible and unclear, how vague and murky are the ideas one gains as a rule in this way! The general formulae that can embrace the historical life of mankind and nations become progressively more empty of concrete content the wider the horizon of observation is expanded, until in the end they are reduced to obvious trivialities. I therefore prefer to illustrate the interdependence of military organization and the organization of the state in a single concrete example. I have chosen for this the development of the Latin-Germanic peoples since the decline of ancient culture, a development that runs right up to the circumstances and interests of the present day.

I should like to begin, however, with a few general remarks by way of orientation.

All state organization was originally military organization, organization for war. This can be regarded as an assured result of comparative history. Larger groups of people united in the more solid structure of the state, primarily for defensive and offensive purposes. Out of this martial organization there first developed a more severe government with coercive power over individuals, and it increased in strength the more frequently wars were waged. All free men capable of bearing arms were warriors; on the side they probably also hunted or raised cattle, but agriculture and housekeeping were left to women and slaves. The assembly of warriors was the political assembly; the supreme commander became the head of the state; whoever was not a warrior had no place in the political community. But then there came a period, as agriculture expanded, as men took root in the soil they cultivated, as the population increased, as communications and technology advanced, as trade developed—in short, as the conditions of economic life changed—when a separation of military and commercial activity set in, a division between the class that fought and the class that fed. The armed forces became a special part of the whole, and its organization a special aspect of the organization of the state.

The questions that now arise are these: What place is occupied by the organization of the army in the general organization of the state? To what extent does it influence political institutions as a whole? How far do the economic requirements of the whole community or even of individual classes impose limitations on the demands of the warrior class to dominate public life? How in general do class contradictions interweave with the contradiction between military life and commercial life? What balance between the two does the state organization provide?

Herbert Spencer distinguishes in this regard two basic types of state and social organization, which he calls the military and the industrial. The structure of the military type, with strong coercive powers, with centralizing despotism, with regulation by the state of economic and private life, has as its regulative aim merely the maximum achievement of military might while the freedom and welfare of the individual must take second place. On the other hand, in the industrial type of society, these very aims of individual freedom and welfare, if not cramped by severe pressure from outside, provide the structure of public intercourse and thus impress on the community the character of voluntariness, of decentralization, and self-government, of individual latitude in all realms of life.

These are ideal types, which perhaps have never been purely realized in the history of mankind. Reality has witnessed almost everywhere mixtures of both elements. The military type, however, has been particularly prominent in many states, ancient and modern, among civilized and uncivilized peoples. Spencer points to the Empire of Dahomey, to the Peruvian Inca Empire, to ancient Egypt and Sparta, to Prussia and the German Empire, and to Russia. The industrial type develops only under especially favorable conditions, very slowly and not so obviously. England and the United States in particular are examples, with their militia system, self-government, the principle of individual freedom of movement, compared to the more tightly supervised life of the military states of the Continent.

Spencer goes on to suggest that the general trend of cultural development tends toward the gradual dislodging and ultimate replacement of the military type by the industrial type. He is not blind to the fact that there can be powerful and lasting retrogressions in this course of development and that everything depends on whether wars become rare and are waged increasingly only on the edges of the civilized world, on whether peaceful commercial activities prevail over military activities. But he is of the opinion that the world is, by and large, moving in this direction. We hear in him the voice of the England of Cobden and Gladstone, the spirit of a politics and world-view well satisfied, its commercial predominance threatened by no competition to speak of, and therefore pacific and humanitarian. This mood has in the meantime changed markedly in England and the rest of the world, and I wonder whether statesmen like Disraeli or even like Cecil Rhodes and Chamberlain believe or have believed with the same assurance in the peaceful progress of states toward the purely industrial type. Perhaps Spencer's types are only the polar opposites between which the political life of mankind takes place, at times drawing closer to one, sometimes to the other pole. In the four thousand years of human history that we look back over today there has been unquestionably a great increase in commercial activity but really no diminution in the readiness of states for war.

In referring to this problem I should like to point out that I do not conceive of the "organization of state" in the narrow, constitutional, and juridical sense that deals only with the distribution of the state's functions and powers among its various executive agents. If we want to find out about the relations between military organization and the organization of the state, we must direct our attention particularly to two phenomena, which conditioned the real organization of the state. These are, first, the structure of social classes, and second, the external ordering of the states—their position relative to each other, and their over-all position in the world.

It is one-sided, exaggerated, and therefore false to consider class conflict the only driving force in history. Conflict between nations has been far more important; and throughout the ages, pressure from without has been a determining influence on internal structure. It has even often suppressed internal strife or forced it into compromise. Both these forces have manifestly worked together in the design of the military order and the state organization. In the ancient world, once a balance among the social groups (Stände) had been achieved or was evolving, the Hoplite phalanx of the citizenry took the place of the single knights who fought on horseback or in chariots. Where this arrangement was subsequently rigidified, as in Sparta, no further extension of the state's power and range took place. But wherever the community was sufficiently adaptable, as in Rome, the pres-

sure of the foreign situation forced a progressive extension of the
citizenry with political rights, because greater masses of soldiers
were needed. It was at heart this joint operation of external
pressure and internal flexibility that enabled Rome to progress
from city-state to world empire.

Roman history provides also a particularly clear example of
the way in which an army's composition and organization are
influenced by the shape and size of the state's territory. The citizen militia, subdivided according to the ownership of property,
corresponds to the simple city-state; the progressive conquests
in Italy are accompanied by systematic military colonization; in
the great struggle for power and survival with Hannibal, the
old principle of universal military service comes to be fully applied in practice. When the city's rule is subsequently extended
beyond the Italian frontiers, when distant provinces like Mace-
donia, Africa, and, above all, the two Spains with their unruly
and bellicose population have to be administered and kept in
order, then military requirements are increased and the propertied class can no longer cover them. The place of the citizen militia is taken by a standing army composed largely of proletarians;
and the payment of salaries hitherto made only occasionally to
replenish troops becomes the general rule.

This standing army and the necessity, brought about by the
expansion of the empire, of sending field commanders with long-
term commands into far-flung provinces—and the personal influence that victorious *imperatores* gained over the troops in these
long wars—undermines the republican constitution. At first officials of the republic, these commanders become independent
lords feuding among themselves. In the long run even the ideas
of restoration with which Augustus imbued his reign could not
have prevented the transformation of *imperator* into monarch,
and of Rome into an empire in which the Roman citizenry—that
is, the Italian population—still held a privileged, ruling position
but which increasingly lost its national Roman character. Thus
in Rome the standing army created the monarch, just as else-

where the monarch created the standing army. Both are intimately connected to the development of the city-state into a world empire.

The great problem as to what it was that caused this empire and along with it ancient culture to collapse has not been solved by anyone in a clear and plausible way. Obviously there are many reasons for it, but I should like to mention here only one of them. The Roman Empire was not overpowered by other foreign powers—there was no neighboring power that even approached her might. It was a world empire in an altogether different sense than what we mean today by world power. It was a universal state, one that held sway over the whole civilized world. There was no question of a society or system of states, of a number of coordinated states maintaining a balance of power among themselves, compelled by their constant tension and rivalry among themselves repeatedly to exert all their forces so as not to be dislodged from their place. The wars on the frontiers no longer touched upon vital questions of power and survival; they did not mean much more than the colonial wars of England or today's war in South-West Africa. The heavy pressure from without had eased. The tension in foreign affairs which had goaded the Roman state on from conquest to conquest had relaxed ever since these conquests had absorbed the whole civilized world.

In comparison to modern armies, the quantitative strength of Roman armed might relative to the population of the Empire was slight. Even this relatively small number of troops increasingly lost its national Roman character. The principle that only Roman citizens might serve in the army had already long since been circumvented by the granting of citizenship to foreigners who enlisted. Augustus had still strictly distinguished these citizen legions from the foreign auxiliaries, and under the Julians the legions were still made up largely of Italians. This ceased with Vespasian. The Italians in fact became exempt from military service, as they were already from direct taxes. The legions made up for this by recruiting in the provinces and their distinction from the auxiliary divisions became more and more blurred. Despite the continuing principle of universal military service, the army was in fact replenished mainly by volunteers and recruits, and only as a subsidiary measure did the civil authorities proclaim a general levy. But substitutes were allowed and in practice they were the rule. For a long time the Praetorian Guard in Rome, at least, had still represented the dominant Italian element. With Septimius Severus this too ceased. The *Palatini* who replaced it were recruited from the provincial legions. The universal conferral of the rights of citizenship on all subjects by Caracalla put a final constitutional end to the privileged position of Italy within the world empire.

This mercenary army, made up of a mixture of nationalities only superficially romanized, had no connection with the Empire except through the person of the supreme commander, the Emperor. It even had its own special religious practices—different from the civic cult—among which the worship of the divinity of Caesar played a conspicuous role. It was a power unto itself, and, in the absence of a strict law of succession and a firmly established principle of legitimacy, the elevation of the Emperor depended on that power. Only military discipline held the whole structure together, and with the end of the dynasty of the Severusses that discipline ceased doing its job. During the incessant mutinies in the fifty years between Alexander Severus and Diocletian the traditions of the old Roman army were destroyed and its organization collapsed. In the fourth century the legion became something altogether different from what it had been before. On the frontier the soldiers lived no longer under the old strict camp discipline but scattered about on farms with their wives and children. Recruits were provided by the great landowners who had moved from the towns to the country and administered their estates themselves. Hordes of purely barbarian Germanic peoples joined the army; from then on, we can say, the army became increasingly Germanic. The Empire was, it may be said, initially barbarized by the army. The result was that the old constitutional edifice, at least in the West, began more or less rapidly and completely to crumble.

This is the point of departure for a new period in the history of the Latin-Germanic peoples. On the one side there is the crumbling universal Roman Empire leaving remnants of its culture and civilization; on the other, the Germanic tribes, in youthful freshness and vigor. These two factors set in motion the great historical process that has continued up to our day. I now want to give you a sense of that process with a quick overview of its various phases from the point of view of how the political and military order conditioned and influenced each other.

We can distinguish three great epochs in this process, in which definite types of military and state organization appear linked together: the epoch of the tribal and clan system, at the dawn of history, the epoch of feudalism in the Middle Ages, and the epoch of militarism in the modern period. This last epoch yields a double image of the absolutist military states on the one hand and of freer systems with predominantly militia-type defense arrangements on the other. I should like to give here only cursory treatment to the first two epochs, and to speak rather more fully only of the third. We shall see that we can further divide this epoch of militarism into three periods, distinguished by the following phenomena. In the first period, from the end of the fifteenth century to about the middle of the seventeenth, the mercenary system was not yet firmly and permanently integrated with the political institutions, nor was the organization of the state itself yet solidified into the absolutist-centralist state toward which it was moving. During the second period, from about the middle of the seventeenth century to the turn of the eighteenth and nineteenth, there developed on the Continent the full-fledged absolutist-military states on the one hand, and, on the other, England, with its militia, Parliament, and self-government. Finally, in the third period, in the nineteenth century, there emerged the interrelated principles of universal military service and the constitutional order of the state; in addition, it must be remembered, the militia system was continued and naval forces assumed greater significance.

We do not know much that is very certain about the first epoch. It is sufficient for our purposes to realize that we are dealing with a social organization in which the state and the army are virtually identical units. The oldest political system of the Germans had an associative-federative quality; and if the somewhat bold assumption is correct that we can regard century (*Hundertschaft*), clan (*Geschlecht*), and tribal settlement (*Gauansiedlung*) as identical, then we have before our eyes in concrete form an association of clans (*Sippenverband*) that is both a political community and a military body. In any event, there is no doubt that in some form or other the organization of the state as well as the military organization of the time depended on the cohesion of clans, and corresponds to what we otherwise, from historical and ethnographic evidence, know about the organization of primitive life. The Germans went into battle as a clan, and the close solidarity produced by blood-relationship, neighborliness, and a complete community of interest may well have provided their tactical formation, the *cuneus* or boar's head (*Eberkopf*), with a substitute for their lack of true military discipline as the Romans knew it. How far the blood-relationship was still a reality, and how far it worked only as an idea, is not very important. What is important is that there was a feeling of community, a natural bond of association, which welded fighting men and the places of their settlements together into a military and political unity.

Besides this associative element of organization, the element of authority was not lacking, emerging sometimes strongly, sometimes weakly. It appears in the system of chieftains, in the principate, as Tacitus presents it, and, above all, in the position of the duke at head of the *civitas* in times of large-scale war. Even in Tacitus' time, the system of chieftains here and there passed over into the rule of a king, but this did not much alter the basic cooperative character of the polity. Nonetheless, in succeeding centuries the authoritarian element in political arrangements forged ahead while the associative element lost strength. Already in Tacitus' time the military organization shows embryonic beginnings of this in the *comitatus:* the system of followers that singled out a famous chieftain or military leader to be the focus of a hand-picked warrior band tied to him personally, by a peculiar bond of fealty in which the old family bond was replaced by membership in the lord's household.

With the expansion of the originally small political units into great tribal alliances embracing a number of *civitates*, with the beginnings of warrior migrations of whole peoples or the storming over the Roman border of a single tribe, royal power was fortified and became a general phenomenon while the associative bond of the old clan units, especially after their settlement on Roman soil, became more and more rare. In the Frankish realm of the Merovingians, which was not really stormed by a conquering people with an elected military king, but in which a ruler from an old family with the prestige of sacral origins—a brutal despot—led the attack, the royal power developed particularly strongly. Accordingly the attempt was made to extend to the subjects as a whole the authoritarian organization enshrined in the institution of the military retinue. The Merovingian king had not simply a close-knit, exclusive, mounted retinue, in the *antrustiones* but also his great vassals, who originally stood in a similar personal relation of service and loyalty to him,' forming as it were a retinue of inferior rank. In the end he demanded of all subjects oaths of loyalty and service (*fidelitatem et leudesamium*).

This attempt to transform the collapsing associative organization of military and social life into an authoritarian organization did not succeed in this form. Rather, hardly a century after the seizure of Gaul, we find a powerful landowning class emerging, an outgrowth of the Roman *possessores* or of royal grants of land, probably chiefly arising from the sub-leaders who as counts had to represent royal authority in definite districts, in peace as well as war. These landlords in turn surrounded themselves with enormous retinues that they ruled and provided for in a military, patriarchal style as *seniores*. Presumably this circumstance was the fruit of a marriage of the Germanic service-and-loyalty relation in the form of the retinue and the Gallo-Romanic patron-client relation—not to exclude the influence of the Roman private soldiers in the service of great landholders. Even the great clerical landowners maintained these military retinues, and the ecclesiastical system of benefices provided the best means for furnishing warriors with land without completely giving up such land. Possession depended not merely on continued fulfillment of service but on a renewal of the grant between the parties as well. Through this connecting of vassalage with a benefice, of service with a fief, the Frankish feudal system got its peculiar shape.

The clever policy of the managers of the Arnulfingian household knew how to attach this institution to the central authority, thereby lending at least partial success to the earlier trend toward authoritarian organization of the armed forces. Thus, in contrast to the idea of a mass of roughly equal subjects, the feudal system presented a looser form of authority transmitted and weakened through several intermediate grades. In a society based on a natural economy, where the population was gradually passing from a military to an agricultural life, where communications were still undeveloped and a landed aristocracy with dependent people had become more firmly established, this form of authority was the only one that offered the possibility of having the fighting forces required by the age—that is, mounted troops with a high degree of individual training. Of course a large part of the usefulness promised by this form of organization of state power was lost again as fiefs gradually became hereditary; but this change was actually a more apt expression of the relations of the highest authority to the aristocracy, which was still after all relatively independent. In this form feudal institutions were to exert a decisive influence on military and political life for centuries, and on social relations for even longer.

In military terms the feudal system meant the gradual supplanting of the old levies (largely infantry), by heavily-armed cavalry whose success depended not so much on the shock of a mass attack in tactical units, as on the bravery and skill of individual knights in single combat. The old levies did not altogether disappear, but they lost their military importance. With the economic and social changes that set in after the settlement of Gaul, with the population striking firmer roots in the soil, with the rise of a relation of dependence between peasant and lord, the old cement of the German army, the bonds of blood and comradeship, lost their strength. And with the primitive communications of the prevalent natural economy, there was no other way of creating a disciplined soldiery. Foot soldiers were not completely absent from medieval wars; they survived principally in the towns, where later the guilds were organized in military fashion. But, at least in the earlier centuries, their importance was secondary to that of the knights.

A great social change was intimately connected to this change in the nature of war. The feudal system implied an enduring social differentiation, a world-historic act of division of labor and occupations, and thus the beginnings of the formation of a comprehensive class structure. The military vocation was segregated from the commercial; both became hereditary. The knightly estate confronted the peasant estate in the position of a ruling class; for the knights were connected to the landowning class, while the peasantry, whose occupation had ceased to be military, sank farther and farther into servitude or into various degrees of dependence.

The social effects of the feudal system lasted longest. They lasted on the Continent, notwithstanding many limitations and diminutions, up to the time of the French Revolution—in other words, they persevered long after the military and even political system of feudalism had in the main been superseded.

In political terms, the feudal system meant a peculiar form of state organization very different from what is typical of a modern state. The feudal state lacked the attributes of sovereignty—that is, independence beyond its borders and exclusive rights within them. The whole of public life was dominated by the idea of a graduated pyramid of governing powers, each unrestricted in its own sphere, but owing to the higher power service and obedience within strictly defined limits. The states were not yet fixed in area, consolidated in themselves, or sharply distinguished from each other. Because of the extensive Continental lands he ruled, the King of England was the vassal of the King of France; the Emperor claimed supreme authority over all of Western Christendom; the Pope, finally, claimed that all Christian kings were his vassals, and actually some countries recognized this claim.

Domestically, the principle obtained of *chaque seigneur souverain dans sa seigneurie:* the state's power was not yet concentrated in one point but was still dispersed among various centers and effective at the top only in a highly diluted form. It was a kind of state organization intimately tied to the form of military organization but, like military organization itself, resting on ties between large groups of peoples, on the isolated existence of each region caused by the prevailing natural economy and by the undeveloped state of communications. Warfare, economics, and politics conspired gradually to change this circumstance. The towns became centers of more active trade; political life became more integrated first in individual provinces and then in large states, in the beginning only on the surface. The Papal See hadn't been any more successful with its idea of universal rule than had the Emperor with his secular idea of supremacy. By the end of the fifteenth century, France, England, and Spain had all gained a certain internal consolidation, and by the same date at least some territorial states in Germany and Italy were assuming more or less definite shape. Once more, this process was accompanied by remarkable changes in military organization.

At approximately the time of the Crusades, the custom of paying salaries was insinuated into the feudal military system. It appeared earliest and most obviously in England, then in France and Italy, and finally in Germany. The basic precondition for this was the extension of trade in a money economy; but its immediate cause was the political need of the rulers to deploy their military might more effectively. There was nowhere a reduction in the feudal military obligation. In the great campaigns, such as England's in France, and Germany's in Italy, special compensation had always been demanded and awarded, in the form of money or grants. In England as early as the twelfth and thirteenth centuries the obligation to military service came to be systematically discharged by the payment of scutage, partially against the vassals' will. In this way the King acquired the means to recruit knights for pay, and he could dispose over them much more freely than over his vassals. In France, the *hommage lige* with its unlimited obligation appeared, in Germany the institution of *Ministerialität*. Ultimately the payment of wages and mercenaries won the day everywhere, particularly in Italy. Thus, preparation for war became a financial question, and after the fourteenth and fifteenth centuries we find the rulers striving to exact payment rather than military service from their vassals and other subjects in order to prepare themselves for war. This became a prime cause of the development—or at least the more frequent convocation—of assemblies of the Estates, Parliaments, *Etats-généraux*, and *Landtage*. The feudal system with its numerous isolated centers of authority was displaced by the system of Estates, with the uniting of the Estates into corporative bodies for common participation in the affairs of the province or the state.

The feudal elements, however, reacted vehemently to this monarchical and Estates principle of creating political unity. They opposed this incipient consolidation of the state and its authority. They held fast above all to their right of feud—for the feudal system by no means precluded private wars. With the entry of wage payments on the scene, the firm bonds of feudal obligations had also loosened. Individual great lords in all countries in the fifteenth century maintained large armed retinues, veritable private armies: the *grand seigneurs* in France, the *grandees* in Spain, the lords in England, the princes and cities in Germany. In Italy the system of the *condottiere* began to blossom with mercenary knights, many of whom were foreigners, often German. All this was in direct opposition to the endeavors of the monarchs and the Estates in the direction of state consolidation.

So long as this feudal license prevailed, the regular functioning of the monarchical-Estates system was inconceivable. In England, favorable conditions did not prevail until after the warrior part of the aristocracy had exhausted themselves in the Wars of the Roses and worn each other out; Henry VII and his successors strictly forbade private armies and actually did away with them. In France the principle was advanced in 1439 that only the King had the right to recruit troops and to raise taxes for this purpose. Thus, recognition for the nobility's right of feud disappeared, and the King's exclusive sovereign right in matters of war was established in principle. In a similar fashion Ferdinand and Isabella in Spain by using the holy *Hermandad* organized a monarchical peace-keeping force, so that the *grandees* gave up their private armies. In Germany, after the endless feuding between princes, knights and towns, the perpetual *Landfriede* of 1495 put a stop, at least in principle, to this feudal anarchy. In Italy only the invasion of foreign powers and the establishment of foreign rule led to some measure of order.

The feudal reaction was still not completely overcome. This happened really only in England. Spain still had its revolt of the Communes in the sixteenth century. In France, feudal and anarchic tendencies allied with Estates and constitutional tendencies in the Huguenot Wars and still in the Fronde of the seventeenth century. Nonetheless, although political consolidation was not complete, a certain amount of it was achieved in the three Western kingdoms in which a more or less strong monarchical authority and corresponding Estates institutions originated. Meanwhile in Italy, partly under foreign rule, absolutist tyrannies predominated. And in Germany the territorial princes secured full independence from the Emperor in the conflicts of the Reformation and the Thirty Years' War, and the territories with their monarchical and Estates systems developed into veritable states.

The waning fifteenth century can be considered the end of the feudal age. From then on, we enter the third great epoch, that of militarism. Somewhere on the borderline there came into being an important institution that could be ascribed equally to the feudal or the militarist age—the ordnance companies of Charles VII of France. From the standpoint of the art of war these were thoroughly feudal units: an army of knights with auxiliaries, organized in the usual way in lances (*Lanzen*). From the standpoint of political organization, however, they were something new: the first standing army in Europe based on the King's exclusive sovereign right to make war. This was an epoch-making arrangement on the Continent, and was imitated by Charles the Bold of Burgundy and Maximilian of Austria.

It will be of interest to cast a glance at one of the great theorists on the threshold of the new epoch, one who linked the art of war and statecraft—Machiavelli. This reformer of political science discussed military organization and its relation to the state's organization and policy in a very instructive way. His political ideal was indeed the national unification of Italy, which he conceived of as a federated state rather than a unified state. It was clear to him that a republic would not be equal to this task, that only a prince could complete it, and that it would require extraordinary military exertions. But for military organization, his slogan was "No foreign mercenaries, no *condottieri!*" These had been the ruin of Italy, he said, and had made her ripe for rule by foreigners. The new Italy should rest, in his opinion, on an arming of the populace and on universal military service, though not of course in the form of a standing army—such seemed to him financially impossible anyway—but in the form of a militia to be summoned only in wartime and in peacetime to practice the use of weapons only on holidays or in leisure hours.

One can see that Machiavelli's idea is not so far-reaching as to warrant the occasional claim that he was the prophet of the principle of universal military service in the modern sense. His idea really harked back to antiquity, to Livy; and in practice Machiavelli's own experiment with such a militia when he was Secretary of the Florentine Republic was no success. Nevertheless, hidden in it was an idea with a promising future, as we shall see when we become aware how the idea of the militia kept its importance in later times. What Machiavelli wanted was by no means his own contrivance; it had already taken shape elsewhere in the world. He knew of Charles VII of France's attempt to form a peasant militia of *francs-archers* (Freischützen). This militia was to supplement the ordnance companies, to provide infantry alongside the cavalry, and was set up and armed in the parishes. I do not know whether Machiavelli was acquainted also with the English model for these *francs-archers*, those bowmen who had given the English such a decisive initial superiority over the French armies consisting solely of hordes of knights in the wars of the fourteenth and fifteenth centuries. This institution, however, goes all the way back to the old English militia, formed in accordance with Henry II's *Assisa de armis habendis in Anglia* of 1184. Almost at the same time as peasants disappeared from German armies, the free population of England—to the extent that it did not lay under feudal obligation—was organized for defense of the country in classes according to their landed property, recalling the timocratic system of the citizen militias of antiquity. This was an essential part in the system of self-government that was established under Henry II. Self-government and militia went together. The fact that in England the feudal system with its bondage of the peasants had not completely displaced the freeholders and indeed was disappearing since the middle of the fourteenth century, formed the social background to this development. For this reason the English militia had held its own and had developed so strongly that these archers could on occasion be used even in foreign wars. In France, on the other hand, the same institution did not work out so well. It produced no reliable soldiers, and with the land organized under the prevailing feudal system it seemed dangerous to arm the rural population. Louis XI therefore abolished the peasant militia and in its stead took on Swiss mercenaries, who became the nucleus of the French infantry. Nevertheless, it is interesting that on the threshold of the epoch of militarism the idea of a militia—its complement as well as its contrast—became prominent.

Actually the advance in the art of war and military organization which made possible the development of militarism on the Continent derived from the peasant militias. The Swiss became the great teachers of all nations. The secret of their military success against the armies of knights—the Austrian in the fourteenth century, the Burgundian in the fifteenth—lay in their understanding of how to form a tactical body—that is, how to move and deploy a large mass of troops according to a unified plan and for specific war aims. Not until such methods were successfully applied did usable infantry once again arise and eventually prove itself superior to the individual combat of knights. This superiority did not lie in having firearms—they still did not play a decisive role with the Swiss—but rather in their tactical solidarity. This solidarity of the Swiss Confederates in turn was not yet based on drill but was based on the permanent habituation to war and, in particular, on the moral and political factor of a living, ordered community, which tied the feeling of common solidarity among neighbors to the recognition of the authority of a leader. In other words, it was something akin to the moral power that animated the old German *cuneus* and turned it into a tactical body. This capacity for organization founded on a sense of community, a comradely solidarity, can be found throughout the period of feudalism in other German lands, where free peasants had stuck to their community organization; I have in mind, particularly, the *Ditmarschen*. Among the Hussites national and religious fanaticism played a similar role.

Swiss tactics won the day. They prepared the way for an end to feudal warfare and made the infantry, rather than the cavalry, the decisive and determining factor in modern war. Their effect was felt in all Continental countries. But while the French were content to take the Swiss into their pay, the Spaniards and the Germans shaped their systems of warfare after the Swiss model with their own men. The German imitation was the *Landsknechte*, which were recruited largely from sturdy journeymen and could make use of the cooperative traditions in the guilds and journeymen's unions for their discipline. Their leaders followed the model of the Italian *condottieri*.

These mercenary armies, which mainly waged the wars of the sixteenth and particularly of the seventeenth centuries and then came to be drilled systematically under great organizers like Maurice of Nassau and Gustavus Adolphus of Sweden, became the standing armies of the seventeenth and eighteenth centuries. By and large, the older mercenary armies of the sixteenth and seventeenth centuries had not been institutions of state. Since they had been raised only as an extraordinary measure and for specific temporary goals, they were not tied to the state and its constitution in any lasting or systematic manner. Not even the armies of Maurice of Nassau or Gustavus Adolphus of Sweden were an exception. The new type of military organization thus began outside the organization of the state. There was no place for mercenary armies in the political order, whether of a constitutional or of an Estates character, which had developed after the end of the fifteenth century in opposition to feudal military anarchy. The spirit of this political order was pacific, and directed to prosperity and order rather than to military might. This was the case in the German territories as well as England, and this spirit manifested itself also in the French Estates-General of the sixteenth century. But on the Continent the ideal

of a pacified political society, engrossed in the pursuit of prosperity and culture, died on the vine. The great political antagonisms of the day did not allow it to develop. Ever since the
violent rivalry between France and the Habsburgs had been kin-
dled—a contest that lasted almost two centuries and was a
struggle for supremacy in Europe in which the old medieval imperial idea lived on—there had been no lasting peace in Europe.
When in the middle of the seventeenth century, the France of
Richelieu and Mazarin triumphed over the Emperor and Spain,
it became decisive to resist the tendencies of Louis XIV toward
world domination. The constant rivalry between the Great
Powers, which was still mixed up with confessional differences;
the permanent political tension that invariably provoked further
military exertions, in order that single states could preserve their
independence and thus the basis of all prosperity and culture; in
short, power politics and balance-of-power politics created the
foundations of modern Europe: the international system as well
as the absolutist system of government and the standing army of
the Continent. England, with her insular security, was not directly exposed to the danger of these wars. She needed no standing army, at least not one of Continental proportions, but only a
navy which served commercial interests as much as war aims.
In consequence she developed no absolutism. Absolutism and
militarism go together on the Continent just as do self-
government and militia in England. The main explanation for
the difference in the way political and military organization developed between England and the Continent—one which became
more and more distinct after the middle of the seventeenth century—lies in the difference in the foreign situation.

In the Continental states the army became the very backbone
of the new centralized greater state. In order to enable the
French crown to fight Spain and Austria, Richelieu suppressed
with force the particularism of the provinces and thus created
a unified absolutist state, such as was hitherto unknown. The
German *Landsknechte* of Bernhard of Weimar then formed the

basis of the greatly enlarged French army that fought the Spanish War to a finish. In similar fashion the Great Elector of Brandenburg welded his ancestral land together with Cleves, East Prussia, and all other territories that were united in personal union under his scepter into a united state only after a struggle with the Estates over maintenance of the standing army. The Prussian state of the eighteenth century actually rested more on the army than upon its disconnected territories. Austria and Spain in general showed the same tendencies, if not with the same results. Everywhere the system of *condotta* faded into the discipline of the monarchical army. The colonels ceased being private military entrepreneurs, and became servants of the state. The sovereign, and not the colonels, henceforth appointed officers; he himself took the chief command. A hierarchy of service grades was created, culminating in the monarch. His military commissaries took charge of maintaining and quartering the army, of regular payment of wages, and of provisions in the field. Only in the specific matter of the economics of the company which the captain directed did some remnant of the old military entrepreneurship survive through the eighteenth century, in France as well as Prussia. The captain was to look out for the replenishment of troops and the military preparedness of the company. He got for this a lump sum for which he did not have to give any further accounting. Above all, he had the recruiting in his hands, almost like a private concern.

In France the salability of officers' positions lessened somewhat the severity of monarchical discipline. There was no question of this in Prussia. In general the trend away from the old salaried army is clear: the result was the socialization of the army. But just as the army had developed outside the state's framework, so it continued to occupy a special position in the state, with its own military police, judicial, and religious system excluding the civilian agencies. The army was, as it were, a foreign body in the state. It was an instrument of the monarch, not an institution of the country. It was created as a tool of power politics in the foreign sphere, but at the same time it served to maintain and extend the sovereign's power at home. Any resistance to this vast royal instrument of power became impossible in the country. The army embodied most clearly and most palpably the new idea of state—that of the powerful, centralized, absolutist greater state.

Maintenance of the army became the chief task of the state's financial administration. This in turn led to unprecedented extension of the tax burden and consequently to a peculiar economic system that aimed at increasing the stock of ready money and at the same time at fostering and stimulating production artificially, especially in industry. Economic life could not be left to itself, because it was supposed to serve the ends dictated by *raison d'état*. This kind of thinking resulted in the full-blown system of commercial regulation that is associated with mercantilist economic policy. Power politics, mercantilism, and militarism are all related.

The absolutist military state developed into the tutelary police state, which understood the *salus publica* inscribed on its banner, not in the sense of the individual felicity of its subjects but in the sense of the preservation and strengthening of the state as a whole. At the same time the institutions of the army insinuated themselves in an important way into the realm of civil administration. This was particularly evident in Prussia, generally the classic example of the militarist state. The entire administrative organization there was keyed to military aims and served them. Out of the military commissaries came the actual provincial police agencies. Every minister of state was also called minister of war; every councilor in the administrative chamber, every tax councilor, was known also as war councilor. Former officers became provincial councilors, even presidents and ministers. The administrative councilors were recruited in large part from senior regimental quartermasters and judge advocates. The lower ranks of the bureaucracy were to be filled so far as possible with retired non-commissioned officers and disabled veterans.

In this way the whole state acquired a military cast. The entire social system was placed in the service of militarism. Nobles, burghers, and peasants really existed, each in his sphere, only to serve the state—they all had to *travailler pour le roi de Prusse.*

Not without harsh coercion, not without many violations of the strict letter of the law, was this new order of things established. To the champions of "the good old days" and of the old law and the old Estates order this seemed like a revolution from above. Everywhere the crown had to cope initially with more or less dogged resistance from the nobility. Louis XIV's rule had a distinctly bourgeois cast, similar to Frederick William I's rule in Prussia. But the struggle with the nobility was nowhere a struggle to the death. It ended in compromise, and everywhere in the eighteenth century we find the nobility becoming the support of the new monarchies. This alliance of absolute monarchy with the nobility is a characteristic feature of the whole *Ancien régime.* It rested, on the one hand, on the crown's leaving untouched the social privileges of the nobility and the old social order of the Estates and, on the other hand, on the nobility's gradually taking over the officer corps in the standing army. The two were intimately connected. Feudal memories were deliberately prodded back to life and used to give moral and political cohesion to the officer corps. One can say that the feeling of vassalage, presumed dead, turned out to be one of the moral factors that helped to build the spirit of the modern officer class. In Prussia the exclusive right of the nobles to possess manors was maintained so that they would remain able to produce replacements for the officer corps.

Replenishment of man power was in principle still based on volunteer enlistment. Natives of the country were still supplemented by large numbers of foreigners, in France as well as Prussia. The old idea of a militia did not, however, altogether disappear. In France there had been repeated attempts ever since Francis I to organize a peasant militia alongside the standing army for the defense of the land. Even in Germany we find from the end of the sixteenth century an effort in individual territories to set up a territorial defense corps (*Landesdefensionswerk*). It is noteworthy that in this case the organization of these militias was connected to the system of territorial estates. The East Prussian *Wibranzen* of the seventeenth century were an example of such a militia of the local Estates. In Hanover during the seventeenth and eighteenth centuries an Estates militia existed side by side with the monarch's standing army. In France, however, the militia became a purely royal institution under Louis XIV. After 1688 they succeeded in organizing it after a tolerable fashion. As a rule it was earmarked only for the defense of the country, and consisted of special units, but on occasion it was used also to fill out the ranks of the field army in foreign wars.

In Prussia, too, in this period, and particularly in the War of the Spanish Succession, new attempts cropped up to set up a royal militia. Significantly, it was to be made up only of peasants of the royal domains—apparently one did not yet dare to recruit subjects from the nobility. We do not find in Prussia the actual consignment of recruits by the Estates, as was the practice in the Austrian provinces. But even in Prussia it became customary to impose on the local authorities, which were partly in the hands of the *Estates*, a specific number of men to be furnished, though the requirement could be discharged in cash and ceased altogether when the army was considerably increased under Frederick William I. The militia was suspended, even the name was forbidden. The King wanted to have only his powerful standing army. Voluntary enlistment was not enough to maintain it, and so they experimented for a while with impressment. When this created much ill-feeling throughout the country, provoked resistance from the rural landowners, and drove young men to flee over the border, the King formally and publicly forbade it— though he had no objection to his captains' procuring bodies from the manorial districts if they could do so without causing any fuss or violence.

At this stage a certain solidarity of interests became manifest between the captains and the noble estate-owners, since they had the same social background. It was the captains, not the king, who took charge of recruiting. The captains had an interest in recruiting natives as much as possible, because they made better and more reliable soldiers, did not desert so often, and also cost less than foreigners. Beyond this, these men, once they were trained, could be given leave for part of the year so that the captains could save the price of their wages, and the estate owners did not have to go without the necessary laborers during harvesting. A manorial lord who was himself an officer or who wished to give up a few men to an officer who was a relative or a friend, could naturally dispose of them as much as the King once did with his own peasants for the militia. Even this system of recruiting had something of the look of a militia, however, for trained men generally spent only two months with the colors, during the great exercises. The rest of the time they were home on leave. Thus, without any express legal prescription, conscription became common practice in the countryside, and the King sanctioned this practice in 1733 by assigning to individual regiments and companies specific recruiting areas, the so-called "cantons."

The Prussian system of cantons therefore rested on a dovetailing of a mercenary army and militia, based on the one side on the monarchical discipline of the standing army and on the other, on the division of the population into estates. Just as the nobility made up the officer class and had a moral obligation to do military service, so the sons of peasants were expected to fill the ordinary ranks. The age-old feeling of the nobleman's superior rank over the peasant, the habit of one rank to command and of the other to obey, the patriarchal element that was then an inextricable part of social relations and inspired in the ordinary soldier confidence in the Junker's leadership—all this provided a strong foundation for military discipline, in which Prussia was farther advanced than any other military power. Naturally, thrashing played a role in military training, just as it did at home on the farms, but the hard, cruel punishments that were thought indispensable as a supplement (such as running the gauntlet) were designed more for the foreign rabble than for the cantonist soldiers, and stemmed from the traditions of the mercenary armies.

The canton system has, not without justification, been called the precursor of universal military service: without the military education of the lower classes, and the habituation to military service it provided, Prussia would hardly have been the state in which this principle had its first successes. The spirit of the canton system was, however, very different from that of universal service. The canton system was based on the social structure of the time, the system of Estates, which the absolutist rulers of the *Ancien régime* had maintained—on the distinction between privileged and non-privileged classes. Universal military service was based on the idea of the equality of all citizens before the law.

With this idea, which so clearly presents the connection between political and military organization, we enter upon the third contemporary epoch, the epoch of militarism.

The driving impulse behind the general change that now occurred came from the French Revolution. In the Revolutionary Wars France integrated itself into a nation with a unified political consciousness. The French revolutionary armies became something different from what the armies of the *Ancien régime* had been: a nation in arms, inspired by national enthusiasm and democratic ideas of liberty, faced the old mercenary armies of the absolutist states. Excellent strategists saw how to form reliable troops out of this new material; and the genius of them all, Napoleon, created with it, on the foundation of the altered political and social order, new strategy and tactics with great implications for the future. The methodical warfare of the old days, with its preference for maneuvers over battle, with its slow, cautious movements bound to the requirements of a central system of stores, seeking more the exhaustion than the crushing of the enemy; with its rigid linear tactics, conditioned by the need for discipline to hold the troops together; and dogged at every step by the ineradicable scourge of mercenary armies—desertion— this old approach now changed into more powerful and daring strategy and tactics. This new system moved masses across half- continents with unprecedented speed; replaced central stores by on-the-spot commandeering of supplies; replaced linear tactics with column attack and dispersed fighting, trusting in the spirit of the men, and holding to only one objective—to locate and an- nihilate the enemy forces. With these new methods of warfare Napoleon overwhelmed the states of old Europe and forced them to appeal to the same spirit that had made this military system possible in the first place—the spirit of voluntary effort, of pa- triotism, of spontaneous interest in the defense of the country—in short, the military and civilian public-spiritedness of a nation. The necessity of restructuring military organization in accord- ance with this spirit led, among all peoples capable of it, to a corresponding restructuring of state organization.

Yet France, which under Napoleon achieved the greatest suc- cesses with the new military organization, corresponding to changes in the public spirit, was not able to give this organiza- tion itself the proper shape for it to be considered the full ex- pression of the new political and social principle. Regard for the propertied classes meant that the system of conscription still countenanced substitution. One dared not carry out the idea of universal military service in all its implications. This happened only in Prussia. The classic land of old absolutist militarism ef- fected the earliest and purest realization of the modern idea of universal service and thus set the standard for all modern mili- tary powers. The prerequisites for this were the freeing of the serfs and the suspension of the Estates' privileges; the result was an irresistible trend toward constitutional political freedom.

The immediate consequence was a totally altered position for the army in state and society. Foreigners disappeared from the army. The position of the soldier ceased being a life-long profes- sion. It became a normal stage in the life of every able-bodied citizen. The division between warriors and the citizenry—the fighters and the feeders—was overcome. There occurred, as it were, a reversion, at a higher level of civilization, to an orginal state where in principle each man was a warrior—an elimination or correction of that historic and fateful division of labor through which in the age of feudalism a ruling and a serving class arose. The individual in the modern state receives a two-sided education, one military and one civilian. The whole system rested on that altered concept of the state, whose germ was the awakening of political consciousness in the population, the image of the state becoming an affair not merely of the rulers but of the ruled and being conceived of as a community, a corporate collective personality. This too is a reversion—to the age-old associative idea of the state, which of course in Prussia stood in still unresolved tension with a highly-developed authoritarian organization.

This dual aspect of the *raison d'état* found its genuine expression in the original distinction between the *Linie** (regular army) and the *Landwehr*† (territorial defense army). The *Linie* continued the traditions of the old standing army with its monarchical organization and discipline; the *Landwehr* continued more the militia idea—the notion of the nation in arms. Scharnhorst and Boyen tried to breathe a distinctive spirit into the *Landwehr* different from that of the regular army, and their efforts met with enthusiastic endorsement from patriots of the Wars of Liberation. The *Landwehr* was supposed to be a formation of its own, to be commanded all the way up to the captain by *Landwehr* rather than professional officers; its units were supposed to con-

---

* The regular, active, peacetime army that comprised professional soldiers and conscripts performing their military service.
† A Prussian military institution divided into two groups. The first comprised those up to 32 years of age who had completed their active military service and had returned to civilian life but were still obligated—from time to time—to brief military exercises; in case of war, this group would be integrated in the *Linie*. The second group comprised those between 32 and 39 years of age who had done their military service; in case of war they were employed for purposes of occupation or in territorial defense.

form to local civilian administrative units and to absorb something of the spirit of self-government that was then projected for the civil administration.

A clear illustration of how far these tendencies went is provided by E. M. Arndt's *Catechism for the German Landwehrmann,* published in 1813. The spirit of blind, unconditional obedience was to disappear from the *Landwehr* according to this account. The national idea was to have primacy over military discipline, and the *Landwehr* was to fight only for the great national possessions. This was a spirit similar to that which animated the Spanish army after the insurrection of 1808. That army had even waged a war of liberation without a king. It was a spirit that could easily degenerate into the ticklish phenomenon of a political army, as happened to the Spanish army which, with its *pronunciamentos* and its involvement in political party struggles, became the curse of the country. In Prussia matters did not reach this stage; the basic element of monarchical authority in the old military state was far too strong. After 1819 the *Landwehr* became increasingly integrated into the regular army, until with the reform of 1860 it actually disappeared in its old unadulterated form. Thus universal military service achieved full and final realization not as an extension of the militia idea but as an extension of the institution of the standing army. A modern militarism developed that took over essential features from the old.

It is extremely interesting to observe how this phenomenon was connected with the decisive change in the Prussian constitution. It can be said that in a certain sense universal service was intimately connected with the idea of a representative constitution. A representative constitution—that is, the participation of the people through its representatives in the functions of state—was the necessary result of that change in the political atmosphere which called for universal service. The statesmen who made universal military service part of their program had in mind also self-government and a representative constitution. Admittedly the introduction of universal service was not accompanied by an immediate realization of these plans, but a representative constitution was still the needed complement to the new political and military system. In Prussia this constitution—much to the radicals' chagrin—left untouched the relations between the Crown and the army. The army still owed allegiance to the King, and not to the constitution. The Crown therefore possessed a real source of power that assured it the upper hand in political life and could not easily be reconciled with the theory of parliamentary government as that had developed in England. It was for this reason that the reform of 1860, which both greatly increased the size of the army and organized it in a more strictly monarchical way, was accompanied by that constitutional conflict whose central question was whether the Crown or the Parliament should have jurisdiction over the army, whether the budgetary rights of Parliament included the power to challenge the army budget from year to year.

The advocates of parliamentary rights pointed to England. There, since the Revolution of 1688, the small and only recently created standing army was legally based only on annually renewed parliamentary approval. Not simply the means of maintaining the army but also its power to command and to execute military discipline and justice depended on these annual resolutions of Parliament, and each year it was expressly stressed that the standing army was illegal without this parliamentary approval. The statutory armed forces of the country were the militia and the navy. They did not stand on such precarious legal ground because they could not endanger the liberties of the country. It is true that the militia was the weapon of the propertied classes for maintaining existing conditions and the public order, but the navy was a popular institution, the celebrated and successful instrument of the English polity of trade and maritime power, the real bulwark in the nation's defense, free of any absolutist and militarist vestiges, and free of the suspicion that an absolutist monarch could ever use it to overthrow the parliamentary constitution.

The standing army in England was therefore in an exceptional position, by reason of the special circumstances and history of the country. A Continental power like Prussia could not make its armed forces dependent on the resolutions of changing parliamentary majorities. With this conviction, the government fought the constitutional crisis of 1862–66; and the result was that the principle of a parliamentary government on English lines did not carry the day in Prussia. The Prussian system of constitutional monarchy, in contrast to truly parliamentary government, corresponded to the structure of its military organization, which continued to leave the army in the monarch's hand. This system was duplicated in other German states, and, by analogy, carried over into the Empire.

Thus, through the reform of 1860, military organization was finally brought into harmony with the political, constitutional principle of the predominance of the Crown. Considerations for the social structure of the state and for the training for the higher professions that had nothing to do with purely military considerations and requirements, lived on in the institution of one-year voluntary service with its preferential position for those liable for the draft from educated and well-to-do classes. How intimately the education of the people was connected with military institutions can be clearly seen in the oft deplored influence which the proof of eligibility for one-year service exercised on our school system. The abolition of this institution has been demanded from the point of view both of the educational system and of military instruction, up to now without success. France, which took over universal military service from Germany in 1872, has gone beyond the German example and made military service, like citizenship, equal for all.

Moreover, in our officer class the aristocratic principle has persisted, to a degree unknown in France, even though the former privileges of the nobility have been abolished here. An aristocracy of education and wealth has replaced the aristocracy of blood. Besides, this class is set apart from the non-commissioned officers in principle, despite individual exceptions, as strictly as the higher bureaucracy is from the lower. Indeed, the rank of subordinate and lower officials still derives much of its character today from former non-commissioned officers who were provided for by means of civilian jobs. Militarism still pervades our political system and public life today, generally in a very decisive way. Even Social Democracy, which in principle is against everything connected with militarism, not only owes to it the discipline on which its party organization largely rests, but also in its ideal for the future it has unconsciously adopted a good measure of the coercion of the individual by the community, which comes from the Prussian military state.

It has often been asserted that there is an inherent relation between universal military service and universal suffrage, in the sense that they appear to be two sides of the same equation. This is scarcely borne out by history, though the equation is not idle. A phenomenon repeatedly encountered in history is that fulfillment of public obligations leads in the long run to acquisition of public rights. Whoever puts himself in the service of the state must logically and fairly be granted the regular rights of citizenship. To be sure, universal, equal, direct suffrage would not be an automatic consequence.

Doubtless there is something democratic in the principle of universal military service, but only in Hardenberg's sense when he recommended, in his great reform Memorandum of 1807, "democratic institutions under monarchical government." The monarchical element clings to modern militarism, even where it has vanished from the constitution of the state itself. Republican France has still been unable to achieve a complete balance between its state organization and military organization. Militarism and republics do not get along too well together. The army's existence always remains a threat to the republican constitution; for the army by its nature demands a monarch at its head, while the President of the Republic is by nature a civilian. On the other hand, the anti-militarist trend in radical politics cannot be stopped. Be that as it may, the centralized administration of the state, the fully developed bureaucratic spirit that makes itself felt even in modern institutions of self-administration, is in accord with the organization of the army. The Republic is young, but the French people and their history are old, and it is not only pressure on the foreign front but historical habit and the tenacity of tradition that maintain militarism in France.

Just as in France the lack of a monarch, so in Austria-Hungary the lack of a unified state was behind the tension between the political and military organization. The modern army was created for the unified monarchical state. The failure to impose a real political unity in the Habsburg Monarchy could be borne so long as the army belonged after the old fashion to the monarch and not to the country. But with the era of constitutional government and universal military service the forces of nationalist separatism have been increasingly astir, and the question now is whether use of German as the standard language in the army will hold its own and with it the unity of the army. As it is, the *Honved* army in Hungary stands alongside the standing army in somewhat the same way as the militia supplements the mobile troops in England, or as was once intended by its founder for the territorial defense army alongside the regular army. But the *Honved* is even more distinctly set off: it is the Hungarian national militia alongside the standing army of the Emperor.

Even Russia has been unable to avoid the military and political necessity of introducing universal military service, though it hardly harmonizes with her internal constitutional arrangements. It was a decree of an absolute ruler that created the institution there (1874) out of consideration for the respective strengths of European armies, and not out of any impression that the time had come for an awakening of the people to political consciousness. Still, the liberation of the serfs had preceded it, and it was followed by the natural and, as recent events have shown, successful drive toward creation of a constitutional state. There is a certain similarity in the sequence of these events in Russia and

Prussia: first, liberation of the serfs; second, universal military service; and finally a representative constitution.

The success of Prussian and German arms made the introduction of universal service a political necessity for the Great Powers everywhere on the Continent. England, however, was able to escape the necessity. She contented herself with streamlining her army organization in 1871 by abolishing flogging and the sale of commissions. Even to the present day she has not switched to universal service. With good reason, it seems to me. The English army's primary task is to fight colonial wars, and universal service is not really designed for colonial wars. We ourselves send only volunteers to South-West Africa, and there are those among us who are calling for a special colonial force, based on volunteers. Here, once again, we see how nation-building and the political and military tasks it involves influence the structure of military organization. A colonial empire like England needs a different army from those of the Continental states. It is true that the Continental powers are more and more becoming colonial powers; and it is not impossible that in the future the same kind of compromise and *rapprochement* between British and Continental institutions will take place in military organization as has already occurred in political life: that is, England would be infused with something of the spirit of militarism while the Continent would edge in the direction of a militia and navy. The limited stability of peace today is in itself a step in the direction of the militia idea, and one already senses that the increasing size and importance of navies will eventually alter the entire nature of both military organization and public life.

At the present time, to be sure, the army and the militia stand opposed to each other. The militia system has been developed best in Switzerland, where—unlike England, and even America—no standing army is maintained as well. The Swiss of course provided the model for the standing armies of the Continent, but they themselves never went over to a standing army. The reason for this lies not so much in the lack of financial resources—the

Swiss militia is, relatively speaking, as expensive as our standing army—but chiefly in the nature of the political system, which cannot be reconciled with militarism. The monarchical traits inherent in militarism have been missing in this federative, cooperative, political system from the very beginning. There is no clearer example of how the organization of the state and of the army determine each other. At the same time an important factor must not be overlooked. Switzerland is, in international law, a neutral state; and the nature of the country is such that it can be defended like a huge fortress. Switzerland occupies an exceptional position, in much the same way as the island kingdom of England and the North American Union. This combines with the associative character of the political system and makes these three states the chief representatives of the type that Spencer has called "industrial."

Of course, the considerable expansion of the navies of England and America in recent decades severely qualifies this attribute and makes it more and more doubtful. We could even speak of "navalism" as a companion to the old militarism, and it is certain that this phenomenon will greatly increase in significance. It is clear to see and to be expected, however, that a military system whose center of gravity is in sea power will influence the organization of the state in its own peculiar way, different from the way of the Continental military system. Land forces are a kind of organization that permeates the whole body of the state and gives it a military cast. Sea power is only a mailed fist, reaching out into the world; it is not suitable for use against some "enemy within." Land forces have stood since the beginning in more or less intimate alliance with the propertied classes; they still carry something of a feudal tradition in them. Sea power lacks all feudal vestiges. To an eminent degree it serves the interests of trade and industry. Its place is with the modern forces in life, simply by virtue of the vital importance that technology and capital have in its development. Sea power is allied with progressive forces, whereas land forces are tied to conservative tendencies. Moreover, in our day development of sea power means a commitment to international politics—that is to say, to a Great Power policy, whose sphere of interests, through the extension of world-wide commerce, covers the entire surface of the globe. Thus the individuality of single states is weakened and a general adjustment of differing political and military institutions is beginning to take place. The opposition between land powers and sea powers, between peoples that govern themselves and peoples that are governed from above, will become less and less rigid and obvious. The military and the industrial types of society will probably experience not a sharpening of their differences, but a gradual blending and increasing similarity of institutions. That the world is not yet ready for eternal peace events of the recent past have once again clearly demonstrated. In the foreseeable future, matters will remain as they have been throughout history: the form and spirit of the state's organization will not be determined solely by economic and social relations and clashes of interests, but primarily by the necessities of defense and offense, that is, by the organization of the army and of warfare. This, I believe, is the lesson we can draw from an historical consideration of developments up to the present time.

6

THE ORIGINS OF THE
MODERN MINISTERIAL SYSTEM:
A COMPARATIVE STUDY

This article, which was published in the *Historische Zeitschrift*, Volume 100 (1908), and represents the expanded version of a lecture given at the Tenth Congress of German Historians in Dresden in 1907, can be regarded as Hintze's first publication in the field of comparative history. It is true that some years earlier he had compared the Austrian and Prussian eighteenth-century bureaucracy in a lengthy essay ("Der österreichische und der preussische Beamtenstaat im 17. und 18. Jahrhundert," in *Historische Zeitschrift*, Volume 86, 1900), but the article on the ministerial system expands comparisons over the whole of European history.

Hintze emphasized that, despite their different modern forms, the ministerial systems of the European countries had a common basis, and he explained with great care in what ways and why the developments in the various European countries differed. In his later comparative studies Hintze continued to maintain that the society of Latin-Teutonic states was a unique formation and that therefore only comparisons among phenomena with this Latin-Teutonic society could be fruitful and produce valid results. In the present article, Hintze is almost exclusively concerned with establishing the causal connections that brought forth different results despite a common point of departure; in later comparative studies he gives more weight to the role of the functional factor in shaping an institution. Consequently, he recognized that non-European institutional patterns can be instructive, and so gives a certain amount of attention to them, although the European world remains the focal point of his interest.

Briefly, Hintze's comparative approach is more fully developed in later studies than in this essay, which stands at the beginning of Hintze's work in this area. And yet it is an article of unusual richness, which one is inclined to call the "definitive" treatment of the problem under investigation. Of course, in certain questions of detail, scholarship has advanced beyond Hintze's factual exposition. Hintze's remarks on British politics in the eighteenth century show that the article was written before Sir Lewis Namier and his school had embarked on their re-evaluation of the policy of George III and of the role of the British Parliament in the eighteenth century. We have become aware that "political parties" and "party politics" were regarded as being destructive and as having no justifiable existence much longer than Hintze assumed, and the story of the emergence of a government's parliamentary responsibility is undoubtedly less direct and more complex. We might also have some doubts as to whether the story of the development of modern political institutions can be fully understood without greater reference to political doctrines and political ideology. But it is hard to imagine that there will be another scholar who is able to master this immense mass of dispersed material and to present it in a unified whole.

It seemed unnecessary, even inappropriate, to provide a vocabulary, for Hintze himself left most of the technical terms in foreign—i.e., non-German—languages, because it was frequently important to show that, despite differences in the terms, they indicated a similar or identical institutional development.

My intention in this study is to present a comparative survey of the rise and growth of the modern ministerial system in some of the important states of today. This does not involve a detailed account of the results of recent research but rather a construction of general lines which, taken together, may permit us to explain and to understand the present by reference to the past. I am of course aware that such systems are only the form in which history and politics develop; they are, as it were, tools created by the mind and the will of the rulers. Like real tools, however, these instruments of political activity have their history, too, and they survive those who created them. Even though at various times they serve diverse ends and are activated by differing impulses, they nevertheless embody a strong political tradition. They keep public affairs for generations in the same path, and changes in these forms can be brought about only by some very powerful impulse. The story of the development of the ministerial system reflects the over-all course of political development of which it is a part.

The ancient world had no experience of a ministerial system in the modern sense, despite a few rudiments of it; the system is equally alien to the East—at least until the imposition of modern imitations. The system was produced by Western civilization, a civilization Latin and Germanic in origin; it was brought into existence primarily by the centralized monarchical state, though its elements date far back into the feudal hierarchy of the past. Its growth was furthered and shaped particularly by the modern notion of *raison d'état,* which flourished in the sixteenth, seventeenth, and eighteenth centuries, and also by the constitutional struggles that took place between the seventeenth and the nineteenth centuries. It was political life, both internal and international, that brought into existence this instrument of modern government. The influence of states upon one another was as important here as the factor of common origin and parallel developments resulting from common roots.

A historical examination of a comparative character clearly shows that despite great differences in detail and in general (the English Channel, e.g., marks a particularly obvious division) the modern ministries are formations of a very similar nature. As a whole, a ministry is a board composed of heads of departments who administer the various areas of government activity and the government as a whole, in behalf of the head of the state, and are responsible to a popular representation. King and Parliament are the two focal points in political history which determine the trajectory that indicates the development of ministries: monarchical government created these institutions, responsibility to Parliament gave them shape and transformed them.

In the most advanced states the ministries were transformed from a corps of civil servants exclusively dependent on the King, into parliamentary committees whose appointment by the head of state was a mere formality: this determines the degree of collegiate unity and cohesiveness among the ministers. The stronger the personal will and energy of a monarch on whom the ministries depend, the weaker the structure of the ministry as a whole; and likewise, the stronger the element of parliamentary control, the stricter the bond that unites the ministers into a collective body. The self-governing monarch needs councilors, and they must appear as a united body only when representing government before a parliament. Parliamentary party government needs a united and cohesive ministry as its executive arm. In the first instance the single departments are often of greater weight than the ministry as a whole; in the second, the importance of departments is secondary to that of the Cabinet's general policy.

The single departments existing today—i.e., ministries for Foreign Affairs, War, Marine, Finance, the Interior, and for all those

special fields that in the course of the last century have branched
off from the Ministry of the Interior—this entire structure of numerous specialized departments has everywhere much the same
basic features. Of course, the degree of ministerial cohesiveness
and the exact delimitation of functions varies and, for instance,
differs between England and the Continent. Moreover, because
of particular political developments, the principle of dividing the
work according to geographical areas has continued to exist in a
few countries, next to that of division according to fields of governmental authority. In the separate ministries, as a rule, the former collegiate type of organization has given way to a more hierarchical type, such that a single minister assumes responsibility
for affairs—though in England this bureaucratic transformation
of offices has not developed so sharply as on the Continent.

Many of the features peculiar to England are of particular
value in a comparative study, because they are historical remains
to which analogies can be found in the earlier stages of the Continental administrative development. As on a geological map that
indicates all the various layers, we can find in the English Cabinet all the combined historical elements that have formed the
ministries of today: the great offices of the court, the Secretaries
of State, and the collegiate Privy Council that gave the framework to the entire ministerial system of government. These are
the three separate roots from which the modern ministerial offices developed, though in the single countries they may have intertwined and forked in various ways. This process of growth can
be understood only if we go back to the twelfth century and
briefly consider the older institutions, for it is only if we take a
comprehensive look that we can recognize in full clarity the
common origin of the institutions that developed on both sides
of the Channel.

In every case it was the court of the King or Prince that became the kernel from which, together with central authorities,
ministries were to grow. The sovereign had a permanent *entourage,* a number of knights and churchmen who assisted him in

carrying on the business of government. From time to time this permanent court was expanded into a *curia solemnis* or *curia de more;* this generally happened concurrently with the great feasts of the Church, but it happened also whenever the sovereign summoned his vassals and liegemen to his presence, whether to serve him by deeds or advice, or merely to recognize by their presence that they owed him their loyalty. At such assemblies particularly important affairs of government, of both legal and extra-legal nature, were frequently enacted: these meetings formed the basis for the development of Estates and parliamentary bodies. The proper court, however, embraced the permanent councilors and servants of the sovereign, without firm organization or order of business, and a lengthy process of differentiation took place before a Council of State emerged which formed the receptacle for the growth of modern ministries.

The process of differentiation was one of remarkable uniformity in the various states; in every case a typical triple formation emerged: of High Court, Exchequer, and Council. In France and England, from the mid-thirteenth century onward, these three offices evolved from the formless court when the regular legal and financial business was entrusted to commissions made up of specially competent councilors and servants. Thus, at the beginning of the fourteenth century, the High Court and the Exchequer emerged as definite separate offices, next to the Royal Council, though their personnel was to some degree identical. In England the earliest and most important of these offices, the fiscal authority—the Exchequer or *curia ad saccarium*—made its first appearance in the twelfth century; in France a High Court, the Paris *Parlement*, appeared after the mid-thirteenth century. The Exchequer was subsequently supplemented by a High Court —the King's Bench—just as the Paris *Parlement* was supplemented by the *Chambre des comptes:* and above both, as supreme government authority, a collegiate council was placed which took firm shape only at the beginning of the fourteenth century. This collegiate council must be regarded as the proper workshop of monarchical government. Its competence was not restricted to political matters, but extended its functions to law and finance as well, and only the ordinary current affairs of the administration of justice and of accounts were left to the other bodies. Anything of extraordinary importance, or anything that the King found particularly interesting for whatever reason, was dealt with not in these bodies but in the Council, in which the full power of the monarch resided and acted.[1]

The same developments can be detected in Germany, but only in rudimentary form; these beginnings were stunted, because the Empire turned from a monarchical united state into a federative republic of princes, and its Imperial head was deprived of the normal powers of government. The High Court of the Empire disappeared in the middle of the fifteenth century; there is, apart from a few traces in the thirteenth century, no real evidence to show that there ever existed a Chamber of Finance for the Empire; while the Imperial Council, though it functioned for some time as an Imperial court, did not produce any Imperial ministers. Maximilian I attempted to reform the central administration of his hereditary lands on French and Burgundian lines; he planned, by means of these offices, to rule the whole Empire, in much the same way as the Capetians managed to extend the rule over their lands to the whole of France. But Maximilian's plan failed; it was only under Ferdinand I that the Council of the Court and the Court Exchequer acquired a permanent character. A special High Court for the hereditary lands of Austria did not exist—the complex of territories was too varied, too lacking in cohesion, to allow a single High Court with assessors for the Estates. But the Council of the Court increasingly developed into an Imperial court wherein the affairs of the Empire as well could be judged; and supreme political direction was given to the Privy Council instituted in 1527 as a "Committee of the Council of the Court."

These Austrian forms subsequently influenced southern and central Germany, and indirectly Brandenburg as well. The Privy

Council of Brandenburg, founded in 1604, was instituted "on the model of other well-founded polities and regiments"; but its creation was merely the last stage in a process of development which, very similar to events in France, went on in the sixteenth century.[2] The beginning of the seventeenth century saw in Brandenburg the distinct emergence of a High Court, a financial office, and a Privy Council exactly corresponding to the triple authority in France of *Parlement, Chambre des comptes,* and *Conseil royal*—as at the beginning of the fourteenth century they had emerged there as separate formations. In each case the subsequent system of ministers was to grow out of the Royal Council, or out of the permanent Privy Council of the prince. The organization of these bodies, however, was a collegiate one, and we must therefore examine the individual court dignitaries for discovering the origin of separate departments.

In the earlier period of court life, before the beginning of the process of differentiation, the great court dignitaries had a role of particular importance in the *entourage* of the prince. In accordance with the pattern of the Carolingian Court, they were entrusted with the daily business of the monarchical and patriarchal manorial household—the Marshal, the Steward, the Cupbearer, the Chamberlain, and the Chancellor. There were many variations in these offices and their nomenclature: in France the Capetian Court had a "seneschal" rather than a "steward"; while in England the *capitalis justicia* was the characteristic court officer of the Normans, and in Germany we find, later on, a *Hofmeister* (superintendent of the household). In England and France the office of Marshal was divided into two ranks, the higher one being that of *connétable,* the lower that of Marshal. The Gentleman of the Chamber (*chambrier*) was assisted by a Chamberlain (*chambellan*) whose prestige was lesser but whose practical importance was greater, for, like his equivalent the German *Kammermeister,* he was chiefly engaged in the financial aspects of the household. Altogether, out of the office of chamberlain the manysided administration of the princely domains has grown.

The old household officers of the heads of the German tribes came to serve the princely government and the princely household. It was a peculiarity of feudal administration that it used efficient household arrangements for the conduct of public business. Household and government were still combined, not separate, in the courts of the feudal age. In the period between the thirteenth century and the sixteenth, French and English court regulations offer a very similar picture of these large manorial households from which later the civil authorities would emerge. The great court dignitaries could be described as the ministers of the feudal age. It is of course scarcely worth remarking that these offices were not by any means the basis of the later order of division into ministerial departments, even though some connection between the old dignitaries of the court and the modern minister of state can be demonstrated.

The fate of these court offices varied greatly from country to country. The greater their prestige and independence, the less could they be filled by servants of the sovereign. In the German Empire the great offices (*Erzämter*) were bound up with the Electorates; the hereditary offices at the court were now filled by the *ministeriales* of the Empire and gradually became mere titles of nobility, and the same happened regarding the hereditary offices at the courts of territorial rulers. In East Prussia, secularization and particularly the Estates movement of 1555 led to a very peculiar development: the occupants of the great court offices, which here were of course not hereditary, came to assume governing power as a *Regimenstrat* (Council of Government) rather in the manner of a collegiate ministry. This Council was appointed by the sovereign, but it administered the land in agreement with an oligarchic clique of noblemen.[3]

As a rule the great officers of the court did not form a corporate entity. In France they were simply pushed into the background as the power of the King increased, for the very reason that they claimed a hereditary right to their offices. The office of seneschal threatened to develop into a new form of *major domo*, and was therefore abolished in 1191 by Philip Augustus; and if at a later date—from Louis VIII onward—we find holders of court offices again enjoying particular positions of confidence at the court of the Capetians, these officers were not the privileged great dignitaries of former times, who lived in princely style, but titled servants of more humble origin, who could no longer endanger the prestige of the Crown. The great court offices survived longest in England, for here the high nobility learned to adapt itself earliest and most completely to the new monarchical state, thus acquiring a strong and durable influence on the conduct of government. These offices remained hereditary in part, even until the six- teenth century; their occupants regularly appeared in their ca- pacity of officers of the court in the Royal Councils that stood in organic connection with the *magnum concilium* of prelates and barons. Still in the sixteenth and seventeenth centuries they were the principal members of the Privy Council, and their traces can clearly still be detected in the ministerial Cabinet of today, even though court administration and the government of the state are now very sharply separated.

In particular three ministerial offices have their origins in the old offices of the court: the First Lord of the Treasury, the Chan- cellor of the Exchequer, and the Lord Chancellor; we could men- tion also the Admiralty and the Master of the Ordnance, a post abolished after the Crimean War. The original occupants of these posts, the Lord High Admiral and the Master-General of the Ord- nance, were created, like their French counterparts the *Grand Admiral* and the *Grand Maître de l'artillerie*, on the model of former court offices, in the fourteenth and the seventeenth cen- turies respectively. The two Treasury ministries stem from the Lord Treasurer, an office that we encounter even as late as in the Stuart period, and which itself came from the *Thesaurarius*, who is shown in the *Dialogus de scaccario* as one of the important per- sons at the Accounting Office, on a par with the Constables, Mar- shals, Chamberlains, and Chancellors under the chairmanship of the *capitalis justicia*. We can say little of the origins of the office—

at the time of the *Dialogue* the post was occupied by its author, Richard, Bishop of London. We might perhaps assume, however, that the *Thesaurarius* came, like the numerous Chamberlains, from the old unified office of the Chamberlains—among its many functions this office had charge of finances and kept the accounts. The *Thesaurarius*, or Lord High Treasurer, as he was later known when the office became the preserve of a noble layman, gave place in the seventeenth century to a collegiate Treasury, of which the two chief members—the First Lord of the Treasury and the Chancellor of the Exchequer—nowadays are members of the Cabinet.

At this point it is worthwhile to make a brief comparison with the counterpart of this office in the administration of France. In the fourteenth century there were several *Thesaurarii* (generally four), called *trésoriers de France*, which term corresponds to the English *Thesaurarius*. But again we know little of how these positions came about. They obviously had something to do with the Royal Treasury (*Kammer*), from which—in the fourteenth century, once the Templars had ceased conducting the financial administration—the personnel of the financial administration was taken; but they had a rather subordinate position. They were entrusted with accounting for and guarding revenues coming from the demesne and royal prerogatives. Next to them, from the second half of the fourteenth century on, we find the *généraux* as chief tax officials. Both groups acquired a common chief authority in the *Surintendant général* when, under Francis I, the *Epargne* (General Treasury) was founded. On the fall of Fouquet in 1661 the office was abolished, and the King himself took over the supreme direction of the financial administration with the help of a *Contrôleur général*. Finally, on the eve of the Revolution, a *Premier Ministre des finances,* above the *Contrôleur général,* was entrusted with the direction of financial affairs. This already was the position of the modern French finance minister; this office, too, can be traced, though only indirectly, to the functions of the old office of Chamberlain.

But it was chiefly through the chancellorship that the old system of court offices is tied to the modern ministries of state. At the old princely courts the Chancellery alone was a strictly bureaucratic organization—it concentrated in itself the business of government and administration with which the court had to deal. When the monarch granted fiefs, gifts, privileges, and similar graces, he had to use the great seal; this afforded the official in charge of the seal—that is, the Chancellor—a kind of constitutional right of legal control over the most important acts of princely government. In England this constitutional control was particularly firmly established and tenaciously maintained; and the Lord Chancellor has remained one of the most respected ministers up to the present day. Under Henry VIII the office passed from clerical to secular hands; it involved the appointment of judges, the administration of justice by equity, and the presidency of the House of Lords, which counts as the highest court of the land. Thus the chancellorship is effectively a department of justice, though the functions of this office are not so strictly delimited as those of these ministries on the Continent.

Developments in France followed a rather similar course. The chancellorship itself was abolished, like the seneschalship, in 1185 by Philip Augustus: it seemed to be a restriction of the King's power, because it was held by a high churchman whose dependence on the monarch was only partial, and who could not, by tradition, be deposed from office. The title of Chancellor appeared again, however; from the end of the thirteenth century onward, the office was held even by laymen—jurists such as Pierre Flote and Guillaume de Nogaret under Philip IV. In France, too, the Chancellors had charge of the great seals and at the same time directed the administration of justice. Until the French Revolution the tradition was maintained that Chancellors could not be deposed: if a Chancellor happened to forfeit the King's confidence, then a solution was found to the difficulty—he was ordered to surrender the great seals. These were given to a specially-appointed *Garde des sceaux*, who proceeded to function in the Chancellor's stead. Finally, in 1791, the modern Ministry of Justice arose from this old office.

In the German Empire the Elector-Arch-Chancellor (*Kurfurst-*

Erzkanzler), the Archbishop of Mainz, won out, after a long struggle, over the Court-Chancellor of the Emperor. In the last centuries of the Empire, the Imperial administration was largely concentrated in the Imperial Court Chancellery, and supervised by Vice Chancellors appointed by the Arch-Chancellor. The Chancellor of the Imperial Court emerged from 1620 onward as an authority for only the Austrian hereditary lands, whereas the Imperial Court Council became primarily concerned with the affairs of the Empire. At a later stage we shall review the importance of this Chancellery in Austrian administration. In Brandenburg the old office of Chancellor was suppressed just when the Great Elector began to weld his disparate provinces into a united state (1650): the title "Great Chancellor" (*Gross-kanzler*), which, after Cocceji (1748), was assumed by the first Minister of Justice, was no more than an imitation of French nomenclature and had no real historical connection with the old office of Chancellor in Brandenburg and Prussia. Likewise, the modern office of Imperial Chancellor is a modern imitation which was meant to arouse historical memories but has no real historical connection with the old office of Chancellor.

Thus, insofar as a connection exists between the modern ministries and the old court offices, it is limited to the departments of Justice and Finance; these officers are members of the Royal Council—the central cog in monarchical government—and the further development of ministries are, in the main, tied to this collegiate council. Again, England was most conservative in her development. Even today, the English Cabinet is, regarded from the constitutional angle, no more than a committee of the Privy Council; whereas, in France, Prussia, and Austria, a complete and fundamental divorce occurred between the Council of State and the ministry. Before the reforms of the seventeenth century, however, the organization of the ministries was always tied to the Council of State, often in a very complicated manner. We shall now briefly examine this connection, so far as space permits.

In France and England, the two most significant countries,

from the sixteenth century on, the Council of State took on a very different aspect from what it possessed in the Middle Ages. It acquired a more strictly bureaucratic character. Of course the members of this Council had always been royal officials, both in France and in England. Whenever the nobility or the Estates attempted to force on the King a council that would restrict his power and force him to conduct his policy in accordance with the Estates' wishes, their efforts were in vain. In England in the fourteenth and fifteenth centuries, the Royal Council recognized a kind of responsibility toward Parliament, but nothing of this kind ever came about in France. In France and England the King was free in the choice of his councilors—although in principle rather than in practice. He had to take into account the eminent origins or position of some people who were thereby regarded as necessary members of the Council; high churchmen often made difficulties in the Council; in England there were still a few hereditary offices whose occupants had the right to attend the Council. The number of men entitled to attend was frequently too large, and several times restrictions were placed on size, or narrower groups were formed. Nor did these inconveniences entirely cease after the sixteenth century, for much depended on the King's energy and his ability in government as well as upon the circumstances of the times. Even later there were still retrogressive developments and distortions of the regular pattern. By and large, however, the Royal Council had become, by the sixteenth century, a reliable instrument of the rising monarchical absolutism, composed of persons who, whether noble or nonnoble, felt themselves to be primarily servants of the king.

Even in the England of Henry VIII—on whose reign we are particularly well informed through the publication of the Council proceedings[4]—the parliamentary responsibility of the Privy Council, as it had still existed in the fifteenth century, had practically ceased. The Royal Council, and not Parliament, gave the government of the country its decisive direction. The Council, however, was in all respects a tool of the monarch. Certain cur-

rent business (probably of very small importance) it was entrusted to handle on its own, but in all matters of any moment its
powers as regards the monarch were merely consultative: the
King was the ultimate decision-maker.

In the sixteenth century at the princely courts a primitive kind
of personal rule of the monarch out of the Cabinet was customary.
In general the King was not personally present at meetings of his
Council of State: even Henry VIII, who on his frequent changes of
residence always took with him a number of councilors, only sel-
dom participated in their meetings, as their protocols indicate.
Even then, daily sessions were held at fixed times of the day, often
in both the morning and the afternoon. The bulk of the business
discharged was concerned with internal affairs, but foreign affairs
and foreign correspondence were increasing in volume and significance. The protracted rivalries and power struggles in the
course of which the Great Powers of Europe developed and established their frontiers had begun; the new notion of *raison
d'état* dominated the monarchs' Cabinets and council chambers.
In these circumstances, as personal instruments of this monarchical policy, the Secretaries of State gained the peculiarly important role they have played since the sixteenth century. They were
the real ministers of old Europe; they appeared in England,
France, and Spain, also in the Italian republics Venice and Florence. It would seem that their origins are to be found in the Roman Curia, in the Papal secretaries of the fourteenth century who
were attached to the Chancellery.[5]

Originally the secretaries were confidential clerks of the King;
in fourteenth-century England they were described as "the King's
clercs" and in France as *les clercs du secret;* later on they were
called in England "the King's secretaries" and in France *secrétaires des commandements du roi et des finances.* They were the
Cabinet secretaries of the King and also formed a link between
the King and the Council. In England,[6] from the middle of the
fifteenth century onward, they were members of the Privy Council; in France, they entered the Council only in the sixteenth cen-

tury, initially without the right to vote and not as equals of the
councilors of higher social standing. At the outset their rank was
rather low, but it rose in the course of the fifteenth and, still more,
the sixteenth century; the English court regulations of these centuries show this clearly.[7] The secretary's proximity to the King's
person at a time when the monarchs were taking a rapidly expanding direct share in internal and external affairs gave to the
office increasing importance. The secretaries not only became an
organ of the absolutist ruler in the Council; they also were entrusted with important negotiations with representatives of foreign powers. They were the men most thoroughly acquainted with
affairs and the intentions of the monarch, the most reliable and
obedient instruments of his will, the ablest and most industrious
experts, the earliest professional civil servants; and as such they
represented a marked contrast to the frequently changing and essentially dilettantist noble councilors.

It was highly characteristic that the title "Secretary of State" in
France was given first to Claude de l'Aubespine, who negotiated
the Peace of Cateau-Cambrésis in 1559, because his Spanish ne-
gotiator already had this title. Yet official doctrines of the internal
administration still referred to the secretaries for a long time as
secrétaires des commandements du roi et des finances, and this
lasted until 1660, when the title "Secretary of State" became common usage.[8] In sixteenth-century England several notable statesmen, such as Thomas Cromwell, William Cecil (Burleigh),
and Walsingham, passed through this post. The first to bear the
title "Secretary of State" was Sir Robert Cecil (1601); but, as in
France, the title passed into regular usage only gradually.

At the outset in England there was only one chief secretary,
but after 1540—perhaps as a consequence of Cromwell's fall—two
were regularly appointed. Under Elizabeth Sir William Cecil was
for a long time the only secretary, but later there were again two.
It would seem that in France, already at an earlier date, a larger
number of royal secretaries was at work: in the *Règlement* of
1547 their number was restricted to four, which meant an in-

crease in work and also in salary. Thus, each secretary henceforth received an annual salary of 3,000 *livres Tournois* (almost twice as much as before), and after 1588, 3,000 *écus;* the number of four was retained throughout the entire *Ancien régime*. Florimond Robertet, who served in three reigns and reached the climax of his career under Louis XII, has been counted as *père des secrétaires d'état,* giving the office greater influence and increasing social prestige. By this time the office was no longer a clerical preserve, but entrusted to learned scribes and jurists.

Florimond Robertet was the first to countersign decrees of the King; and later on, under Charles IX, Nicolas de Villeroy had to sign his name alone in place of the indolent King's. This man, who was removed by Henry III in 1588, has left memoirs[9] that sharply illustrate the nature of the office; a comprehensive Instruction of 1588,[10] is another important source. It clearly appears that the central feature of the office was its occupant's position as Cabinet secretary to the King. The secretary on duty appeared early in the morning in the King's study, bearing a violet-colored velvet attaché case that contained the incoming documents to be opened only in the King's presence. After instructions by the King, the secretary drafted the answers and presented them to the King for his signature; he would then countersign them for verification and control. The Instruction of 1588 specially decreed that secretaries should write nothing other than what the King had commanded; and it is clear from Villeroy's memoirs that correspondence on the side, which many secretaries found necessary in their professional interest or their personal information, aroused the displeasure of the suspicious monarch in those days of political tension and party intrigues. Villeroy held that such supplementary correspondence was vital for any secretary anxious to do his duty properly; and it would seem that things as they developed under Henry IV largely bore out what he said.

We acquire a similar impression of the nature of the office from the correspondence between Henry VIII's secretary, Dr. Pace, and Cardinal Wolsey, published in the first volume of State Papers.[11] Wolsey had complained to the secretary that he was not giving the King a true account of affairs, giving him not the entire text of his letters but merely extracts from them, and including his own ideas in the King's replies. Dr. Pace rejected these reproaches and represented himself as the mere obedient and conscientious scribe of the sovereign. He described how the King carefully read all Wolsey's letters himself, and indicated precisely how the reply should run. Then Pace illustratively recounted the process: he would outline the reply to Wolsey, and present it for the King's approval; if the King disliked it, he would have the secretary come to his private room bearing pen and ink, carefully reread Wolsey's letter three times, note the replies to be made in the margin, and instruct the secretary to compose the reply on this basis.

The crucial fact is that from the sixteenth century on, these Cabinet secretaries were members of the Royal Council. They were not secretaries keeping the minutes of the Council: for this task special clerks existed, in both France and England; before such clerks were appointed, no record was kept. Secretaries of State served as regular links between King and Council: in Council they asserted the will and the purposes of the King, and reported to the King the views of his councilors. Thus they became the proper agents of this numerous assembly, and finally the leading ministers in charge of particular areas of business. In the seventeenth century they ceased to be Cabinet secretaries of the King, a task given to other people;[12] but they maintained the right of personal reports to the King and thus remained in constant contact with the source of power.

The manner in which departments were distributed among the Secretaries of State shows the origins from the writing chamber. The secretaries were divided according to the local areas with which they corresponded. Each secretary had some provinces within the country and a few foreign courts to deal with. This geographical division was preserved in England even when Secretaries of State had long ceased to be mere correspondents and had become leading ministers; still in the eighteenth century a distinction was made between the Secretary for the North and the Secretary for the South: the first dealt with the affairs of the northern counties and the northern states of Europe, the other with those of the southern. Only in 1781, under Burke's influence, this geographical division was replaced by a substantial one: the Home Secretary was distinguished from the Foreign Secretary, internal from external affairs. After the union with Scotland a third Secretary of State came into existence to deal with the affairs of that country, until the Battle of Culloden in 1746 put an end to the intrigues of the Stuart Pretenders. After 1768 a special Secretary of State for the Colonies was appointed, though the post became superfluous after the loss of the American Colonies in 1783; again, in 1794, when war broke out with France, a third Secretary of State for War appeared, and he took charge of colonial affairs as well. In the nineteenth century a special Secretary of State for the Colonies was appointed; the office of Secretary of State for War was combined with the Mastership of the Ordnance as a result of the catastrophic experiences before Sebastopol, and a modern Ministry of War thus came into existence. To this structure was added a special Secretary of State for India, when it had been annexed to the Crown. Thus, all the ministerial posts that did not owe their creation to the old court offices arose out of the offices of the Secretaries of State—until most recently, a new political form, the Boards, appeared.

In France the process was not quite so simple, though it took a similar course. Departmental distribution frequently changed, not always following strict groupings and delimitations. The general rule, however, was that each of the four Secretaries of State had charge of the internal affairs of a number of provinces and *généralités* insofar as these affairs did not fall within the competence of another department (as was the case, for example, with economic administration, which was conducted by the *Contrôleur général*, or with public works, which constituted a

separate department). Each Secretary of State had thus a provincial department charged with internal affairs; but each possessed also a department concerned with a special line of business in the entire country. Toward the end of the *Ancien régime*,
one had charge of Foreign Affairs, the second of War, the third
of Marine, and the fourth of the Royal Household, together with
the clergy and the Reformed Church. These tasks gradually
took the upper hand; even in the eighteenth century there was
talk of a Foreign Minister, a War Minister, and a Minister of
Marine. There was no special Minister of the Interior, for his
functions were distributed, according to the territorial principle,
among the four Secretaries of State. Each of these secretaries
had a *bureau*, in which assistants (departmental councilors)
without special rank but with a special field of competence, together with some subordinate officials, carried on the business of
the department. Similarly, the *Contrôleur général* had financial
intendants to assist him in his work.

It would, however, be wrong to regard these ministers of the
Ancien régime as modern ministers, administering a special area
of governmental activity. They were not yet placed in exclusive
control of their departments, nor were they exclusively responsible for them. The most peculiar aspect of the old order was
that these ministers remained in close connection with the
Royal Council—which possessed merely consultative powers
regarding the King but was the effectively governing, executive
organization regarding the land—announcing the King's orders
and supervising their execution. The Council was not organized,
however, in accordance with the distribution of functions among
the secretaries but according to principles of its own. This aspect
of the matter, which makes the over-all picture of ministerial administration in old Europe difficult to understand, deserves a
brief discussion.

In both England and France we can distinguish a division of
the Council into two parts, a division caused by the jurisdictional
separation that began during the fifteenth century and emerged

clearly in the sixteenth. One section of the Council, called in
France *Conseil privé ou des parties,* was an extraordinary High
Court of France, combining the functions of a supreme administrative court with those of a court of appeals. In the sixteenth
century all the members of the Council of State belonged to it,
and later it still involved the greater part of the councilors, along
with numerous *maîtres des requêtes* whose task here, as in the
royal palace itself, was to examine petitions and to submit them.
In England there is a corresponding institution, the Ordinary
Council, which had its own "masters of requests," though it
never acquired the significance of its French counterpart, since
the King's extraordinary legal powers did not develop to the
same extent as in France and were not preserved for so long, at
least with respect to civil cases. Thus, under Elizabeth, this
branched-off Council disappeared. Neither in England nor in
France did this Court have bearing on the rise of the ministerial
system.

The significance of the other division of the Council was all
the greater. It underwent no further division in England, and
appeared in the sixteenth century as the Privy Council of the
King. This Privy Council assumed a particularly rigid form as
the Star Chamber, when it constituted itself as an extraordinary
Royal Court in affairs of criminal and administrative justice; but
the Star Chamber was abolished, together with all the extraordinary juridical powers of the King's Council during the Puritan
Revolution, and was never restored; we are therefore justified in
leaving it out of our account. Admittedly, many commissions
were formed, and later dissolved, from the body of the Privy
Council; but this did not lead to any permanent separation of
departments. It can, however, be observed that a narrow circle
of councilors whose relations with the King were particularly
intimate, was formed. Henry VIII decreed in 1526 that a fixed
number of councilors must accompany him on his frequent
changes of residence (nine out of the twenty that then made up
the Privy Council). There developed, in his reign, two Councils—

one near the person of the King, and the other in London—and between the two there was regular correspondence. The Secretary —so long as there was only one—remained with the King; but the duties of the most important great Court officials—the Lord Treasurer, the Lord Chancellor, and even the Lord Privy Seal— required them to be in London. Briefly, the restricted Council close to the King was different from the Cabinet Council which emerged in the eighteenth century and in which the great Court offices were represented, although the former may have been the point of departure for the formation of the latter.

Edward VI divided the Council's business among five commissions, one of which was intended to discharge the affairs of state, as they were called, and the King intended to be present once a week at this Council.[13] This ordinance comes from the last years of the young King's reign, and we do not know whether the arrangement left any mark. The term "Cabinet" was given under the Stuarts to the restricted committee of the Council of State, with which the King customarily discussed affairs of state. In 1667 Charles II instituted a division of the Privy Council into seven commissions,[14] the chief of which dealt with foreign affairs; and the name "Cabinet" designated primarily this commission of trusted councilors. In the same year it was decided to give the Treasury a collegiate organization. Even earlier in the seventeenth century the position of the Lord High Treasurer had been dissolved into a commission made up of several officials; the same had happened with the post of Lord High Admiral.

The Long Parliament, because of the association of Presbyterianism with the collegiate principle, intervened in administration by means of parliamentary commissions and gave a great impetus to the formation of collegiate bodies. Under the Republic both the Treasury and the Admiralty became commissions; this was the time when the English navy was effectively brought into existence, and the office of the Admiralty was involved in considerable financial responsibilities. Nonetheless, in 1660 the Duke of York came to head naval administration again in the old form of Lord High Admiral, and when he came to the throne he reserved this post for himself. In 1690, however, the Admiralty was once more transformed into a commission, a system that this time proved permanent. The Treasury's collegiate organization was similarly several times abolished, a Lord High Treasurer being reimposed—this happened in the years 1685–87 and 1702–10; again in 1714, in peculiar circumstances shortly before Queen Anne's death, Lord Shrewsbury was in possession of the office for a few days. From George I's time onward, however, there was no further deviation from the commissary principle. The framework of the Privy Council as a whole became increasingly less important; but within that framework there developed both the offices of State and the collegiate ministries of special departments. This is the characteristic feature of the English system: to begin with, the ministers were agents of the Privy Council, but emerged from it and sought to form a more restricted circle of councilors.

In France, developments were a great deal more complicated. The Council of State itself split up into special commissions, for finance, for internal administration, and for the great and secret matters of high policy, among which foreign affairs took primacy. These divisions were named *Conseil des finances, Conseil des dépêches,* and *Conseil d'en haut:* this last was referred to also as *Conseil secret* or *Conseil d'état.* These commissions of the Council became, in the course of time, distinct departments, and while the *Conseil privé* became further and further removed from the King's person, the departments remained in close touch with him. The rule by great First Ministers, which acted in place of the King in the seventeenth century, prepared the way for the all-embracing royal autocracy that Louis XIV exercised in a grand manner. This was essentially a government in Council, but it was also a Cabinet government, with Secretaries of State and the *Contrôleur général.*[15] The meetings of the Royal Council were always held in the King's chambers, whereas the *Conseil privé,* though it also met in the royal palace, had rooms of its own, and the presidential chair of the monarch remained vacant.

At the meetings of the Royal Council, however, Louis XIV generally presided himself, seated on a *fauteuil*, and the councilors sat around him on tabourets. He would carefully listen to the views of the councilors, and make the decision himself, usually on lines proposed by the majority. The Council met every day before dinner; the *Conseil d'état* met on Sundays, Wednesdays, and Thursdays, and also on alternate Mondays; the *Conseil des finances* met on Tuesdays and Saturdays; the *Conseil de conscience*, which concerned itself with Church affairs and was attended by confessors and high churchmen, assembled every Friday; and the *Conseil des dépêches* met every alternate Monday.

The most important by far was the *Conseil d'état*, to which generally only three persons were invited—originally Le Tellier, Lionne, and Colbert; this was the most intimate, most secret, and highest layer of government. The *Conseil d'état* discussed all affairs of particular importance—policy, war, finance, economic affairs; even legal decisions could be made there, the King appearing as judge, surrounded by his most trusted councilors. The title *Ministre d'État* (Minister of State), was accorded to the members of the *Conseil d'état* and was retained by them for life, even if the King no longer asked for their attendance in the *Conseil*. Participation in this most secret Council was obtained not on the basis of appointment but of *ad hoc* summons. The King presided also over the *Conseil royal des finances*, in which—apart from the Marshal, who was supernumerary, and the Chancellor—three councilors were present, among them Colbert, as *Contrôleur général*, who was the chief member. In this body the budgets were arranged, the *taille* contributions fixed and distributed among the *généralités*, the *fermiers'* contracts reviewed; and this Council acted as final court of decision in litigations on financial matters.

The reports to the King and the administrative details were prepared by various officials. Next to the *bureaux* of the *Contrôleur général* and the financial intendants, we find special collegiate commissions of the Council (also designated *bureaux*) which carried out the work with which the councilors were concerned: the *Petite direction,* as it was called, which dealt with financial administration, and the *grande direction* for financial litigation. These collegiate *bureaux* or *directions* must be carefully distinguished from the real *bureaux* of the Ministers.

The deliberations of the *Conseil des dépêches* had less importance than those of the *Conseil d'état* or the *Conseil des finances.* It met once again under the King's presidency; and the Chancellor, the three Ministers of State, and the four Secretaries of State were present; these last were expected to report on their departments. This was to an extent a collegiate Ministry of the Interior, in which the intendants' reports were presented and where they were assessed. Primarily it dealt with the control of communal authorities, provincial Estates, the clergy and ecclesiastical institutions, agriculture, public works, and similar matters; again, its precise jurisdiction was difficult to define. Not everything could be dealt with in the regular sessions that took place every fortnight; the important aspects of the internal administration of the country, insofar as they were not handled by the *bureaux,* were considered during audiences that the Secretaries of State had individually with the King, usually early in the day between the *levée* and Mass. It was on such occasions that they discussed the affairs of their particular department: Foreign Affairs, war, Church matters, the royal household, and the like. The important decisions on these matters, however, were taken in the *Conseil d'état,* to which the Secretaries of State as such had no admission; in 1661 the War Minister, Le Tellier, was the only Secretary of State to sit in the *Conseil d'état;* the department of foreign affairs was represented not by Secretary of State Brienne but by Lionne, who to some degree resembled a minister without portfolio.

The Secretaries of State did not form a special group among themselves; ministers did not act as a group, had no common responsibility, and had no agreed principles of administration. The King was not averse to his most important servants' regarding one another with ill will and jealousy. He avoided giving any one of them a dominating position, by joining them together in

groups under his own presidency. At the same time he scrupulously avoided the emergence of ministerial solidarity among
them by holding the sessions of each council separately and by
dealing over the heads of these assemblies with individual ministers; merely for the sake of form were such decisions issued as
Arrêts du conseil. Divide et impera was the motto of this autocracy; all the threads of government led to the monarch, a system
that put a strain on the monarch's industry, patience, and governing skill that subsequent kings could not bear.

Louis XIV surrounded himself essentially with men of humble
origin who were incapable of darkening the splendor of his person, who owed him all, and whom he had trained himself, in some
cases, for royal service. This was true of Louvois, his War Minister, who was Le Tellier's son. A reaction occurred under the
Regent, who gave aristocracy again an increasing part in the
conduct of affairs; and later the influx of the aristocratic element
into the higher government posts could not be fended off, even
though the Regent's changes in the organic structure of the government did not last. The nobility regained a dominant position
in the state. True monarchical self-government such as Louis
XIV had exerted could not be maintained. Louis XV tried to
take the reins of government into his own hands on the death of
the last great First Minister, Fleury, in 1743, and to maintain the
old forms; but this produced, on the one hand, a government of
mistresses and favorites, and, on the other, an anarchic ministerial despotism that Frederick the Great sneeringly described as
a government, not of one king, but of four—the *Contrôleur général,* the Minister of War, the Minister of Marine, and the Minister
of Foreign Affairs.[16] As before, there were no plenary Council
sessions, and in any event the large number of councilors and the
lack of a directing authority would have made them futile. The
nodal point of government was the King's person, and the council as it was and remained could not serve in his place. The separate ministers dealt with the affairs of their departments as they
saw fit, and the *bureaux* that prepared the business gained undue

influence. This was the situation in the French *Ancien régime* right up to the Revolution.

The development of Prussia was simpler, and of course also much shorter. Here there were no Secretaries of State and no great court dignitaries. It is true that before Ilgen became minister he had been confidential secretary to the Elector, and that Frederick William I turned certain of his Cabinet secretaries into ministers, as was the case with Boden and Marschall; but this does not account for the rise of ministries in Prussia. The origin of ministries in Prussia was in the Privy Council: the collegiate secret Council became divided according to separate functions, and this division created the ministerial departments of the eighteenth century. In the seventeenth century the Council still formed an undivided unit, and constituted the main instrument of princely rule in the whole state: the Great Elector governed still in and with the Council. He was always accompanied by a number of councilors on his frequent travels and campaigns, and regular reports were sent to him from the councilors he had left behind. If he were at his residence at Cölln an der Spree, he held council himself; the published proceedings[17] make clear that after the matter had been presented and the councilors' opinions been expressed, the Elector himself would speak, summarize the results of the deliberation, and make his decision. He recommended this method of government to his successors in the Political Testament of 1667:

Listen carefully in the Council, note well the opinions of all the Councilors and have proper Minutes kept . . . when you have the Councilors give their opinions, see to it that the first to do so should be the Councilors in the lower ranks and not those of the higher ranks—on account of the senior councilors' authority the junior ones will not freely express their opinions and thoughts, for they are often derided and scoffed at by the senior councilors.[18]

The Council Ordinance of 1651 created a core for Cabinet government, but the core was not developed; nevertheless, government was not entirely absorbed in the Council. The Elector advised his successor on lines that he himself had found best in the course of time:

Conclude no important business in the presence of the Councilors, for secrecy is necessary; keep such affairs to yourself for your own consideration, call in once more a councilor and a secretary, ponder again over the opinions you have heard and decide on their merits; be like the bees, suck the best nectar from the flowers.

Presumably the Elector himself followed this course, as outlined to his successor, in the later part of his reign—when the proceedings are fully published, we will know. The government in council, as conducted in the first decade of his reign, obviously was not maintained; in this the development of the Council itself played its role. In its relation to the Elector it was of course a deliberative and consultative assembly; as regards the outside world it appeared in different guise, as chief executive authority. The Executive could be made effective, however, only if certain branches of the administration—chiefly the administration of the domains and of taxation—which stood in close relations with the local authorities and the central authority, were developed into a specialized organic structure; and once these departments were created, they established themselves as separate authorities outside the Privy Council's collegiate framework. Hence the origin of the central offices for administration of the domains of taxes and of police—offices consolidated into a General Directory in 1723.

Around the same time, Foreign Affairs—in which the maintenance of secrecy was of special influence—was entrusted to a committee (*engere Konferenz*) of two or three Privy Councilors. Over a long period of time, the old and experienced Ilgen had carried this burden by himself; but on his death in 1728 a special department of Foreign Affairs with three ministers was constituted. What remained of the functions of the old Privy Council was mainly the administration of justice and Church affairs. Thus, under Frederick William I the central authority was divided into three great ministerial departments; stemming from the old Council of State, they automatically acquired a collegiate organization. As a rule, Foreign Affairs was conducted by two to three ministers; justice by three to four who at the same time looked after Church affairs. In the General Directory there were at the outset four directing ministers whose functions were divided along provincial lines, and who administered internal and financial affairs.

Frederick the Great added a number of specialist ministers for commerce and manufactures, for the financing of army needs, for customs and excise, for mining and metallurgy, and for forestry. All business was to be dealt with collectively, although this principle could not be carried out in practice. There were no ministerial *bureaux* of the French type; only the two Privy Councilors in the foreign department were comparable, although in fact they were only expediting secretaries. In the General Directory the councilors who reported on departmental affairs were colleagues of the directing ministers, and had a voice equal to theirs in plenary sessions. The Department of Justice had no such councilors: everything that was not strictly Chancellory business had to be done by the ministers themselves. The ministers together continued to form the Council of State, and members introduced to and sworn into this body were accorded the title "Minister of State" (*Etatsminister*). But the Council of State was now merely a notional framework of government designating the ministers as a special class of person, not as a group of men engaged in a common task giving a rank rather than establishing a bureaucratic agency. It held no further regular plenary sessions, and was no longer a center of governmental activity.

After Frederick William I, the unity of administration was represented only by the Cabinet of the King, and he communicated with the ministers only in writing. The King usually spent his time in Potsdam, or was otherwise absent from Berlin; the ministers sent him their reports from there, and he then made his decisions by recording them in the margin or by issuing a Cabinet order. This method of government was continued under Frederick the Great, and under him autocracy was developed to the highest possible degree. He personally conducted correspondence with his diplomatic representatives at foreign courts. The department of Foreign Affairs was called "Cabinet ministry," yet it remained utterly distinct from the Royal Cabinet, although the Cabinet minister saw the King more frequently than did his colleagues in Justice or General Administration. The King as a rule received the ministers of the General Directory only once a year, at the beginning of the fiscal year; in the course of a morning in Potsdam the budgets were fixed and general administrative principles discussed. But otherwise there was only written communication in which the Cabinet took the initiative and gave the directions. Even the great reforms of the administration of justice carried out by Cocceji and later by Carmer were due to the King's initiative. He refused, in principle, to interfere in judiciary affairs, at least in civil cases, and proclaimed as an axiom that in courts the laws alone should speak, and the monarch be silent. The administration of the army, insofar as it was not purely economic in character, was carried on by the King in person, from his Cabinet, with the assistance of an adjutant general; only after his death was a specific central authority created, the Supreme Military Council (*Oberkriegskollegium*).

The King found this type of government superior to the government in council that prevailed in France; he explained his views on this in the Political Testament of 1752.[19] Wise political decisions could not, he felt, come from collegiate deliberations: a political system, like its philosophical counterpart, is the produce of one head. The ministers would always intrigue against one another, and mix up their private inclinations and dislikes with the interests of the state; their discussions in council, lively as they may sometimes have been, served more to obfuscate affairs than to offer enlightenment on them; and in any case secrets are never really kept if so many people are in the know. He had in mind the deterring example of France: the degeneration of the French governmental system was a permanent warning for him, and he passed it on to his successors, enjoining them to avoid governing by ministers.

With this type of autocracy, ministers were naturally only instruments of the monarch; they were expected to inform him of affairs, without his having to rely exclusively for this on them, and they had to direct and control the execution of his orders. They were not to present ideas and programs of their own; they existed purely as handymen for the monarch, and if they differed in opinion with him, they would have to be content with the *gloria obsequii.* They were neither departmental heads, the main departments being collegiately organized, nor did they form together a collective body of any solidarity.

One would expect that, under Frederick the Great's weaker successors, who were unable to deal with the burden of work that this type of absolutism involved, the ministers would have obtained a position of greater independence and responsibility. There was a tendency toward this, but it was impeded by changes that occurred in the Cabinet of the King. Under Frederick the Great the Cabinet secretaries with whom he worked had in reality been mere royal scribes; under his successors, and particularly under Frederick William III, they became the real advisers of the King, or, as Hardenberg once said, "Ministers in Secret." The perseverance with which Frederick the Great's successors clung to the old forms of autocracy thus resulted in a degeneration of Cabinet government. The old form of government from the Cabinet had been a real monarchical self-government, whereas the new form, government through the Cabinet, preserved former appearances but left all power in the hands of irresponsible agents, for they could always cover themselves by reference to royal commands; unlike the ministers, they had no professional connection with the executive agencies, and unlike the old Secretaries of State, they remained strictly separate from the ministers. This perverted system of government was notoriously responsible for the catastrophe of 1806.

In the eighteenth century France and Prussia were well on the way to being unified states, if they had not already become such. This cannot be said of Austria, and this essentially explains why the development of ministerial authorities there took a different course. As in France and in Prussia, the Privy Council was the chief consultative body for the ruler of the Austrian monarchy, but it did not, as elsewhere, become the very center of government.[20] It had in the first place no organic relation with local authorities. To a large extent the various territories preserved their administrative independence, using the remnants of the Estates institutions; consequently no modern provincial authorities which might have served as agents of the Privy Council in the provinces came into existence until the middle of the eighteenth century. Correspondence with the territorial authorities centered exclusively, as in the past, in the Court Chancellery (*Hofkanzlei*), which had maintained an independent existence next to the Council, and which permitted the local administration of the various territories and their Estate institutions a freedom of activity that existed neither in the France of the intendants nor in the Prussia of the provincial commissariats.

A second factor that gradually undermined the importance of the Privy Council was the eminent position of the Court Chancellor; he not only headed the Chancellery but also sat in the Council, of which he was the most important member, the true representative of political tradition and the monarch's most trusted servant. The Privy Council of the Emperor was composed of nobles whose approach to affairs was distinctly amateur, and among them the Chancellor was in reality the only truly modern official. Under his direction the matters to be discussed were prepared in the Chancellery and they were presented to the Privy Council through officials of the Court Chancellery. In consequence the Privy Council gradually became dependent on the Court Chancellery and in particular on its chief, the Chancellor. This position resembled that of the European Secretaries of State; and as Secretary of the Imperial Cabinet and member of the Privy Council, he became a kind of Prime Minister. Thus it happened that the Court Chancellery he headed developed into the very center of administration.

The old form of Chancellery administration, under which the

Chancellery was a unit independent from the agencies of the Council, was preserved longer in the case of Austria than in any other country; after 1654, however, the Chancellery itself assumed collegiate forms and became the agency deciding and executing administrative measures; it acquired greater practical significance than the Privy Council as the proper executive authority of the whole Empire. It had originally separate departments for Bohemia and Hungary; but as administration became proportionately more intense in the second half of the seventeenth century, provincial autonomy won out even in the highest government agency, so that a Bohemian and a Hungarian Chancellery were established as special offices side by side with the Austrian Chancellery, and we find later special court chancelleries for Transylvania, Italy, and the Low Countries. The office of Austrian Court Chancellor was doubled under Joseph I, the first having the Imperial household and foreign affairs in his charge, the second *provincialia* and *iudicalia*. These positions, and not the Privy Council or its Confidential Committee, were the effective centers of government.

When, after the War of Succession, Maria Theresa attempted to reform administration because increased administrative unity was hoped to provide greater military and financial power, she abolished in consequence what remained of the old Privy Council, and developed the new ministerial authorities out of the Court Chancelleries. By separating Justice from administration, she created a "Joint Austrian and Bohemian Court Chancellery" and a "Supreme Office of Justice" for the Cisleithanian lands; furthermore, a "Chancellery of the Household, the Court, and the State" (*Haus-, Hof-, und Staatskanzlei*) was split off from the Austrian Court Chancellery and charged with foreign policy and household affairs. The Hungarian territories kept their special organization, only the old "Court Chamber" (*Hofkammer*) and the old "Court Council of War" (*Hofkriegsrat*) remaining in existence as supreme authorities common to all the territories. This left the Habsburg Monarchy at a longer remove from modern types of ministerial organization than Prussia and France; only in one respect was the Habsburg Monarchy in advance of the other two: the removal of the old Council of State as supreme governing authority. Maria Theresa constituted a new Council of State in 1760 as a consultative body without executive power,[21] and this may well have served as a model for the subsequent Councils of State that emerged in France and Prussia; it is not known, however, whether that was really the case. We may omit from the present context the precipitate centralizing reforms of Joseph II, for later the Monarchy essentially returned to Maria Theresa's organization, which existed until the recent transformations. Here, too, unity lay only in the self-governing monarch's person, though there was no Cabinet government of the autocratic temper of Frederican Prussia. The Austrian system was characterized by regular personal communication between monarch and ministers, partly by means of individual audiences, partly through conferences where several administrative chiefs were present: ministers took a much more significant share in government than was the case in Prussia. The State Chancellor, from Kaunitz to Metternich, generally had the decisive influence on foreign policy. Maria Theresa had originally intended to make the Council of State a regular consultative body at the Crown's service in all matters of internal administration, and to leave the executive power to the ministers; but this was only imperfectly realized. In the end the Council of State became significant only as regards the preparation of the great reforming laws and the over-all supervision of administration. Maria Theresa did not carry on any "government in council" of the type associated with Louis XIV or the Great Elector of Brandenburg; those ministers who were not present in the Council nonetheless continued to influence the Empress's decisions. In the course of his reign Joseph II put an end to the collegiate sessions of the Council of State, preferring to consult single state-councilors in addition to the ministers. His method of governing came close to the more autocratic form of govern-

ment from the Cabinet: with Kaunitz he had chiefly written contacts, he surrounded himself with secretaries, and restricted his
contacts with the ministers. This contact did not wholly cease,
however, nor did the personal influence of the ministers. This was
true of both Joseph II and his successors, in spite of the increasing importance of the Cabinet.

There was no question here of a collegiate ministerial solidarity; only very occasionally did ministerial conferences take place.
In the order of organization of the higher authorities the departments of Foreign Affairs, the Interior, of Justice, Finances, and
War took clear shape; but their functions extended partly over
the whole monarchy, partly over parts of it, and the organization
vacillated between collegiate and hierarchical notions—or, as it
was said in Austria, between *gremial* (by groups) and *präsidial*
(presidial) conduct of affairs. In the supreme office of Justice, judicial administration and court proceedings were not yet separated for reasons of principle. But the same was true, throughout
the entire eighteenth century, for Prussia, at least so far as the
penal code was concerned.

If we survey the activities of Continental absolutist rulers from
the viewpoint of ministerial organization, we can see that an important step forward was taken in the gradual transformation
of the separate departments into specialist ministries charged
with particular branches of administration, and in providing
increased strength of executive energy, mainly through establishing an organic connection between district and local agencies.
Ministries were not only the seat of the sovereign's advisors but
also the heads of an administrative body. But modern unity, and
relative independence, were still lacking, just as were rational
clarity and simplicity in the delimitation of their functions. The
principle of specialization was nowhere fully asserted; it still
overlapped with the old territorial principle of division. The old
idea of collegiate bodies—an idea that came from the Councils of
State and was retained in part in the institutions of those Councils—came into conflict with a new principle, that of the exclu-

sive authority, direction, and responsibility of one minister for his department. Collegiate solidarity of the ministers was utterly unknown: any unity the administration possessed lay purely and simply in the person of the monarch, and otherwise there was no unity. Autocratic absolutism had no interest in permitting such a consolidation and strengthening of the ministerial authority that it could function independently. It wanted a suitable instrument likely to follow all impulses from above and to carry out the details of administration according to the established pattern.

In the ministerial circles we find tendencies toward an increase in the importance and independence of their offices, and toward a clearer and more rational organization of the bureaucratic apparatus. Moreover, the spirit of the times at the turn of the eighteenth and nineteenth centuries worked in the direction of stronger and freer development of personality as well as a rational, planned, and lucid shaping of the administrative order. The France of Louis XVI and similarly the Prussia of Frederick William III saw all kinds of experiments aiming at reforms in the arrangements of the ministerial agencies: in France, however, only the Revolution, and in Prussia the era of reform after 1806, has made realization of these efforts possible. The Continent was far advanced beyond England regarding the internal structure of the ministerial agencies, both the delimitation of functions and the organization of departments. But after the end of the seventeenth century, the influence of parliamentary institutions produced new, epoch-making changes in the position of the ministers, which served as a model later on the Continent.

In England the year 1679 can be considered the beginning of a new phase in the history of ministerial development. A strong parliamentary opposition had again come into life; closer supervision of financial affairs was brought in with the introduction of an appropriations clause; the growing influence of Parliament in general enforced a stricter cohesion of the ministerial offices. The "Cabinet," henceforth an assembly of departmental heads, separated from the Privy Council as a permanent commission and adopted stricter collegiate solidarity.[22] We meet here for the first time a typical phenomenon: increased responsibility to Parliament compels the ministry as a whole to greater unity. The Crown's interests were at harmony in this respect with those of Parliament. It is true, the "Cabal" ministry was attacked; the new institution was purposely deprived of a base in statute, but it was nonetheless ultimately accepted as an inevitable prerequisite for effective parliamentary responsibility of the ministers. The Cabinet was at that time an instrument of the royal prerogative, and such it was to remain even after the Revolution of 1688, despite the strengthening of the parliamentary factor that accompanied the revolution. William III was the master, as far as the ministers were concerned; he personally conducted foreign policy, and asserted his will in the ministry. Parliament still regarded the King's ministers with mistrust, trying both to make them more responsible to Parliament and also to exclude them as far as possible from any influence on Parliament.

The Act of Settlement of 1700 established that in the future, after the accession of the House of Hanover, questions of government should be deliberated in the Privy Council and that the assenting members of the Council of State should be required to countersign the monarch's decrees of government; that, furthermore, the ministers of the King, like other officials, were to appear before the House only on being summoned by the Commons. These arrangements were suspended, however, before they could be put into practice. Parliamentary control had effectively made Parliament a second government, and the ministers themselves gradually became the trusted agents and leaders of the parties. This turn toward parliamentary government developed slowly and by no means steadily during the eighteenth century, and was completed only in the nineteenth. It began when the two Hanoverian kings ceased to conduct affairs in person: George I spoke no English at all, and George II did not speak it well enough to negotiate with English ministers in the

Cabinet Council, as William III had done. Besides, circumstances firmly bound them to the Whigs, and it thus happened that the chiefs of this party, who formed the ministry, introduced a new type of government the essence of which was that the ministry —closely united under the leadership of a Prime Minister—was virtually independent of the King, managing affairs in agreement with the majority of the House of Commons. The party and class rule, established in the era of Walpole, was shamelessly plutocratic, and provoked a reaction that brought Pitt to the helm.

Pitt regarded himself as a Whig, but he fought the selfish rule of a clique consisting of a small group of great landowners and capitalist magnates, who exercised power under the Whig name. He associated himself with Bolingbroke's Tory notion of a "Patriot King" who stood above party for the *salus publica;* Pitt wished to conduct affairs as the servant not of a party but of such a King. The personal self-government remained excluded, and the ministry still remained leader of the parliamentary majority. Pitt considered desirable that one prominent member of the Cabinet—the First Lord of the Treasury or the Chancellor of the Exchequer—should belong to the Lower House and direct the government party. If the first Lord of the Treasury (who usually was the Prime Minister) was a peer, then he had his position in the Upper House, in which the Lord Chancellor presided. There thus began an organic connection of ministry and Parliament, and particularly with the government party in the Commons. This is the feature that strikingly distinguished the English ministerial system from its Continental counterparts, and has remained peculiar to it until today.

George III, the first of the Hanoverian Kings to be born and bred in England and to feel with pride that he was English, attempted to reconstitute a personal rule such as William III had conducted; but his attempt failed, because of the heavy-handedness and the failure of the American policy and because of the common resistance of the two parliamentary parties, which in the meantime had been effectively transformed. Both the Tories and the Whigs rejected the King's attempts at personal rule, the Whigs seeking a purely parliamentary party government in which the majority party would provide the King with ministers; the Tories wanted to preserve the Crown's freedom of choice in appointing and dismissing ministers, and took the line that Crown, Lower House, and Upper House were to some extent three equal powers in politics which must achieve a balance among themselves: they argued that a ministry that had the Crown and the Lords on its side might govern at least for some time even against a Commons majority. In the dramatic contest between the younger Pitt and Fox (1783), Pitt won through with this new Tory principle; he returned to the approach of his father, but became a Tory, even in name. He defended the prerogative of the Crown against the Whig doctrine of parliamentarism; but personal rule by the King remained excluded, and George III's repeated mental disorder, which terminated in utter madness, favored this system of government just as did the limited personal talents of George III's successor.

It was in reality the ministry that conducted the government, standing as a special third power between Crown and Parliament; Pitt's successors were however unable to preserve their independence from parties to the same extent. From 1783 to 1830 there were Tory governments; but the change of government in 1830 represented a victory of the Whig doctrine; and when the Cabinet again changed in 1835 even Peel, a Conservative minister, had to recognize the fact that no ministry could govern England against the will of the majority of the House of Commons. This established the system of parliamentary government according to which the government is identical with the ruling committee of the majority party. Appointment by the Crown became a mere formality, and so did membership in the Privy Council—of which formally, even today, the Cabinet is a committee. If the government is outvoted on an important matter in the Lower House, it returns its mandate, and the Crown, acting on the Cabinet's advice, entrusts the leader of the Opposition with the formation of a new Cabinet whose members, if they are not so yet, automatically become Privy Councilors.

The role of the Prime Minister implies that the Cabinet will act in uniformity—a characteristic phenomenon of English public life and an innovation that stems from the parliamentary responsibility built into the English ministerial system in the eighteenth century. This responsibility assumed a different form, since Parliament became itself an element in government: the old form of ministerial indictment, in form of impeachment, disappeared, since a vote of no confidence was enough to procure the resignation of the Ministry, or that of a dissenting member of it. The Cabinet as a whole, as a collegiate body, and not single departments as on the Continent, set the political course. This fact, which was related to the weakening of the monarch's power, was an object of emulation for liberal politicians on the Continent. In the formation of the single departments, however, England remained far behind the Continent.

Burke had proposed certain reforms in 1780 aiming at a stricter unification of the ministerial departments and a more sharply defined limitation of their functions. Such reforms, which, as he hoped, would organize financing, accounting, and budgeting in a clearer and less confusing way, pointed to the example of Frederican Prussia. Pitt took up these reforming tendencies, but realized them only partially: it was only in the nineteenth century that the English ministerial offices were properly consolidated and marked off from each other. Furthermore, as a significant consequence of the cohesion and concentration which parliamentary responsibility requires, the collegiate ministries, the commissions, were altered in their bureaucratic organization and received a pyramidal structure: individual members of these collegiate bodies—for instance, the Chancellor of the Exchequer and the First Lord of the Admiralty—were members of the Cabinet and as such became principally responsible for their department and obtained the decisive voice in its conduct. The ministerial departments did not, however, become bureaucratically organ-

ized; even the Boards established after the 1870s (the Board of
Local Government, the Board of Trade, the Board of Education,
etc.) represent a kind of mid-way stage between collegiate
and hierarchical organization, a commission with a head but
without strict subordination of the other members under the
responsible departmental head, as is usual in Continental ministries. Not only in the Cabinet as a whole but also in the single
ministries, more reliance is placed upon agreement than upon
orders from above. Nonetheless, this change shows a closer ap-
proximation to the Continental pattern.

If collegiate solidarity of the council of ministers was first realized in England, France preceded England in creating the structure of the modern departmental ministries. I cannot go into the
attempts at consolidation made before the Revolution.[23] The
really decisive change occurred only after the transformation of
the *Etats généraux* into the *Assemblée Nationale,* after the storming of the Bastille and the night of August 4, a few days after the
entry of Necker into his second ministry; obviously the need for
dealings with a parliament changed the entire organization of
Conseils and *ministerial* agencies at one stroke into a single assembly of departmental chiefs. A royal Règlement of August 9,
1789,[24] achieved this *Réunion des Conseils:* the *Conseil des dépêches* and the *Conseil royal des finances* (to which the *Conseil
du commerce*—a Royal Council in the eighteenth century that
ranked with the three others—had been joined some years before
the Revolution) were united with the *Conseil d'état* and henceforth bore simply the latter's title. The *Conseil d'état* thus swal-
lowed up the other councils.

The Almanac Royal of 1790 gives a list of its members:[25] apart
from the King at its head, there were four Ministers of State,
among them the *Garde des sceaux,* who took the Chancellor's
place, and Necker, the First Minister of finance; furthermore the
four secretaries of state. Their departments already deserve
the name "specialist ministries," one being for Foreign Affairs,
the second for Marine, the third for the royal household, ecclesi-

astical affairs, benefices, civil appointments, and the internal administration of almost all the provinces and *généralités;* the fourth department of the Minister of War, however, administered the newly acquired provinces and frontier areas of strategic importance. The designation "Minister of the Interior" does not yet occur; but the third department, that of Count St. Priest, who also countersigned the *Règlement* of August 9, was essentially a combination of ministries for the royal household, Cults and Public Worship, and the Interior.

At the same time the single ministries were reorganized on a bureaucratic basis; their divisions into special *sections* under heads and *premiers commis* suggest the structure of a modern ministry. The *Constituante* did little to alter this structure. The Decree of April 27–May 25, 1791[26] abolished only the two Ministries without Portfolio (a Marshal and an Archbishop), supplanted the Chancellorship by a Ministry of Justice, and fully consolidated the Ministry of the Interior, which acquired this designation. The description *Conseil d'état* was preserved for the ministers as a whole. The essential contribution of this decree was its definition of ministerial responsibility and of the constitutional positions of the ministers. These prescriptions were inspired by the principle of the separation of the executive and legislative power. The ministers were agents of the executive power, appointed and dismissed by the King, but they were responsible also to the legislative assembly. Their responsibility was a personal one of each individual minister; the single departments were the center of gravity in the regular administration, the *Conseil* emerging as some guarantee of unity, but in an essentially subsidiary way. Its chief function was general political direction: the great political decisions, acceptance or rejection of the laws resolved by the legislative; general planning of political proceedings, general disposition for campaigns and the like—all such issues belonged under the competence of the *Conseil*. The Constitution of 1791 altered none of the essentials here: where the ruling notion was the principle of the separation of powers, there could be no question of parliamentary government.

This principle, and the constitution as a whole, did not prove to be permanent, but the structure of the six specialist departments remained as a basis for further development. The Convention of course in its turn abolished the ministries, and handed over their functions to executive *comités*, with the *Comité du salut public* at the top. The Directory, however, returned to the system of specialist ministries, even though the positions of the ministers were effectively subordinate to that of the Directory, which took main responsibility. This was, in essentials, the ministerial system of the Consulate and again of the First Empire. Napoleon I conducted a kind of government from the Cabinet: the specialist ministers, whose number was increased by him to eleven, were no more than handymen of the Emperor. He communicated with them through the Secretary of State, Maret, who was a kind of Cabinet secretary with ministerial rank—similar to the position of the Secretaries of State in the absolute monarchy. There was as little chance of the ministry's developing a corporate solidarity as of their becoming responsible to a legislative assembly. But an essential novelty that supplemented the ministerial administration of the Napoleonic epoch was a Council of State that had no part in administration and was separated from the ministry. This Napoleonic Council of State clearly served as a prototype for the Prussian one of 1817 and similar institutions in other lands; it was primarily entrusted with the preparatory deliberation of laws and a section of it served as an administrative High Court. This form of State Council has been preserved until the present day.

The Constitution of 1814 again introduced proper constitutional responsibility, and the July Monarchy even saw some kind of parliamentary government, though the ministry tended to influence the formation of the Chamber far more than the Chamber did the ministry. Napoleon III returned to his uncle's principles, rejected any notion of ministerial solidarity, and employed ministers merely in consultative and executive functions. These ministers had little to do with the popular representation: in the assembly they could not be called to account, and the preparation of new laws was done as in the times of Napoleon I, by commissioners of the *Conseil d'état*. From 1860 onward, however, Napoleon III found it necessary to adopt more constitutional procedures, and this naturally affected the ministers' positions, for they henceforth were required to answer questions in the legislature; in 1869 they formed a *conseil*. But it was only with the Republic that a properly parliamentary form of government was established, such that today—as is the case in England—a Prime Minister forms the Cabinet from suitable elements taken from the majority party. Since then France has had rapidly changing parliamentary ministries, and current business is dealt with entirely by the professional officials in their *bureaux*. Each ministry is divided into sections in accordance with its principal functions, and the sections are divided again into *bureaux*. This is a clear and logical organization: it has existed since Napoleon's time and has frequently been used as model.

In Prussia[27] Stein demanded, even before the catastrophe of 1806, the end of government from the Cabinet and the establishment of a collegiate council of five specialist ministers. He was obviously thinking of the French Ministry of 1791, although the legal position of such a Prussian ministry would have been widely different from that of the French—because of the lack of a contribution in Prussia. The great alteration that Prussia would have had to undergo, were such arrangements made, was the limitation of royal self-government. It is comprehensible, therefore, that the demands of the reformers met tough resistance on the part of Frederick William III and that he gave in only step by step. The Cabinet was not abolished, though it lost its baneful influence. The King entered upon direct and constant contact with his ministers; and the concrete ministerial organization was formed in close connection with the former institutions. The principle of division according to functions was completely realized, however, and the single ministries acquired a hierarchical form in place of the old collegiate one. The plan which Stein, after the improvizations of the first years, left behind as a well-considered organizational scheme provided for a return to the old combination of Council of State and ministries. In contrast to the situation existing before 1806, he intended that the unity of government would reside in the revived State Council. The ministers were to be mere agents, executive organs of this larger body, in which all the administrative chiefs were to be represented with equal voting rights, together with the royal princes and particularly trusted persons. This Council of State was to be the real supreme government agency; the ministers were merely departmental chiefs and executives.

Stein's evident intention was to counteract ministerial capriciousness or incompetence by means of this institution: for the ministers were not as yet restrained or driven into action by parliamentary responsibility; only the monarch possessed any degree of control over them. One may doubt, however, whether this grandiose plan could have proved itself, if executed, even if Stein had taken part as Minister without Portfolio, as was his intention. Without him it proved to be wholly impracticable, the outcome of it being the Dohna-Altenstein ministry; this was indeed a collegiate ministry of five departmental chiefs, but it was unable to cope with the difficult situation, so that in 1810 there was a return to a Prime Ministerial system; in fact this had been the position enjoyed by Stein, and Hardenberg before him, in the years 1807 and 1808. The Council of State thereby lost any character as supreme government agency; it was to serve only to draft laws, and this is the way in which it came into being in 1817. Hardenberg, as State Chancellor (*Staatskanzler*), had the right to demand information and accounts of their administration from all the ministers, to suspend any of their orders that seemed to him inadvisable pending decision by the King, and, if necessary, to give directives over the heads of the ministers— and they had quite simply to resign themselves to them. These arrangements contained something of the spirit of the Napoleonic ministerial arrangements, only in this case the weight lay rather with the Chancellor than with the monarch. The Chancellor controlled all contacts of the ministers with the King; all their reports had to be forwarded through him (he usually minuted them in the margin for the King's perusal); and reports of the ministers to the King took place in the presence of the Chancellor.

The Chancellor of State thus acquired such complete power that the ministry's collegiate organization, which was established without any particular decree, became rather meaningless. The weekly conferences of the entire Ministry were not of central significance; the real business was done in the single ministries, and above all in the Cabinet—a name given to the conferences held by the King with the Chancellor of State, to which specialist ministers were summoned only individually and occasionally. Nonetheless, Hardenberg hoped that after his death the office of the State Chancellor would cease and the collegiate nature of the ministry would be reinforced; it is clear from his papers that this was the purpose of the Cabinet Order of 1817. In his lifetime, however, the State Chancellor preserved his own preponderant position in its entirety, despite the increase in the functions of the ministry. In 1819 Humboldt attempted, with the aid of Boyen and Beyme, to overthrow the Chancellor, in order to establish a direct connection between the person of the King and the ministry that was to be headed by a Minister President; but he failed.

Although after Hardenberg's death the office of a State Chancellor soon disappeared, the old system still left the custom whereby one of the Ministers—who was in fact styled Cabinet Minister—acted as go-between between the ministry and the monarch, a custom that came to an end only with the establishment of the United Diet, and effectively with the creation of a constitution. The constitution altered nothing in the organization of the ministry, and nothing of any note in its functions; but parliamentary responsibility nonetheless enforced a stricter cohesion of the ministry under a Minister President; the Cabinet Order of September 8, 1852, granted Minister von Manteuffel, as Minister President, a somewhat limited general power of direction as well as control over discussions of departmental affairs of the single ministers with the King. Even with these powers,

however, the position of Minister President in Prussia by no
means corresponds to that of a Prime Minister in England, or in
France, or in any other parliamentary country.

Bismarck once stressed this very heavily in the Chamber of
Deputies. The position he created for himself vis-à-vis his ministerial colleagues was not any different from that of a Prime
Minister—except perhaps vis-à-vis the War Minister, who always
remained in close touch with the King. But this position existed
by virtue of Bismarck's forceful personality and the authority
he gained from possessing the King's confidence, and not by virtue of the regulations in the Cabinet Order, to which he had recourse only when his position began to weaken. Even the greatness of his influence cannot conceal the fact that the person of
the monarch is the center of government; for the King of Prussia
never ceased to rule himself. Consequently the ministry has remained a corps of civil servants, a royal collegiate council of the
old style, which assisted the monarch in his government but did
not restrict him by parliamentary devices, still less supplanted
him in the government. The greatest importance in affairs belongs
not to the government as a whole but to the single ministries.
The Ministry is of course organized collegiately, but its collegiate sessions are not of central significance for the conduct of
political affairs; it is concentrated in the personal contact of the
Minister President and the single ministers with the King; this
involves a certain control by the Minister President on the lines
laid down by the Cabinet Order of 1852. Frederick William IV
once asserted to Minister President Camphausen that the Ministry must present a united front to the country at large, and also,
naturally, to foreign powers; but the King must always have to
deal only with single ministers; they ought not confront the King
as a solid collective, fixed in its resolves, for the King must not
be put in the position of having to give way before a unanimous
opposition or, alternatively, to dismiss the entire ministry.

This principle seems to have been realized in Prussia. Here the
King does not merely reign, he himself governs; the ministers are

primarily his servants, selected of course with an eye to the parliamentary majority with which they have to get along; but they do not depend on this majority, and their aims will always be to create the majorities that will enable them to rule. The differences between a monarchical-constitutional and a parliamentary government is thus reflected in the diverse structure of the ministries: the parliamentary form of government knows a cohesive, united Cabinet, led by a Prime Minister, whereas the monarchical-constitutional government, in which the personal rule of the monarch has left its traces, has a system of ministerial conferences, in which not the attainment of collegiate decisions but the manifold relations with the sovereign and the strength of the influence of individual ministers are essential. To the outside world, particularly vis-à-vis the popular representatives, this ministry appears as a unit, as the main representative of the policy of the government.

The course taken by most of the larger federal states was similar to that taken in Prussia. In Austria-Hungary only the Revolution of 1848 brought a rather sudden transformation of the ministerial agencies, in the constitutional pattern of a responsible collegiate ministry. There was at first, however, as little substance to this as there was to the Constitution itself; after 1851 it was replaced by a ministerial conference of the old style, where there was no trace of parliamentary responsibility nor indeed of collegiate solidarity. Finally, after absolutism and the idea of a centralized, unified state had been abandoned, all kinds of experiments were tried, but none of them resulted in arrangements of permanence. Finally, after the Compromise with Hungary in 1867, separate Austrian and Hungarian Ministries of State were called into existence, while an Imperial Ministry took charge of Joint Affairs. All these ministries were collegiate, and responsible to popular representatives; but they lacked the solidarity that marked the English Cabinet, they did not decide on questions of government by majority votes, and they were regarded as consultative and executive organs of the monarch. In particular the Joint Ministry was supposed to maintain and give expression to the spirit of governmental unity. The present crisis shows the difficulties of this task. It would seem that Hungary is gradually developing a system of parliamentary government with ministers from political parties, whereas in Austria this is hardly possible because of the nationality conflicts, and the government there remains a ministry of civil servants. For the rest, the abnormality of the state's structure makes conditions distinctly complicated and peculiar. Figures such as that of Hungarian Minister at Court or Austrian *Landsmannminister* (representatives of the nationalities in the ministry) show how, next to the constitution, the historical origins of a state have shaped the nature of the ministerial system.

In the German Empire, parliamentary government has asserted itself as little as in the component federal states, but even here we can detect an important deviation in the structure of the ministerial system caused by the manner in which the state originated. Administration in the Empire is constitutionally concentrated in the person of the Imperial Chancellor, on whom the Secretaries of State, the holders of the Imperial offices, are dependent. The cause is the federal character of the Empire, which required, in the interest of vigorous action, the concentration of executive power in the authority of a supreme Minister. A collegiate Ministry functioning next to the Federal Council (*Bundesrat*) would have been an excessively clumsy and complicated institution.

Politicians who demand the creation of responsible Imperial ministries generally demand also a unitary reform of the constitution. Similarly, the political responsibility of the Cabinet of the United States of America is to such an extent inferior to the President that it resembles the Napoleonic system rather than a constitutional. This is the result of the early institution of strong and responsible Presidential power, which was intended as a counterweight to particularist ambitions; but it is also due to the principle of the separation of the legislative and executive powers which, in contrast to the monarchical France of 1791, has proved practicable in the United States at least up to a point. In this case there can be no question of parliamentary ministers. In Switzerland the Federal Council owes its existence to a republican distaste for the exercise of power by any single person; this Council combines the functions of a ministry with those of a Head of State. It may be said that, in general, the typical ministry of today grew out of a monarchic, unitary state, and thus cannot easily be reconciled with a federal state or a republic that has no monarchical history; in such cases, it must undergo considerable alteration.

This concludes my remarks on the subject. We have covered a period of five hundred years in a very brief survey; and in conclusion we must deal with a general question. Can we observe a general, dominant trend that might indicate the direction of future developments? Well aware that caution must be exercised, I should like nevertheless to stress one point: it is unmistakably true that the formation of the ministries of state and of government depends on the groups of the political society which possess the greatest moral strength and in which state ethos, national consciousness, and political energy are most alive—in short, where the will and the capacity for leadership are most powerfully expressed. Clearly, these circles gradually extend to that degree to which the idea of the state permeates the people as a whole and makes them able to act as a united body. At the outset the seat of government is identical with the person and the Court of the King; then, in England, a Parliamentary self-governing aristocracy developed, and on the Continent, ministerial rule of civil servants became prevailing. Where in political life the free forces of society gained the upper hand, there is a parliamentary form of government, and the ministerial structure is correspondingly transformed; there is even an occasional tendency to pass from parliamentarism to pure democracy, where the will of the politically organized people directly determines the men who are to direct public life. This is the case not only in

Switzerland and America, but also in England, where the parliamentary ministry is developing further and further into a popular dictatorship of the Prime Minister: similarly in France, where parliamentary government is placed above a military-bureaucratic state machinery that is being progressively democratized, though without sacrificing its military-bureaucratic elements. In Germany and to a degree in Austria as well, the military and bureaucratic organization, the true backbone of the political body, is still so firmly tied to the monarchical head that Hardenberg's old motto "democratic institutions under monarchical government" has not yet lost its importance. German political development is almost three hundred years behind that of Western states; and even though the original lag in the level of political culture seems to be rapidly lessening, an impartial observer cannot avoid becoming aware that the population of the German Empire, and likewise of Prussia and the other Federal States, has not by a long shot achieved that measure of national solidarity, of practical conciliation of the social and religious conflicts, by which a people becomes capable of determining its own fate. In future centuries such development will take place also in Germany so long as it is not interfered with from the outside; but for the near future it would seem impossible that, considering the exposed geographical position of Germany, the immense tension among our parties, the splintering and the inconsistencies of middle-class politics, a parliamentary government, let alone direct democratic rule, should be suitable for Germany. The energy of national consciousness is centered in our governments, the monarchical institutions, the army and the civil service, rather than in the masses of the people; thus, a majority of nationally conscious citizens regards the vigorous maintenance of these institutions the best guarantee of satisfactory development. This and not a false reactionary policy, is the reason why a ministry of civil servants as organ of a monarchical-constitutional government has remained in existence in Germany and will remain in existence in the foreseeable future.

7

THE COMMISSARY AND HIS
SIGNIFICANCE IN GENERAL
ADMINISTRATIVE HISTORY
A COMPARATIVE STUDY

In 1919, when this article was published, the Prussian Administration was organized in a strictly hierarchical way. Its head was the Minister of Interior; under him, at the head of the provinces into which Prussia was divided, was the *Oberpräsident*. The provinces were divided into *Regierungsbezirke* (districts) headed by a *Regierungspräsident*, and the *Regierungsbezirke* were divided into *Kreise* (counties) headed by a *Landrat*. There is a certain parallel to the military hierarchy, with generals as commanders of corps, lieutenant generals as commanders of divisions, and major generals as commanders of brigades. It is evident that Hintze's study tried to understand and explain the genesis of a strictly hierarchical centralized administration, independent of popular representation, without self-government; and this attempt led him to recognize in the Prussian phenomenon only a particular form of a general European development that resulted in the establishment of modern bureaucracies. The article is detailed and technical, therefore, in its first part, which deals with Prussia; the second half offers a masterly survey of developments all over Europe.

In its emphasis on the crucial importance of the bureaucracy for the emergence of the modern state, in its demonstration of the importance of power politics for its internal organization, in its separation of English developments from those on the Continent, this essay touches upon some of Hintze's most fundamental ideas, and is one of his most characteristic products. The article is a strictly scholarly but clear presentation of the result of extensive research in sources, and as such hardly needs an explanation. It is a work abounding in technical expressions. If they are translated the German word is given in parentheses; if the German word is left untranslated in the text an explanation will be found in the glosses. Quotations which Hintze gave in the original language are not translated, because Hintze evidently believed that their exact wording was significant.

The institution of the commissary as an extraordinary organ of state power in contrast to ordinary officials and agencies has received no thorough consideration in the theory of modern administrative law, even though in practice it plays a role of some importance, albeit complicated and theoretically hard to grasp. Its importance was much greater in the administrative history of the period from the fifteenth to the eighteenth century, when it lay at the heart of the great monarchical reforms that created the modern state. It is my intention in the present study to trace its widely ramified manifestations in various countries and various periods (as far as the present incompleteness and uneven depth of research will permit) in order to direct the attention of my colleagues to this object of study in comparative administrative history. It has as yet hardly been touched as a whole, and closer examination certainly promises to enlighten us further.

I

It is no secret that the eighteenth century Prussian administrative organization derived its characteristic features from the commissarial authorities that had chiefly developed out of the military commissaries. The military commissary appeared simultaneously with the emergence of new mercenary armies as the supreme commander's appointed watchdog over his interests in all their various forms. In Brandenburg, as in Germany as a whole, he appeared first in the seventeenth century as successor to the old recruiting officers (*Musterherren*), supervising the captains, colonels, and generals who, under the *condotta* system, led the troops enlisted for the supreme commander, half as military officers and half as financial speculators. In accordance with the military hierarchy and the division of the units, military commissaries emerged with various degrees of rank and jurisdiction, as *Generalkommissarien, Oberstkommissarien,* and simply commissaries. They were supposed to make sure that in the mustering of troops, the general, colonel, or captain had filled his quota of men, that the troops were all present and in good order, and that they were receiving the right wages. In particular the General War Commissary (*Generalkriegskommissarius*), the head of military administration as a colleague or subordinate of the general or field marshal, was to ensure that provisions, weapons, and munitions were in ample supply, that fortresses were in a sound state for defense, that justice in the army was properly administered and that taxes (*Kontributionen**) regularly flowed in.

Beside these military commissaries proper, who accompanied the army and the regiments, there were so-called district commissaries (*Landkommissarien*), who looked after the interests of a particular geographic region (*Provinz, Amt,* or *Kreis*) in matters concerning movement, quartering, fighting, or encampment of troops. Particularly they supervised and managed the collection and use of taxes (*Kontributionen*) raised for military purposes. As a rule these district commissaries were "decreed," but paid by the local inhabitants; they were named by the sovereign, but sometimes (as in Brandenburg with the military commissaries) following nomination by the Estates. Occasionally, to distinguish them from the recruiting commissaries (*Musterkommissarien*), they were known as troop commissaries (*Marschkommissare*), but the designation "military commissary" was also applied to them. After about 1660 many of their functions passed over to the true military commissaries, who now became permanent bureaucrats simultaneously with the formation of a standing army. Together with their military administrative functions, these bureaucrats took over supervision and control of taxation,

---

* *Kontribution.* A tax levied on peasants for the purpose of maintaining the army.

which involved far-reaching police responsibilities and administrative jurisdiction.

The same agencies that were concerned with maintaining the army and ensuring a regular inflow of taxes were also made responsible for maintaining and developing the prosperity of the population and their ability to pay taxes—above all, they had to take care of the provisioning of towns and the commerce among them. Thus military administration became inseparably entangled with civilian and police administration; the whole internal police system that gradually developed from this bore a militaristic cast. This was the distinguishing mark of the Prussian administrative system, setting it apart from those of other German states such as Saxony, Bavaria, and Austria, where the war commissary remained to a large extent a purely military, partly extraordinary appointment without becoming organically bound to the regular civil administration.

In Prussia this new civil bureaucracy of the commissarial authorities was constructed on three levels: the General War Commissary (*Generalkriegskommissar*) in the central office, the Higher War Commissaries (*Oberkriegskommissarien*) in charge of individual provinces, and the plain war commissaries and tax commissaries (*Kriegs- und Steuerkommissarien*) in the local office. Corresponding to the juridical structure of the administration these plain commissars came in three kinds: *commissarii loci* (local commissaries) for the towns, after the introduction of the excise tax; county commissioners (*Kreiskommissarien*) for counties ruled by nobles (*ritterschaftliche Kreisverbände*), which only gradually came to be regular administrative districts; and, occasionally, as district commissioners (*Ämterkommissarien*) for the sovereign's domains, which really did not belong to the counties. The *commissarii loci* developed later into the tax councilors (*Steuerräte*) of the towns. In the course of time, the county commissars became increasingly dependent on the monarch without losing touch with the interests of the local Estates; at the beginning of the eighteenth century they fused with the

Estates county directors (*Kreisdirektoren*) to form the new office of *Landrat*.* The importance of district commissioners diminished as responsibility for the welfare of the inhabitants of domains devolved on the new provincial agencies.

Out of the Higher War Commissions which in the beginning administered taxes in the provinces together with the organs of the Estates, developed, in some places earlier than others, the provincial boards (*Kriegskammern*) or Commissariats that gradually took over the administration of taxes from the Estates, and police administration from the former provincial "governments" (*Regierungen†*). In 1712 the General War Commissariat (*Generalkriegskommissariat*), the central authority, was organized as a board and its old subordination to the military command ceased; this organizational structure was transferred to the provinces, consolidating the growing administrative jurisdiction of these agencies. Finally, the Commissariat was fused with the administration of royal domains, and became the General Directory (*Generaldirektorium*) and the Boards for War and Domains (*Kriegs- und Domänenkammern*).[1] Thus these commissaries, originally an extraordinary post, developed during the first half of the eighteenth century into regular officials and board-like agencies. But the whole spirit of the bureaucracy had simultaneously changed in a peculiar way.

In the seventeenth century, and even into the eighteenth, an older and a younger stratum can be distinguished in the Prussian bureaucracy. The older layer, as most clearly represented in the provincial governments, belongs to the era of territorial rule by the Estates; the more recent layer serves the aspirations of the new military-absolutist centralized state, and its most important representatives are the agencies of the commissariat. These agen-

* *Landrat*. The official at the head of the administration of a county. The Prussian *Landrat* was originally the chief executive of the central government on the local level.
† *Regierungen* (governments). Governmental organizations which the Estates had established for the administration of a territorial unit. With the rise of absolutism they were gradually superseded.

cies had no roots in the old provincial constitution and law. Their attitude toward the old order of public life was unsympathetic, indeed decidedly hostile. They became the chief implements for destroying the old system of government by Estates and for building the new absolutist military state. They dispensed with a legal, publicly recognized foundation; they got the principles for their actions from secret instructions, disclosed neither to the province at large nor even to the old agencies. They emerged with the standing army merely as tools of the monarch's will, without a public decree defining the nature and scope of their authority. The whole apparatus, which rested only on the monarchical right of decree and which ran counter to the Estates and territorial custom in myriad ways, appeared to the countryside to be, like the army itself (whose care was its primary task), an extension of the conditions of war into peacetime: a slow revolution from above directed at the overthrow of the old territorial rights.

The old authorities, who found themselves ousted from one position after another, saw this daily increasing and encroaching power as an illegal usurpation, although they recognized that behind it was the irresistible will of the sovereign as military chief. Gradually men became used to this new way of governing, whose political necessity finally forced itself even on the adherents of the old order, and whose impressive successes at home and abroad could not be denied. But it was not really an administrative law, based on public legislation, but only a monarchical administrative order, whose fundamental rules were known only to the immediate participants. Thus the "police state" replaced the older territorial state of Estates rule which, although undeveloped and serving the interests of the ruling class, was unmistakably a state based on law. The sharp antagonism which perpetually arose between the Boards for War and Domains animated by the spirit of the commissaries, and the old provincial governments relegated in time to the position of higher courts, and which fed on conflicts of jurisdiction that no department regulation could completely set aside, illustrates the silent but dogged battle the idea of the state-by-law (*Rechtsstaat*) fought with the idea of the police state throughout the eighteenth century. The idea of the state-by-law lost so much ground in this process because its adherents were unable, owing to the particularism and limited powers of the provincial Estates to cope with military and political necessities and with pressure to form a greater state.

If at the time the ordinary courts, the provincial governments, had been left the right of arbitration in questions of jurisdiction, the monarchical reforms would not have advanced. These ordinary courts could only give judgment based on the old provincial law, the *Rezesse** and public decrees, while the standards of the new monarchical administrative system lay in secret instructions known only to the administrative officials themselves. Therefore, administrative jurisdiction in the broadest sense was left to them. Not until Frederick the Great reformed the judicial system did the constitution of the courts and the spirit of the judiciary become compatible enough with the new institutions of a centralized state that the idea of the constitutional state could once more gain ground. The turn of events was heralded by the *Allgemeines Landrecht†* and led to the general and definite transferring in 1808 of all trials to the ordinary courts through suspension of "closet justice" (*Kammerjustiz*) and to the long-sought goal of "separation of justice and administration." Although the new provincial governments of 1808 grew out of the old Boards for War and Domains, they rested, unlike the latter, from the outset on public law. Nonetheless they can be regarded as direct suc-

---

* *Rezesse*. Written agreements between prince and Estates, which establish the results of a meeting of the Estates.

† *Allgemeines Landrecht*. The Prussian law code which Frederick the Great had ordered to be compiled and which became the basic law in the Prussian states in 1794. The law was to be simplified, freed of legal subtleties, and made comprehensible for the layman; it was to provide a synthesis of the old German, Roman, and natural law. By providing a single code of law for the scattered provinces of Brandenburg-Prussia, it was a significant step toward the creation of a unified state.

cessors of the former commissariat authorities that came to life
with no legal basis and originally consisted only of single commissaries, with extraordinary and temporary powers. It was
mainly these commissaries therefore who caused the great upheaval that created the modern administration of the Prussian
state.

The office of *Oberpräsident* in nineteenth-century Prussia affords a significant example of the process by which the commissary became an ordinary bureaucrat. The *Oberpräsident* grew
out of the Civil Commissioners (*Zivilkommissare*). During the
French occupation after the Peace of Tilsit, these Civil Commissioners had to deal with the foreign army leaders in single
provinces or in groups of provinces, and had to work with them
in provincial administration.[2] They were originally intended as
permanent commissaries of the ministry in the provinces. Only
later were they assigned a regular administrative activity as *Regi-
erungspräsidenten,* and only through the reform of 1883 did they
become a special echelon between the provincial government and
the ministry, which at the outset they were certainly not supposed
to be.

II

So far as I know, no one has yet observed that there is a striking
analogy between the process that created the administrative
structure of the French *Ancien régime* and the emergence of the
Prussian commissary—although, as might be expected from the
peculiar spirit of the French bureaucratic organization, the external results were very different. I have in mind the process that
led to the establishment of the provincial intendants, of which
G. Hanotaux[3] has given such an illuminating and thorough account.

The intendants occupied the same place in the administrative
system of old France as did the Boards for War and Domains in
old Prussia. The very different structure of these two agencies
does illustrate the fundamental antithesis between the organi-

zational principle of boards and the principle of hierarchical offices—the characteristic difference between the German and French systems of administration. But the origin of both institutions is the same. They can both be traced to commissaries who, possessing extraordinary powers, without legal basis, accompanied the armies and their leaders in wartime. As an adjunct of the military administration they decisively influenced the civil administration as well, transforming it in a monarchical, centralized direction until they themselves became permanent locally fixed agencies. So it was with the *intendants de justice ou d'armée,* or—to give them their full title—*intendants de justice ou des finances et des vivres en telle armée.* These appeared in the wars of Henry IV from 1589 to 1600, again in the unrest after 1614, and once again under Richelieu. They were obviously nothing but military commissaries assigned to the commander of an army to provide for maintenance and order among the troops, and at the same time to assert more effectively the authority of the King against the local authorities and the inhabitants of the province for whose subjection or pacification the army was intended. When the campaign was over, they generally stayed on in the province to complete the establishment of the monarchical order. The content of their "commissions," which were generally sent to them individually (in the form of *lettres closes,* and not to the agencies in general, in the form of *lettres patents*), varied according to circumstances and was flexible and multifarious. But the essential feature of all of them was the combination of military and civil functions, resting on extraordinary powers.

On occasion these intendants received two special "commissions," one issued for financial tasks and military supply, the other for judiciary and police duties in the army and in the province at large; occasionally these two powers were combined. Once military operations were over, the civil powers naturally predominated, and empowered the intendant not only with extensive supervision of all local agencies but also with the discretionary right to intervene in the practical exercise of their power. The intendants had a right to claim the chairmanship and the casting vote in all civil agencies, even in the courts; they could exert judiciary power wherever they wanted, even arbitrate conflicts of jurisdiction and other questions of competence between agencies; they exercised comprehensive police powers, particularly in superintending towns and parishes, in accepting and dealing with complaints about the local authorities. They held all this power with no other titular right than the plenary powers known only to them and given them by the King, which they carried with them, and without any other legal course of appeal except to the Royal Council, out of whose midst they came. As a rule, after all, they were *conseillers* or *maîtres des requêtes*.

The intendants were also, like the Prussian commissaries, pioneers of the police state that undermined the bulwarks of the old legal order: hence the resistance, from the very beginning, of the parliaments to these "extraordinary commissions, not verified in the sovereign courts." The magistrates saw in the intendants usurpers of office and instruments to overthrow the existing condition of law, because they exercised the most comprehensive official functions "without an edict" and "without paying a fee," and often saw fit to interfere in the ordinary jurisdiction. At the time of the Fronde, when the intendants had become particularly hateful as compliant agents of a dishonest financial administration, resistance to them escalated into an insurrection. Abolition of the intendants became the battle cry of the rebellious magistrates. Their retention was perhaps the clearest evidence of the completeness of the victory won by absolutism. Under Louis XIV and Colbert the provincial intendants came to be an ordinary publicly recognized office, but the antagonism between them and the parliaments lasted up to the Revolution. The old legal order proved in France, as in Prussia, inadequate to the aims of power politics and monarchical reforms; but it did not cease to protest against the police state that had grown around and above them.

The provincial echelon was the focal point for this conflict, but the difference between "commission" and "office" also made itself felt in the center and in the periphery of the bureaucratic state. The *Surintendant des finances* and his assistants, the financial intendants of the central administration (who otherwise had nothing to do with the provincial intendants), both developed out of control commissaries.[4] Even the office of Secretary of State, the real minister of the *Ancien régime*, rested on a mere commission, in contrast to the office of *Conseiller d'état*. At the local level the intendants had their *sub-délégués:* "commissary of commissaries." The entire bureaucracy of early-modern France was split into two layers: one whose members held their office by virtue of a simple commission and could therefore be dismissed or transferred arbitrarily and were perpetually and effectively dependent upon the central power; and another whose positions were designated as *érigés en titre d'office*. These were, next to the municipal agencies, the positions in the judiciary and financial administration, and also in the Council of State. They were all acquired by purchase, according to the old usage systematically developed in the sixteenth century, or, after Henry IV, even acquired by heredity. In any case these positions were much less dependent upon the central government than those based on mere commission and acquired without payment.

To this system, too, Prussia offered a counterpart: through contributions to the Army Pay Office (*Rekrutenkasse*), the judiciary and municipal offices under Frederick William I had become as good as purchasable, whereas this was not the case for the commissariats and boards.

There was also a remarkable similarity in the conduct of the monarchical administration with regard to the cities in the France of Colbert and in the Prussia of Frederick William I. In both places an investigation aimed at regulating debts led to general supervision of finances and finally to complete abolition of communal independence. Colbert made use of the intendants in this effort, while Frederick William used special commissaries; even later in Prussia it was still through the *commissarii loci* (*Steuerräte*) that the municipal officials were bureaucratically supervised.[5]

In France as well the modern form of administration rests to a large extent on the idea of *commission* as opposed to *office*. It is true that the intendants were eliminated by the Revolution. They were, however, the prototypes of today's prefects. The process to which the intendants owed their existence was repeated with striking similarity by the activity of the Convention's commissaries during the Terror. Out of them arose the Napoleonic Prefects, just as the intendants had once arisen from the military commissaries of the civil wars.

The history of administration in Spain offers a further parallel to the rise of the French intendants. The Spanish intendants of the Bourbon period are a fairly faithful copy of the French: they developed from the military commissaries who accompanied the French regiments in the War of Spanish Succession, who took over civil jurisdiction and financial administration as well as finding provision and billets for the soldiers. In 1718 their office was declared permanent, was afterward abolished, and in 1749 was permanently restored.[6]

The institution of the commissaries had its effect in a great number of European states, almost always in the service of political absolutism. In Denmark it came in the period of absolute monarchy—that is, under Christian V toward the end of the seventeenth century—and involved a general transformation of the old independent boards into commissions that were more pliable instruments of the royal will.[7] In Sweden, too, under Charles XI, we can discern a similar dissolution of boards (*Kollegien*) and a preponderance of commissions.[8] It has wholly different significance, of course, that in England, after the Revolution of the seventeenth century, the old court offices of Lord High Treasurer and Lord High Admiral were dissolved into commissions: here it was Parliament, by now the real holder of power in the land, that created the more pliant and dependent form of these important administrative offices.

III

The army intendants from the period of Henry IV, the regent Maria Medici, and Richelieu were, as Hanotaux has indicated, merely a special example of the *commissaires départis* sent from the court into the provinces to serve the aims of the royal government. In peacetime throughout the sixteenth and even the seventeenth century, *maîtres des requêtes* from the Royal Council generally rode a circuit on horseback through the provinces as "eyes and ears of the king" to supervise the local officials, hear the complaints of the locals, register their impressions, take notes, and on their return make a report to the government. In troubled regions like Corsica in 1550, or in any time of unrest such as the period of Huguenot hostilities, they were, as "intendants," given more far-reaching tasks and plenary powers of an executive nature. They looked out for the monarch's interests in assemblies of the provincial Estates, kept a secret watch on the governors, parliaments, and financial officials, pursued rebels and state criminals, and otherwise carried on special government business. In war they also appeared as army intendants with extensive plenary powers. So it is that we see the military commissary with civil power develop, so to speak, organically from the wider institution of the *commissaires départis* under the pressure of wartime necessity. It was characteristic that, as under Henry IV, the normal *commissaires royaux* replaced the intendants as soon as peace was restored but that, in 1610, on the outbreak of his last war, which came to an abortive end with the murder of the King, military intendants (in Champagne) immediately reappeared.

It is not impossible that the French institution carried its influence into Germany, where we have exact information on the War commissaries only after the beginning of the seventeenth century.[9] On the other hand, we do have hearsay evidence of their existence in the armies of Charles V[10]; and it is also striking that the intendants in France appear to have had nothing to do with actual recruiting. For this purpose there were probably special, more subordinate officials.[11] Be that as it may, we can assume that the general institution of commissaries developed as bearer of extraordinary powers of the government, which broke through the established hierarchy of the old administrative system and served as new tools to accomplish new and extraordinary administrative tasks. Even in Prussia we find that simultaneously with the war commissaries, commissaries not attached to the army simply cropped up in the administration as in the reform of the municipal constitutions and the reorganization of local administration in East Prussia.[12] And not every war and tax commissary involved in the introduction of the excise tax had earlier accompanied a regiment. The concept of the commissariat is more general: the actual war commissary is merely an important special type.

Hanotaux disclaimed any attempt to trace the commissaries to their origins: in his painstakingly detailed researches, his attention was focused on the intendants of the sixteenth and seventeenth centuries. But in an investigation of the wide international context we cannot avoid this task, and it is in no way disposed of by saying that this was an ordinary and natural phenomenon that occurred everywhere. In the last analysis nothing in the historical world is self-evident. Clearly we are dealing with a phenomenon that was somehow shaped juridically. Indeed, the apparent all-pervading importance of the contrast between *office* and *commission* in the French bureaucracy of the *Ancien régime* is an indication that at some point there must have been a theoretical formulation of this difference.

At this point it seems appropriate to consult Bodin, the first great systematizer of state and administrative law in modern times, who also made a special study of the French institutions of his day. And in fact we find a detailed theory of the institution of the commissary in his *Six Books of the Commonwealth*, Book III, chapter 2, entitled "Des officiers et commissaires."[13] As Bodin himself emphasizes, it is the first theoretical treatment of the

problem. It apparently became as basic to the French administrative law of the *Ancien Régime* as was his theory of sovereignty
to constitutional law, although I have been unable to find recognition of this in the work of any French administrative historian.
The theory of commission has therefore not had the bright career of the theory of sovereignty; but for our purposes it is well
worth our while to give it a closer look.

In his usual way Bodin begins with a precise definition: "An
officer is the public person who has an ordinary charge defined
by law. The commissary is the public person who has extraordinary responsibilities limited by a simple commission." He
draws a further distinction between two types of officials and
commissaries: "Those who have the power to issue orders, or
magistrates, and those subordinate officials who can only take
cognizance of the facts or execute orders." We should add that in
the third chapter of the book he conceives of and treats Magistrates only as a sub-group of ordinary officials; he does not include the commissaries with their power to issue orders. All officials and commissaries are public persons, but not all public persons are officials or commissaries—not for example Popes, bishops,
or priests, whom he wishes to differentiate as *bénéficiers* from the
officiers.

There are two features that differentiate the concept of *commissary* from that of the *official:* first, the extraordinary character
of his mission, and second, the lack of a legal basis for it. To this
latter point Bodin attaches the greatest significance. He expressly
stresses that an edict is required "for the institution of ordinary
public responsibilities under the aegis of an office; otherwise,
there is no office, if there is no explicit edict or law." He explains
that it is customary in France to make public such edicts concerning creation of new offices, even the most trivial ones, in the
sovereign or lower courts. They are sealed with green wax and
contain a clause indicating the permanence of the office "to all
those present and to come." In contrast the letters patent of the
commissions are sealed in yellow wax and lack the "aspect of

perpetuity."[14] He maintains with great determination that the King cannot increase the number of judges and subordinate officials (such as sergeants, criers, trumpeters, land-surveyors, meat inspectors) in any agency without a special edict, which must be made public, examined, and registered.[15] Most important is the legal basis:

It is not necessary to have parchment to write, green wax to seal, or magistrates to publish the edicts concerning the institution of an office: for writing, sealing, verifying are not the law any more than other acts or contracts. . . . However, in whatever way the offices are instituted for ordinary and public responsibilities, it must be done by law.

That is the difference between *office* and *commission*. In order to understand it more readily, says Bodin, one could perhaps say that "an office is like a lease which the proprietor cannot terminate until its term is expired; a commission is held at will, a precarious loan that the lender can call in at any time he chooses." The nature of the commission is such that it lapses as soon as the task to which it relates has been carried out. It can also, however, be withdrawn even before completion. At this point Bodin quotes an old "Judgment of the court, taken from the classified register of Olim." Certain persons not attached to the court had been sent with commissions as bailiffs to the *grand jours* of Troyes, where a deputation of the Parliament held court. They continued to act as bailiffs even after the end of the *grands jours*, but they were prohibited to do so by a decree because they were not "officers."

Bodin considered it dangerous to suspend all magistrates and make use of commissaries with absolute power to reform the institutions of state. At least this had not worked out well in a republic like Florence; it was probably better suited to a monarchy. In this connection he cites an example from the period of Charles V's regency in France, when at the behest of the Estates-General of Paris fifty *commissaires-réformateurs* were sent throughout the land to inform the Estates and the government about misconduct of officials, who then were all suspended.[16]

Bodin has another case in mind, where apparently the difference between *office* and *commission* was blurred: the *Commissaires de Chastelet et des Requestes du Palais*.[17] These were really *officiers*, in spite of their being called *commissaires*. But Bodin speculates that the explanation of this is that they began as mere commissaries, and that this name was retained when they became *officiers* ("*furent erigez en tiltre d'offices ordinaires et perpetuels*"). Henceforth they are not commissaries, for otherwise they could be dismissed by the Court (Parliament?) "which the king himself could not do, except in the three cases which are in the ordinance of Louis XI which concern all the officers of the realm."[18] This emphasizes the irremovability of officials (except by a court) as a characteristic hallmark of the French officer as opposed to the mere commissary.

Office and *commission* are therefore conceptually distinct, even though they might be united in one person: the majority of commissions are given to officials, but the official cannot, within the framework of his ordinary office, function as a commissary. The so-called *commissions excitatives*, through which an official is instructed to carry out the duties of his office, are not true commissions, unless they are to contain clauses not altogether consistent with the law, and relying merely on the authority of a prince or superior, as for example when a judge is instructed to proceed first with more recent cases and to leave the older ones in abeyance. In such cases we are dealing with a real commission (which in Bodin's opinion is clearly extra-legal). If in this way a conflict occurs between the commission and the office, then the decision the officeholders make has priority, just as the status of officer takes precedence over that of commissary.

In this connection Bodin stresses the hateful aspects of extraordinary commissions, but equally their necessity in cases in which misconduct of officials is to be investigated, in which judgment must be pronounced on numerous court cases that have accumulated as a result of a civil war, or a decision must be made in matters in which the majority of officials of an agency or, for that matter, the entire agency has an interest. He clearly speaks from the experiences of his own times. In the first case he points to the distant example of Venice and Genoa, where annually, or every five years, *syndici* were deputed as commissaries to investigate possible official misconduct. In the last case he spins out a memory from his own life as an official (he was *avocat du Roi* at the court of Laon). In 1570 he was charged with a commission by Charles IX, relating to a general reform of the administration of the royal waters and forests in Normandy (the better part of the domain possessions there). Bodin managed to arrange the affair in such a way that the president and councilors of the Rouen Parliament were excluded from taking part in the investigation, and although they, as he says, moved heaven and earth to reverse this arrangement, the matter remained as it stood, and in the end they had to resign themselves to it. The first president and twenty-two councilors were excluded from the investigation, and likewise the entire municipal council of Rouen, because of the claims they themselves were making against the King. In this instance, therefore, administrative jurisdiction in the royal domains took the form of an extraordinary commission, since the ordinary courts of the province were considered prejudiced in these matters.

Having discussed the content of the concept of the commissary Bodin goes on to determine the range of the concept. He distinguishes between commissaries "for the government of provinces, or for war, or for justice, or for other things that concern the state" (probably thinking, among other things, particularly of ambassadors). One sees, therefore, that commissaries are used in all branches of state administration. Had he taken account of the Protestant states he could have included also the church by virtue of the ecclesiastical commissions for visitation, from which, in the Protestant states of Germany, the consistories developed, and in England the High Court Commission, the very name of which is an indication of its origin.

Bodin further distinguishes between commissions that emanate from a sovereign prince, or from ordinary authorities (magis-

trates), or from commissaries which the prince has deputized.
For commissaries appointed by the monarch can delegate part
of their charge to other persons if it is not expressly forbidden
in their commissions, except in matters concerning the interests
of the state (as in diplomatic negotiations for peace, alliance, or
similar questions) or the life and honor of an individual. In this
connection the later intendants' *subdélégués* come to mind: they
were appointed by the intendants themselves—a particularly important example of application of the commissaries' right to give
commissions. Bodin himself remarks at one point that until the
time of Philip the Fair in France the magistrates had appointed
their dependents to subordinate offices. Philip the Fair took these
powers from the *baillis* and *sénéchaux,* says Bodin, while the
seigneurs with powers of jurisdiction were allowed to continue
to appoint their sergeants and notaries in their own territory.
Moreover, the *procureur général du Roy*—who looked out for the
King's interests in courts in the manner of a Crown Solicitor
(*General Fiskal*)—in earlier times appointed his subordinate fiscal
official, the *advocat du Roy,* at his pleasure. "Afterward this particular commission of the magistrates took on the force of a very
honorable office appointed by the prince." (One recalls that
while writing his book Bodin himself occupied this post in
Laon.)

Bodin also distinguishes between commissaries who are simultaneously officials and those who are private persons (who naturally through their commission also become public persons).
Among the officials he also differentiates between the commissaries whose commission bears on the duties of their office, and
those for whom it does not. Yet another distinction is drawn between commissaries whose authority is final and not subject to
appeal to the authority that gave the commission, and those
whose judgments are open to an appeal to the prince or to the
authority designated in the commission. Finally, there are commissaries with and without executive power, as was emphasized
at the outset.

The commission lapses if the one who conferred it dies or re-
vokes it, or if the commissary, during the period of his commission, is appointed to an office equal in rank to that of the magis-
trate who gave the commission. The formal revocation of the
commission by letter of the sovereign who bestowed it takes
effect whether or not the commissary is informed. Anything done
by the commissary after the revocation of his commission is invalid. That is the strict law. Reason and equity of course demand
that the commission remain in force until the commissary is informed or otherwise comes to know of its revocation.[19] To avoid
such difficulties the Secretaries of State (in France) were in the
habit of including in commissions and in all related writings the
clause "on the day of notification of these writings," a clause
that must be supplied as a matter of course even if left out on
occasion.

A commission lapses with the death of the sovereign who issues
it, assuming no mitigating factors. This is not the case, for example,
when, in a legal matter, litigation has already begun. The
commissary must then see the matter to its conclusion. Matters
are similar if a general acting on a commission hears of the sovereign's death at the beginning of a battle. The ordinary officials,
on the contrary, remain in office even after the sovereign's death.
After the death of Louis XI the Paris Parliament decreed that
officials should remain at their posts as before, until word should
arrive from the new King; here they were following an old edict
of October 1381 (after the death of Charles V). To be sure, the
Toulouse Parliament acted differently on the death of Charles
VII, suspending all hearings and decisions until a letter from the
new King arrived. Bodin disapproves of this procedure because
the office persists by law just like royal power.[20] The different
treatment reaffirms the difference between *office* and *commission:* the office is permanent or at least has a fixed term, and is
based on law; the commission has a transitory character, and is
based on a simple order. Therefore it lapses on the death of the
person who gave the order, while, to suspend an office, a special

act is necessary. When in 1544 the positions of fifth and sixth president in the Paris Parliament were abolished, it occurred through a special edict, just as in 1560 Charles IX abolished all the new offices created after the death of Francis I at the demand of the Estates General of Orleans. Even the office of clerk of the registry in the Parliament was similarly done away with in May 1544 (by request of the chief registrar) by a special edict, just as it had earlier been established by one. If a commission is combined with an office as such, it is transferred to the successor in office.

According to Bodin, the power of officers is in substance stronger and more extensive than that of commissaries. The magistrates in particular can interpret the laws independently, while commissaries are bound by the text of their instructions, unless it contains a clause (*selon les personnes, à la discrétion, à la prudence, à la volonté*) which gives them greater freedom of action, as is especially desirable for ambassadors and military personnel. Naturally this is always granted with the proviso that it does not work to the detriment of the community. One sees that Bodin had not yet encountered the effectiveness of the military commissaries as they developed from Henry IV's time on. He did not even remotely suspect the eminent importance that the institution he so carefully described was to acquire in the administrative law of his own and other lands. The direction of his thought was not toward establishment of absolutism but toward a monarchical legal order. He saw in the commissions a residue of an earlier circumstance, when the people were still ruled without laws. They were a necessary instrument of government but one that had to be used with caution and confined as much as possible. Transformation of commissions into offices was a process in which he had full confidence and for which he had sympathy. He knew that commissaries were indispensable to prevent or curb abuse of office, but the idea that a whole system of offices, so far as it touched on real administration, should be reformed in the spirit of the commissary, was totally alien to him.

IV

What conclusions are, then, to be drawn from Bodin's presentation of the origin of commissaries? There is no simple answer to this question. Bodin says nothing expressly about it. But basic to his thought is the view that temporary and informal transference of authority to a deputy is the simplest and most primitive way in which a ruler can use others to make his will felt, and that therefore commissaries are really older than legal ordinary officials. Accordingly, he selects his examples from the whole range of his historical reading, particularly from Greek and Roman history, which, after the manner of sixteenth-century writers, he does not hesitate to throw together with modern history. In particular the Roman dictators, the decemvirs, the *quaestores parracidii*, the provincial governors are for him characteristic representatives of the commissary type. Here we leave him.

Antiquity is a world of its own, and it is enough for us to note that neither Aristotle's *Politics* nor Roman Law boasts a fully developed theory of the *commission*.[21] If we limit ourselves to more recent political and legal development, it is clear that the concept of the commissary gains greater juristic precision and becomes a legal institution that can be theoretically defined only when it can be set off from the concept of the ordinary official. The whole theory of the commissary as Bodin presents it rests on their opposition to the officers: the *officium* had to be developed first before there could be any question of the *commissio* in any legal theoretical sense. Here we meet head-on the problem of the rise of the *office* in the feudal, hierarchical, medieval world, which in no way has been thoroughly explained and which we cannot go into here.[22] It might only be pointed out in passing that the example of a hierarchy of offices in the Church had a considerable, though not always sufficiently appreciated, influence in state institutions. Hinschius laid particularly great stress on this influence.[23]

Canon Law (apparently in connection with the traditions of Roman state administration) did not only create a developed system of administrative agencies but, says Hinschius, gave currency to "the concept of office." As opposed to the later Germanic conception of *office* as essentially a useful private right this concept saw *office* as a complex of certain rights and duties to be exercised in the public interest. It gave currency as well to the basic principle that the officeholder might be removed from his position only under certain conditions and by a prescribed procedure. "Its hierarchy of officials and the law governing them was the model for the so-called absolutist state." He is also inclined to assign to "the example of the Church, which, in accordance with dogma, had to ascribe to officials alone the ability to govern and considered the laity merely the passive objects for the execution of the mission given to the officials," indirect responsibility for "that well-known notion of the all-wise government and of the limited understanding of its subjects, as well as the notion that the activities of officials and government are independent tasks detached from the interests of the people." In any case the international context of medieval administrative law which, rightly, has been recently emphasized, evidently has its strongest roots in Canon Law.[24]

But given the concept of *office,* the concept of the commissary immediately emerges with greater legal precision, particularly in sources of ecclesiastical law. For his distinction Bodin cites Roman and canonical sources side by side: *Leges* from the Digests and the Codex of Justinian, *Capitula* from the Decretals of Gregory IX, plus such legists and canonists as Bartolus, Baldus, Jakob Butrigarius, Johann Andreae, Felinus, Hostiensis, and others. If we look more closely at his citations we find only the barest rudiments of the theory in the Roman sources, as in the sentences on *iurisdictio mandata* in the Digests and in the Justinian Codex.[25] The most important source proves to be the oft-cited section 29 of the first book of the Gregorian Decretals: "Concerning the office and power of the delegated judge." Next in importance are the commentaries of the jurists named above.

We therefore are led in the main back to Canon Law for development of the theory. The doctrine of *iurisdictio delegata* forms the basis of the theory. "The first development of this institution and a particular theory concerning it," says Hinschius,

dates from the first half of the twelfth century. In the second half, at the time of Alexander III, the principle of delegation already appears, for all intents and purposes, to be in extensive usage and fully developed in theory. . . . From the beginning of the twelfth century we have only a few, after Alexander III a large number, of Papal rescripts, in which matters brought directly before the Pope for investigation or even decision are transferred to other churchmen, particularly bishops, abbots, and the like.[26]

This repeated the process which in earlier centuries had already led to the development of Papal legates. Even the rise of the significant position of the archdiaconate, believed in the Middle Ages to have *iurisdictio ordinaria*, Hinschius tries to trace back to a jurisdiction originally delegated by the bishops as a commission. Between the *legati* of the earlier epoch and the *delegati* of the twelfth and thirteenth centuries there is an unbridgeable gap in canonical theory; it might rest on the fact that the power of the legates had in the meantime become *iurisdictio ordinaria*. Both times, however, it was the stimulation of the later Roman Empire that initiated Papal commissaries. On the first occasion, it was direct adoption of the Byzantine institution of Imperial commissaries as mentioned in the *Codex Iustinianus* and the *Codex Theodosianus*.[27] On the second, it was the confluence of the remarkable growth of Papal power in the twelfth century with the blossoming of the Roman school of jurists in Italy,[28] which led to development of the new institution of the *iudices delegati*.

The practice of the Papal Curia is found at the same time at the Imperial court, in both Germany and Italy: the Emperor appointed delegate judges of the same type and with the same attributes as the Popes.[29] Thus this institution infiltrated the German legal system. We find it in the Imperial court (*Reichshof-*

gericht) from the twelfth century (1159) onward, and after the fourteenth century with increasing frequency, until under Frederick III it became almost standard practice to appoint commissaries to cope with or to make decisions in legal matters.[30]

We cannot say exactly when the name *commissarii* is first used to designate those entrusted with extraordinary powers by authority; throughout Canon Law they are still called *delegati*. By the fifteenth century the name is in general use, in France and in Germany.[31]

Like the Pope, so also the bishops appointed commissaries; and like the Emperor, so also the princes. It is well known how significant these commissaries became for the structure of the judiciary in the German territories: Stölzel has shown the effect of these princely commissaries on the rise of a learned magistracy.[32] As late as the seventeenth and eighteenth centuries the significance of extraordinary commissions in German civil procedure was very great; only more recent judicial legislation has abolished them as a matter of principle.

Up to the sixteenth century, however, the application of the institution of the commissary in Germany did not extend very far beyond the realm of actual legal proceedings, particularly civil proceedings, just as in canonical doctrine they remained limited mainly to the court system. In their dealings with the Estates, which do offer many analogies to court proceedings, the Emperor and the princes had themselves represented by commissaries. When in 1495 the common penny (*der gemeine Pfennig*) was decided upon, the Imperial Treasurer sent commissaries from Frankfurt throughout the Empire to collect the taxes assessed by princely officials and priests;[33] but, like the tax itself, these commissaries did not last. Maximilian I in a decree of February 18, 1502, speaks in entirely general terms of his "Commissaries and vicars in the Holy Empire, Italy, the Upper and Lower Austrian and Burgundian lands and elsewhere," with particular reference to the financial administration.[34] The commissions of visitation at the time of the Reformation have already been mentioned. It was only with the military commissaries of the seventeenth century and their successors that the institution of commissary began to have a more far-reaching effect on all realms of political life, though naturally only in the separate territories.

In the Western states, which developed administratively much earlier than Germany, commissaries had already gained greater significance for general public administration by the Middle Ages. It is certainly no accident that the institution began its significant development in England and France in the twelfth century at the same time that Emperor and Pope were beginning to make greater use of it. Here, too, its basis was the power of the courts; but from this there soon developed an abundant administrative activity. In France the *baillis* were to all intents and purposes already royal commissaries, sent from the court into the country to supervise the *prévôts*,[35] the old local overseers or trustees; until, after the so-called Testament of Philip II August (1190), at first a few, and later many, of them became permanent officials, as middlemen between the court and the *prévôts*. But as soon as the *bailli* acquired local jurisdiction, he in his turn had to be supervised for the court by traveling commissaries. These were the *inquisitores* of St. Louis' time, whom Ducange and some more recent writers after him have interpreted as successors to the Carolingian *missi*.[36]

The *missi* of Franconian times[37] clearly had the character of commissaries. They belonged to the same epoch in which Papal legates developed whose official name was originally *missi*. Therefore we can scarcely rule out a powerful ecclesiastical influence, the more so as a spiritual and a secular *missus* always traveled together. But that the institution of *missi*, of whose later existence we know nothing, had a direct influence on the *inquisitores* of Louis IX is doubtful. A less remote connection is at hand: the legacy of the canonical institution of *iudices delegati*. The same connection suggests itself for the itinerant justices who appear in England after 1131 and in particular with Henry II.

They were, as we know, the beginnings of local self-government, in the form of commissions of local inhabitants for the purpose of dispensing justice, assessing taxes, and recruiting for the various classes of the militia.[38] The effectiveness of these commissaries, the *iudices itinerantes,* like that of the French *inquisitores,* is allied to the introduction of the inquisitional procedure in the courts, for which the model proceedings in the Franconian royal courts set the standards.[39] An influence of the institution of the *missi* in a similarly indirect form, through the medium of the canonical *delegati,* cannot be completely ruled out, since the *delegati* were themselves a reiteration of the old Papal institution of *missi,* institutionalized as legates.

In France these *inquisitores* were first succeeded by the *commissaires-enquêteurs réformateurs* of the fourteenth and fifteenth centuries,[40] to which Bodin's fifty *commissaires réformateurs* of 1356 belonged and who under Charles VII were still unpopular with the provincial officials.[41] They in their turn gave way in the sixteenth century to the *maîtres des requêtes de l'hôtel.* These were officials employed by the Royal Council, so-called to set them apart from the *maîtres des requêtes du palais* attached to the Paris Parliament. The *maîtres des requêtes de l'hôtel* were sent through the *généralités* to supervise the local officials' administration of justice and finances and to report on the abuses they came upon. As *maîtres des requêtes* they were ordinary officials, but on their rounds they appeared as *commissaires départis* and *commissaires enquêteurs.*[42] They were in the sixteenth century the most important form of commissary that Bodin knew; but beyond them commissaries had spread to all areas of public administration, and no doubt it was French administrative law that was the most important of the sources from which Bodin drew his general theory.

In the area of court proceedings, commissions had become as widespread in France as in Germany, especially in the form of royal commissaries acting in the sovereign's interest or on a request of the parties on particular legal matters. The privilege of *committimus* gave the particular individual in question a *forum privilegatium* before the designated court, whether it was that of the King in his *hôtel,* or that of Parliament in the *palais.*[43]

In the area of police functions the *commissaires du châtelet de Paris* have already been mentioned. These were perhaps connected to the *inquisitores* of Louis IX's time.[44]

In the area of financial administration commissaries had been utilized in many ways at least from the fifteenth century.[45] Already in the fifteenth century a distinction was made between *office* and *commission* among the financial officials.[46] In the great financial Ordinance of 1445 (article 16) it was forbidden to draw up and seal commissions in financial matters without an order of the King and the *trésoriers* or *généraux;* and only steady and solvent personnel could be taken on as commissaries in financial administration.[47] In article 20 of the same Ordinance *commissaires esleuz* (*élus*), *etc.* are mentioned,[48] and the *règlement* of 1454 (article 46)[49] also speaks of "letters of commission sent in behalf of the King to the commissaries, elected or otherwise, about the matter of assistance." Thus *élus* were then still royal commissaries, perhaps paid by the inhabitants of dioceses or *pays* from which they had earlier (after 1355) been chosen. Even the tax collector (*collecteurs des tailles*) had a commission.[50] The right of sub-delegation appears in a prescription of the Ordinance of 1452 that the *élus* can at their own cost and risk maintain *commis* as their deputies, whose powers were of course limited.[51] This specifically French institution of the *commis* kept by certain higher officials (for example, at a later date by the minister-Secretaries of State), which so signally distinguished the bureaucratic system of the French *Ancien régime,* was an extension of the right to delegate. These *commis* were nothing other than *subdelegati,* like the *subdélégués* of the intendants. Even the clerks (*greffiers*) of the *élus* had in the fifteenth century their *commis* or *commissaires.*[52] We are already touching on the realm of military administration when we read of *commis* or *commissaires du contrôleur des guerres* or of the *maréchaux de France*[53] or of the *commissaires pour lever les che-vaux pour l'artillerie,* which the Ordinance of 1517 (article 19) presumes to be in existence.[54]

The commissaries sent with extraordinary powers into the provinces from the court in Savoy-Piedmont in the fifteenth and sixteenth centuries must have had considerable importance. The Estates records published by Sclopis[55] show that the Estates complained at almost every meeting of the Diet between 1440 and 1536 about these extraordinary tools of the sovereign's power, who repeatedly intruded not only on the judicial but also on the police and financial jurisdictions of the ordinary authorities without the extent or nature of their commissions' being known. In 1440 the Duke was obliged to recall all his commissaries at a request of the Estates, but they later reappeared in many capacities. In 1489 at a complaint of the Estates of Piedmont the concession was made that, from then on, commissaries should show their commissions to the ordinary officials (*officiarii ordinarii*) before performing their duties; but this does not seem to have been invariably complied with. Perhaps the *referendarii* who appear in the seventeenth century at the head of the provincial administration and who later developed into intendants were successors to these commissaries as regular officials assigned to a particular place.

V

One group of commissaries not mentioned by Bodin, for which he had no example in the France of his day but which elsewhere was of great importance for the development of administrative institutions, has to be particularly emphasized here. They are what in Germany were called territorial commissaries (*Land-kommissare*). In the monarchical states we can distinguish two main groups of commissaries: those from the court, and those from the territories. The court commissaries were persons sent from the court into the provinces to assert royal authority or otherwise to serve the goals of the central administration; they were instruments of centralization and absolutism, trailblazers for the monarchical bureaucratic administration. The territorial commissaries were as a rule also appointed by the sovereign, but chosen from the leading inhabitants of a territory (*Land*) or entity with communal character. On occasion they were even elected directly and merely confirmed in office by the King. Their primary task was to serve the interests of the inhabitants of their region and to reconcile these interests with the monarchical political order. They did not make a life vocation of public service but served the public good as honorary officials and were not therefore so exclusively instruments of the sovereign as the careerists in his service. They were the bearers of modern local self-government, which rests on delegation of the functions of the state and of the highest authority to unsalaried active inhabitants of a community. In England the members of local commissions who assist the itinerant justices in court, in tax assessment, and in recruiting for the militia, can be designated as "territorial commissaries."

Even the later office of justice of the peace, which was established as such between 1327 and 1360, had a precursor in the thirteenth-century commissions for keeping the peace (*conservatores, custodes pacis*). It is just this common origin as territorial commissaries that gives the Brandenburg war commissaries and county directors—the later *Landräte*—their much touted similarity to the English justices of the peace. The institution is even more widespread: territorial commissaries are to be found in Hanover into the nineteenth century,[56] and in Denmark from the time of the Estates' reaction to Christian IV's arbitrary rule (1638) until the establishment of absolutist administrative organization.[57] That in France, too, the *élus* between 1356 and 1439 and beyond must be seen as territorial commissaries has already been indicated[58]; by Bodin's time they had long since become purely royal officials, no longer selected from among the local inhabitants. Where the tension between such commissaries and the royal power was too strong, where they entered into direct opposition to the monarchical rule, as in Denmark, they were disposed of by the strengthened monarchical power without leaving a trace. Where, however, they accommodated themselves to the monarchical order and served its aims, as in England, they developed into the most important agents in local self-government.

The English justices of the peace stood in clear opposition to the ordinary local officials—the sheriffs—in whom neither the King nor the residents had sufficient confidence to entrust to them the expanding tasks of police administration, with its manifold implications for economic life. The Crown always resisted the demand for election of justices of the peace by the local inhabitants: the justice of the peace was to be a delegate of state power and to remain as such. The institution in itself was created by statute but justices of the peace did not gain a *jus quaesitum* to the office, as did the sheriffs, who farmed the revenues of the counties. The appointment of justices of the peace was called a "commission"; and until the great upheaval of the Puritan revolution they could be dismissed by the Star Chamber —that is to say, the superior authority—without ordinary due process. It was not until the eighteenth century that they became the independent figures one usually thinks of.

VI

To summarize, the total significance yielded by the commissaries in the general administrative history of modern states is this. Wherever public administration came up against new and extraordinary tasks, which the ordinary officials did not have the equipment to cope with, at first extraordinary officeholders were outfitted by commission with power adequate to these new tasks. Then in the course of time these extraordinary officials readily became ordinary ones if the need that had brought them into existence persisted and made a regularly functioning office desirable. In this way the primitive district administration of bailiffs and officeholders throughout Europe was displaced by a new organization of the district bureaucracy: by organs of self-government like the justices of the peace in England, by local administrative boards like the *Steuerräte* and *Landräte* in Prussia, by individuals of a strictly bureaucratic nature like intendants or prefects in France. Everywhere it was commissaries—either court or territorial ones—who effectively shaped these new structures in their initial stages; and they showed a trace of that influence for a long time, in places even up to the present day.

The institution of the commissary was especially a means of exerting monarchical discipline and the authority of the absolutist state in administration. We have seen that this institution had served for centuries to protect the system of offices from the danger of private corruption, and finally on the Continent in the seventeenth and eighteenth centuries to transform the system in accordance with modern *raison d'état*. In the same way as a *beneficium* was attached to ecclesiastical office (*officium*), an estate or salary went with a secular office. The earlier corruption of the system of offices by claims of a right to investiture was matched in the more modern post-feudal administrative system by a tendency on the part of tenured officeholders to exercise and enjoy their office, with all its appurtenances, more as a vested right than as a public duty. The entanglement with local, particular aspirations and class interests, the obstinate clinging to outworn customs and legal arrangements, often turned the district offices, particularly in times of far-reaching monarchical reform, into focuses for an invincible passive resistance to action generated from above. The great process of centralization and amalgamation on which the modern, uniformly administered state rests had this as its greatest obstacle to overcome throughout the Continent. In this struggle to establish a new order of state the *commissarius* became the most effective instrument of the state's power.

Without a *jus quaesitum* to his position, without ties to the local centers of resistance, without the fetters of superannuated legal ideas and traditional notions of office administration, only an instrument of a higher will and the new idea of state, unreservedly devoted to the prince, empowered to act by him, and dependent upon him, no longer an *officier* but only a functionary: the commissaries represent a new type of public servant corresponding to the spirit of absolutist reason of state, who did not completely supplant the old officialdom but, in amalgamation with it, after a long struggle, effected profound changes in its nature which have their impact to the present day.

After this great accomplishment the commissary in its pure form was naturally unable to play the same role in the modern constitutional state as had been the case in the seventeenth and eighteenth centuries. One of the two defining characteristics of the commissary, which Bodin advances—the lack of a legal basis for his activity—can be reconciled with the principles of a constitutional state only insofar as this activity remains within the legal limits of the authority of the one who gave him the commission. Without ranging too far into enumerating the many uses of commissaries in present-day public life, I might mention the representatives of the government in parliamentary bodies; the commissions for taxation, military recruitment, examinations, economic and social investigations, and, among a host of other public matters, for the preparation and execution of reforms of all kinds. In fact the main burden of all parliamentary and corporate work is carried on in commissions. But it seems to me much more relevant to point out how fundamentally even current administrative law reflects the influence of the spirit and position of the old seventeenth- and eighteenth-century commissaries. The old difference between *officier* and *commissaire* is the basis for the difference in legal position of the judicial and political officials: the one greatly independent of, and the other more dependent on, the state even if the original distinction has been modified and refined past recognition in the modern constitutional state.

The peculiar legal position of ministers can be explained also in terms of the survival of the legal form of commissarial offices. In old France the Secretaries of State—the ministers of the *Ancien régime*—counted as straight *commissaires* and not as *officiers;* despite government by boards the situation was similar in old Prussia. The reason for this was that the monarchs did not want to be bound to these most powerful of their servants. In England, on the other hand, because of their greater responsibility to Parliament, the ministers as such became simple "commissioners." After the Puritan revolution, and ultimately after 1688, the most important ministries—the Treasury and the Admiralty—were in the hands of a number of commissioners, instead of being entrusted to the old great offices of Lord High Treasurer and Lord High Admiral. The modern English Cabinet, which has no legal claim to existence and which, consistently with the nature of Parliament, has a transitory character, can be called a true commission as distinct from a fixed office. All constitutional ministries have something of this commissarial character. Finally, even today, we can gauge how important the use of commissaries in place of ordinary officials might be in the lower ranges of public administration, if we imagine that the chairmanship of the district tax assessment commissions (*Steuerveranlagungskommissionen*) in Prussia was assigned, instead of to the *Landrat,* to a tax official deputized *ad hoc* who would be entirely free of the ordinary officials' almost inevitable involvement with local interests, social power relations, and personal considerations.

8

THE PRECONDITIONS OF
REPRESENTATIVE GOVERNMENT IN
THE CONTEXT OF WORLD HISTORY

This essay is Hintze's last extended study in the field of comparative history. It was preceded by an article on "The Character of Feudalism," in which Hintze asserted that changes in military organization were the main reason for the origin and development of feudalism. The importance of the individual warrior gave rise to an economic organization in which the agricultural work had to be carried out by dependent peasants; the military structure strengthened the position of the warrior-lord in such a way that he could claim and acquire immunities for his possessions. Empires extending over large areas were particularly susceptible to such a splintering of power; accordingly, Hintze regarded the area which the Carolingian Empire had covered as the soil most suitable for the full development of feudalism.

Undoubtedly Hintze's essay directed attention to significant features in the rise of feudalism. Nevertheless, later important studies devoted to the problems of European feudalism (for instance, Marc Bloch's masterly and comprehensive treatment) and more recent investigations of this phenomenon in non-European countries have shown the limitations of his approach. It seemed unnecessary, therefore, to reproduce Hintze's study of feudalism in this volume—particularly since a portion of it is available in English translation in Fredric Cheyette, ed., *Lordship and Community in Medieval Europe* (Holt, Rinehart & Winston: New York, 1968).

As Hintze himself remarked, the essay "The Preconditions of Representative Government," although a sequel to the article on feudalism, can stand by itself. Although this study may seem of greater value and interest today than the article on feudalism, it must be remembered that the problems of the system of Estates, which stand in the center of Hintze's investigation, have been studied no less in recent years than have those of feudalism. On the contrary, it is enough to point to the long series of *Studies Presented to the International Commission for the History of Representative and Parliamentary Institutions,* which began in 1937 and has already reached the fortieth volume, to realize the increased attention which historical scholarship has given to the problems of the Estates and of the origins of representative government. Nor can it be claimed that Hintze's references to the scholarly literature demonstrate a particular interest in recent investigations. Rarely does he quote from historical monographs from the 1920s, and when he does—as in the case of Hölzle and of Asakawa —fortuitous circumstances like his membership in the Berlin Academy or on the Editorial Board of the *Historische Zeitschrift* seem to have directed his attention to these recent books. Most of the writings to which he refers in footnotes or which he mentions in the text (for instance, Wundt's *Völkerpsychologie* or Jellinek's *Allgemeine Staatslehre)* had been published before the First World War.

Nevertheless, although Hintze's interest in contemporary historical studies of a specialized nature seems to have been limited, the present article reveals that he was deeply interested in recent developments in one particular field of scholarship—sociology. The essay clearly shows the impact of two sociologists whose works had come out—either for the first time or in revised or collected form—in the 1920s: Franz Oppenheimer and Max Weber. The ideas of Max Weber, appearing in his *Wirtschaft und Gesellschaft* (1922) and in the *Gesammelte Aufsätze zur Religionssoziologie* (1920), were especially influential in the composition of Hintze's essay; Hintze does not intend to present new historical discoveries but to examine or reexamine the validity of modern sociological propositions on the basis of the historical facts known to him.

It is this approach that gives Hintze's article its lasting importance, despite our greater knowledge of the existence and functioning of Estates and representative institutions. Historical monographs and specialized studies have only limited significance for the two broad questions which Hintze raises and discusses in his article and which result from consideration of the difference between the sociological and historical approaches. The first problem that is most clearly posed concerns the role that the system of Estates played in the development of modern constitutionalism, and how it can be related to the larger process of European institutional and constitutional development. The second question, closely connected with the first, had concerned Hintze since early in his career: the question of the extent to which the assumption of historical individuality and singularity is compatible with the pursuit of comparative historical studies.

The representative system of government that today gives the political life of the whole civilized world its distinctive character traces its historical origins to the system of Estates of the Middle Ages. This system in turn has its roots—if not everywhere nor exclusively, at least in the most important countries—largely in the political and social environment of the feudal system. In principle there are of course many differences between the medieval system of Estates and the representative system of today; nevertheless, they are links in the same continuous historical chain. The doubts recently expressed about this[1]—from a focus, significantly, on the system of Estates of the German provinces—must pale before the example of the constitutional development of, say, England. There it is hard to determine the line where the system of Estates passes over into a system of representative government. The French Revolution threw into sharp relief both the historical continuity and the difference in principle between the system of Estates and the modern representative system, in that the Third Estate burst apart the newly revived Estates system and constituted itself as a modern popular assembly, the "National Assembly."

Nowadays the representative system is concomitant with the republican form of government. It originally arose, however, in monarchies, wherever the monarch, representing the unity of the state, opposed the Estates, representing the manifold private interests that had to be repeatedly woven anew into a unified front. This dualism is basic for the system of representative government. In modern political life it appears in the polarity of *state* versus *society*, of the unity of interest versus the diversity of interests within a people.

In the constitutional history of France, Germany, and England, we commonly assume a periodization in which the era of Estates follows right after the era of the feudal state, and is then followed, with or without an intermediate stage of absolutism, by the modern constitutional era of the representative state. For a long time comparative history did not advance beyond this limited view. Eastern Europe was merely occasionally drawn into the existing scheme, which by and large seemed to fit Eastern Europe only in a qualified fashion.[2] Of late, however, sociologists have begun to apply this same scheme, again with some qualifications, to the political development of all peoples, without regard for the various cultural groupings. This attempt at sociological construction demands a reply. I am thinking here particularly of two modern German authors, Wilhelm Wundt and Franz Oppenheimer. Wundt, in Volume VIII of his great work on social psychology, employs the era of feudalism and the era of Estates as regular stages for all peoples on the way to modern political organization. Oppenheimer, in his comprehensive *System of Sociology*, whose volume on the State has appeared in a new edition, takes the same line at least with regard to what he calls the inland states in contrast to the maritime states, by which he means chiefly the states of the ancient Mediterranean culture. I have examined the arguments for this thesis and have found them untenable for such a general application.[3] Max Weber himself was a long way from accepting evidence like this; and yet his various explications betray noticeable gaps regarding this very problem of the system of Estates and require complementation.

One has to concede that feudalism did appear outside the European realm, although with the concept in its present undefined condition we must set out the various types of feudalism in a much clearer way than has hitherto been the case.[4] As for the system of Estates, on the other hand, it remains my conviction that they are limited to the cultural realm of the Christian West. Even those countries outside the world of Western culture which did undergo a feudalistic stage—such as Japan, the Islamic states, perhaps also ancient Egypt in the transition from the Old to the Middle Kingdom, and Mycenaean Greece—show no trace of a real system of Estates. With the *polis* the ancients traveled a completely different road in the development of their states and institutions. In the Christian West, however, the phenomenon of Estates was rather common not only among the Latin-Teutonic peoples but also in the purely Germanic Scandinavian North, as well as among the Slavs and the Magyars. In the West they lacked full development only in those regions where the municipal structure of the states of the ancient world still exercised considerable influence, particularly in Italy but also in other parts of Southern Europe. In southern Italy feudalism and the system of Estates were not indigenous but had been introduced through the Norman Conquest. Without the invasion the municipal form of organization would certainly have predominated there, just as in northern and central Italy. The ancient city-state, constituted, as Jellinek says, "on monistic, purely corporative principles, on the social basis of a sharp differentiation between free men and slaves," was no more compatible with a feudal Estates organization than was universal empire at the opposite end of the spectrum, where the corporative element was completely suppressed by the monarchical.

The feudal and Estates system had its real origin in the Latin-Teutonic heart of modern Europe, as represented by the building of the great Frankish empire. From here it radiated in various directions but it was directly transmitted only in part. As a rule certain beginnings and rudiments were already in existence that needed only to be recast or brought to fuller development. England, for example, which in Anglo-Saxon times showed possibilities for development of this kind, became through the Norman Conquest the classical exponent of a particularly strong and promising feudal and Estates system, distinguished by its early amalgamation of feudal law with common law. The northern states and Poland and Hungary were absorbed into the same development. I would only stress in passing the remarkable Aragonese influences on Hungary recently demonstrated by Professor Marczaly.[5] In fact the system of Estates extended beyond the narrow circle of the Christian West and of the Roman Catholic Church. Konstantin Jirecek has detected rudiments of it among the Serbs and other South Slav peoples.[6] As for Russia, Maxim Kovalevsky's illuminating study has established beyond doubt the existence in the sixteenth and seventeenth centuries of not simply an Upper House of Magnates—the Boyar Duma—but also of a Lower House of service nobility and urban merchant patricians, mainly from Moscow and its environs. This body was frequently convoked under the name *Zemsky Sobor* and enjoyed important advisory functions. One recognizes, of course, as Russian historians such as Klyuchevsky and Milyukov have emphasized more heavily than Kovalevsky,[7] that we are dealing here with a much weaker form of representation in Estates than in the West. In Russia the Estates were princely organizations and lacked the inner strength and corporate independence of the Estates in the West.

The question now arises, How is this remarkable fact to be explained—that the system of representative Estates appears regularly as an indigenous phenomenon in the Christian West but does not appear in the rest of the world?

Naturally, the two comprehensive systems that ruled and typified the political and social life of the West in the Middle Ages offer themselves immediately as means of explanation: feudalism and the Christian Church, specifically in the form of the Roman Catholic hierocracy. It is a fact that we can detect in both important motives that lent assistance to the development of the system of Estates. A third factor, however, closely connected to the other two, enters in: the peculiar form of nation-building in the West. This produced a constant competition between the individual states for power and prestige, without ever leading to a general unification in a universal empire. Because of this competition the states were prompted toward increasing rationalization and consolidation of their political machine (partly with instruments inherited from ancient civilization and transmitted by the Church). On the other hand this process triggered its opposite: a corporate reaction.

We are presented, then, with two closely related phenomena of world-historical nature: the European state system and the modern sovereign state, both of which are confined to and peculiarly indigenous to the Christian West, as is the representative system of Estates. We might even go so far as to claim that without this state system and its tendency toward constant rivalry, without the modernization that went with it—that is to say, the consolidation and rationalization of state operations—even the representative system of Estates would not have appeared. It did not exist in a vacuum; and it can be completely understood only in relation to the structure of European political life that had been gradually developing since the later Middle Ages, achieving fruition in the sixteenth and seventeenth centuries. In the background, more or less hidden, was the omnipresent influence, on modern Western history, of the ancient world, particularly of the Roman Empire, making itself felt through the agency of the Christian Church.

Of course the Roman Empire itself could not provide any direct model for the medieval Estates, because of its municipal structure and especially because of its absolute monarchical mode of government. It is true that the diarchy of Emperor and Senate, as it existed under Augustus, showed a certain similarity with the dualism of the system of Estates, but still its significance was fleeting and influenced the modern world of states not as a matter of immediate historical continuity but only as a humanist echo of the past. Still, it was this kind of thinking that prompted countries like Poland and Sweden in the sixteenth and seventeenth centuries to call their Upper Houses "Senates," and it is the reason that even today nations like the United States and the French Republic use the same term for their upper chambers.

Much more important was the indirect influence previously underrated in this context, that the Roman provincial Diets—the *concilia*—exercised on the development of the representative system in the Christian West as the presumed model for the Christian Councils. The work of Konrad Lübeck[8] shows at least in all probability that first in the East and then in the West of the Empire these *concilia* provided the stimulus and the model for Diets primarily intended to foster the cult of the divine Emperor but which in connection with this task possessed some representative functions.[9] It also shows that first in the East and later in the West they provide the stimulus and model for the periodic convocation of synods of the Christian parishes of a region. This significantly enhances our basic perception that the organization of the Christian Church followed to a large extent the model given it by the Roman Empire. I would also like to emphasize the fact that the word *repraesentatio* is used for the first time in its modern meaning by Tertullian, who is often cited as our earliest source on the old Christian Councils.[10] As for the significance of these Councils for the development of the medieval representative assemblies, we shall discuss them later. For the moment it may suffice to point to the testimony of Nicholas of Cusa, who regarded the internal historical connection between the German Diets and the ecclesiastical Councils as obvious, treating these Diets simply as the secular counterpart of the Councils.[11]

Feudalism is a concept that still needs to be clarified and is rather complex. One must, as von Below[12] taught, distinguish it from the genuine system of fiefs. The system of fiefs is a clearly definable legal concept, whereas feudalism is more a sociological type or the collective term for such a type. The system of fiefs is the narrower, feudalism the broader, concept. But what one wants to embrace under feudalism beyond the system of fiefs is still subject to debate. In this regard I part company with von Below. These questions, however, are a problem unto themselves that I have dealt with specifically elsewhere.[13] Their solution is in any case not of vital importance to our present topic. After all, there is no general and necessary connection between the feudal system and the system of Estates. There are feudal systems that never led to a system of Estates, as in Turkey and Japan. On the other hand, a system of Estates arose in certain countries that had no system of fiefs, such as Hungary and Poland. What we are dealing with here, as we shall see, is variation among types, both within the feudal system and within the system of Estates.[14] In any case the factors growing out of feudalism or affecting the development of Estates through feudalism can be rather clearly ascertained without broaching any further the problem of feudalism itself.

There are two factors of this kind. In the first place there is the special, peculiar character, conditioned socially and psychologically, of the bond existing between monarchical sovereignty and subjects and lying at the foundation of the Western feudal state. The basic idea was that dominion, which rested originally on leadership rather than on repression, was exercised in the name of and with the consent of the people, whether expressly given or tacitly assumed. It meant that the ruler also behaved as the representative of a whole people who were duty-bound to obey but to whom he himself was in some way responsible so that it was a matter of reciprocal obligation between ruler and subject, of a linking of the two, if not in formal law, at least in custom and tradition. This idea received its strongest expression among the Germanic peoples and gained among them, in time, real juridical validity.

In the second place there was the exemption of certain persons or groups from the direct effects of public authority, and the transfer of public, legal powers to these very persons or groups, the upshot being isolated local self-government. This was mainly the result of that legal institution known as "immunity," a term that, as an aspect of the real system of fiefs and of manorial lordship, is usually associated with the concept of feudalism. As we know, it is an institution that grew originally out of the privileged legal status of the Imperial domains in the Roman Empire and was subsequently accorded to the extensive holdings of the Church, and finally extended to secular local authorities with a feudal Estates-like character. All the privileges that made up the peculiar legal foundation of the Estates government depended on this institution. In a certain sense one can call these privileges the forerunner and pace-setter for modern personal civil rights, usually argued for only on the grounds of natural law, because they delineated the positive, personal, and civil rights of individual groups of subjects. These rights depended on being either granted or usurped and on subsequently being expressly or tacitly recognized.

Tied to these elements of a primitive notion of a state based on law and of a rudimentary form of individual civil rights of individual privileged groups of subjects was the peculiar form of nation-building in the West owing to the fundamental and universally important dualism of Church and State, which ultimately produced a state system based on international law. These states were forced by competition and rivalry progressively to consolidate and to rationalize their respective government operations, a process unrivaled in world history and of important, wide-ranging consequences. In this work the standard-bearer of the process of modern nation-building—the princely power—naturally availed itself primarily of those elements of the population whose possessions and whose authority on the local level made them especially capable of financial and military contributions and therefore capable of assisting the princely power in the new type of state.

These elements were the so-called Estates. They were to begin with the born and sworn councilors of the sovereign, with whom he treated the *ardua negotia regni* in periodic court assemblies often held as an adjunct to some high Church feast day. To the degree, however, that the sovereign increased his claim to financial and military contributions for his policies and at the same time occasionally still tried to avoid the increasingly irksome participation of the notables, the Estates, as though by way of compensation, demanded for each increase in the contributions an increase or reinforcement of their privileges. To the degree that the consolidation and rationalization of the new state operations reinforced the purely ruling organs and functions at the court and throughout the land, those privileged groups of subjects felt themselves equally compelled to combine and to form a united front to maintain their liberties and privileges within the consolidating state. In the end they received most of what they demanded. This process can be most clearly seen in their reaction to higher and more regular taxation, the most important aspect of the consolidation of state operations and the driving force in the development of the system of Estates.

This kind of consolidation and rationalization of state operations we find only in the West. In order to grasp the contrast between modern state operations and those of the ancient Oriental culture, we need only to think of the justice dispensed by the Turkish Kadi, which was based on considerations of economy and expediency according to principles provided in the Koran, but is worlds apart from the spirit of a rational administration of justice. Or one need only think of the administrative methods of the Chinese Mandarins, with their literary, humanistic education, exercising their office on the basis of Confucian teaching, without any real administrative or economic expertise. It was apparently the Church, especially the Roman Catholic, steeped as it was in the spirit of rational jurisprudence, which was of crucial influence for the Western political world. Behind the Church lay the civilization of antiquity, particularly the administrative and legal order of the Roman Empire. Roman law became a powerful lever for modern state operations. It was therefore the creative synthesis of two intertwined world-historical civilizations that produced the peculiar political development of the West.

II

Let us now consider more closely various aspects of this outline. I shall begin with what I like to call the germ of a primitive notion of the state based on law. It is the idea, particularly strong

and clearly developed in Germanic law, of the reciprocal obligations of the ruler and his subjects instead of the one-way street of
the ruler's prerogatives and the subjects' duty to obey. It is the
idea that the relation of ruler to ruled is restricted to the confine-
ments of law or tradition. That was the idea of liberty that Montesquieu found in Tacitus' *Germania*,[15] and to it he tried to trace
the parliamentary constitution of England—an interpretation, by
the way, which had a long history before Montesquieu, as a recent special study has shown.[16] The idea was later taken up by
Guizot and Eichhorn, and .even recently Spangenberg, in his
work *Vom Lehnsstaat zum Staendestaat*,"[17] has expressly en-
dorsed it—although, in the form in which this thesis has been
generally presented to us—insofar as it offers a specifically German and racial predilection—it is hardly tenable.

We find a similar basic idea among the Slavic peoples, and
Schrader[18] goes so far as to claim that it is a common Indo-
germanic idea. Among all of them, he discovers, the twin pil-
lars of the political order are, as in Tacitus, the princes and
the assembly of the inhabitants of the land. Even this, however, seems too strict a geographical limitation. There is much
the same basic idea in Hungarian tradition and elsewhere. A German missionary[19] has even undertaken to demonstrate that it existed among the West Africa tribe of the Eve in Togoland. Alfred
Vierkandt[20] describes the constitution of all primitive peoples in
the same vein. We are dealing not with a special racial predilection but with a general and typical phenomenon among peoples
who have reached the level of a primitive tribal constitution.

Montesquieu himself was far removed from any narrow racial-
psychological interpretation. He preferred to use the influence of
his beloved "climatic" factors, by which he meant the natural
basis of what Karl Marx later termed "the economic structure of
society." It seemed to him that the birthplace of Germanic freedom was the primitive life and culture of the forest. He was
thinking in this context chiefly of the contrast with ancient Mediterranean civilization with its city-state, or with the great ancient

river civilization in Egypt, Mesopotamia, and China, with their great patrimonial empires tending toward bureaucratic administration. Differences in conditions of settlement and other material bases of culture are certainly of great significance for our problem; yet, as we shall see, other and more important factors were involved. We might even speak of a general socio-psychological predisposition that emerges almost everywhere in typical forms on the cultural level of a primitive tribal or clan constitution but which, with the progress of civilization, has been able to develop freely to higher forms only in certain places. The problem, then, requires this formulation: What are the circumstances that have determined that this original germ of a primitive idea of state ruled by law came to full development not in the larger part of the world but only in the Western cultural realm?

Here, as we have already said, the conditions of settlement played a part. In the ancient city-state, bound as it was to the sea and to the coastal civilization of the Mediterranean, this germ of an idea developed quite differently than it did in the great inland regions of rivers and forests. But beyond this there was another decisive circumstance that often completely stunted its growth. This was the excessively strong development of the office of ruler through its alliance with religion and the social tendencies to which religion gave rise. The whole of Oriental civilization, ancient and modern, is permeated with this. The ruler is either a god walking on earth, as in ancient Egypt or among the Accadian Assyrians or in China and Japan; or he is at least the special protégé and agent of the gods, as the Kings of Babylon protected by the Marduk, as the Achemenids by the Ahura Mazda, or by the other local gods of the regions they had conquered, or as the Caliphs of the Islamic states were as successors to the Prophet; or he is deified through the ancient process of apotheosis, as were Alexander and the Roman Emperors. The result everywhere is enormous strengthening of the temporal authority by the spiritual, or even the idea of the unity of Church and State, as in the Roman Empire after Constantine and in the

Islamic empires. Easily allied to this was the trend toward universal monarchy and toward the unlimited absolutism of the ruling power. In all the cases mentioned both occurred, and the germ of the idea of state based on law became stunted.

This trend is not absent in the West either, particularly among the Germans. The Anglo-Saxon kings all traced their lineage to Wotan, and even the Merovingians boasted of a divine origin which, even after their conversion to Christianity, conferred on them a very effective magical and sacral consecration, now supplemented and reinforced by the legendary anointing of Clovis from the ampulla brought from heaven. The fact that the Carolingians, unable to establish for themselves a sacral tradition of this type, found it to their interest to create intimate links with the Roman Catholic Church in order to make up for what they lacked in legitimacy by spiritual anointment, and to legitimize their usurpation of the Crown, is an historic turning point. But consecration by the Church limited from the outset the character of the ruler, by committing him to divine law. The title *Dei gratia*, which became more and more common with rulers in the entire West after Charlemagne and whose meaning has been subject to considerable debate, does entail this commitment above everything, and thus a weakening of the heathen magical and sacral character of the ruler's office, and security against perversion of the office into tyrannical arbitrariness or universal omnipotence. Church doctrine therefore assimilated the German idea of the state based on law, preserved it, protected it from ruin. At the same time, however, it combined the idea with ecclesiastical ideas of the *jus divinum* and its reminiscences of ancient ideas of natural law and particularly of Stoicism. In this way Christian doctrine created a theory of Christian social organization that was later developed in the thirteenth century, after the rediscovery of Aristotle and his absorption by way of Thomas Aquinas into the teachings of the Church, into a comprehensive system that dominated the medieval world. It became the spiritual soil in which the system of Estates in the West was nourished.

In order to achieve fruition this development required the fulfillment of certain conditions. It could happen only after the Church, with the help of the Cluniac movement, had freed itself from patrimonial and feudal dependency on the protective secular power which, because churches were regarded as property, threatened to rule the Church throughout the West, particularly in the empire of the Saxons and Salians. The investiture struggle had to be ended, and the Church had to become an autonomous institution under the strong leadership of a papacy arrogating to itself hierocratic claims that soon brought about conflicts with the emperors and later also with other secular powers. This long-lasting conflict, reaching from the eleventh century to the close of the Middle Ages, was one of the most important factors in world history and was of the utmost significance in the rise of the system of Estates. The political and social theory of the Church was in large part an accompaniment of this struggle between *sacerdotium* and *imperium*. It was a weapon forged and used with great success in the intramural ecclesiastical combat of the eleventh century. One need mention only the names of Manegold of Lauterbach or John of Salisbury. The admixture of natural law from the ancient world introduced into Germanic law the alien idea of a kind of popular sovereignty, of a delegation of the Crown by the people. This ingredient lent new and strong support to the old German right of resistance against illegal power. I shall not go farther into this, for it has been clearly and accurately outlined by Gierke and also, recently, by Fritz Kern[21] and Kurt Wolzendorff.[22] I would only like to stress that the Roman Church, by virtue of the factors defined above, came to have a clear and decisive preference for the principle of election in the appointment of secular rulers. The early Middle Ages witnessed in Germanic law and elsewhere a competition or combination of the two principles—hereditary right and election—whereby election really had a magical and ritual origin; it was not based on the idea that among the claimants to the Crown one would arbitrarily become the ruler, but it assumed that election would find the man who had the true right to the Crown. Through the influence of the Church hereditary right was forced into retreat. The principle of election was favored; the magical character of the act of election transformed it into a church ritual so that participation of the Church became a necessary part of the procedure. As a rule it was the great ecclesiastical lords who took the lead among the electors of Kings and it became general conviction that after the election the Kings in their government would chiefly rely on those who had elected them.

In general the high Church dignitaries were advocates of the Church's conception of a limitation of secular power by divine law and of a form of Christian society based on this law. This meant that something of the basic Germanic ideas of law that had been implanted in the Church's teachings could be carried over to non-Germanic peoples insofar as they had developed similar conceptions although in a weaker, even obscure, form; the Poles seem to be an example of this. One has to realize in this context that the chancelleries forming the center of the whole primitive machinery of state were in the hands of ecclesiastics, that the procedures and ideas of these chancelleries passed from country to country, from court to court, and that in this way a certain uniformity of thinking about politics and administration was established which gave way only much later to the advancing differentiation of national characters. Just as with *Dei gratia,* countless other formulas traveled throughout the West, and with them went the Church's doctrine of a Christian society, which became the seedbed of the system of Estates.

The example of Church Councils in the Middle Ages was also of great importance in the development of assemblies of the Estates into regular institutions. In the Frankish kingdom the court Diets which the King held with the notables and which in part developed into formal Diets of the Empire, had their beginnings, on one hand, in the old military review—the March-field, a recasting of the old Germanic local community gatherings, and on the other, in the national Councils or Synods of the Church. The latter exercised a decisive influence. A Synod of the Church held under King Pippin in 755 at Verneuil[23] resolved that two Synods should be held a year, the first in March, in the presence of the King, to be held wherever he convoked it (thus, by old established custom coinciding with the March-field; in this particular year the March-field was postponed until May, and this forced the Church, too, to postpone its assembly), the second at the beginning of October at a place to be agreed upon by the bishops in March. "Presumably in imitation of the two synods decided upon then," Brunner says, "the custom arose of holding two court Diets every year."[24] These are the two assemblies Hincmar of Reims speaks of in his work *De ordine palatii*.

The spring assembly was held in May and coincided with the May-field. It was a formal Diet of the realm, made up of the temporal and ecclesiastical notables of the realm, and, in the background, the horsemen, to whom all the resolutions were customarily communicated. The autumn assembly was a smaller one of specially trusted ecclesiastical and temporal advisers and great lords for the purpose only of discharging important business and of preparing with this smaller group the agenda for the next spring assembly. Thus, although the Council and the Diet were in theory separate, they in fact came down to the same thing. Alongside the designations *placitum generale* or *conventus generalis* as applied to the greater assembly, there were also *concilium* and *synodus*. The assembly, according to Hincmar's description, split into two *curiae*, one ecclesiastical and one temporal, which sometimes met apart and sometimes met together. The spiritual curia was separated from time to time into a special assembly of bishops and a special assembly of abbots. That the King convoked and dissolved the assembly derived from temporal usage; that the assembly was limited to the questions put before it by the King and possessed no initiative of its own corresponded to the conciliar tradition. The formulation of the agenda and of the resolutions of the body certainly lay in the hands of clergymen.

We have here, therefore, an institution that derives from two sources: Germanic tradition and ecclesiastical statute. We may assume also that the model of Church Councils was a heavy influence in consolidating the position of these representative bodies as institutions and in lending them their corporative structure. From the standpoint of legal history the Carolingian *placitum generale* or *concilium* must be regarded, as Brunner says, as the seed of the Estates and parliaments we find later in Western and Central Europe. Here, too, there was no unbroken continuity, but the tradition remained alive, and the same forces and the same tendencies were at work which later under different conditions shaped the Diets and Estates.

The influence of Church Councils on the court Diets and local assemblies made itself felt even more strongly than in the Frankish state in the Visigothic realm, which, indeed, had a half-ecclesiastical quality. Even after the collapse of Arab rule this influence was so important in the new Christian kingdoms of the Iberian Peninsula that Marina, the father of Castilian legal history, chose to trace the origin of the *Cortes* directly to the Councils of the Church.[25]

Similar to what occurred in the Frankish realm, a blending of ecclesiastical and temporal elements took place in the local assemblies of the Anglo-Saxon realm. In the *Witenagemote* the bishops stood beside the *Witan,* and here too there developed division between a spiritual and a secular curia.[26] In the Anglo-Norman realm—which after all was established with the help of the Curia—the bishops (who were soon all Normans) continued to exert decisive influence in the court assemblies out of which the original parliament of prelates and barons arose. Before the Commons, the real representatives of the towns and the shires, had been added to this great Royal Council and it had become the *parliamentum,* in England representative assemblies of the Church in which not simply bishops and other prelates appeared, but also representatives of the Cathedral chapters and of the founders of ecclesiastical institutions (*Kollegiatstifter*) as well as of the lower diocesan clergy in the form of procurators (proctors) of the diaconates and the archdiaconates. These assemblies were known as *convocations*.[27] They were summoned after the beginning of the thirteenth century, no longer exclusively and directly by the King and no longer for the whole country but separately, by the archbishops, at times at the behest of the King, for the two Church sees of York and Canterbury, to work on Church legislation.

These convocations acquired great political importance after the conflict between Pope Boniface VIII and the French King Philip IV over the taxation of the clergy by the state. The Bull *Clericis laicos* of 1296 extended to the clergy of England the ban on paying taxes demanded by the King; but then followed the compromise on the basis of the Bull *Romana mater* of 1297, which included England in the permission to pay these taxes if the payment was voluntary. Thus the clergy's privilege to approve taxes was clearer and more extensive than that given the secular Parliament by the *confirmatio chartarum* of 1297,[28] and the clergy did not fail to make use of it in its convocations, little to the satisfaction of Edward I. The King tried, in consequence, to draw the representatives of the clergy away from these assemblies and into the secular Parliament by charging the bishops in the so-called *praemunientes* clause of their summons to Parliament, to bring along the heads of the Chapters, the archdeacons, one representative for the lay clergy for each cathedral, and two representatives of the diocesan clergy.[29] But this attempt failed. The representatives of the clergy never appeared numerous enough in Parliament, and finally after 1332 stayed away altogether. They preferred to make their appropriation for themselves in the convocations, which maintained this function until 1664. Nonetheless, the proctors of the clergy were summoned regularly in the fourteenth and even in the fifteenth centuries.

The treatise concerning the *modus tenendi parliamentum*,[30] which dates from the mid-fourteenth century and deliberately emphasizes the representative character of the lower House compared to the ecclesiastical and temporal lords, lists among the three *gradus sive genera* of which the *communitas parliamenti* consisted, in first place the *procuratores cleri*, in second place the knights of the shires, and in third place the *cives et burgenses*. These three groups of representatives, in opposition to the lords, are characterized as men *qui repraesentant totam communitatem Angliae*. The *procurates cleri*, who were chosen by order of the bishops in the diaconates and archdiaconates of their dioceses, had been active in the convocations before the Commons was added to Parliament, and may well have provided the model for the secular representation of local units in the assemblies of the land. The representative idea had already been realized in the convocations long before the knights of the shires were summoned to Parliament by King John in 1213, and the representatives of the *civitates et burgi* in 1265. It was apparently imparted by the conciliar tradition, and did not require first a juridical framework made up of specifically Germanic legal ideas.

Hatschek, who tries to show that this is the case, denies—wrongly, as it seems to me—the representative character of the convocations.[31] He is obviously thinking in terms of the modern concept of popular representation, as it has existed since the French Revolution, rather than of the specific medieval concept of representation of Estates. His derivation of the representative principle from the old Germanic legal principle of the separation of guilt and liability[32] I find neither clear nor convincing. This principle, a consequence of the associative idea, provides only the formal possibility for the legal construction of a representative relation but does not suggest a sufficient reason for its development.

In the course of his argument Hatschek does correctly stress that the peculiar character of representation in England, in the beginning a duty and not a privilege, is to be explained by the severe pressure of the state which turned the old cooperative associations into passive and duty-bound service associations and imposed joint liability on them for whatever their legal representatives had granted, more or less under heavy pressure, to the

King in the way of contributions and services. Those who appeared in the county court passed as the representatives of the shire, and those who had failed to answer the summons were regarded as having given their consent, by virtue of an arbitrary legal fiction. In the general assemblies, the Parliaments, however, representation of the towns and shires by delegate burghers and knights was based on no different principle than the representation of the diocesan clergy by the proctors. If we, like Stubbs, conceive of the rise of Parliament as a concentration of local administrative machinery, this process could well have been stimulated by the older example of representation in the Church, even if later the process was reversed and the convocations were influenced in many particulars by the fully-developed secular Parliament (for example, in the division into two Houses). Thus, the argument would run, the assemblies of the Church would have provided the hidden historical connection between the old *Witgenagemote* and the Parliament which Freeman and other English legal historians assumed to exist, though on the basis of inadequate knowledge of sources and in an untenable form.

Therefore the substantial influence of the conciliar institutions of the Church on the development of representative assemblies is at least very probable not only in the successor states of the Carolingian Empire, but also in Spain, and above all in England. In any case it was everywhere very significant that the members of the ecclesiastical councils were simultaneously eminent, and often leading, members of secular provincial or Imperial assemblies. We can assume, as a general rule, that the high clergy were also the leaders of Estates movements of the Middle Ages. The fact that in the German territories the ecclesiastical curias were less important and were partly even lacking—a fact von Below gives great weight[33]—proves nothing against the general importance of the influence of the clergy so widely attested to in earlier times and in larger political surroundings. The German territories were, after all, small and abnormal formations and cannot be made the basis for generalizations in constitutional history.

Consonant with this, we find the Roman Curia striving in many places to create Estates and constitutions. What in general was at stake here was the limitation of secular power and the gaining of leverage for the permanent influence of Church policy. This point will be developed farther on.

In the teachings of Thomas Aquinas no real theory of a system of Estates is to be found or to be expected.[34] In my view, no such interpretation should be given to the famous passage in the *Summa Theologiae,* in which, dealing with mixed constitutions, the monarchy is complemented by *principes* representing the aristocratic principle, and by the people, who elect or are entitled to elect them, representing the democratic principle. What is at issue here is a constitution for the entire Christian West as a great comprehensive unity. Monarchy is the universal rule of the Pope supported by the Emperor, or the Emperor himself as bearer of the secular sword. The princes are the individual kings of Christendom, who are largely elective monarchs. Here too we see the Church's preference for the electoral principle. It provides the soil for a system of Estates, not the system itself. Not until after the conciliar period when the Church of the Popes, having ascended to absolutism, passed through a great constitutional crisis in which the conciliar principle opposed Papal supremacy do we find a general theory of Estates among ecclesiastical writers. Thus that famous passage in Nicholas of Cusa's work[35] to which Gierke so often refers.[36] This passage concerns Imperial and provincial estates in all European states. It is no accident that the century of the great reforming councils was also an age of advance for the secular system of representative estates, particularly in the Holy Roman Empire. The constitutional counter-movement, so-to-speak, against the rule of Popes who had ascended to absolute power in the thirteenth century unleashed similar efforts in the secular world, and high ecclesiastics often took the lead in them. The *Concordantia Catholica* of Nicholas of Cusa presses home forcefully the parallelism of these ecclesiastical and secular movements, which affected the entire West.

The doctrine of corporations, created by canon lawyers from a mixture of German and Roman legal ideas, came too late to enable us to ascribe to it any really significant influence on the rise and early development of the system of Estates. The corporate body as a legal reality is of course a great deal older than the theory of corporations; yet the theory was still very important for the later development of the law of Estates. And it had still another important and far-reaching effect. The older and more genuine corporative structure retained a pronounced polar tension as a result of the dualistic notion of *prince* and *people,* of the princely authoritative institutions and the corporative territorial representation, so that the prince and his subjects often confronted each other as two compromising or quarreling parties. The newer doctrine of corporations, by contrast, brought to the state a new conception of an organic entity, a kind of secular *corpus mysticum,* with the image of head and limbs that belong together and form an organic unity. We need only cite Marsilius of Padua and, once again, Nicholas of Cusa. It is interesting to see how this doctrine altered the conception of the role of Estates in government as early as the fourteenth, fifteenth, and especially the sixteenth century, and how it changed into the more modern constitutional and representative form. The famous doctrine of the Holy Crown of Hungary[37] was based on the influence of these factors, which can be detected as early as the end of the fourteenth century. Rudiments of a similar conception are occasionally to be found elsewhere, as for example, in France and in Sweden. Even in Elizabethan England a contemporary theorist advocated the idea that King and Parliament belong together like head and limbs, and must work together as a unit.[38]

III

The second aspect under which the uniqueness of the Western system of Estates can be explained derives from the fact that the Estates do not indicate simply an economic and social differentiation of the population such as we find in every highly devel-

oped civilization, but privileged—i.e., legally and politically privileged—groups of the population. We are dealing, that is, not
simply with priests, knights, peasants, artisans, merchants, as can
be encountered in various forms everywhere also in the East, but
with the peculiar creations of a clergy and of a prelature—which is
unique to the Roman Catholic Church—of a more or less highly
privileged, corporatively united aristocracy of great lords and
knights, and of a growing homogeneous bourgeois class in privileged urban communities.

Now we find—apparently in contradiction to our thesis—at an
early stage in Indian history a structure of Estates which agrees
rather exactly with the Western scheme of "fighter, feeder,
teacher" as it was developed in the political theory of the seventeenth and eighteenth centuries, in accordance with Scholastic
and humanistic formulations and even with really existing conditions. We find this in the teachings of the oldest Indian law
books, those of Manu and Yajnavalka, which mention four *varnas*,
—the Brahmins, Kshattriyas, Vaisyas, and Sudras—of which the
first three were privileged classes of the Aryan conquering people and the fourth was a servant class of subjugated dark-skinned
indigenous inhabitants including all other foreign non-Aryan elements.[39] This three-fold division of the Aryans into priests, warriors, and producers corresponds fairly closely to the Western
scheme of clergy, nobility, and Third Estate (teacher, fighter,
feeder). It, too, is for ancient India a scholarly sociological construction which reduces the real circumstance of numerous classes
to an ideal typology. Perhaps this very plausibility theory of estates
in ancient India might have influenced Western social doctrines in
one of those great global historical connections of which there are
several examples.

What really lay at the basis of the Indian system was the development of a priestly and a warrior aristocracy within an already
highly civilized Aryan master-race which many centuries before
Christ had invaded India from the northwest and had established
its rule in a multitude of small kingdoms only brought together

into a great empire in the fourth century B.C. The Aryan people was not able to preserve its own peculiar culture and civilization in its genuine form. Despite all restrictions of taboo, some mixing of races was inevitable between the Aryans and the indigenous races, which were at a much lower cultural level, with a primitive system of tribes and clans. This altered the structure of the population fundamentally and brought about the replacement of the old Aryan class structure by the new caste differentiation so characteristic of India. The model of a primitive clan society, together with ethnic differences, hereditary professional specialization, magical and ritual prescriptions for marriage, food, and avoidance of the unclean, combined to make a system of social differentiation embodying the whole sacral law, which by its very rigidity excluded class structure on Western lines. The constant rivalry between the two upper classes—the Brahmins and the warrior-aristocracy—in which at first the warriors had the advantage despite the teachings of the priests, ended in the complete disappearance of the warriors so that the Brahmins were the only old class that was transferred to the later order of castes. However, Chandragupta, the ruler who completed the extension of the Magadha Empire in the time of the Diadochi of Alexander the Great, was far from being a scion of the Aryan master-race, but belonged to the Sudra caste. His successors favored Buddhism, and this caused the old Hindu beliefs to retreat and made its individual doctrine of redemption independent of the caste system. But the caste system itself lived on in undiminished strength.

The main facts that concern us in this development—and it frees the present thesis of any apparent contradiction—are not only that the original Aryan structure of Estates disappeared in the face of the Indian caste structure, but that even the old Indian Estates structure, whether we regard its theory or its practice, completely lacked any connection with political representation. Moreover, the status of the higher Estates rested not on legally recognized privileges but merely on custom and tradition of a magical and ritual nature. That is to say, we have before us no true political and social legal order through which certain claims might be asserted against the power of the state (which did not yet exist in India anyway), but only an order of rank regulated by religious custom and tradition and maintained and interpreted by the priesthood in its own interests. It is characteristic of the whole system that there is much talk of the giving and taking of gifts but not of specified contributions like duties and taxes. This really is something essentially different from the system of corporate privileges in the West. It has the rudiments of the Western system, but they did not develop.

Castes exist only in India; but a similar impact on the social structure, in the sense of excluding the formation of legally and politically privileged classes, results also from the maintenance of the old clan system with its cult of ancestry and its manifold functions that create a kind of self-government outside the state —proof of the differentiation of the Orient from the West. For instance, the lack of real, privileged classes in China is apparently related to the retention of such a clan system spanning the whole range of Chinese culture with a net of strong family bonds. The clan system performed the service of a kind of local but also more far-reaching self-government in a patriarchal spirit of community, so that the development of special privileged classes ran into great obstacles—not to mention the fact that the subjective claims of individual groups to rights against the authority of the Emperor and his organs of government would have seemed an offense against piety. It is striking that China failed altogether to develop any knightly warrior-aristocracy, the heart of the Estates system in the West. Even the literati, the aspirants to office out of whom the Mandarins developed and who took special examinations and were filled with the spirit of Confucian piety, were anything but a privileged class that might serve to represent the people and, in certain circumstances, form an opposition to the government. In China, instead of control and opposition by representative Estates, we have periodic uprisings of unorganized masses against misgovernment and oppression, uprisings to which the Mandarins involved had often to be sacrificed. Such movements were based not on any doctrines of natural right but rather on custom and tradition, and their real power lay in that very fact.

Of course China did not totally lack the associative union of particular occupational classes. Here, too, the merchants and especially the artisans had their guilds and corporations, which were of great importance. But we really have no exact knowledge of the structure and spirit of these associations. We have no right to assume that they are sociologically identical with their Western counterparts. We gather that the principle of a paternal, authoritarian leadership and of cooperation in fraternal solidarity asserted itself in them in a way similar to what we know of the more familiar Russian *Artell*.[40] But this principle stems from the spirit and the habits of a community of families or clans and is fundamentally different from the Western and especially the Germanic "voluntary union" that sprang from an already strongly individualist social order and presupposed a fully developed sphere of personal rights for the individual members of these associations.

With this we come to the fundamental problem of the social-psychological difference between East and West—that is to say, to the difference in personality structure. In the East, personality remained trapped in the traditional bonds of family and clan, while in the West it developed into full individual liberty, independence, and activity within the framework of a greater social circle. What is relevant here is the distinction between *community* (*Gemeinschaft*) and *society* (*Gesellschaft*) which Toennies has taught us and which even before the differentiation had been made was used by jurists when they distinguished a relation based on status and a relation based on contract. While the East remained frozen in the status relationship of family and clan of a primitive community, the privileged classes in the West, and thereby the whole system of Estates, rested on an evolving though by no means fully or finally established modern social order that at first strengthened the authority of the head of the household in a single family in place of the old clan unit and then produced with the *privilegium* an enhancement and enrichment of the sphere of personal rights. This led to claims of subjective rights against the state and created, through the transition from a status relationship to a contract relationship, the possibility of an alliance among the individual privileged legal units which constitutes the basis for the formation of recognized units and of the actual political system of Estates.

Such a development as the West displayed was possible only in a relatively modern political and social order that no longer depended on the traditions of the tribal and clan system but on the rational spirit of positive legal statutes that came not only from the Roman commercial law of the ancient Mediterranean basin but also from old Germanic law and from the Canon Law of the Roman Church, nourished in the Teutonic and Latin spirit. It was an order depending on a legal and political theory which, owing much to Aristotle and the cosmopolitan doctrines of the Stoics, had worked Christian and Latin-Teutonic views of law and morality together into a normative system of natural and divine law that stood behind the positive law of individual peoples, completing it and regulating it.

How different the spiritual assumptions of the non-Christian and non-Western peoples were from this is perhaps most clearly shown by the example of Chinese high culture, with its Confucian political and social order. It was based not on rational law but on traditional mores, not on personality but on family bonds, not on an individualistically oriented society but on a clan-like spirit of community. Because of this it knew of no public subjective rights accorded to the individual, but only of subordination to tradition and, above all, reverence for paternal authority in every form, and for the older generation in general. In this soil, naturally, no system of Estates could grow, even disregarding the theoretically unlimited power of the state exercised by the Son of Heaven.

This unlimited state power itself grew out of the age-old patriarchal forms of the tribal and clan system, where there was no division between spiritual and secular authority and where the head of the clan or tribe was at once priest and protector of the cult of ancestry and the leader in temporal matters.

If in China—as we have already noted—there was no separate privileged warrior class like the knighthood in Western states, this is also connected to the early incidence of hired or pressed armies, maintained and equipped at state expense, since this precluded self-equipment or self-training of single warriors or private bands of warriors. This phenomenon, widespread in the ancient Orient, of the bureaucratic administration of armies wherein even slaves were trained and equipped as warriors has afforded Max Weber the basis for his attempt, sketchy as it is, to explain the absence of a system of Estates in the East.[41] It is an attempt that does not cover the problem in all its scope and depth, but it is still worth our attention and deserves closer consideration.

According to Weber's analysis, the necessity in the ancient river cultures—Egypt, Mesopotamia, China—for supervising masses of workers in a unified and systematic way in great hydraulic projects, to regulate the rivers and to irrigate the land over wide areas, called into being bureaucratic state administrations functioning within a system of natural economy. This administration then entered upon the area of military affairs and stifled or prevented from the outset the self-equipment and self-training of single warriors prevailing everywhere in the West. It was on this very principle, however, that feudalism in the West was based; in fact feudalism originally was an attempt to bring under state control the proliferating private military enterprises. But when the self-arming and self-training class of knights that had been formed as a result of this attempt encountered increasing demands dictated by the political interests of the princely overlord, the knights united in an effective coalition through which they secured privileges for their class. These privileges gave the knights a favored legal and political position and frequently some kind of participation in the government of the developing state. This possibility for highly-trained and self-equipped warriors to combine among themselves and to wrest privileges from the sovereign, was especially successful where there was no real feudal law, as in Poland.[42] Here the nobility's privileges as a class were all acquired, both before and after the General Privilege of Kosice in 1374, through the pressure a coalition of self-arming knightly warriors were able to apply on the sovereign war lord when he was in critical straits.[43] On the other hand, we see that everywhere in the West the development of a standing army created and maintained, outfitted and trained according to the system of bureaucratic administration at state expense, spelled the death of the feudal political and social order of Estates.

We may thus probably assume that the absence of a privileged warrior-class, and thus of the chief motivating force in the Estates movement, was related in the East to the early incidence of a military administration that was centralized and bureaucratic. But this is not a fully satisfactory explanation. It is contradicted by the fact that a system of fiefs and a feudalistic political order did develop in the East—not of course in China, but elsewhere in the Near and the Far East, despite the bureaucratic military administration, and even partly because of it. Particularly in Japan and the Islamic states this feudalistic order closely parallelled the Western system. But the fact is that here it failed to develop into a system of Estates but rather compromised with an absolutist monarchical political order so that neither the warrior-class nor any other outstanding group possessed legal and political privileges that would have enabled them to coerce the central authority or to play the role of representatives of the subjects.

Japanese feudalism, in many respects similar to the Western form, differed from it essentially through the legal nature of the feudal contract.[44] The Latin-Teutonic contract was based in principle on the equality of rights and the reciprocity of both parties. The Japanese was based on a much more severe dependence of the vassal on this liege-lord than was usual in the West. This was consistent with the Confucian doctrines that had also become standard in Japan and led to the liege-lord's being granted a kind of paternal authority over his vassal. This is ultimately explicable by the fact that the Japanese vassal relation of the *kenin* had been originally a client relation within the larger units of the clan, which often took in strangers as younger sons or brothers in the earliest stages even through the symbolic act of blood-brotherhood, and, especially in times of family feuds or internal unrest, used them as armed retainers.

How different this is from the German retainership which was the point of departure for the later vassal relation is obvious. According to the testimony of Tacitus, this was based on the declaration of a free man to his peers in a public assembly whenever one of the chiefs asked in that company for volunteers to assist him in one of his wars or raids. In Japan, by contrast, a patriarchal relation from the outset was at the basis of the relation; and even later, when it had weakened, it still never became a relation between two equal contracting parties. Everywhere the feudal contract was a status contract, a synthesis of a contractual and a status relationship: it was a contract aimed at a fixed typical status relationship. In Germanic law, the status relationship was that of a free man, whose status, through voluntary subordination to a military chief, who looked out for his livelihood, was not lowered but rather raised, particularly when the chief was a prince or a king. In Japanese custom, however, the status relationship was that of younger son or brother in a family whose head was the liege-lord. This involved a much greater dependence, to which the common reverence of ancestors lent sacral reinforcement. It is in this context that we can explain why later, when these origins were long forgotten, liege-lords allowed their vassals, as an honor, to assume the lord's family name and to wear the family crest on their helmets. The whole entourage of vassals of a great lord were called his *han*, a word meaning roughly "fence," recalling the *hag* that played a role in the German feudal system (one thinks of the *Hagestalden*—unmarried retainers—placed and fed in the *hag* of the liege-lord, as against those vassals who with their families were settled on special landed properties). The Japanese *han* was often translated by the English word "clan."

Professor Asakawa,[45] a great expert on Japanese constitutional history, inveighs against this translation as an anachronism. It is certainly true that in the Tokugawa era, which he particularly has in mind, in the seventeenth century, the era of the real clan state lay a thousand years in the past. However, even if from the seventeenth century onward the word *han* meant no more than the mere extent or realm of a feudal principality, this still does not exclude the fact that in earlier centuries, when the extensive sub-infeudation and the territorial consolidation of feudal principalities were still largely incomplete, it probably meant more the personal relation of the entourage of vassals to the lord, which can be conceived of as an extension of the lord's household. That is the interpretation advocated by Karl Rathgen[46] and by Tokuzo Fukuda.[47] For the purpose of the present study it is of primary importance that the feudal contract in Japanese law involved an extensive subordination of the vassal to his lord, and a considerable patriarchal authority for the lord; therefore, the legal dualism so basic to the system of Estates in the West could not develop.

The priestly class in Japan qualified even less for Estates representation than the warrior-class, the less so as there were two different, competing religious systems. The Shinto priests had to care for the ancestral cult of the Imperial house. From them could emanate an impulse toward a later restoration of Imperial power, but not toward the organization of local authorities nor toward the limitation of the central authority. Such a tendency toward Estates squared with the Buddhist spirit just as little. It was absorbed in the care of individual souls; and where it was politically active it could establish and govern a theocratic community in the isolation of the high Tibetan mountains but was not capable of any constitutional participation in a secular state government. Buddhism as well as Shintoism thoroughly lacked the rational and legal Christian spirit that the Christian Church, particularly the Roman Catholic Church, had appropriated as an inheritance from the Roman Empire, and which enabled it to play such a significant role in the political life of the West.

The dualist spirit that produced the Estates system in the West was also lacking in the feudalism of the Islamic states.[48] Here, fiefs were originally a reward for distinguished Arab warriors, and later a substitute for mercenary payment to Turkish soldiers and their commanders. There was no personal relation of vassalage; it was replaced by the religious obligation of fighting for the faith. The *Sipahi* did form a privileged class of mounted warriors, but it was not able to gain the same political significance as the Western knighthood, because its particular class-feeling was never more than a not very effective reinforcement of the much stronger common feeling of joint responsibility that animated the entire community of faithful Moslems and bound the faithful in principle to the ruler in a relation of loyalty that precluded the dualistic principle of Estates as in the West. The Islamic state was above all a religious community, and the spirit animating it was heavily influenced by the traditions of the systems of clan and tribe. They were still very much alive when it was founded, and they lived on for a long time.

The entire aggregate of priests and teachers, the *ulema,* did form with its numerous divisions and grades a privileged class, though more in fact than in law. Yet this group could not exercise the political function of representation of the people or the country, because it was itself an essential and important part of the machinery of state government. Church and State formed here a complete unity animated by a patriarchal spirit, and allowed no dualistic principle of Estates to arise as it did in the West.

A formation of a wholly different type was the ancient city-state of the Mediterranean countries, but even this rested to a large extent on the clan system and thus provided no favorable possibilities for the development of privileged classes and for a representative constitution based on them. In fact the clan system of these city-states had its special features. Max Weber pointed out with great emphasis that the nature of the Western city, especially of the *polis* of ancient Mediterranean civilization, rested on an act of fraternization among citizens, and that this was possible only where the original clan system did not display so great a degree of exclusiveness resulting from ritualistic taboos and restrictions on the individual as was the case among the Indian and equatorial peoples.[49] Where, however, the possibility for the sacral union of different clan units existed, then this became, in conjunction with a union for defense and settlement, a firm basis for the building of the state.

The ancient city-state was, in its original germ, a confederation of clans within a tribe or a group of tribes possessing a common shrine and the basic institutions for a common political life, and it clung tenaciously to its basic tribal structure. It even formed the basis for its organization of Estates, which was quite different from that on which the system of Estates among the Latin-Teutonic peoples was founded. Members of the old clans were originally the only citizens to possess full political rights, forming the patriciate. Class struggles were directed toward the extension of these rights to the unpedigreed or immigrant plebeian population. In the homogeneous closed community which thus developed and which had got rid of an earlier monarchical leadership, there was no duality that would have favored the rise of representation of the citizenry by privileged classes. The institution of slavery reinforced this tendency toward the legal and political homogeneity of the citizenry. There were, certainly, differences of interest and party, but no privileged classes in the medieval sense.

The clan system tends to disappear in proportion to the development of feudalism. Feudalism is based on the household authority that dissociates itself from the clan and breaks it up. On the other hand, associations like the curias of Rome or the Attic *Phratriae* or the Spartan *Obei* are more suited to maintain and strengthen a clan system, on which they are modeled. These artificial new forms, which originally seem to have been connected with the system of military organization, are generally found wherever a tribe or group of tribes has become a state without passing through the intermediate stage of a large feudalistic kingdom. This is the case in the West, as, for example, in Poland and Hungary. The Polish *szlachta* seem to have been put together out of such defensive associations of traditionally free clansmen, the *nobiles*.[50] A formation corresponding to the Greek *Phratriae*, the *bratstvo*, is attested to among the South Slav tribes.

In such communities, which are not really feudal, the nobility is the totality of all clansmen fit for military service, not really a special class. The old territorial and ethnic units hold together tenaciously, and by virtue of their semi-autonomous constitutions give the state an aristocratic and federalist character that favors the local position of lordship of the nobility. This nobility of course was differentiated into higher and lower levels, but the higher nobility was distinguished only by its special titles and dignities and as well by its large holdings. What finally did give the nobility even here the stamp of a privileged class was the successful attempt, mentioned above, of these self-armed and self-trained warriors at wresting legal and political privileges from the monarch and chief commander at a favorable moment. The form of the state favored such an endeavor, since it had nothing of the concentrated form of a city-state in which the monarchical head could easily be disposed of, but was a state extensive in area, with a composite, almost federal character whose unity was only realized in the monarchical leadership. Because of this the monarchy remained indispensable, even if it was always weak as compared with the nobility in their local units.

These states whose people made a direct transition from the life of the tribe to the life of the state, without passing through a stage of feudalist empire, could be called simply "privilege-states" as opposed to "feudal states." They contained the pre-conditions for the rise of a system of Estates in this very system of privileges. Otherwise, the nature of the constitution in these states was essentially different from that developing out of feudalism.[51]

In the feudal West, which had given birth to the typical Franco-Germanic system of Estates characteristic for the Continent, the system of clans generally no longer played a role. It had disappeared almost entirely. The chief reason for this lies apparently in the long, bellicose migrations of the Germanic tribes, who settled down on the soil of the Roman Empire, with its long-standing civilization. The cooperation of the Church and the rising monarchical central power went a long way toward completely eliminating the remains of the clan system. It was not monarchy alone that was at work here. In China a great comprehensive monarchical state had been able to come into being without the clan system's ever having been eliminated. Thus it may be assumed that in the West it was chiefly the Christian Church which had forced the elimination of the remains of the clan system. The Church had very weighty reasons for opposing the clan system. In the first place, the system had ingrained heathen vestiges in its ancestor worship. In the second place, it clung to the idea of blood vengeance, or managed the system of atonement that took its place, in an irrational way inimical to the spirit of ecclesiastical law. In the third place, it possessed exclusive control over family law, which the Church itself aspired to control, and it preserved above all the communal property of the clan by forbidding the freedom to make a will—which was of greatest interest to the Church, because of bequests to ecclesiastical foundations.

The united effort of the Church and its ally, the Kings, succeeded in eliminating the clan system everywhere in the West, and this meant a powerful expansion of the possibility for developing representative Estates.

Of similar importance was the fact that the Church in the West promoted the mixing of the races in a wholly different sense than the religions of the East with their tabooistic and ritual restrictions and bonds. The Christian Church, particularly the Roman Catholic Church, eliminated magic more and more from the regulation of social relations in favor of a rational configuration of social law. Max Weber has indicated the far-reaching consequences, for social history, of the Christian principle of common meals which St. Paul introduced when he did not shrink from eating with the uncircumcised at Antioch, thus abandoning the ritual separation of Jew and Gentile and asserting the common life of Christians of both traditions.[52] This was the basis of the Christian community; in regions with no ancient municipal tradition this Christian community in turn was of fundamental importance for the origin of urban communities such as the East never saw.

In this context we must also mention the gradual abolition of slavery in the Christian world. This took place largely for economic reasons and was related to the transition from the money economy of the ancient Mediterranean city-states to the natural economy of the inland medieval communities; but this material factor was still very fundamentally supported by ideal motives emanating from the morals and law of the Christian Church. What was at issue here was less the generally oppressive social condition that was the lot of the slaves in ancient times or of the bondsmen in the Middle Ages than the question whether these people could be legally classified as persons. For on this depended the possibility of representation, which was basic to the system of Estates. One can only represent persons, not objects. The medieval lord of the manor could be regarded as the natural representative of his bondsmen, but the Roman *possessor* could not be regarded as the representative of his slaves.

If at its apogee ancient civilization failed altogether to produce the category of popular representation, then the institution of slavery surely had a large share in this. After all, it was only because a large part of the population consisted of men without legal status that the system of direct democracy, embracing all citizens with rights, could develop and maintain itself without popular representation, the need for which was neither felt nor satisfied. In the great urban centers of the later Roman Republic and of the Empire there was a mass of proletarians but there was no citizen class depending on free labor. The slave economy not only ruined the peasant class but also prevented the rise of a commercial middle class. It bears the burden of blame for the social disintegration of the ancient world. The ultimate victory of Christianity rested in no small measure on the fact that in the communities of the faithful a new spirit of social community was called to life which bridged the gap between free man and slave and proved itself indispensable as a strong and durable cement in the building of a new political society.

Thus the Christian Church as a community of believers contributed widely to establishing the preconditions for the Western system of Estates. Beyond this, however, the priesthood of the Christian Church, which was distinguished from the priesthood of all other religions by its hierarchical organization, nurtured in the Roman Empire and based on natural law, became the model of all privileged classes in the West. Because of its sacral character, and as a repository of what remained of ancient education and culture, the clergy occupied a highly privileged position vis-à-vis the barbarian state authorities that succeeded the Roman Empire. So long as this position was purely personal in nature, and attached only to the clerical office as such, it could not of course serve as a model for the secular Estates.

The clergy had or acquired large land holdings and received immunity by virtue of their position as manorial lords. This privilege continued the tradition of the exceptional position accorded to the Imperial domains in the Roman Empire; it afforded the clergy freedom from interference by state authorities, and with that soon even their own jurisdiction. That is to say, they secured a transfer of the state's sovereign rights, the nucleus of all subsequent granting of privileges in the West. Following the Church's

example, this immunity was sought after and secured by the secular notables. It was the basis for the whole system of privileges
that everywhere characterized the state based on Estates. Where
there was a system of fiefs, immunity was attached to it; but
even where no real system of fiefs existed, immunity generated
the conditions for the rise of privileged classes and for a system
of Estates as, for example in Scandinavia, Poland, and Hungary.
In Sweden[53] nobility was constituted by freedom from taxation
and from the other burdens and impositions of the state, granted
to those landholders who provided military service on horseback
(*frälse* is equivalent to immunity). In Poland[54] and Hungary[55]
the system of immunity of the Church operated as a model for
the system of privilege of the nobility regarding both local sovereignty and self-government and the limiting of services to the
King. The position of the nobility here rested on privileges and
not on feudal law. Only late in the game did these privileges
come to approximate to some degree a feudal system, by way of
the so-called *banderiatus* and *avitacitas* system under the Angevin Kings.[56]

In Russia,[57] where a peculiar feudalism of a more ministerial
character developed, it was the very lack of such privileges that
gave the nobility—from the highest boyars to the lowest retainers
—the characteristic coloration differentiating it from Western nobility. A reason for this is the fact that the Church had not been endowed with privileges of immunity to the same extent as it had
been in the West and that the immunities it possessed were curtailed or withdrawn after the Church was converted in the sixteenth century into a national state Church under the protection
of the Muscovite Tsars. Thereafter the privileges of the Russian
clergy were more of a personal kind. After the ascendancy of
the Muscovite Tsars the power of the state was too strong to
yield its sovereign rights easily. The attempt of Patriarch Nikon
to open the way to something like an Eastern counterpart to the
Papacy in Russia collapsed pitiably in 1666. When in the seventeenth century serfdom was introduced under the patrimonial

authority of the manorial lords, it occurred in a way that did not free the nobility from the threat of government intervention in their estates. On the contrary, it meant the determination of the noblemen's relations with their serfs through police regulation, an additional elaborate regulation of their service obligations, on which of course their whole position depended. Milyukov emphasizes that the Russian nobility in the time of the *zemsky sabor*—that is, in the sixteenth and seventeenth centuries—was not by any means a privileged class. It became that only in the eighteenth century under Catherine the Great, when representation by Estates had long since vanished. That explains the weakness in Russia of the system of Estates of the sixteenth and seventeenth centuries.

The importance of immunity for the constitution and autonomy of the towns in the West is already familiar to us. It set the town apart from the mass of subjects as a region with a special law and administration. As a corollary to this, the town was still identified with the concept of *community*, of a corporative association of free and equal citizens. The ideal type for such an association of citizens was originally a *conjuratio*, a sworn union. It was an association bound together by oath for mutual protection and support. This origin cannot be vouched for everywhere in the Middle Ages, since in more recent foundations of towns we often enough have no knowledge of an act of *conjuratio*. Wherever the model of an urban community existed, its spirit and essence could be transferred or appropriated without such an explicit act. Nevertheless, the construction of an ideal type must be based on the assumption of the existence of a sworn union. But towns like these exist only in the Christian West. Certainly there are extended settlements at the great centers of commerce near princely residences or around the centers of administration and defense outside the Christian West. But although they might carry the name of town, they were not really towns in the Western sense, not the residence of a privileged middle class, and therefore not inclined to serve as one element

in a system of Estates. Even in the Christian West, urban communities in this strict legal sense were really indigenous only
to the realm of the Latin-Teutonic peoples. They were carried
over to Poland and Hungary by German colonization and always
remained there a weak and not fully valid branch of the representation by Estates. In sixteenth- and seventeenth-century Russia there were no towns at all in the Western sense. This, too, is
one of the reasons for the weakness of the system of Estates in
Russia.

The importance that the aspect of association held in the Estates system also rested on the character of Estates as politically
privileged groups. It was not in itself the sole basis for the system—this had already been provided by the cohesive bond of
the state—but it was at least an indispensable component in a
genuine and powerful Estates system. Association was often the
lever for acquiring privileges. On the other hand, equality of
privilege furthered in turn the unity of an Estate and its corporative exclusiveness. The alliance of different Estates among themselves served to maintain the privileges of each individual Estate,
and bred that solidarity in defense of the liberties of the land
that emerged in times of conflict. For this reason I prefer to rate
the factor of association in the Estates much higher than does von
Below, who, of course, had only the German territorial Estates
in mind. He is quite right that the cohesive bond of the state
was the main foundation for the Estates system; but the system
of association was also of fundamental importance.

The system of association was strikingly absent in Russia, and
that is apparently connected to the lack of real privileges.
Neither the Estates as a whole had a sense of solidarity, as testi-
fied by Kovalevsky's extracts from the richly informative documents of the Sabor of 1642,[58] nor did the individual Estates. The
Russian clergy lacked that imposing exclusiveness and discipline
displayed by the celibate clergy of the Roman Catholic Church.
The higher clergy, monastic in origin, stood in sharp contrast to
the married, and generally uneducated, lay clergy who formed

a kind of hereditary caste and enjoyed little prestige. Even the bishops and abbots, who owed their positions largely to the Tsar's favor, were scarcely fit to be an important factor in representing the people or region. It is true that they were called in to the great assemblies of the land from time to time, as in 1642; but they did not really belong to the *magnum consilium* of the Boyar Duma, and did not, as a body, entertain any political ambitions, even if individuals did at times exert significant influence. In 1642 they expressly stressed their readiness to give the Tsar's policies their loyal support, but they preferred, as hitherto, to limit themselves to their spiritual functions.

The boyar class was deprived of this sense of solidarity in the course of the jealously fought battle of its members over the ordering of families by rank, determined only by past and present service and as manifested in the sixteenth and seventeenth centuries in the so-called *mestnichestvo*. Their attitude was that of a dependent servant group, not of a proud privileged class. Had the Estates system really been merely an organization forced into being by the state, as von Below suggests, then Russia would display its ideal type. In truth, however, Russia displays only an incomplete deviant variety of the system, and it is for this reason very instructive, because it shows where the real motive power of the Estates lay. The system of association in itself, without the fundamental cohesive bonds of the state, naturally did not create the system of Estates; but within the bonds which the state had more or less sharply established, it represented an essential condition for the creation of strong, politically capable Estates.

IV

As I have shown elsewhere,[59] the feudal system is not a universal stage that all human societies must pass through in their social and political development. Similarly, the Estates system cannot be regarded as a universal and necessary extension of the feudal system. As we have seen, there existed in the East feudal systems that could not by their nature develop into an Estates system. On the other hand, we find systems of Estates in the West that did not evolve from a real feudal system. This does not rule out the fact that in the rest of the Western states the feudal system and the system of Estates were closely allied, or even that Estates can be regarded as a continuation or final phase of feudalism. But it does seem clear that factors besides feudalism were at work in the rise of the Estates system. We have already indicated repeatedly the historic importance of the constitution of the Christian Church in this context.

Connected to this, at least partially and indirectly, is the phenomenon we must now examine closely. This phenomenon, which is characteristic of the modern age, is the progressive consolidation and rationalization of state operations. Where feudalism dominated uncurbed as in the German empire, the political organization, already loose enough, disintegrated easily and more or less completely. On the other hand, we find lasting systems of Estates capable of development only where to a certain degree the strength of political bonds has been preserved or restored and where, within this framework, a political life of some intensity, guided by rational calculations, developed. The main reason for the uniqueness of the Estates system of the West is the fact that it was a phenomenon accompanying the peculiar form in which states originated in Western history. Outside the Christian West the formation of states tended, as a consequence of the bond between secular and ecclesiastical power, toward universal monarchy, which in the interior encouraged absolutism. The peculiar constitution and politics of the Church, with its opposition to the state, was the fundamental cause for the failure of such a universal monarchy to develop in the West. It caused nation-building to develop in the direction of a diversity of coordinated state structures that recognized each other's independence. It promoted what later after the sixteenth and seventeenth centuries was called the European state system.

This later stage in Western nation-building was preceded by

an earlier stage whose main outlines begin to show after the twelfth century. It partly still carries an aura of the more loosely structured small territorial state in comparison to the later stage of greater national states, but it can nonetheless also be regarded as a nascent system of states, for which the Roman Catholic Church provided the coherent framework. On the whole the community of faith institutionalized in the Church later transposed itself into a society of states based on treaties and natural law. International law was merely the medieval religious cultural community in secularized garb resting on the *jus divinum*.

The driving forces that produced this peculiar form of political life were twofold. There was on the one hand the constant rivalry among the states, the constant competition for increased power and prestige; on the other, the moral necessity for these conflicting states perpetually to come to terms again and to find a *modus vivendi* in order not to go beyond the scope of the ecclesiastical and religious cultural community, and later beyond the scope of the civilized society of states sustained by international law. On this overarching psychological and political structure rested the general disposition for creating a system of Estates. In the constant battles, which were not battles to the death but only for the extension of power and for a variety of advantages, the rulers found themselves thoroughly dependent on the good will of those strata of the population capable of military and financial contributions. This good will naturally had to be rewarded or even bought by giving full consideration to their economic and social interests but also by giving concessions and liberties of a political nature like those enshrined in the privileges of the Estates—the basis of the Estates system.

The active elements of the population who helped to build the state also gained a share in its government. That was a direct consequence of this kind of nation-building and politics. Thus the French and English Estates systems developed most particularly during the protracted war to settle the boundaries of their spheres of power in the fourteenth and fifteenth centuries. Similarly the Estates system of the Nordic states developed in the fifteenth and sixteenth centuries during the wars that followed on the dissolution of the Union of Kalmar; that of Poland, in the struggle with the Teutonic Knights and Russia; that of Hungary, in the struggle with her South Slav neighbors; that of the German territories, in the internal strife of the Empire in the fifteenth century in which their boundaries were by and large definitely set for the first time. It is characteristic that Hungary's wars with the Turks, or the Spanish kingdom's conflict with the Moors, did not have the same effect of endowing the Estates with extensive privileges: these were wars against the infidels, which Christian duty and self-preservation simply compelled one to enter. Otherwise it was fully possible for a country that was not well disposed toward its ruler simply to place itself under another lord somewhat in the way that the Prussian Estates deserted the Teutonic Knights for Poland or the Sicilians forsook the House of Anjou for that of Aragon. The right of resistance, to which Estates everywhere more or less explicitly laid claim, covered the possibility under certain circumstances of "placing oneself under another lord."

A significant exception is the state of affairs in Renaissance Italy, which has been regarded as the prototype for the European state system. Here the constant rivalry among the individual states did not yield any system of Estates within the rival states. The explanation for this is not hard to come by: almost all these states were city-states, or at least states with a thoroughly municipal structure. The municipal structure, as we have seen, precludes the development of a system of Estates.

There is another, though only apparent, exception to which we must devote some attention. I am referring to the later epoch of the European state system, when, in connection with the struggles that brought about the transformation of a conglomeration of small states into a centralized larger state, absolutism appeared and curtailed the functioning of the Estates system. This, however, was only a transitional state resting on the fact that the

Estates system had in many places become a hindrance to the development of greater states. As soon as this development dictated by political necessity had been completed, we find a revival of the representative principle, together with the awakening of a national political consciousness within these centralized great states, in the new form of a constitutional system. But, we cannot go into this any further here. It is a complicated process that is a story in itself.

What mainly interests us here is the earlier era, when the developing national states, still divided into small states, coexisted in the coherent framework of the community of the Church. We must point out in this context the fact that in the course of the bellicose rivalries of this time the Roman Church, sometimes by conscious policy, sometimes by its mere existence and by the conflicts of its hierocratic ambitions, lent everywhere visible encouragement to the process of nation-building and the related process of the development of an Estates system.

Even though canonical theory always maintained the idea of a universal empire, the Curia still contributed much to preventing the rise of any real universal hegemony of the Emperor. This we see in the Popes' successful efforts to take such states as Poland and Hungary out of the protective sphere of the Emperor and into their own, and later particularly in the time of Innocent III, in the development of a systematic policy to make as many states of Christendom as directly dependent on the Papal throne as possible, like the Normans in Southern Italy, Aragon, and Portugal, and England under King John. That the Curia also directly favored and even required the establishment of a system of Estates, is proved by its behavior in Hungary between 1222 and 1232, and again in the fourteenth century, as well as from its policy in the Naples of Charles I and Charles II. In Hungary the occasion was the conflict that led to King Andrew II's promulgation of the Golden Bull. The King was in the process of making the great nobility real masters of the realm, by granting them disproportionately large crown lands. The *servientes*—the middle and lesser nobility—rose up against this. The Curia likewise came out against the overly powerful higher nobility and did much to ensure the King's promulgation of the *magna carta* of Hungary, the so-called Golden Bull, which especially benefited the lesser nobility.

Of course, the machinery of the right of resistance which it created was in the long run not convenient to the Curia. When the law was renewed in 1232 the Curia tried to alter its provisions so that in the event of the king's breaking his promises, he was to be directed and held to the fulfillment of his promises by the ecclesiastical authority. When in the fourteenth century the first two Angevin Kings of Hungary, Carobert and Louis the Great, attempted once again to rule without the participation of the Estates, it was chiefly the bishops who lodged a complaint to the Curia in Rome to bring about Papal intervention to restore the system of Estates. In the Kingdom of Naples the Curia deliberately exerted pressure on Charles of Anjou to hold parliament. The assemblies of the notables that the Emperor Frederick II on occasion convoked cannot really be regarded as parliaments. But Charles of Anjou attempted to carry on without any such assemblies and resisted the Pope's imprecations. Under his successors, however, after Sicily had fallen to Aragon in 1282 and and 1283, things changed under a steady stream of Papal admonitions, and an Estates system was established in Naples too.[60]

Most important of all, the Curia was involved in more or less all the great rivalries between the states, and we can prove its part in almost all the great crises that led to the development of a system of Estates. Still, the political constellation was changeable. In the German Empire the investiture contest provided an occasion for the strengthening of the princes' opposition to the Emperor which we must regard as the basis for the liberties of the princes and the Estates. The famous privileges accorded to the spiritual and temporal princes by Frederick II in 1220 and 1231 likewise have for their background the opposition between Emperor and Pope. To the privilege of 1231 was attached the

Imperial statute that, though it had no immediate legal consequences, can still with justification be regarded as the signal for
the coming territorial system of Estates. In the battle with the
Curia in 1338 the electors agreed to a demonstrative common
action which was an important step on the way to a formal constitution of the Imperial Estates. In France, Philip IV had assembled the Estates-General of his realm in the Church of Notre
Dame in 1302 for a similar demonstrative act in his conflict with
Pope Boniface VIII. This likewise marked a new age in the history of the system of Estates in France.

In England the Magna Charta of 1215 resulted from the political situation which arose from the subordination of the anathe-
matized King John to the Pope as liege-lord in 1213 and from the
victory of the Papal cause in the battle of Bouvines in 1214. The
result was a double squeeze from Pope and King, whose immediate and palpable result was the common exploitation of the
English Church by both these powers, who eliminated the claims
of the spiritual and temporal magnates for control over the
churches in their lands. Thus, the prelates and barons united under the leadership of Stephen Langton, Archbishop of Canterbury, over whose appointment Pope and King had earlier fought,
and obtained the famous charter of liberties which opened with a
guarantee of free canonical elections in England. Thus, not only
the conscious policy but the whole hierocratic constitution of the
Roman Church manifestly aided and abetted the rise of the Estates system in the West. Where there was no such Church, as in
most of the East, or where it was politically weak as in Russia,
there was no such powerful impetus.

If we now look at this connection between the formation of
states and the Estates system from the point of view of domestic
politics, we shall be led to the fundamental difference between
the older, more extensive state organization that was characteristic of the Carolingian Empire and the whole early Middle Ages,
and the later, more intensive organization that made itself felt
in the small territorial states, not only in Germany but also in

France (particularly Normandy) or smaller national states such as early England, which closely resembled the territorial states. The extensive state organization, which rested on a disproportion between the size of the state and the instruments available at this cultural level, led to a fragmentation of rule and with it to a feudalism that carried within itself disintegrating tendencies. The more intensive state organization overcame this kind of feudalism through rational and functional institutions that at first strengthened the authoritarian element in political life, and led —partly under preservation of feudal forms—to a veritable feudal absolutism. By the same token, however, it evoked a reaction by corporate elements and thus encouraged the development of Estates systems.

In the beginning the ruler consulted from time to time his *magnum consilium* of prelates and barons. Eventually, however, he created for himself permanent organs of his ruling will in the typical three central agencies: the Council, the High Court of Justice, and the Exchequer. From this arose the *concilium continuum,* confronted by the parliament of prelates and barons as a separate body. A corresponding local administration was organized under the central administration. A more intensive and rational management of legislation, finances, and general administration got underway.

The strong influence of the Church on the development and functioning of this whole organization has to be especially emphasized. Bracton, the father of English jurisprudence, was a priest, as was the author of the *Dialogus de Scaccario;* the administration of the treasury in France was conducted and organized in the beginning by the Templars. Even the transformation of local administration from a feudal to a bureaucratic form could use the *officium* of the Church as a model. The important institution of commissaries had been worked out in canonical practice according to the spiritual and temporal model of the Carolingian *missi.* The canonists had followed the legists; Roman law had the most powerful influence on the rationalization of state operations. All these were influences possible only in the West and in the final analysis rested on a cultural synthesis of the Latin and Teutonic strains, in which the Church played mediator. These impulses were altogether lacking in the non-Christian world. In Russia they were—at the very least—highly attenuated by the Byzantine spirit of Caesaro-Papism, which asserted itself, after some vacillation, in the seventeenth century.

This increasing intensification of state organization and the strengthening of authoritarian and institutional aspects in political life led, wherever the old original idea of law had survived and the beginnings of privileged groups existed, to a more or less marked reaction of the corporate spirit against the one-sided reinforcement of the institutions of control. The result was the evolution of a regular system of Estates. In details these developments took various forms. In England feudal absolutism succeeded in saving the counties from feudal disintegration, they remained in the service of the state as associations for the fulfillment of obligations and the discharge of burdens, and the powerful privileged elements were persuaded to take their share in the growing tasks of a more intensive local administration. Accordingly, the principles of rulership and of association became fruitfully reconciled in the area of local administration; and the growth of the parliamentary system here appears as the progressive concentration of the local administrative machinery. In Poland and Hungary, where there was a powerless, often foreign, elected king, the more or less highly privileged nobility made the old territorial units—*Voivods* and the *Comitats*—into the domains of their class influence, and the Estates system became the foundation of a kind of republic of nobles, with a monarch at its head. Wherever, as in France and Germany, local administration was restructured after the dissolution of the old county and regional units in a patrimonial spirit and the prince's bureaucratic authority gained the upper hand, the corporate reaction of the nobility in the development of the Estates system emerged most clearly.

Out of the primitive right of resistance, and its rough and ready reprisals, there developed the subtler preventive methods of cooperation by the Estates in legislation, of the granting and administering of taxes by the Estates and its agencies, of a system of grievances and petitions against abuses of the princely authorities. Thus arose the representative system of Estates, in its various types. It was the prototype of the modern constitutional system, which has conquered the whole civilized world and which has culminated nowadays in parliamentarism, which seems to have entered into a serious crisis in view of the great changes in the world's political and social structure that have emerged from the Great War. If, however, the representative system has by now spread over the whole world, partly even in the Soviet and Fascist systems, it is still not a universal invention of mankind, but developed as an indigenous phenomenon only in the Christian West in the prototype of the Estates system. This process was, however, dependent on conditions so closely tied to the whole course of world history that we must not speak here of a general sociological law but of a singular historical process, extending throughout the entire West, whose results were subsequently carried over to other lands.

HISTORY AND THEORY

9

THE INDIVIDUALIST AND
THE COLLECTIVE APPROACH
TO HISTORY

In this brief article, published in the *Historische Zeitschrift,* Volume 78 (1897), Hintze presents, for the first time, his views on historical theory. He touches here upon problems that occupied him throughout the remainder of his life: whether the historian could formulate universal laws of history; whether such an aim was compatible with the historian's particular task of demonstrating the unique and individual characteristics of a historical event; and whether and to what extent comparisons in history are valid and fruitful. Hintze would frequently return to these questions, in essays on questions of historical theory (see, for instance, the following essay, "Troeltsch and the Problems of Historicism") and in investigations of historical events. As the point of departure for Hintze's further reflections on the theoretical problems of history, this early article is of great interest.

The article was Hintze's contribution to the great debate that went on in the world of German historical scholarship during the 1890s and is usually called the *Lamprecht Streit.* Karl Lamprecht, in a series of articles that began with one entitled "Alte und neur Richtungen in der Geschichtswissenschaft" (1896), asked German historical scholarship to take a new course. The historian ought to aim at the discovery and the establishment of historical laws so that history, like other sci-

ences, would be based on the principle of strict causality. This would
become possible through application of the insights of social psychology. In Lamprecht's view social psychology provides criteria that can
enable the historian to identify different historical periods because
each epoch of history has a sociopsychological life of its own. This can
be described and defined through analysis of the artistic and literary
forms of expression and through examination of the common elements
of the political and social customs of a period. A causal explanation of
historical development is feasible because—to quote from Lamprecht's
American lectures, entitled *What Is History?*—there is "a regular course
of sociopsychological development within great communities of men,"
so that the various periods of history are causally interconnected. Lamprecht stated that these new aims of history would also require a new
methodical approach that would fully incorporate the study of literature, art, and almost all forms of human activity into historical investigations. Lamprecht called the new history he advocated "cultural
history." (It might be remarked here that in the translation of Hintze's
article the terms "cultural history" and "culture" are used when
Hintze writes of *Kulturgeschichte* and *Kulture;* now we would probably use "social history" for what Lamprecht called *Kulturgeschichte.*
It ought also to be mentioned that at the time when Lamprecht's
essay appeared the phrase "mass psychology," which is used to translate Hintze's *Massenpsychologie,* was a descriptive term, lacking pejorative connotation.)

Lamprecht's views were vehemently attacked by a number of the
leading German historians of the time; as a consequence of the
Lamprecht Streit, Lamprecht became entirely isolated and for decades
his ideas remained without influence on the development of German
historical scholarship. The almost unanimous rejection of Lamprecht's
ideas was caused primarily by the firm hold the Rankean tradition
had over the mind of the German historians. Lamprecht refrained
from attacking Ranke directly, but his call for new historical methods
and approaches was a clear challenge to the Rankean tradition.
Lamprecht's demand for cultural history was in contrast to the
emphasis Ranke and his disciples placed on the political content of
history; his thesis of the existence of general historical laws denied
the Rankean view that the historian was concerned with unique and
individual events and developments; and Lamprecht's assumption of

a steadily broadening and improving psychological understanding was in opposition to Ranke's theory that ideas of each age were unique, equal in value, so that each period of history was "equally near to God."

In his Memoirs, entitled *Erlebtes, 1862–1919*, Friedrich Meinecke stated that Hintze's article was the "best" contribution made in the debate about Lamprecht. In the light of the hostility and ferociousness with which Lamprecht's adversaries carried on this debate, it is clear that Meinecke wanted to indicate that Hintze's contribution was the only one that tried to do justice to Lamprecht's position. It is a sign of the independence of Hintze's mind that, in contrast to almost all other German historians, he recognized the importance of the questions which Lamprecht had raised. In this article Hintze refers briefly to Emile Dubois-Reymond, the famous psychologist who argued that science and scholarship must be freed from metaphysical assumptions, and to Wilhelm Dilthey's psychological studies, which had just then been published. They are additional proof of Hintze's belief that historical studies must keep in touch with the discoveries and the progress made in other fields of learning, if history were to avoid becoming rigidified in a traditional position.

Professor Lamprecht has published a lengthy article entitled "Was ist Kulturgeschichte?" in the *Deutsche Zeitschrift für Geschichtswissenschaft* (Number II); here, with greater clarity and more completely than before, he sets out his views on the objects and methods of our discipline. This essay is, to my mind, by no means the worst that has been written on this subject; it contains much that is of value even for men who would not, in principle, accept Professor Lamprecht's point of view. But though his basic principle is correct, his one-sided application leads him to conclusions which, if we are to establish the truth with proper sobriety and care, cannot remain unchallenged.

What essentially is at issue is the old debate on the existence of historical laws. Are historical events of such a general nature that they can be arranged in a typical pattern of normal development, or have they, for the most part, only a unique character? This is a great question underlying any discussion of historical method, and which seems to me to have been the true driving force for what Lamprecht has to say.

Recently there has been much discussion of the relation between method and general viewpoint (*Weltanschauung*). Lamprecht, with his rigorous empirical approach, denies that any such relation exists. As far as elementary methods of discovering facts are concerned, he is certainly right. But he himself has always indicated that method implies definition of the aims—indeed, the ultimate and highest aims—of research; and he would admit that this definition is usually arrived at by a hypothesis which grows from subjective intellectual and emotional needs and which empirical research can only confirm to a limited extent.

Such intellectual needs—though they affect historians to varying degrees, depending on their individual intellectual habits
—cause the recurrent and inescapable question of typical patterns
in historical development. Today this discussion no longer centers
on the crass opposition of the materialist and idealist interpretation of history. The conflict has been transferred from the field of
metaphysical speculation to the calmer regions of psychological
investigation, where the issues are no less sharply contended but
where there is more hope of reconciliation.

The contrast of individualist and collective psychology is the
point of departure for Lamprecht's entire investigation. Because
he overemphasizes this contrast, Lamprecht has been led to conclusions that are one-sided and therefore incorrect. In my opinion Lamprecht has, strangely enough, overlooked the one-sidedness and inadequacy of these two psychological approaches; only
a combination of the two reveals the true nature of the object.

Social psychology represents perhaps the most significant advance in the Humanities (*Geisteswissenschaften*) since the end
of the last century. Its roots are in the era of our idealistic culture; when Hegel talked of "the objective spirit" and Jakob
Grimm of "the soul of the people" (*Volksseele*), they had in mind
collective intellectual forces which they deduced from the existence of a mass psychology. In its heyday classical philology
was saturated with such notions. The confluence of the ideas of
Wilhelm von Humboldt and Herbart produced a school of national psychology (*Völkerpsychologie*) which ethnology and
linguistics have put to better use than history. Under the influence of Comte and Spencer these notions have been developed
in a more realistic direction; in France, Taine expressed them
in a way that can be considered almost canonical, whereas Gustav Freytag has popularized them with a specifically German
coloring. The German idealistic one-sidedness of earlier times
has been redressed by expert, empirical investigation of the science of politics and lately economics. To me at least it seems
that Lamprecht's "German History," despite all the objections

that can be raised, marks a distinct advance in this direction. The author's theoretical views which he now presents to us and which only gradually have taken shape in the course of the work, do not allow us to conclude, as has often been done, that his approach to history is a one-sidedly economic one on lines of the Marxist school. He—and indeed all modern thought, in Germany and throughout Europe—differ from these rather outdated views because the crude objectivism of the Marxists is separated by an enormous gulf from the subjective, psychological approach, a characteristic product of all modern culture. If the Marxists maintain that rigid "objective" forces, namely, the conditions of production, dominate history in a mysterious and inexplainable manner, we now conceive of these conditions as results of mass-psychological processes in which ethical norms, too, play a part.

This is the paramount importance of the social approach. History knows no driving forces other than those carried out by man, not only man as an individual but, above all, man in historical connections; they produce the collective intellectual forces that are the living center of all institutions.

Of course this all depends on how one envisages the processes of mass psychology. Even Friedrich Engels once said that the developments which depend on the conditions of production must first go through the minds of men in order to have effect. But he saw the psychic stage through which they had to pass as a passive medium producing the same reaction in every case, and for this reason entirely negligible. Lamprecht does not make this crude mistake. In place of "objective" conditions he regards the forces of the collective psyche as the determining factor. But he has given no attention to the question of how these forces arise and change; for him the life of the individual and the life of society are separate entities having no organic connection. The "subjective" antithesis of the individualist and the collective interpretation becomes for him the "objective" contrast between an individual and a collective sphere of life. Moreover, he believes that in examining collective action within social groups and organizations which have a collective spirit, he can eliminate the individual aspect (although he recognizes its existence); he regards the members of groups as equal in value so that all of them are ruled by the ideas, emotions, and desires common to the group.

Such an interpretation may well be justified in certain cases and within certain limits; but as a general method of procedure it is one-sided and therefore misleading. For the common motivating ideas that rule the life of a close-knit human community have their ultimate origin in the psychology of individuals. The common motivating forces are expressions of the common element in individual attitudes and are forged into an accepted intellectual system (*objektive geistige Macht*). Even where they are reinforced by being embodied in institutions, they are not permanent and immutable factors, but change constantly as a result of alterations in the individual impulses which prompt them. The more primitive the social development, the more it imposes uniformity on the individuals of a community, and the individual cannot liberate himself from the beliefs of the community; nonetheless, all progress is based on differentiation, and on the contrast between the mind of the individual and the mind of the community. The individual factor cannot be disregarded in its effect on the development of the collective mind; it must be seen not only as the source of the specific character of a group, it is also the most vital factor in its further evolution.

These considerations are of importance for the following reasons.

Lamprecht distinguishes between what eminent persons can achieve as individuals, and what happens as a result of the activity of the community. The former belongs to the realm of the "singular," and the latter of the "general." In the first case, freedom (in the sense of inner determinism) prevails, and in the second, necessity (in the sense of demonstrable causality). I consider this separation erroneous. In my opinion they are both rather opposite poles of a continuous and basically homogeneous series—the poles between which all history revolves. The individual factor makes itself felt in the collective development; it is reflected in the growth and transformation of language and custom, of economics and law, just as it is reflected in the founding of states and in conflicts between nations—less apparent, but not for that less important. And on the other hand, even the conscious activity of a historical personage is confined within those narrow boundaries that are set by the development of public opinion and the conditions it has created.

All history is based on more or less conscious individual activity; and the individual life is always part of a communal life, more or less governed by the collective forces at work. Between what might be called the organic growth and evolution of historical societies and the apparently free action of a will in public life there is a difference of degree not of principle. The role of the individual factor may be seen in the sum of countless small actions which, by themselves, do not go far beyond the customary but, taken together, have considerable importance; the individual factor makes itself felt also in outstanding actions— though, in order to have historical importance, they need to be supported by and accompanied by a similar disposition of smaller or broader groups of society. The psychological attitude of broader groups produces what we usually call the historic ideas. I see no reason to abandon this term; that they are not transcendental forces, but inherent in society, will surely be recognized by all historians, whatever their leanings. I am unable to discover anything mystical in Ranke's conception of these ideas. Of course, in the last instance, we are always confronted by an impenetrable mystery—the mystery of life, which science and learning cannot solve. Even Dubois-Reymond has talked of the riddles of the world: are we for this reason to call him a mystic?

All causal analysis of historical developments must stop where it penetrates to the qualitative essence of individual life, the ultimate origin of historical events. The problem of individuality which we encounter in all strata of historical life can be pursued to earlier generations, but can never be solved. Its solution is beyond even the new methods of analytical psychology, as recently Dilthey seems to have convincingly demonstrated. Moreover, attempts to explain the origin of human self-consciousness in terms of simple psychic elements are somewhat irrelevant to the historian: with the means at his disposal, he cannot explain how individuality originates. The historian deals with people whose consciousness is already fully formed. We can understand them only by an act of artistic insight, founded on careful research, and this has been recognized also by Lamprecht as justified and necessary for historical interpretation.

In recognizing that a psycho-physical entity is the basic element in all social structures, we do not return to the one-sidedly individualistic interpretation of society prevalent in the last century. We are merely establishing an organic connection between the psyche of the individual and that of the group. We are aware that strong individuality whose activity has often determined the fate of peoples is rooted in the collective psyche; but we are also aware that the collective psyche is created and nourished through the actions of individuals, and that the existence of an outstanding individuality would be impossible without that latent individualism that even the most primitive societies possess.

There are in history no events of an entirely general nor of an entirely individualist character. Everywhere there is cooperation and conflict between the life of the individual and the life of society, and their relation is varied, depending on the changing strength and compatibility of the two components. Altogether the process is an extremely complicated one; it can be described and analyzed; but there is no way of rationally explaining the whole on the basis of a few simple elements.

I cannot therefore agree that there are two different historical methods, the collectivist and the individualist; nor do I accept that there are two different historical disciplines under the names of political and the so-called cultural history. However, I agree with Lamprecht—and this may practically be most important—in the view that historical scholarship must be placed on the broad basis of thorough and profound research in social psychology. This is, I think, progress beyond Ranke, just as the so-called political historians Sybel and Treitschke represent progress in a related direction. To use a geographic metaphor, we want to know not only the ranges and summits but also the base of the mountains, not merely the heights and depths of the surface but the entire continental mass. This is an enlargement of previous scholarly endeavors, not the overthrow of historical scholarship. As it appears to me, it will not result in the establishment of a regularly recurring pattern of events but in the comprehension of an altogether singular historical development. In what we call universal history—i.e., the connected cultural development of ancient and modern peoples—the single nations represent distinct stages in the development of a wider whole, rather than the recurring pattern of a recurring national development.

In the present state of our historical knowledge it is not possible to construct the standard pattern of national development, unless we are to content ourselves with vague biological analogies. There is unquestionably a natural tendency toward such a standard pattern; but it has never gone beyond beginnings that belong to a very early age, when the single peoples had not yet become part of the world historical development. The nations that form the subject of history are no mere products of nature, but of world history—this is true above all of the English, French, and American nations. The historian cannot separate nation and state in the manner Lamprecht suggests: the nation forms the state, but the state in its turn forms the nation and has an all-pervading influence on its cultural life. The economic consequences of mercantilism are a case in point. Contrasts between nations and states and their union form the process of world history; they are large, all-inclusive individualities rather than specimens of the same general type. A parallel development, like that of the Latin and Germanic peoples, is based on common cultural foundations that are not gifts of nature but attainments of world history. This view, which Ranke has brilliantly presented to us, will not be destroyed by placing historical studies on a wider basis. The development of world history is not merely a by-product of national developments but has an independent character; created by nations, in its turn it creates them. It comes into being through a distinct and universal process of mass psychology; it often interrupts national developments, and after nations have become entangled with each other, it affects them to a profound degree. The effect of universal cultural forces is not limited to renaissances, receptions, or "diosmoses"; by living under the sway of the same universal cultural forces, nations have a common life like individuals living in the same social group. This meeting and intermingling of national and universal developments makes it impossible, in my opinion, to contruct world history as a comparative history of nations; world history is and remains a great process with a unique character of its own.

10

TROELTSCH AND THE
PROBLEMS OF HISTORICISM:
CRITICAL STUDIES

The following article, which was published in the *Historische Zeitschrift*, Volume 135 (1927), is cast in the form of a criticism of Ernst Troeltsch's work, *Historicism and Its Problems;* it should immediately be said that Hintze considers not only the ideas which Troeltsch had expressed in this book but also Troeltsch's views presented in a collection of essays, *Deutscher Geist und Westeuropa* (1925), and in lectures published under the title *Der Historismus und seine Überwindung* (in English translation, *Christian Thought: Its History and Application*). Moreover, Hintze's essay transcends the purpose of discussing Troeltsch's ideas. It has a wider scope. It provides a general statement of Hintze's views on historical theory. In this article Hintze resumes discussion of the questions which he had treated in his earlier study, "The Individualist and the Collective Approach to History"; his treatment here, however, is more comprehensive and systematic. It includes an examination of the validity of the attempts of the philosopher Heinrich Rickert and his school to separate the methods of the cultural sciences from those of the natural sciences; it examines the usefulness of Max Weber's sociological ideas for the work of the historian; it considers the significance of Spengler's notions for the writing of comparative history; and it probes not only Troeltsch's ideas on historicism but also those of Hintze's Berlin colleagues and friends, Friedrich Meinecke and Eduard Spranger.

Hintze's mastery of the trends of research allows him to illustrate, with concrete examples, the consequences of different methodological approaches for the analysis of the past. The article is so rich that a detailed explanation of the allusions and references within a limited space is hardly possible; because of this compactness, the article is not easy to read and was difficult to translate. This is particularly true for the last sentence, in which Hintze, without quotation marks, uses two famous passages from Goethe poems and, by means of these citations, indicates that he rejects Troeltsch's optimistic confidence in the ideality of cultural and ethical advance and expresses his belief in an individualistic ethic that follows its own values whether they are accepted or condemned by the outside world.

Historicism as a Philosophy and as a Methodology

The following observations are intended not as a belated review of Troeltsch's already well-known work[1] but as an attempt on my part to define my own attitudes to the basic ideas in it. Unfortunately the work was not completed, and presumably for this reason it has not received the full critical attention that its real importance would have justified. It has of course been overshadowed for some time by Spengler's *Decline of the West*, which has operated on the sensibilities and imagination of a wide reading public in a completely different way than this by no means dry but nonetheless thoroughly scholarly book. In spite of Spengler's essentially literary character and Troeltsch's academic character, the two works still bear an intellectual resemblance to each other. Their similarity is evident not in their approaches, which are in fact disparate, but in their common origin as products of a time when a long-dormant interest in the philosophy of history, revived and heightened by the terrible experience of the Great War, demanded solutions to the riddles the sphinx of world history had posed.

Following Schopenhauer and Nietzsche, Spengler believes in an inescapable law of universal growth and decay and awaits with defiant resignation the tragic disintegration of our Western culture. Troeltsch stands in the tradition of German idealism that began with Leibniz and reached fruition in Ranke and Hegel. Convinced that there is a rational meaning in world history, and motivated by an indomitable ethical impulse, he works toward a living synthesis of culture which will define and clarify the entire intellectual legacy of the West in relation to the development of the human race as a whole. Drawing on productive moral forces at work in this legacy, he hopes to point the way to new goals, invoking the motto, "We bid you hope." Had this work been completed as Troeltsch had planned it, it would doubtless have had a powerful and enduring influence. I cannot share Troeltsch's unquestioning optimism. In fact, I tend toward Spengler's view in many respects, although with considerable reservations, both general and specific. I do believe, however, that Troeltsch's effect on the general public would have been more beneficial than Spengler's has been. It is often necessary to conjure up illusions, and even deceptive hopes, in order to waken and mobilize dormant moral forces. As everyone who knew him can attest, Troeltsch combined an indestructible idealism with the exceptional gifts of leadership necessary for this task.

But Troeltsch's work remained uncompleted, and we have only the rudiments of his synthesis of culture and of its practical and ethical applications. Troeltsch entitled the first part of his study "The Methodological Problem in the Philosophy of History." In terms of the book's actual content, this title strikes me as too limited. A more suitable one might be "conceptual foundations," a phrase that in fact occurs in the preface. In any case, this first part goes beyond a mere formal methodology of history. Troeltsch also submits to thorough review the material philosophy of history insofar as this position, with its logical and epistemological presuppositions, its metaphysical underpinnings, its connection with the realm of values, ethics, and social philosophy, is even tenable for the modern consciousness. These sections are surely the most original and stimulating in the book. We might well regret that Troeltsch's consideration of these questions was interrupted by a comprehensive critical analysis of the philosophy of history since Hegel, an analysis that takes up the greatest part of the existing book. This analysis was essential to Troeltsch's effort to clarify his own thinking, and it is an admirable scholarly performance, erudite, original, and imaginative. But it diverts the flow of the author's own thoughts and leaves the reader with the perhaps not wholly justified feeling that Troeltsch chose to deal with the problem of historicism historically, offering a history of philosophy, not a philosophy of history.

"Historicism" is a relatively new term, and its meaning is not quite clear. It has, it seems to me, come to be associated with Nietzsche's well-known essay, "The Utility and Futility of History." The term originally had something of a pejorative connotation, which implied that viewing the affairs of man from an exclusively historical perspective leads to skepticism, relativism, or purely aesthetic contemplation, weakening the will and crippling the capacity for action. The term has entered general usage completely or at least partially stripped of its pejorative overtones. The word now denotes either a methodology or a general philosophy of life that is sometimes regarded as a substitute for metaphysics. Troeltsch did not make as sharp a distinction between these two meanings as I think desirable. He declares that in discussing historicism we must sever the word from its pejorative connotation and use it in the sense of a fundamental historization of all our reflections on man, his culture, and his values. So understood, historicism is the opposite of naturalism, defined by Troeltsch as "a system of laws which ignores all qualitative and immediate experience in comprehending the entire scope of reality." This definition places an emphasis on historicism as methodology, but it does not clearly separate this aspect of historicism from a concept of it as a general philosophy of life. These two ideas are, of course, related, but it still seems to me both desirable and possible to draw a distinction between them. What prevented Troeltsch from making this distinction was the belief, inherited from the school of Windelband and Rickert, that systems of value show a close, fundamental, and indissoluble bond with methodological categories, even though, as we shall emphasize later, Troeltsch freed himself on one important point from Rickert's theory of value.

We shall soon discuss the relation of value system to the methodological categories that constitute historicism. For now we should simply note that Troeltsch did not completely succeed in ridding the term "historicism" of its pejorative connotations. "The fundamental historization of all our reflections on man, his culture, and his values" leads again and again down that path of skepticism and relativism that Troeltsch hoped to close off. Time after time the ghost of "bad historicism" appears and must be exorcised by a good and true historicism—that is, a historicism imbued with and dominated by ethics. At the end of this book Troeltsch describes the purpose of his work and of the philosophy of history itself as an attempt "to overcome history through history." We might recast this phrase to read, "Historicism must overcome itself." With this in mind, we are equipped to understand Troeltsch's last work, *The Overcoming of Historicism*, which contains some of the ideas that would have been more fully developed in the second part of the work under review. We do not know whether Troeltsch himself chose this title, but its meaning, briefly, is this: Historicism has as its subject the course of history; and man's moral conscience, rooted in the ethics of the culture in which he lives, ought to channel and direct the course of history in such a way that it absorbs these ethical tendencies without running counter to history's natural flow. This strong emphasis on the ethical element in Troeltsch's concept of the cultural synthesis and of the continuing historical process affects his view of historicism itself: the general philosophical function of historicism, which is to provide the materials for both the cultural synthesis and the historical process, takes precedence over the purely epistemological function and hinders its clear emergence. The emotional element in Troeltsch's thinking absorbs the cognitive element. In the interests of a clear methodology, I should prefer to conceive of historicism as nothing more than another mode of thought, another set of methodological categories.

There is as yet no precise demarcation of the area covered by the concept of historicism. Is it limited to the romantic context and the organic-historical school of jurisprudence to which Ranke shows ties, or does it embrace also the historical dialectic of Hegel and Karl Marx and even the evolutionary theory of the

positivist school? Troeltsch treated all these schools and many
others under the aspect of historicism so that the problems of
historicism could appear simply as problems in the philosophy of
history. A stricter and narrower view of the term "historicism"
would limit its application to the great intellectual transformation that began with Vico, Herder, and Rousseau and culminated
in German romanticism, in the historical school of jurisprudence,
and in Hegel and Ranke. This narrower view was not foreign to
Troeltsch. Indeed, he used it as the basis of one of his most important theses, one that is only touched upon in the present work
but receives thorough treatment in a number of lectures and
essays.

This thesis claimed that there is a basic difference between
German historical thought on state and society and the historical
thought of the West European and American peoples, which is
based more on natural law and the rationalism of the Enlightenment. It was this basic difference that the wartime propaganda
of our opponents transformed into a difference of "mentalities,"
claiming that in the German view power took precedence over
justice while the tendency of Western civilization was to protect
justice from abuse at the hands of power. It was Troeltsch who, in
this clash of minds above the field of battle, discovered a specifically democratic means of winning the masses to a war originally
alien to them and of discrediting the enemy; but at the same time
he expressly emphasized the legitimate core of this opposition of
"mentalities" as he understood it. He believed that the mode of
thought of Scholastic philosophy, which was based on the idea of
natural and divine law and related to the Stoicism of the ancients,
had taken on secular form, becoming reason and natural law in
modern philosophy.

This philosophical position, including the moral code that
went with it, dominated even in Germany up to Kant's time. Outside Germany, this position has held its ground in the West up
to the present day, even though in the course of the eighteenth
century another mode of thinking, empirical and historical in

nature and emphasizing positive law, attached itself to the rationalistic mode. From this amalgamation the Positivism of the nineteenth century arose. In Germany, on the other hand, romanticism discredited natural law and reason; they were supplanted by a specifically historical way of thinking characterized by new notions of individuality and of a developing collective spirit. In Hegel's case particularly, all this became a sublime but one-sided historical and dialectical monism that conceived of the entire world process as a unified movement. This was an absolute contrast to that Western dualism of *ratio* and *empirie*—of reason and history—which coexist independent of each other.

In his *Idee der Staatsräson* Meinecke shows that these two different mentalities give rise to different understandings of *raison d'état*. In the Western view, *raison d'état* implies the principle of an unconditional predominance of state interests, which coexists with and is independent of the moral code of Christian, rational natural law. In the German interpretation, as expounded by Hegel and the political theorists he influenced (e.g., Treitschke) the contrast between *raison d'état* and ethical demands disappears to a certain extent, since *raison d'état* is seen as belonging to a vast process of history, which in turn is interpreted as the working out of divine reason. Consequently, there is no sharp distinction between power and justice; and ethicized power and right have their place in the divine order. Meinecke felt that the gap between the German and Western modes of thought might be bridged if the German monistic system could be framed in a more dualistic shape and if the ethical demands arising from the old natural law could counter the rationalized, but fundamental, instinctive drives that underlie the course of political life. This dualism should not be allowed to take on the sharply contrasting shape it assumed in the West. It should instead have the character of a polar opposition subject to a single universal principle.

There is an obvious relation between this subtle thesis of Meinecke's and Troeltsch's idea of the overcoming of historicism. They both show historicism to be a specifically German mode of thinking. True as that may be, I find that the underlying difference between German and Western thought, though certainly present, has been exaggerated much more than it would have been without wartime propaganda. In the first place, Western thought is not a monolithic structure that stands in opposition to a similar structure of German thought. There is, for example, considerable difference between French and Anglo-American thought. Moreover, the importance in the Western countries of empirical historical thought, which often combined with rationalism and natural law to form utilitarianism and positivism, must not be underestimated. Similarly, in Germany, the influence of the law of reason, as taught by Kant and Fichte, has never quite been eliminated (the Fries school is a case in point), and the old system of rational natural law as it occurs in the teachings of the Church has persisted unchanged, particularly among Catholic thinkers. To this we must add the considerable effect of positivism in the second half of the nineteenth century, an effect neither to be denied nor wished away. Then, too, there is no lack of German influence upon English or French historical and philosophical literature. Carlyle and Seeley, Renan and Taine, and, more recently, Bergson are obvious examples. Germany by no means stood alone in her concept of *raison d'état*. The doctrine of power and national egoism was far more readily accepted and far less scrupulously applied in Machiavelli's homeland than it ever was in Germany; yet Italy was never a target of enemy propaganda. A philosopher of history like Croce is evidence of a possible compromise between Western and German thought. Thus, I consider an exclusively German and idealistic interpretation of historicism to be altogether too restricted. I believe that today we can widen the concept of historicism to include Marxism and positivism. This would naturally involve shifting the emphasis from the category of individuality to that of development.

Troeltsch saw in naturalism the antithesis of historicism. This view reflects his tendency to define historicism as a general philosophical position. If we take an opposite view and see historicism as a methodology, we would choose pragmatism as the contrasting position. By pragmatism I mean the dominant historiographical principle before the advent of the modern "historical" mentality. This pragmatic principle still exists together with, or rather within the framework of, modern ideas. Pragmatism sees the meaning and coherence of past events primarily in terms of the purposeful actions of individuals; it is justified in doing this as long as it limits itself to political history and, within that discipline, to the major actions of statesmen and nations.

It is no accident that modern historical thought has developed together with what one is wont to call "cultural history" as opposed to "political history." It is even less an accident that legal history was the main bearer of the new historical idea in the Germany of the restoration period and that, besides the jurists, it was theologians, philologists, and philosophers who were sooner and more profoundly influenced by the new idea than historians themselves. Even social and economic history did not grow out of history of the old school but apart from it, under the influence of research in economics. As historians began to focus on areas where the actions of individual personalities were not so predominant as in politics but where the power of anonymous vital forces, linking the individual to the community, work in a mysterious way either above or below the level of human consciousness, the more attractive and less objectionable became the idea of an irrational historical design, which soon assumed the name of "development." To supplement the no longer relevant individual personalities, new historical agents were created to carry this "development": the "national soul" of the Romantics, the "objective spirit" of Hegel, or the means of economic production of the Marxist school.

Nowadays we tend to see all history as "cultural history," a concept that includes "political history" as well as constitutional and economic history, the history of art and literature, the history of religion and of ideas. Rickert's distinction between the humanities and the natural sciences has fostered this tendency, and Troeltsch conceives of history purely in these terms. Troeltsch regarded old-style political history, which described situations, deeds, and events, as a pre-scientific or purely specialized effort of practical or perhaps artistic value. Even in Ranke, to whom he attributed almost canonical significance, it was not the richness of concrete events in the national histories that was of historical and philosophical interest to Troeltsch but the general remarks on intellectual currents in history and on the significance of historical constellations and epochs. He was of course drawn also to Ranke's idea of a community of Teutonic and Latin peoples and to Ranke's scheme for a world history. Jakob Burckhardt, whose less optimistic temperament was basically foreign to Troeltsch, did, however, offer him much more than Ranke in terms of the philosophy of history, because Burckhardt's selection and treatment of historical subjects was in keeping with the dictates of "cultural history." I rather suspect that the greatest part of recent historical research was of little interest to Troeltsch, whose central concern was the philosophy of history. The only contemporary historian with whom he was profoundly in sympathy and to whom he obviously owed a great deal was Meinecke, whose devotion to the history of ideas obviously appealed to him.

Apart from Meinecke, the economists, sociologists, theologians, philosophers, and art historians contributed most to the growth of Troeltsch's theories and intuitions. Troeltsch's notion of historicism stands in clear contradiction to what I have called "pragmatism" and therefore bears little relation to most contemporary historical research. "Political history," coping with its ever-increasing mass of documents and other sources, is hardly concerned with historicism, and contributes little to the solution of its problems. Political history is synonymous with pragmatism, whose concern is to investigate the acts of statesmen and other influential individuals. This kind of political history has its legitimate uses even though its approach is fundamentally different

from that of "cultural history." Political history can, however, be
treated as part of cultural history, particularly if it is subdivided
into special topics, such as military history, diplomatic history,
constitutional and administrative history. This is certainly the
modern trend. While this schematic method is developing, however, there still persists a powerful and seemingly irresistible tradition of narrative history.

In this tradition the actions of sovereigns and governments in
war and peace constitute the essence of national destinies and
give shape to cultural life. The narration of these events takes on
the quality of a great universal epic. In ancient Greece, in the
age of the *polis*, historians like Heredotus and Thucydides assumed the role played by Homer in the heroic age. The modern
world is no different. When Ranke described his work as an
effort "to tell the tale of world history," he clearly had in mind
the remark of the medieval German poet Gottfried of Strassburg,
who described a fellow poet, Wolfram, as *vindaere wilder maere*,
a "teller of strange tales." Here we find the essentially artistic inspiration of Ranke's efforts in scholarship; for though the web of
vital national interests and the universal tendencies he described
carried his work far beyond the bounds of art, Ranke never lost
sight of the concrete, living material that was his subject. This
awareness of the vital whole is utterly foreign to the purely scientific, systematic method even when this method is applied to
the study of human culture. Jakob Burckhardt's descriptions and
observations, for example, have nothing of this epic quality, although Burckhardt was certainly able to present historical figures and cultures in a vivid way. But a certain measure of pragmatism is invariably involved in this epic style. As in Ranke's
case, this epic quality exists together with historicism but is not
wholly absorbed by it.

Before the emergence of historicism, naturalism had hardly
any influence on the writing of history or on the concept of history. Even a philosopher like Leibniz, who used mathematics so
effectively in metaphysics, was far from allowing it any influence

on the historical studies he is known to have pursued with such
interest. Pragmatism reigned supreme. It was more at odds with
naturalism than with the historicism that later replaced it. In
historicism there is much that is kindred with naturalism. I have
in mind here the organic principle to which the positivists merely
gave a more rigorous biological shape. For this very reason, it
seems so necessary in our day to make a new and much sharper
distinction between the natural sciences and the humanities, particularly between the natural sciences and history. For Troeltsch,
as for others, the theory of historicism serves essentially to secure
the historian's independence and autonomy against the doctrine
of naturalism. But Troeltsch loses sight of the problems raised by
pragmatism. The relation between pragmatism and historicism
receives no extensive consideration in his work, although it seems
to me that this relation is of crucial importance at the present
time.

The notion that historical events can be explained in terms of
psychological motivation is one that derives from pragmatism.
J. G. Droysen, who had strong pragmatic leanings despite his
contact with historicism, once remarked that the historian's task
was "to understand through research" (*forschend zu verstehen*).
Even a modern sociologist like Max Weber sets himself the task
of understanding the nature of a society in terms of the psychological motivation of individual actions. He allows organic explanations derived from the nature and function of sociological
structures to serve only as preliminary orientations and aids to
analysis. Troeltsch has no interest whatsoever in these psychological methods. He is so suspicious of experimental psychology,
of its naturalistic presuppositions, and of its misapplication by
positivist theoreticians that he flatly rejects all psychological
methodology. The new "psychology of the humane sciences,"
based on entirely different presuppositions and so successfully
applied by Spranger, has some validity for Troeltsch, but he does
not appreciate its significance for the philosophy of history. He
regarded spiritual and intellectual processes and phenomena as

given units that defy analysis, and he viewed with suspicion any attempt to break them down, to see them as complex entities produced out of simple psychological elements. He took a firm stand against attempts of this kind, and claimed that this new "psychology of the humane sciences" could and must learn a great deal from history, but not vice versa. That there is give and take here he stolidly refused to acknowledge. Consequently, his theory does not accord the problem of understanding the importance it seems to me to deserve.

We might call Troeltsch's method "pneumatological" in order to distinguish it from the psychological. He sees intellectual life not as a continuation, intensification, or transformation of psychic life but as an entirely separate realm. There is no psychologically mediated connection between the individual and the course of history. He likes to speak of the spirit's "invading" history, and he has in mind something like divine revelation. The metaphysics underlying his theory of historicism leans heavily on Leibniz and Malebranche and has a distinctly religious note. Troeltsch's epistemology derives from Malebranche's doctrine that through God we understand what is foreign to our own minds; but Troeltsch made no psychological exploration of this field. His methodology of history, too, was profoundly influenced by Malebranche's doctrine.

Historical Logic and Value Systems

Following in the footsteps of Rickert's pioneering work on historical logic, Troeltsch undertook a logical analysis of the phenomenon he described as "the historization of our thought on human affairs." In doing so, he discussed the two concepts fundamental to specifically historical thought: the concept of individuality and that of development.

Individuality here does not refer merely to individual personalities but to the principle by which we can separate one object of historical study from another. The world of history—unlike that of nature—has no elements that can be conceived of as the basic units involved in complex phenomena, elements whose interaction is governed by abstract, general laws. The individual, taken in isolation, does not constitute an historical object; even biography must deal with the individual's intellectual and social environment. The basic units in history are individual totalities in which psychic processes and certain natural features combine to form living wholes. These units are not made up of individuals and their environment in the biographical sense but are instead collective individualities: peoples, states, classes, estates, as well as cultural periods and trends, religious communities, and all kinds of complex processes like wars and revolutions.

These individual totalities include the concepts of both originality and uniqueness. They cannot be explained in psychological or causal terms. They burst forth from hidden regions far below the level of human consciousness as fully formed entities, only to be fit into the categories that our physical and psychic apparatus provides. The experienced reality of such individual totalities is transformed into historical concepts by a process of selection that not only lifts the object out of the flow of things but also stresses only its essential or characteristic features. These features must, however, imply in turn the countless details, inferences, and evaluations associated with the object by experience and imagination. In this way a general concept suggestive of the concrete arises, a concept wholly different from concepts the sciences use in classifying or describing natural phenomena. The origin of this historical concept derives from the value or meaning that is immanent in the totality in question and that we can grasp only by virtue of our own ability to perceive value and meaning. By means of this value relation, we form an idea of the essential features; and because of this relation, what we see as the "essential" is synonymous with what Eduard Meyer has called the "fruitful" and the "permanent." The individual totalities we have been discussing are not modeled on psychological patterns but arise spontaneously whenever human thought focuses on the realities of the past.

Since historical situations are never stable but are in constant flux, the concept of historical individuality necessarily entails a concept of continuing growth or development. The unity of meaning and value in a given historical object appears as an historical trend or idea and renders the progress of the individual totality intelligible. Furthermore, it brings several such totalities together, creating a larger cultural context. The continuity of meaning, value, or idea that dominates the whole and that is initially grasped by an intuitive act is the crucial point here. An empirical psychological method can demonstrate certain causal connections within such a historical totality, corroborating the existence of a structure originally perceived intuitively. But the overwhelming amount of detail involved makes it impossible to carry this method through. Underlying this whole process is the historical view of time which, unlike that of science or mathematics, sees time measured and divided not by spatial movements but by changing patterns in historical constellations. This concept of historical development, like that of historical individuality, is an abstraction derived from concrete experience. It suggests only historical change as such, the continuing vital force that moves in and produces everything. For every upward movement there is a downward one, for every flowering of civilization, a decay.

"Development" in this sense should be clearly distinguished from "progress," which philosophers of history have defined as a cumulative process that carries everything forward and propagates it. It should also be clearly distinguished from Spencer's biological concept of evolution, which, with its alternation of integration and disintegration, merely added a new factor to the natural chain of causation. The genuine concept of development is proper to history and not to developmental psychology. Its uniqueness and originality have something of that spontaneous illumination about them that we normally associate with religious inspiration. Psychology is out of its depth here, be it a psychology of the humane sciences or a psychology of a phenomenological stamp.

By introducing the concept of value, which seems for all practical purposes to be synonymous with "meaning," Troeltsch's methodological considerations of individuality and development take on an ethical or even metaphysical cast and lead us to the heart of the most difficult problems in the philosophy of history. The conceptual structure of a researcher's logic seems to be determined, or at least influenced, by close contact with his subject matter. A philosophy of identity underlies this notion. From the perspective of this metaphysically oriented epistemological presupposition, Troeltsch deals with a number of problems, e.g., the tension between the objective and the subjective mind, the concept of the subconscious, creativity in the human being, the meaning of freedom and chance, the possible existence and nature of historical laws. We must give all these questions further consideration if we are to come to a critical assessment of Troeltsch's views.

First, it seems to me that the methodological problem is more closely intertwined with the metaphysical one than is necessary. Troeltsch often describes the latter problem as "epistemological," expanding the term beyond its usual definition. We can arrive at abstractions based in concrete experience, abstractions necessary for forming historical concepts, without reference to value and meaning. These abstractions do not provide categories of classification but of typology, as Heinrich Maier has described them. Further, these abstractions are not necessarily involved in defining the historical object, although they do give rise to the concept of development as well as of individuality.

In defining objects of historical study we must differentiate between actual objects and possible objects. Possible objects present no problem for the philosophy or even the logic of history. The choice of an object for historical study depends on several factors: the historian's personal interest in a particular field, the need for work in a given area, the nature and accessibility of source material. These factors have no essential significance for the philosophy of history and would be of importance only for a specialized theory of historical methods. Any aspect of a past human society, viewed from the perspective of time, can be an object of historical study. The concept of the individual totality is, of course, crucial to determining an object of historical study; and I would suggest that the only decisive criterion for defining an individual totality is its comprehensibility as a unit of life. Troeltsch used this phrase but he did not ascribe to it the significance I think it has. The defining of objects of historical study is, in my opinion, an act of intuitive, not rational, thought. The historian's thinking here is not logical but analogical. The concept of the individual personality underlies this analogical thinking and has, I believe, a much greater significance for history than Troeltsch allows it. In the early epic form of historical writing, the "hero" assumes the same leading role he had played in the epic itself; and by analogy to the individual personality, the imagination apprehended or created the collective personalities of race, nation, state, class, religious community, church, and the great cultures of both West and East. Personification is a very powerful urge in the human mind, seizing upon the seemingly inanimate and expressing itself everywhere, as in the grammatical genders of language.

The intellectual act that creates these collective personalities for the historian must of course reflect a true image of the real object if it is to leave any permanent impression on our consciousness; and this image must be open to empirical, rational, and analytical corroboration. If we subject our image to rational analysis, we come to realize that an intuitively grasped "unit of life" presents itself, rationally speaking, as a "unit of meaning." "Unit of meaning" of course can be as ambiguous as the word "meaning" itself: it can be used in a nominalistic or realistic sense; it can refer to the meaning of a word or the significance of a thing. Ordinarily, no clear distinction is made between the two. Understood nominally, the phrase "unit of meaning" suggests only a vague sense that various things are somehow related and that they may be brought together under a single name.

Understood realistically, it would signify a grasp of the nature of that relation and therefore of the nature of the things themselves, taken singly and together. We need only the first meaning to define an object of historical study, although this first meaning certainly directs us to the second. The second meaning, however, presumes a thorough study of the object whose status as object has already been provisionally established. The definition of the object is only provisional, but through study it can be corrected and refined or perhaps proved invalid.

A unit of meaning is not, however, necessarily the same as a unit of value, just as the meaning we give a word or a thing does not necessarily carry a connotation of value. The unit of meaning in a historical object is usually apparent in its name. The Italian Renaissance and the French Revolution are historical objects that surely contain meaningful values, but the unit of meaning expressed in the names of these objects does not necessarily reflect these latent values and leaves room for different value judgments of them. This becomes even clearer in the case of such broad areas of study as "Roman history," "German history," and the like. The sense of value can be and must be distinguished from the unit of meaning.

To be sure, some values are associated with all historical objects to the extent that these objects are part of human cultures that are in turn inconceivable without a system of values. In most areas of cultural life involving both material and spiritual factors, the meaning of an historical object such as a nation, state, or institution is based on the purpose that object has in the culture. Purposes, of course, embody values. To this extent, meaning is equivalent to value, and value suggests whatever is felt to be beneficial to the life of an individual or of a social group. "Values" in this general sense can refer to material goods or to cultural goods. They can be primarily instinctive or primarily spiritual in nature. This distinction, which is of fundamental importance in ethics, is of no particular significance to the concept of unity of meaning. Since all human purposes aim to fulfill the demands of life in one way or another, every collective purpose may be regarded not just as a unit of meaning but also as a unit of value. However, Troeltsch's idea of special ethical values in a culture must be dismissed. The phrase "unit of meaning or value" is simply a rationalized transcription for "unit of life," a unit that is grasped intuitively, not rationally.

To conceive of a historical object as such a unit of life, we do not have to undertake a detailed analysis of that object's purpose and the particular cultural values it reveals. If I take the Roman people or the German people as an object of historical study, I do not have to know, or to demonstrate in detail, what constitutes their particular character or inherent sense of values. This would involve an endless and hardly feasible analysis that would only serve to show how inadequate scholarly means of perception are. The macroscopic evidence for the existence of a unit of meaning suffices; the microscopic investigation of details remains the task of research. Macroscopic evidence suffices also to prove the existence of larger historical units such as epochs or major events. Who would attempt to reduce the unity of meaning in the Renaissance or the French Revolution to a short formula? The historians who coined these concepts would never have dreamed of doing so. They perceived the unity of meaning in these complexes as a vital unit that could be intuitively grasped. In attempting to present the vivid reality of these complex processes, they proved the correctness of their original intuitions and occasionally refined their views to conform with the indefinite and ever fluctuating contours of the historical object. In any case, it is not the value inherent in an individual totality, especially not any specific ethical value, that qualifies a totality as an object of historical study. Since all history is ultimately concerned with human culture, all such objects are characterized by some kind of values. But the kind or degree of these values, the difference between vital and cultural values in Rickert's sense, plays no role in defining historical objects, since "culture" is used here to include the material and economic goods of a civilization as well as its more narrowly defined "spiritual" goods. All culture rests on the indispensable foundation of nature and stands in opposition to it only insofar as it is a particular modification of nature.

The historical object as individual totality, then, is grasped intuitively as a unit of life. It is the task of rational inquiry, employing empirically gathered materials, to demonstrate the unity of meaning in the historical object. Any relation to a value structure is general and incidental, since all life and all cultures have some kind of inherent values, and it is only in this general sense that values bear on the delimiting of an object of historical study. When we define such an object, we do so only in relation to a basic notion of values, not to any specific values as such—in relation, that is, to a higher ethical and "cultural" value as opposed to a mere "value of life." The category of individuality that we apply in defining an historical object is purely formal, an abstraction drawn from experience in the realm of historical life. Its content is not determined by individual values of life or cultural values.

The category of "development" offers a close parallel to this. Here the historical object appears in motion, not at rest. Thus the category of development provides simply one more aspect of the object in addition to that offered by the category of individuality. Just as the category of individuality is analogous to the unity of life, so that of development is analogous to the process of life, which is familiar to us also from our own experience. Epochs and complex events such as the Renaissance, the French Revolution, and the Great War can be understood just as well, or perhaps even better, as chapters or crises of life, rather than as units of life. They are phases in a larger development and at the same time units of life, inasmuch as the same constantly changing unit of life underlies the life process in all its phases. Basically, "development" is only a modification of the general concept of historical time, which acts as a form for perceiving the continuity of life and the division of that continuity into particular segments.

Fundamental to this idea is the analogy of the ages of man—childhood, youth, maturity, and old age. All historical consideration of peoples, states, and cultural communities makes constant use of this analogy. Thus we can say, contrary to Troeltsch, that biological and psychological development—patterns familiar to everyone from experience—provide the model for the concept of historical development. Development can take the form of ebb and flow; it can lead to both fruition and to decay. The terminological question of whether it is better to separate the concepts of *development* and *decay* as Spranger does is still far from being settled. If we accept this distinction, we at once feel the lack of a concept that conveys the sense of uninterrupted change common to both growth and decay.

The concept of development differs from the pragmatic view of historical connection, although both are projected against the background of historical time. It differs by virtue of the fact that pragmatism takes into account only individual wills acting purposefully in concert or in conflict, while the concept of development involves the special historical configurations or individual totalities we have just discussed. It differs further because, under the pragmatic conception, the more or less arbitrarily set purposes of the actors and their rationally chosen means of achieving them govern the entire course of the action, whereas under the concept of development the idea of an unconscious purpose, immanent in nature and not subject to the arbitrary will of individuals, is crucial: a purpose that automatically governs historical processes although, in particulars, causal connections can be demonstrated. Inherent purpose here does not suggest a conscious human attitude toward specific ethical values—an attitude that may well underlie particular "ideas" or "tendencies" in history—but only a general orientation toward a goal. Like all else in human life, this goal may have a positive or a negative value. It can mean death and decay or life and fruition.

The concept of development is even more ambiguous and fluctuating than the concept of individuality. It is only a schematic construct, designed to facilitate a preliminary, intuitive comprehension of historical constellations that without this aid would be inaccessible to us. Rational scientific research must then clarify and substantiate the existence of these constellations and, if necessary, modify or correct our picture of them. The function and the methods of this research differ according to the various forms the concept of development assumes. I shall devote more attention to these forms in a later section, but for the moment I shall only summarize the results of my arguments so far.

What we call historicism is a new, peculiar structure of historical categories that began to arise in the West in the eighteenth century and achieved authoritative currency in the nineteenth, particularly in Germany, though not in Germany alone. It is characterized by the concepts of individuality and development, which postulate a view of historical reality based on the analogy of the unity of life and the process of life. Historicism was able to win acceptance because the long-dominant idea that rationality originated in the individual consciousness was superseded by the powerful idea of an all-embracing vital force that is beyond the grasp of the individual's rational powers and that includes the individual mind within itself. The opposition of "intuitivists" (*Lebensschauer*) and "formalists" (*Formdenker*) is not a phenomenon of our own time alone. It was clearly present in Herder's later view of Kant; and in a variety of forms and combinations, it has remained with us to the present day.

In general the historicist mode of thought has come to predominate over the individualistic, rationalistic mode, although the latter mode has remained a significant force in both historical research and historical writing. The current predominating view of history, then, sees all life as part of a universal order. The notion of value arises from this view, since all life carries its own values within itself. But the concepts of individuality and development, formed by analogy to the unity of life and the process of life, are not in themselves necessarily related to any cultural values of a higher order. As Troeltsch rightly and repeatedly emphasizes, these higher cultural values have no bearing on the logic of history. They belong instead to the material philosophy of history, where they play an essential role in an ethically oriented cultural synthesis. That they still have a place in Troeltsch's methodology is due to the influence of Rickert's theory of value, even though, as we shall see, Troeltsch largely dissociated himself from that theory. Troeltsch has, however, attenuated these values so much that it is no longer clear whether we are dealing here with higher cultural values or only with general values of life. If historicism is linked to systems of value, then it can easily become associated with a particular philosophical position. But if no connection with any particular cultural values is made, then historicism simply assumes a categorical structure that does not imply any particular philosophical position but can adapt itself to different philosophical outlooks such as idealism or positivism.

The Forms of Historical Development

Troeltsch recognizes only one form of historical development: development governed by what he terms "an idea," that is, a cultural value or a unified complex of such values. Historical development, then, is a process of continual growth by which such a value is realized. This view clearly derives from the principle of a necessary relation between development and higher cultural values and is too limited if we do not accept that logical principle. Furthermore, we cannot agree that historical ideas represent purely intellectual values. What, ever since Humboldt, has been called "ideas," and what Ranke described more accurately as the "material and intellectual tendencies of the centuries," is made up of both natural and cultural impulses.

Everything in history has been shaped and informed by the human mind, and everything arises from natural and instinctive desires. Nevertheless we can distinguish two types of historical events, one governed more by natural and instinctive factors, the other more by intellectual and cultural factors. The first forms the basis of all social reality. It includes blood and race, the divisions and intermingling of races, the growth and decline of populations. *Lebensraum* and the never-ending struggle for survival, economic production and its organizations, migration and colonization, patterns of tribal and family life, social differentiation, the development of occupations and estates, of social friction and the class war, of ruling factions and states—in short, everything that makes up what we ordinarily call "civilization," in contrast to "culture." This is the realm of elemental drives: hunger, sexual desire, and the will to power in all their combinations and manifestations as expressed in the unconscious behavior of the masses. What takes place in this sphere of the "unconscious" is not, of course, a purely natural occurrence. Some kind of shaping intelligence is at work here, too, not in its own terms but in the service of life's needs. Underlying all is the impulse to survive and to further human existence, particularly the existence of social units. But the less highly developed the social differentiation is, the more subconscious and homogeneous the operations of this impulse are. As a result, we can detect patterns of cause and effect similar to those in nature, especially in the realm of biology. But these historical patterns are less clear and rigorous than natural patterns because the mind constantly produces deviations from the norm.

Here we touch on those historical laws Troeltsch mentions and rightly characterizes as empirical rules. Troeltsch, however, tends to make too sharp a distinction between these laws and the laws of nature. Historical laws cannot of course be equated with physical, chemical, or even biological laws. Psychic causality is not of the same order as causality in the natural sciences. But in history we can, by a comparative study of mass behavior, make out certain typical lines of development in which both causal connection and inherent purpose are evident. These trends are vital elements in that complicated process we call "historical development." I feel that Troeltsch errs when he separates the concepts of historical development and biological evolution so sharply from each other.

The biological concept has, of course, two distinct roots. The first is the Romantic concept of organic development as we find it in Schelling, in Adam Müller, and in the historical school of jurisprudence. Here we are dealing with an intuitive apprehension of cultural growth in which the acting agent was thought to be the national soul or spirit. This concept was formed by analogy to the growth of a biological organism with its ancillary spiritual organism. Then there is also a modern biological, or more specifically, ontogenetic concept of development. This concept was formulated in philosophical terms by Spencer, who applied it in a sociological context. It explains causal connections rationally by means of an empirical method, which tries to explain the whole of a social structure in terms of the individuals in it and their interaction. Troeltsch completely rejects Spencer's concept of evolution but is not so hostile to the organic conception. But in the last analysis both these views describe historical and social life as analogous to a biological organism.

The organic concept begins with the whole and tries to grasp its "idea" by means of an act of intuitive thought, conceiving of the individual parts as elements of the organism. The modern theory of evolution, by contrast, takes individuals as the point of departure in explaining the structure of the social organism, proceeding by analogy with the ontogenetic method in biology. Both these modes of procedure are limited, and both fail to achieve their purpose. One requires the other as a complement, and both are necessary to the practical work of the historian, if only as analogies. The intuitive grasp of individual totalities as organic units of life leads, on the analogy of the organic process, to the concepts of birth, growth, fruition, maturity, and death. Rational, empirical investigation offers support to this intuitively grasped process by setting up a causal framework in which individual facts are ascertained, assessed, and related to each other in accordance with the information at the historian's disposal. I do not regard the organic view as intellectual in origin and as a concept transferred from the intellectual realm to the natural one. It originates instead in our experience of the life process as we see it in human life with its inner psychological aspect and in the life of animals and plants as well. Because of this the organic concept, especially with its evolutionary complement, can help us toward an understanding of the processes with which the world of the unconscious, the widest and deepest stratum of historical life, confronts us.

From this naturally and instinctively conditioned source of historical and social reality emerge the "material and intellectual tendencies" that govern and shape conscious historical life. The mode of intellectual development is different from the organic mode we have been considering up to now. Organic development is characterized by constant and continuous growth, by changes that are often so minor as to be unnoticeable but that nonetheless accumulate until their joint effect becomes strikingly evident, and by a general orientation to a single goal. In the conscious world of the intellect, however, historical development takes place by way of contrast and contradiction, conflict and compromise, struggle and catastrophe. In contrast to the model of evolutionary development stands the dialectical model whose essence is represented in Nicholas of Cusa's *coincidentia oppositorum,* the reconciliation of opposites at a higher stage of development.

Hegel reduced this dialectical principle to the formula of thesis, antithesis, and synthesis and at the same time transformed the pattern of thought processes into a pattern of historical development. But if we put aside the universal and metaphysical implications of this Hegelian formula and take it only for what it is—i.e., a subjective thought process—then it is difficult to understand what essential influence it could have on historical reality. Indeed, what is called the dialectical rhythm of historical events is not characterized by the clash of opposing forces but is instead a matter of contrasting principles that can be traced to basic psychological phenomena. But the Hegelian system may well have made such a deep impression on historians over a long period that even those who are unfamiliar with the system as a whole or who disagree with certain parts of it are still led to see historical processes as analogous to thought processes. The result has been an exaggerated application of the Hegelian pattern. Examples come readily to mind. An obvious one is the excessively sharp contrast that many historians claim to see between the *Ancien régime* and the French Revolution. Hegel did, of course, live through a period in history where there were clear-cut contrasts and syntheses in process. The sequence of *Ancien régime*, Revolution, and Restoration provides a textbook example of the dialectical principle and doubtless had considerable influence on the formulation of Hegel's theory. One can choose to emphasize the existing contrasts here, as Taine, Max Lehmann, and Hans Delbrück do; or, like Tocqueville and Ernst von Meier, one can allow them only secondary importance and emphasize instead the continuity of mores and institutions. But it seems to me that the real origin of the dialectical concept of historical development does not lie in Hegel's intellectual construct, much as this construct may have influenced modern historicism, but in man's awareness of a basic dichotomy between nature and mind, between necessity and freedom, between the world of instinctive drives and the world of the rational mind.

There is a need in the human mind not only to create opposites and to resolve them but also to comprehend them as necessary but not eternal divisions in a basically unified entity that encompasses all life. This is the real origin of the dialectical *coincidentia oppositorum*, a principle that permeates the dogma and philosophy of the medieval Church. Through the doctrine of the Trinity and of the sacrament of penance, this dialectic has had a lasting effect on the intellectual life of the West. The same principle is at the heart of Greek drama. With its conflicting characters and attitudes, its dialogue or "dialectic" in the basic sense, its dynamic plot, its *peripetia* and *catastrophe*, Greek tragedy reflects the principle of dialectical development, just as the epic reflects the principle of evolutionary development. This comparison is not an idle one, for there is, I believe, a definite relation between historical study and these literary *genres*.

There are, then, two distinct forms of historical interpretation, an evolutionary one, working primarily with unconscious and instinctive factors, and a dialectical one, working primarily with conscious, intellectual factors. The first proceeds steadily in one direction, the other erratically by means of conflict and resolution. These two interpretations can be compared to the old geological theories of Neptunism and Plutonism: in the one, water is the formative agent, its slow, steady action building layers of sediment; in the other, volcanic activity is the creative force with its sudden explosive power and crystalline formations. Just as the earth's surface has been shaped by a combination of these two forces, so historical and social reality has been shaped by the interaction of evolutionary and dialectical development. We cannot afford to neglect the importance of either one for history. Neither one alone enables us to understand the crust of culture that has formed above the chaotic, instinctual life of the human race. We cannot understand this historical process by the use of strictly logical conceptual models but only by a flexible application of the patterns outlined above. The clearest and most significant products of this approach are "historical ideas," Ranke's "material and intellectual tendencies of the centuries," in which Troeltsch saw the essence of historical development. We can better conceive of those ideas, however, as providing the content for the forms of historical development we have just discussed above.

We usually catalogue the various epochs of history in terms of these ideas or tendencies: we speak of Renaissance, Reformation, Jesuit Counter-Reformation, Enlightenment, Revolution, Romanticism, Restoration, Nationalism, Capitalism, and Socialism. To the extent that these entities have played a significant role in historical reality, however, they are not creations of the mind alone but of intellectual and instinctive forces working together. The mind alone cannot affect historical reality. To make itself felt it needs the constant assistance of forces that originate in the mass subconscious or come from the upper strata of society. But these forces alone do not determine the kind and direction of historical tendencies any more than does the mind alone. Hegel had an intellectual bias and regarded history as an emanation of the universal spirit; Marx, with his materialistic bias, regarded all history as a function of economic structure. Neither of these views offers the impartial observer a satisfactory explanation of historical phenomena. Ranke took a step in the right direction when he characterized them as "material and intellectual," but he did not elaborate on their origins. The German idealists, including Humboldt, whose theory of ideas derived from Schelling, tended to see historical trends originating in a realm beyond human ken and bursting forth from the hidden regions of subconscious life in the form of sudden revelations. Troeltsch, too, subscribed to this view.

It seems to me that the origin of historical ideas could be brought from mystical darkness into the brighter light of historical understanding by means of a psychology of the humane sciences. The central problem here would be the relation between individual and community, between the subjective and the objective mind. Troeltsch threw some light on this problem, but he never really attempted to solve it. He recognized that the collective spirit cannot be explained as the mere interaction of isolated individuals and, conversely, that individuals are not mere derivatives of the community. He contents himself with noting the fundamental tension between individual and community, which he apparently believes to be as much a matter of mutual dependence as it is of opposition, and regards it as a basic phenomenon that cannot be further clarified. This position is consistent with his distaste for psychological explanations of intellectual processes. But I find myself at odds with Troeltsch on this point. In my view, providing such explanations is the essential task of history.

The initial step in any investigation is a study of the individual mind, because it is more accessible and intelligible to us than the objective collective spirit. This does not mean, however, that we can expect to explain the collective spirit that makes up our cultural consciousness by studying isolated individuals in their relations to others of their own kind. No matter how far back we trace the development of our culture, we never reach a point at which individual consciousness is wholly independent from a collective spirit. The relation between individual and community, their mutual dependence, appears as the starting point of all human culture and so of all history—if indeed we are justified in using the term "starting point" at all. But if we trace the development of our culture, we discover that the great transformations to which the collective spirit has been subject can be primarily ascribed to leading personalities or small groups of such personalities. These transformations can be ascribed, that is, to highly gifted individuals who are, of course, formed by the collective spirit of their times but who, by creative acts of intellect, give that spirit new content or direction—or indeed, sometimes even reverse it and revolutionize it.

Troeltsch lays great stress on this individual creative power, but he sees in it, as in historical ideas themselves, simply the inexplicable eruption of intelligence (*Geist*) into the natural-real world. Thus, he simply avoids the issue of a psychological explanation. He avoids it because he is afraid of slipping into a causal explanation of intellectual acts, thereby compromising the freedom of the mind and surrendering to a naturalistic philosophy. He prefers to consider the question of the gifted individual, and of historical life in general, in terms of the theological concepts of election and predestination, and he rants against the shallow thinkers who speak of determinism and predestination in the same breath. Of course, we will never be able to explain the mysteries of individuality, and especially of gifted individuals, simply in terms of heredity, tradition, and similar factors. But I must confess that for me belief in the unlimited validity of the principle of sufficient reason is more satisfying than belief in a totally incomprehensible and arbitrary election as the mainspring of all historical development. The consciousness of freedom consists in the awareness of acting from motives that are not dictated by powers alien to our own minds. This sense of freedom is not impaired by the theoretical possibility that our natures are determined by circumstances which, for all practical purposes, are beyond our cognitive powers.

Another important point bearing on the relation between the individual and the collective spirit is not mentioned in Troeltsch, and he doubtless would not subscribe to it. The collective spirit is not a reality in the same sense as is the individual mind. It is real only to the extent that it affects the individual mind. Its influence is remarkably powerful, but it ceases to be effective if the values the collective spirit propounds are called into question. All human learning and culture, all historical movements and traditions are nourished at the wellsprings of the collective spirit. But the real bearers of this culture and this history are only men themselves—always, of course, in the context of their social relations and stratifications. Actualistic theories of the soul to the contrary, ideas and tendencies lack the tangible psycho-physical reality of men. Ideas have only a functional reality, and even that reality is valid only in the individual mind that produces the ideas. Their relation to specifically human views, needs, and values alone proves that they originate in the human mind. An eternal world of ideas, existing above and beyond human life and providing mankind with an occasional revelation, is a supposition incompatible with the nature of the ideas that emerge in history.

If it is to have effect in the world of history, an idea must initiate a movement. From historical experience we know that a movement takes shape only when tangible and instinctive forces emerge which are in harmony with a given idea and its probable consequences. Then, if interests formed in this way are to become effective in turn, leaders must give them coherence and di-

rection. These leaders can be regarded as exponents of mass
needs and popular instincts. They are Emerson's "representative
men," and they stand in contrast to the gifted creators of new
ideas, whom we could call "heroes" in Carlyle's sense of the
word. In reality, of course, these two human types may well appear in one and the same figure. In any case, an idea or tendency
becomes effective in history only by virtue of a combination of
spiritual and material factors.

How such a combination comes about, the phases a movement
passes through in its development—information, propaganda,
agitation in small, then in larger groups until an irresistible mass
action is underway—the transformation of the idea itself by its
alliance with real interests, all this cannot be presented in general terms, at least not in this study. Research into just these
matters makes up a large and essential portion of the historian's
work. All I want to emphasize here is that the ideas behind historical development, Ranke's "material and intellectual tendencies," are not revelations from a realm beyond human life but
products of human communities and their individual leaders. I
do not mean to deny the mysterious and inexplicable aspects of
creative production. Droysen's famous "X" remains, but to my
mind historical research should aim at reducing that "X" to a
minimum. If that is not our purpose, we may as well abandon
painstaking scientific research and, as Spengler put it, "poetize"
about history. In that case, modern historians could never measure up to Schiller or Shakespeare.

For Troeltsch the concept of development, which is the focal
point of our discussion here, is both specific and universal. That
is to say, it can be applied to specific individual totalities or to a
whole group of such totalities which may well span considerable
time and space but always remains only a part of world history.
But the concept can be applied also to history as a whole to the
extent that the human mind is capable of grasping the whole of
history. Universal development in this later sense is of special
concern to Troeltsch, and we will have to give it further consideration here.

For the philosophy of history this concept of universal development is of central importance, but it belongs to the metaphysical realm and has no immediate significance for the specialized work of the historian. Historical development that is accessible to research is specific in nature. Careful historians like Ranke prefer to speak not of "development" but rather of "tendencies of development." The concept presumes a closed and undisturbed cultural context, but such a clearly defined historical object is rarely, if ever, found. The history of ideas and institutions, however, often constructs connections that assume an immanent principle of development and closed, continuous process of development that presumably shape the entire individual totality. But as a rule, events having no connections with this immanent principle often interrupt, interfere with, or otherwise lend new direction to the process of development. Taine, for example, explains the French Revolution in terms of conditions within France and depicts it as a pathological crisis in the French body politic, thereby neglecting the effects of enemy invasion and of the military situation in the European power struggle. Aulard, who gave a clear historical account of these factors, said that Taine's method was tantamount to describing the Commune of 1871 without mentioning that the victorious German army was surrounding Paris at the time.

This approach is less obviously present, and perhaps for that very reason more often present, in studies that conceive of cultural development as the legal and political history of well-defined and highly individualized peoples. Wellhausen has written a history of the Jews in terms of their religious mentality and has presented that history as an essentially closed process of development. Eduard Meyer, on the other hand, stresses the numerous influences that the neighboring peoples and the major Near Eastern powers exerted on Israel's development. The main school of English constitutional history neglects the transformation of old England into the new unified state of Great Britain, although the revolution of the seventeenth century was obviously related to the Scottish Kings' accession to the English throne, even if at first the bond was created only through personal union. Similarly, German constitutional historians tend to see German development as purely autonomous and to neglect the influence exerted on it by other nations. External factors of this kind must always be kept in mind whenever the concept of development is involved. For Troeltsch, who was primarily interested in universal development, this whole question was of little importance, and he gave it only passing attention in some observations he made on the subject of "coincidence" in history. In any concrete discussion of development, however, this issue is a central one.

Another matter that Troeltsch himself sometimes touched on points up what I would like to call the conflict between, or at least the confrontation of, pragmatism and historicism—i.e., the conflict between a methodology based on the principle of purposeful action and one based on the principle of development. I have in mind here what Troeltsch called "overshooting the mark" and what Wundt termed the "heterogony of intention." This is a familiar phenomenon: an individual sets out to accomplish a limited task but is then forced to embark on much larger enterprises that may well be left to succeeding generations to complete. The final result may then seem to be either the realization of a grand design—a design completely lacking at the beginning of the action—or as something quite different and more ambitious than what was originally intended. In such cases we usually speak of "the natural course of things."

This phrase suggests the autonomous working-out of processes that are advanced by unconscious, instinctive drives but that are set in motion by conscious intellectual acts. Either a positive impulse or the removal of some hindrance can initiate such processes, and the direction these movements subsequently take may not reflect the intentions of their originators but may go far beyond them or stray far from them. The men who propagated the ideas of 1789 had originally hoped to create a community of free men under a liberal constitution and a federation of free nations; but once launched, the revolutionary movement led to military dictatorship and imperialistic ambitions. Ranke described the situation that existed shortly before the outbreak of the revolutionary wars in a formulation that he wanted applied only to a specific moment in recent history: "Politicians worked for peace, but the universal contradictions were bent on war." Mommsen credits Caesar with a comprehensive political program; Eduard Meyer proves to the contrary that circumstances forced Caesar to work slowly toward his ultimate goals. Augustus did not intend to create the Roman monarchy of the Caesars, nor did the Capetians of France or the Great Elector of Brandenburg-Prussia set out to create centralized states.

We could cite examples of this kind indefinitely. Hegel thought he could explain human action in history as a subterfuge of the world spirit which simply turned human efforts to its own purpose. Ranke vigorously repudiated this view, refusing to see men in history as mere puppets set in motion by the world spirit. This Hegelian view was incompatible with the religious elements in his concept of history as well as with his theory of "material and intellectual tendencies." These tendencies represent a balance between instinctive drives and rational, intellectual aims that do not allow any validity to "heterogony of purpose," at least not as a general principle. Ranke's tendencies also represent a reconciliation of the pragmatic idea and the concept of development. But even these two tendencies taken together do not govern the course of history totally and unconditionally. The pragmatic and developmental principles come together in an endless variety of combinations, and we therefore need a variety of approaches, appropriate to different objects of study and at the same time appropriate to the subjective mind of the observer, if we are to make the manifold and complex content of history comprehensible to the human intellect.

So far we have considered historical development only in terms of its movement. We must consider it now in terms of its goal. Progress toward a historical goal can be conceived of in two ways, either as linear progress toward an ideal goal or as a closed cyclical process that can repeat itself on a higher level. Troeltsch thought it desirable to make a sharp distinction between the concept of development, which is a historical concept, and the concept of progress, a concept proper to the philosophy of history. I cannot follow him on this point, because his distinction limits the historical concept of development too severely, leaving it based only on Ranke's "tendencies." Ranke himself, of course, rejected the idea of progress—a favorite idea of the Enlightenment; but what he was rejecting specifically was the idea of general progress in all areas of human life, the steady advance not only of technology but also of culture toward ever higher achievements. He did, however, accept the idea that world history is advancing toward an ideal goal, although he also emphasized strongly that no epoch exists just for the sake of its successor or for the purpose of bringing the ideal goal nearer.

Every epoch has its own justification and value or, as Ranke put it, "stands in direct relation to God." The principle behind this historical advance, which includes all nations but is not dissipated in them, is the "formation, preservation, and extension of the cultural world." Thus, Ranke did not accept the idea of a steady heightening of culture, as the Enlightenment projected it, but he did accept the idea of maintaining the high cultural values already attained and of spreading these values to larger and larger numbers of men. Is this not a form of progress although it is clearly progress in an extensive rather than intensive sense? Hegel did not postulate a *processus ad infinitum* either. He thought that the world was quite near to its final goal of completing the development of the universal spirit. All that remained to be done, then, was to spread the resulting culture. Similarly, the end of Marx's dialectic is reached when capitalism gives way to socialism. The same idea underlies the Catholic philosophy of history: once the divine plan for the redemption of mankind is achieved and Christ's Church is established, all further development is restricted to extending the Kingdom of God on earth until there is "one shepherd and one flock."

This idea of progress clearly differs from the Enlightenment idea, to which the positivists also subscribed. Within the framework of Comte's law of three stages, they believed in progress toward a goal of positivism, democracy, and industrialism. In the one concept of progress, the emphasis is on intellect and culture; in the other, it is on civilization and its instinctive drives. These two basically different views have to be assessed according to separate standards. When a culture has reached its heights, all that remains to be done is to preserve it. Civilization, however, does seem to be capable of progress ad infinitum, since it is rooted in the instinct of populations to increase (we know that the world's population has been growing steadily throughout human history) and in the constantly developing technology that provides the means of survival for this growing population. The concept of development should, I think, be defined broadly enough to take in this idea of progress, too.

Troeltsch did not treat in any detail the cyclical theory of historical development but he by no means ruled it out. The theory has appeared in many forms. Spinoza, Goethe, and Nietzsche conceived of it in universal terms that deprived it of its specifically historical significance. In this concept, history and nature are linked to each other, as they are in the phrase "the eternally recurring ebb and flow" or in the obscure and time-honored expression "the recurrence of all things." As Spranger has shown, this idea first gained concrete historical meaning in Vico's new science, which dealt with "traits common to all nations." Vico tried to prove that all nations developed according to the same laws and passed through the same three stages of the divine, the heroic, and the human. These stages have been incorrectly interpreted as suggesting that individual nations progress through an ancient, medieval, and modern phase. The latter terms, however, apply only to universal history as a whole, not to the histories of individual nations. In the age of nationalism the cyclical view of national development was a popular one. Lamprecht's needless multiplication of typical epochs carried this theory to absurd lengths and brought it into discredit. The currently accepted cyclical theory is no longer applied to individual nations but only to broad configurations like the ancient world of the Mediterranean, the Christian West, Islam, India, and the Far East; it continues to employ the ideas of birth and death, youth and age. Spengler is its most influential advocate.

This view tends to neglect the question of possible connections among these cultures. It is generally assumed that this new theory of cultural configurations has superseded universal history as Ranke saw it; proponents of this theory look down on the traditional scheme of ancient, medieval, and modern as if it were a thing of the past. The actual teaching and practice of history, however, show that we cannot do without these divisions. Furthermore, the theory of cultural configurations and Ranke's notion of universal history are not mutually exclusive but are in fact complementary.

The concept of universal history is the concept of the genesis of Western culture. Modern Western culture grew from the meeting of Northern Europe with the declining culture of the ancient world. The Christian Middle Ages represents the stage of transition. Modern Western culture first developed in opposition to the world of Islam, which was itself influenced by the old culture of the Mediterranean, then by Hellenism and Byzantium. Western civilization defined itself further in the process of colonizing regions once under the control of ancient Asiatic cultures. What effects this colonization will have on the West still remains to be seen. The many peoples and civilizations of the world are gradually becoming one, and Europe and America are leading the way in this process of unification.

The advance of Western history is thus encompassing the entire world. Spengler's greatest error was his failure to see the vital connection between Western and ancient culture; his theory of "pseudomorphosis" cannot compensate for this failure. Spengler argued that a culture adheres to the peoples that produce it. Every culture, he argues, is new and unique, and its transfer to other peoples is an illusion. This thesis is untenable in the extreme form in which Spengler presents it, because it destroys all coherence in human history. The transfer of culture (not simply of civilization) poses a fundamental problem for historicism, and Troeltsch, unlike Spengler, gave it his close attention. His attempts to deal with this problem are closely linked with his efforts to "overcome historicism." But only the ethical will can overcome historicism, and as soon as we are forced to deal with the ethical will, we are forced to consider the problem of value as well, a problem we have tried to exclude from our methodological discussion up to this point.

Standards of Value and the Cultural Synthesis

As we have seen, a system of values is essential to Troeltsch's methodology. For him an object of historical study is constituted as an individual totality only by its relation to a specific value. The same is true of a historical development. But I have tried to show above that such a relation to value, to the extent that it involves any specific value, is not essential to the methodology of history. It is indispensable only for the material philosophy of history, and I suspect that Troeltsch took it from Rickert's theory and applied it to historical methodology merely to bring the material philosophy of history into a closer relation with historical logic and to let that philosophy take rise from methodology. The only way Troeltsch can do this is by drawing problems essential to a material philosophy of history into the field of historical logic. As a result, his philosophical remarks are somewhat less rewarding than his methodological. But this only serves to throw Troeltsch's main idea into strong relief. Today, Troeltsch believes —now that we have left behind the speculative idealism of Fichte and Hegel and the positivist constructions of Comte and Spencer, and now that empirical methods of historical research are so sophisticated and the historian is required to offer concrete support for his assertions of meaning and value—the task of a material philosophy of history cannot consist only in a new, purely theoretic construction of historical continuity, whether along causal or teleological lines. It must instead take a practical turn, a turn that is both ethical and cultural. Working within the context of past world history, we must create a cultural synthesis for the present, a synthesis that will contain the ethical forces needed to perpetuate our culture in the future.

This cultural synthesis informed with the ethical will is central to Troeltsch's whole philosophy of history, and it represents a great critical and creative inventory of all values, creative in projecting tendencies for the future, critical in selecting values from the past. The theory of universal historical development stands in reciprocal relation to the cultural synthesis. The synthesis itself is a summation of world history; but at the same time the pattern we perceive in world history is shaped in turn by the historical values on which our synthesis of culture is based. This ethically oriented synthesis does not uncritically absorb all the historical currents that make their way into the present. It picks up only the most valuable impulses of the past and present, not simply the strongest ones, in its work of advancing culture. Here we are at the heart of Troeltsch's philosophy of history, and we can see now why he placed such extraordinary emphasis on values in historical life. We can also see clearly how he differs from his predecessor, Rickert, the actual founder of the historical theory of values.

Rickert proceeded from the principle that an object of historical study was constituted as an individual totality when a set of historical facts was lifted from the endless amorphous mass of history and given unity through its relation to a legitimate value. Both the value and the system to which it belongs are regarded as extratemporal, universally valid, and therefore absolute. Only in relation to an absolute value does the historian's choice, which otherwise would be arbitrary and subjective, take on substance and become a legitimate object of historical research. In this way the principle of selection becomes the criterion for a historical assessment of the object. The object must be assessed in relation to the same absolute value on the basis of which it was established.

It is to this brilliant theory that Troeltsch owed his ideas on defining historical objects in relation to values. But he rejected its basic axiom, which postulated that these values be absolute. He rejected also the idea that historical judgment, too, must rest on a system of absolute values. He did, however, retain the idea of a historical value judgment and tried to base it on something other than absolute values. He made the justified criticism of Rickert's theory that no road led from the world of values to the empirical facts of history, that individuality in history cannot derive its existence from general, eternal values, and that historical development loses all meaning if it is confronted with a transcendental value system of this nature. But his chief objection, which was related to these other criticisms, was that this view denied the possibility of a cultural synthesis drawn from universal historical development and of creative ethical and cultural goals for the future. These two points were of the utmost importance to Troeltsch.

Troeltsch therefore had to replace absolute, transcendental values with relative and autochthonous ones. These latter values were identical with the cultural and ethical ideals that every historical entity, be it a people or an epoch, produces. But in addition to regarding the historical object in terms of its own values, the historian also has to consider it in terms of the values of his own time. His critical understanding of contemporary values leads to a cultural synthesis of the present. This synthesis is based in turn on the pattern of universal historical development in which the permanent and decisive values of various times and peoples are drawn together. Autochthonous value structures inform the over-all pattern, but at every point in history this universal system of relations presents itself in a different light. Instead of relying upon an absolute value system, the historian must make his judgments in terms of values that are valid for him but are historically conditioned nonetheless. Troeltsch's theory represents a shift in historical thought comparable to the change Einstein's theory of relativity represents in science, and it would have had similar repercussions if Rickert's theory of value had enjoyed so long and widespread a dominance as Newton's law of gravity. Neither Troeltsch's nor Einstein's theory opens the way for unlimited relativism. Indeed, both remain oriented to absolute truths.

Troeltsch's theory deprived the idea of standards of its original meaning. For what does it mean to say that each people and each epoch must be judged only from the viewpoint of its own autochthonous values? If these values are understood as the ethical ideals of a given culture, then we can no longer properly speak of judgment at all; real life invariably lags behind the ideal. Consequently, the historian is not concerned with judging but with understanding the values of the society involved, and history as a discipline is concerned with the affirmation, appropriation, and revival of these values, with reception and renaissance, with cultural and historical relations between peoples and epochs.

Nevertheless, Troeltsch retained Rickert's standards of evaluation and incorporated them into his own theory, but giving them a wholly different meaning. He differentiates between two kinds of standards. The first entails nothing more than an empathetic understanding of the inherent values of each culture, each people, each epoch. Troeltsch frequently equates the "standards" of a historical entity with its ideals. The second kind involves principles of selection by which historical cultural elements have become part of the present culture and by which they are to be included in or excluded from the ongoing cultural synthesis. Thus, these standards arise in part from intellectual syntheses that have taken place in the past and in part from spontaneous choices that express the cultural tendencies of the present.

In my opinion Troeltsch's theory stands to gain in validity if it can be stripped of the false metaphor of "standards," the only element of Rickert's value theory that Troeltsch retained. There is really nothing here to be measured. We are concerned here with questions of quality, not of quantity. More important still, however, is the fact that Troeltsch rejects the idea of absolute standards when he rejects the idea of an absolute, transcendental value system. Standards that arise from a culture and that constantly change as that culture develops are no standards at all, even if they derive from an autonomous cultural impulse.

The metaphor of standards in the world of historical values is justified only when absolute values are postulated and provide a constant frame of reference for the constantly changing world of history. Without the assumption of such absolute values, measurement is impossible, even in a metaphorical sense. The value inherent in a historical object does not measure its individuality but only characterizes it either in its own terms or in relation to our sense of values. All cultural development, seen as more than a mere accumulation of works and achievements, cannot be measured by objective values but must be apprehended by means of a subjective sense of values. And in his argument, Troeltsch is not in fact dealing with standards and value judgments but with the understanding of specific historical and cultural phenomena, with the transmission of cultural achievements from one human community to another, and with the spontaneous, autonomous cultural process that both critically and creatively absorbs and builds upon the entire cultural heritage of the past. All these processes are, of course, closely related to each other, and what is common to them all is not judgment according to set standards of value but the creative production and transmission of cultural achievements, the comprehension and appropriation of ethical and cultural values—in short, the vital principle of cultural development itself.

Troeltsch's emphasis on his theory of standards relegated the central problem of historicism—the problem of understanding the past—to a position of secondary importance. Because he rejected psychological explanation he sought a metaphysical solution to this problem and, indeed, to the general problem of comprehending anything that is foreign to our own being. Here he followed

Leibniz and especially Malebranche. We understand what is foreign to our own being (*hors de l'âme*), including historical entities, by means of a bond with the mind of God. All human minds are contained in the mind of God, and through this common relation a medium of understanding is created. When we see what Spranger, who aims at much the same solution (*Lebensformen*, pp. 365 ff.), achieves by a psychological interpretation and analysis, it becomes clear to us that Troeltsch's fundamental rejection of all psychological methods deprived him of a rich source of cognition.

The transmission of culture from one people to another is one of the great riddles of history. Troeltsch, following Hegel, spoke of a dialectical growth of culture; but to my knowledge he never went into this question in any detail. He more often emphasized that the transference of external "civilization" involves merely external achievements that do not represent genuine intellectual and cultural values and can therefore be readily separated from the culture that produced them. We are forced to the conclusion that whenever real spiritual and cultural values are transferred from one people to another—whether directly through historical proximity or indirectly through a later reception and renaissance—something of the spirit of the people who produced those values is passed on to the people who inherit them. We would be hard pressed to cite a case of an entire culture being transmitted in this way; ordinarily, only a few elements from one culture are passed on to another. Transference takes place if these elements hold special value for another people or, to put it differently, if these elements satisfy the particular cultural needs of that people. But even this kind of partial transference cannot take place if there is no intellectual bond between the two peoples involved. In other words, a process of spiritual education and training is necessary if products of one civilization are to be transplanted into a new environment, and we usually find some influential class performing this educational task.

The clergy of the early Christian Church transmitted Greek

and Latin culture to the peoples of the West. A similar function fell to the humanists of the Renaissance, to the new humanists at the time of Wilhelm von Humboldt, to the legists when Roman jurisprudence was absorbed into European law, and to the legal profession of later periods as well. A "psychology of the humane sciences" is essential if we are to deal with these matters effectively. Troeltsch's "standards," we find, take the form of a cultural need that selects from the life of a declining culture those elements useful to it. The actual conditions of life in the appropriating culture do not interfere with the reception of those elements but tend to make it possible—or indeed even to demand it.

Of the three points we are considering here, Troeltsch gives by far the greatest emphasis to the third, that of the ethical and cultural impulse that undertakes a critical and creative synthesis of past values and so points the way to the future. This cultural impulse expresses itself in spontaneous intellectual activity that is fundamental to the individual consciousness. We might even describe this activity as *a priori*, though this use of the term deviates widely from Kant's use of it. In Troeltsch's thinking, this cultural impulse replaces Rickert's system of values. Its *a priori* nature and the element of activity involved in it are adequate safeguards against the dangers of unlimited relativism and mere aesthetic contemplation, dangers attendant on historicism. I find Troeltsch's fear of relativism in history a little exaggerated. We can openly admit the relativity of all historical phenomena without succumbing to "relativism," for the relativism Troeltsch objects to is a world-view that so misconstrues the dependence of all life, including our own, on factors that lie beyond human consciousness that it completely denies the independence and spontaneous activity of the individual consciousness. If we avoid this particular view, we can safely admit the boundless relativity of all historical life without falling prey to relativism or sacrificing the freedom of the spirit. For freedom is basically nothing more than the consciousness of freedom. To be sure, the recognition of both general relativity and individual freedom implies an antinomy. But this antinomy between necessity and freedom is neither more nor less than the riddle of human existence itself and the source of all philosophical dialectic.

The postulation of spontaneous freedom for the ethical cultural impulse is the central point of Troeltsch's conception of historicism, and to the extent that historicism is equated with relativism, this same point is essential to the overcoming of historicism. Troeltsch likes to speak of a Kierkegaardian leap that we must dare to take, and he even jokingly refers to it as a *salto mortale*. This "leap" had a very special meaning for him, since he did not consider the act of cultural synthesis a subjective or arbitrary one. He stressed the objectivity of this act as much as its *a priori* nature, and he guaranteed its objectivity by basing it on the facts of history. The synthesis must be prevented from becoming a mere construct of the philosophy of history, and it must therefore be based on an understanding of the tradition that is subject to constant review.

Troeltsch repeatedly and eloquently emphasizes that our abstractions from history and our assessments of it must be deepened and corrected by fresh encounters with it and by viewing it in terms of changing values. In this way he hoped to arrive at the most reliable account possible of world history and to create the most complete harmony possible between this account and the ethically oriented cultural synthesis. The cultural synthesis is based on an account of history, and that account is determined in turn by the ethical impulses inherent in the synthesis. The relation between history and the cultural synthesis would thus appear to be a circular and therefore senseless one, but Troeltsch solves this problem, to his satisfaction at any rate, by means of a metaphysical assumption. For him, finite minds share an identity with the infinite mind that reveals itself in the course of history. By interpreting history as the activity of the divine spirit, Troeltsch endows the objective facts of history with a sublime dignity.

I cannot accept Troeltsch's view here. In my opinion the creative life principle that governs nature and history has to be separated from God as we conceive of Him in our own minds. If we regard the life principle as divine, we ought to be aware that nature and spirit are undivided in it and that it is beyond our concepts of good and evil. The division of nature and spirit, of good and evil, is a product of our own minds and arises only because we are intellectually and emotionally constituted as we are. It is not inherent in the world outside our minds, and we indulge in an anthropomorphic illusion if we attribute this peculiarity of our microcosmic inner life to the macrocosmic life principle that we can understand only in its effects upon us but not in its essential reality. It is true, of course, that not only the body and soul but also what we call the mind participates in life. But the human mind, with its reflective consciousness that mirrors not only the outside world but the inner one as well, is unique in itself, and we have no right to project its idiosyncrasies on the macrocosm. The mind is that "creative mirror" (*schaffende Spiegel*) Goethe mentions in the disputation scene of his *Urfaust*. I can think of no more suitable comparison than this to express such a difficult relation.

The creations of our minds are not really original creations but only imitations or modifications of macrocosmic reality and as such are conditioned by the structure of the human mind. They are not identical with but complementary to macrocosmic reality, reflecting our intellectual capabilities as well as our intellectual and emotional needs. The human mind cannot create life; it can only react to life, distinguishing and evaluating, accepting and rejecting, fixing ideas and concepts in signs and words. Its basic function is to meet the needs of practical existence; but when these needs are reasonably satisfied, it soars to the loftier regions of purely intellectual values and ideals. What it creates in this sphere often works against what happens in the real world where the premises of its activity are to be found. This is the origin of the dialectical process. In its own sphere the mind is autonomous; it can be critical of real life and even reject it; but it cannot abolish real life. It can assert itself, refining and humanizing real life, only if it makes some compromises with reality. It can realize its own ideals only by taking real interests into account.

Historical life is governed only to a very limited extent by purely intellectual forces. It is governed to a much greater extent, as are politics and economics, by interests that reflect instinctive drives and that are served by raw power. The intellect often furthers these interests, but then it is obviously a servant, not a master. Where the two forces, real and ideal, achieve a balance, we have Ranke's "material and intellectual" tendencies, but these can hardly be equated with the "activity of the divine spirit."

It is true, of course, that Troeltsch made several concessions in this direction. He admits that the identity of history with the individual human mind is a highly limited one, that the difference between the finite and the infinite mind is not only quantitative —not simply a matter of space and time—but also qualitative, that cognition depends on an anthropological factor as well as on the identity of the known and the knowing, and that there is no completely satisfactory way out of this epistemological dilemma. But his attempt at a solution to this dilemma leads us back once again to Leibniz and Malebranche, to the understanding of what is foreign to us by participation in the divine spirit. Finally then, despite the anthropologically based limits inherent in human thought, historical individuality and historical development remain objects of intuitive perception and constitute, together with the inner movement of the life of the world, a unity of being and meaning, of fact and idea. In Troeltsch's opinion this is the only way to resolve the differences between the "intuitionists" and the "formalists," and it is on this same axiom that Troeltsch bases the pious confidence with which his philosophy of history regards the course of human events, despite all the irrationality, evil, and horror revealed in them.

The limits that anthropology has set to Troeltsch's view of a direct tie between man and God have kept him from the one-sided approach that characterized earlier constructs in the philosophy of history. Eager as he is to expand historical cognition to universal dimensions, he abandons the Enlightenment notion of an all-inclusive history of mankind as well as the German Classical idea of *Humanität*, for which he substitutes his ethical and cultural synthesis. *Mankind* for him is not a meaningful historical entity, for we cannot experience it concretely or grasp it clearly. Accordingly, it shows no historical development. For Troeltsch, historical development, even if it is considered in terms of world history, is limited in application to our own Western culture, which grew from the fusion of ancient Mediterranean culture with the Romanized German tribes and the Christian world. Other cultures can provide comparisons that throw light on our own culture and help us form sociological concepts but they cannot become part of our historical development as Troeltsch's philosophy of history, oriented toward cultural synthesis, defines that development. Troeltsch's perspective excludes not only Far Eastern and Indian culture but also the culture of Islam, which has many ties to the West. On the other hand, however, Troeltsch does tend to see Russia as part of the Western cultural world, and there is no question about the inclusion of America. She owes her origins to Western culture, and she reflects its values more and more, while in Europe our civilization and therefore our culture are being increasingly Americanized.

As long as Troeltsch is concerned only with historical development, his limitation of his field to Western culture seems wise. But in terms of synthesis, his unequivocal rejection of non-European cultures is less fortunate. This rejection may well be a product of the Christian bias in his work, perhaps of a German and Continental European bias as well. A possible synthesis of Western and Eastern civilizations does not seem so remote to the English mind, for instance—as Wells' famous book on the philosophy of history shows. Some German philosophers of history, too, like Max Scheler, hope for a regeneration of metaphysics through

Asiatic influence. All reasonable men will, however, doubtless agree that our first task is to organize, clarify, and strengthen what might be called the European mind.

Influenced by Max Weber and Werner Sombart, Troeltsch takes a much more realistic position than one would expect in his treatment of the Marxian question of superstructure and sub-structure in cultures, a question of central importance in his considerations. He recognizes that intellectual and cultural life is based on a socio-economic, political, and legal substructure, that it arises in conjunction with that substructure and can never become fully independent of it. "It is true," Troeltsch writes, "that the elementary needs of life—nourishment, reproduction, civilization, law and order—determine the individual's life patterns, the life patterns of a community, and the direction of intellectual life as well."

This is particularly true of the modern age—which is, of course, of special importance for Troeltsch's concept of the historical world and for his cultural synthesis of the present. He locates the beginning of this era in the Renaissance, i.e., in the fifteenth century. He sees the sixteenth century and the first half of the seventeenth—the period of the Reformation and of the confessional absolutism that followed it—as a relapse into the attitudes of the Middle Ages, and he considers dating the modern era from the English Revolution and the concomitant end of confessional absolutism. He finally rejects this possibility, however, and returns —quite correctly, I think—to dating the modern period from the fifteenth century. Politically and economically, the essential forces at work in the history of the last five centuries have been the rise of national states; the rivalry among the major European nations; the balance-of-power system; the constitutional forms of parliamentarianism and absolutism; the French Revolution, which replaced the feudal order with modern concepts of state and citizenship; the nationalism of the post-revolutionary period; the development of capitalism with its often related phenomenon of imperialism; and the countermovement of proletarian socialism.

The concurrent intellectual and cultural movements have been the Renaissance, Reformation, and Counter Reformation; European Baroque; individualistic rationalism, natural law, the Enlightenment and Pietism; eighteenth-century classicism and German idealism; romanticism and West European positivism.

Then too, these political and intellectual trends have been accompanied by an unprecedented growth of population, technology, and trade and by the spread of European civilization over the entire globe. The elemental forces of politics and economics follow their own laws; they are our fate. We have to understand them and come to terms with them as best we can. A deeper historical understanding is generally not required where they are concerned; in these areas our knowledge need not go back beyond the beginning of the modern age, although familiarity with earlier times may well be essential for experts in legal and administrative history. Here, an eye for the practical, a knowledge of the present, and a sense of what is possible and necessary are more important than an education in history. Cultural life, however, is completely dependent on knowledge of history. Certain intellectual forces, even when separated from the social and economic structures from which they took rise, have remained a lasting influence on Western culture: the Hebrew prophets and the Bible; Greek civilization in the age of the *polis* —including Homer, whose work achieved canonical status only in this period; ancient imperialism, beginning with the Hellenistic monarchy and culminating in the constitutional and legal structure of Rome; Christianity and the Romanized Germanic culture of the Middle Ages.

These forces can continue to influence the cultural development of the West if we can infuse new life into them through research and study of sources, and so prevent them from becoming mere lifeless abstractions. Their effects on Western civilization are evident in Renaissance, Enlightenment, and Neohumanism, in the Reformation and Counter Reformation, in Pietism, romanticism, and even in positivism. This spiritual continuity must be preserved and carried forward. Our main task will be to build upon the cultural values of our tradition, adapting them to the impulses at work in contemporary life so that we can direct those impulses toward higher intellectual goals. If we can do this, we can initiate a movement that will involve intellectual as well as material forces and will prevent our culture from degenerating into a purely technical, scientific, and materialistic "civilization." In our dreams we wish for a new religious impetus or a great symbolic work like *Faust* or *The Divine Comedy* to provide force and direction to such a movement.

Thus, unless I have misunderstood the rather ambiguous program Troeltsch outlines for the continuation of his work, he envisages the harmonious cooperation of new intellectual forces with the material tendencies of contemporary life, even though these external circumstances cannot but impose serious limitations on the activity of the mind. The path Troeltsch hopes to travel seems to me to be the correct one, but I think the difficulties it presents are much greater than he believed them to be, by reason of the extraordinarily confusing and disturbing complexities and contradictions of contemporary political and economic life.

The forces working for a capitalistic, imperialistic world order and those working for a federalistic, socialistic one present just such a problem. The capitalistic camp seems to have conquered for the time being, but the socialistic one is by no means deprived of its power to resist. Intellectual activity that restricts itself to areas far above the reality of this struggle will be powerless to affect the course of history. But with which side should our intellectual life align itself, particularly in Germany? Should we compromise our national and moral dignity by embracing the capitalism and imperialism of the victorious powers who have condemned us to defenselessness, political impotence, and forced labor? That is clearly impossible. But nearly the entire weight of our tradition prevents us from joining the opposing faction. This dilemma threatens to prevent any resurgence of vitality and any cultural progress in the foreseeable future. But we must have the courage to see things as they are, even if the outlook is hopeless. With all due respect for the optimism that Troeltsch's courageous and powerful work displays, I cannot readily believe that the second part of it, which Troeltsch never wrote, would have been able to show us the way to a more promising future. But the task Troeltsch set for us remains valid nonetheless.

The philosophy of history, or, more exactly, a philosophically oriented approach to history, is just as essential to the historian as it is to the philosopher, and it cannot limit itself to revealing, by means of essentially value-free constructs, a coherent development in European history, thus enabling us to understand contemporary conditions and problems as products of that development; nor can it limit itself to an aesthetic contemplation of the cultural values of the past. We need not dispense with these approaches, for they still retain their validity; but the philosophy of history must assume the additional task of animating an ethical and cultural will that can draw selectively on the values of the past and create ideals for the future, ideals that are not mere castles in the air but ideals that can take on concrete form in the real world. A cultural synthesis of this kind is the task in which we are all engaged with varying degrees of consciousness, hope, and strength. This is the task that prevents us from taking refuge in relativism or quietism. It does not lead us to that intellectual absolutism that Rickert had in mind but commits us, if I may say, to a healthy decisiveness, to clear cultural aims, to the firm resolution not to surrender the individual, national, and supranational forms of our cultural life, but to stand our ground against all hostile powers (*allen Gewalten zum Trotz sich erhalten*) and to develop according to our nature (*nach dem Gesetz wonach du angetreten*).

11

ECONOMICS AND POLITICS
IN THE AGE OF
MODERN CAPITALISM

This article was published in the *Zeitschrift für die Gesammten Staatswissenschaften,* Volume 86 (1929). As Hintze himself says, it is a follow-up of a long, critical report on Sombart's *Modern Capitalism* that Hintze had published in the *Historische Zeitschrift,* Volume 139 (1929), pp. 457–509. In the second article on the subject Hintze restates his views in reply to Sombart's objections.

Sombart's work had first been published in two volumes in 1902, but it was the appearance of a second, revised and enlarged edition (1916–27) that provided the occasion for Hintze's articles. But Hintze's essay also forms part of a broader intellectual discussion that had been going on in Germany since the end of the First World War; and it might be instructive to list together the names of the authors who played an important role in this discussion and to whom references are dispersed throughout Hintze's article.

The most powerful stimulus came from Max Weber's *Wirtschaft und Gesellschaft* and from the series of volumes in which his collected articles were published. Hintze's references to Weber's thesis that the national state represents a guarantee for the survival of modern capitalism comes from Weber's inaugural lecture of 1885, republished in his *Politische Schriften;* and Weber's views on ancient capitalism, which Hintze mentions, may be found in *Wirtschaft und Gesellschaft*. Hintze refers to Schumpeter's view that the mode of life that follows logically from the nature of capitalism necessarily implies an anti-nationalist orientation in politics and culture. Schumpeter's "Zur Soziologie der Imperialismen," which had first appeared in *Archiv für Sozialwissenschaft und Sozialpolitik,* Volume 46 (1919), and then in book form, must be regarded as one of the most important contributions to the then just beginning discussion on the nature of imperialism; recent modifications in our views of this concept are of no relevance to Hintze's discussion, which is directed purely to probing the value of this concept for the problem of historical periodization.

Heinrich Maier was a professor of philosophy in Berlin who, particularly in his book entitled *Psychologie des Emotionalen Denkens,* had given much attention to the logic of intuitive abstraction (*Anschauliche Abstraktion*). Hintze was very much *au courant* on recent research in the field of the French Revolution because his wife Hedwig Hintze was an active scholar in this field. As is shown by the list of books reviewed by Hintze in the 1920s, he had an interest in the literature on the structure of the American Republic. Yet his remarks on America in the present essay probably derive less from Charles A. Beard than from the book by E. C. Miner, *The Ratification of the Federal Constitution by the State of New York* (New York, 1921), which Hintze had reviewed at length in 1925 in *Schmollers Jahrbuch,* Volume 49, pp. 977–82.

Nevertheless, because Hintze's article reflects the intellectual discussion of the post-war decade, it is also a reflection of prejudices aroused by political events. German indignation at difficulties in the question of reparations and at delays in the evacuation of the Rhineland come into the fore in remarks about the League of Nations and French policy. Finally, his distinction between culture and civilization, although without the sharp anti-Western bias revealed in Thomas Mann's distinction of these two terms in his wartime *Betrachtungen eines Unpolitischen,* echoes somewhat the German tradition of a sharp distinction between these two concepts: civilization concerned with the lower, material aspects of life, culture with the higher, spiritual aspects. Although both German and English use the words "culture" and "civilization," their meaning is not identical.

I have already tried elsewhere to give Werner Sombart's great work on modern capitalism the full appreciation it deserves.[1] Sombart, however, has followed this with a reply[2] to his critics dealing with basic principles in which he discusses the relations between economic theory and economic history, and calls for a close and necessary connection between the two, both as a matter of principle and as a way of liberating economic history from political history. This means a clean separation of economics and politics in historical study. I do not consider his arguments to be directed at me personally. The reproaches they are intended to rebut—particularly the charge that he has done violence to history by his theoretical constructions—I have never raised. For purely nonpartisan reasons, however, I regard this as an occasion to present once more a summary of my own rather different view of the relations between economics and politics in the age of modern capitalism.

Sombart rightly claims to have been the first to determine the epochs in economic history according to the various successive economic systems. Previously the arrangement of epochs in political history had been applied to economic history, in Germany by Schmoller and Bücher, but also in France and England. But it seems to me that a historian cannot be satisfied with this complete and fundamental divorce of economics and politics since, in such an approach, theoretical criteria gain excessive importance over truly historical ones. In a predominantly theoretical study, one considers historical and social phenomena in their relation to separate cultural areas such as economics, politics, or religion; and even the historian gains a full understanding of these phenomena only in placing them in the context appropriate to them.

Along with this theoretical approach, however, there is an equally justifiable truly historical approach, the "cultural historical" approach, which recognizes and emphasizes that all experiences and actions of the subjects of history, be they individual men or human groups like nations, form a living unit into which the various cultural systems converge so that their division into different strands is purely theoretical. Economics, politics, religion, art, science, and technology are interrelated, not only in their inception but in all phases of their development as well. Throughout they all display the same "style." The living unit they form makes up what can be called "culture" in the widest sense (including "civilization"). The connection between economics and politics is especially close, however, and politics and economics might be viewed as forming the narrow unity of "civilization" whereas "culture," if used as distinct from civilization, is concerned with the phenomena of intellectual and spiritual life. Whoever presents the history of a single people will distinguish that people's economic development and its political development, not in such a way that he presents an economic history without any inner connection to political history, but in such a way that in the various phases of development economic and political life appear as two sides, or aspects, of one and the same historical process.

This, I believe, is the basic difference between a predominantly theoretical and a predominantly cultural-historical approach to history. One has an abstraction for its object, such as the economy, or capitalism; the other has a living human being or a unity of living human beings, such as an individual or a nation, for its object. To be sure, the abstractions we are dealing with here are of a special kind: they are institutional abstractions that we may, following H. Maier, call "types," as distinct from the "concepts" of the natural sciences. It is easy to associate the "types" of economic life—types such as modern capitalism—with the idea of some living, human agency, as Sombart does with the idea of the Western peoples, or more properly with what he calls the "Latin-Teutonic" group of peoples of modern times. Thus he is not without justification in regarding modern capitalism as a "historical individuality." Strictly speaking, however, it is really only an isolated, overt manifestation of that individual's life. The very category of individuality requires that the economic sector needs to be studied in all its actions and reactions to other areas so that it becomes a full, complete, real, living entity; and an inflexible division of economics and politics makes this impossible.

What is it, then, that turns the "economic systems" into "economic epochs"? It is the fact that these abstractions represent one side, one aspect, of the general life process of human history at a distinct phase of its development. Therefore I, too, believe that the periodization of economic history according to economic systems does not have to be inconsistent with the traditional periodization according to the great epochs of political history. It merely gives the received periodization a clearer and sharper economic dimension. To this extent it certainly marks a considerable methodological advance. And yet we do not forfeit this advance if we recognize that there are unmistakable parallels on all levels between the economic and the political epochs of history. I should like to focus on this parallelism for the age of modern capitalism and of the modern state.

Max Weber has said that the self-contained national state possesses the guarantees for the survival of capitalism. I regard this as correct, even though Schumpeter has tried to show that capitalism and nationalism are by nature antithetical. It seems to me that Sombart has not given this its due significance, for the relation, to my mind, was a fateful one. When he looked into the future of capitalism he altogether omitted mention of the political conditions for its survival. His view on the subject reduces to this: The modern state and modern capitalism stem from a common spiritual and intellectual root; but after they branched out from each other, each developed according to its own laws. These two paths of development run parallel to each other with manifold reciprocal influences and effects; but neither of them could be said to be merely a function of the other. This generalization does not wholly satisfy me, since it neglects the continuous unity of cultural development. There are two essential questions to be asked: first, What is the nature of the common spiritual root? and second, How are we to assess the further relation between the two in the different stages of development?

It seems to me that Sombart has insisted too strongly on the autonomy of economic development, at the expense of the effect of the political factor. What Sombart says remains true: neither did capitalism bring about the modern state, as the Marxists have often claimed, nor did the modern state bring about capitalism, despite mercantilist economic policy and the liberal economic reforms of the nineteenth century. It seems to me equally true, however, that the rise and development of capitalism remains unintelligible without an insight into how it was conditioned by the course of nation-building and by the spirit of politics during the last four centuries. This latter truth runs the risk of being obscured by an all too strict segregation of economic development from political development, and by an all too heavy emphasis on the autonomy of economic life. The unity of the history of civilization is not given its due, although even Sombart recognized it in principle with the assumption of a common spiritual ancestry for the modern state and for capitalism.

We next ask, What is the nature of this common spiritual ancestry? Sombart says that the spirit of capitalism stemmed from the same spirit that, at the end of the Middle Ages, produced the new state, the new religion, the new science and technology. He obviously means the spirit of the Renaissance. He cites the Faustian spirit in order to characterize the drive to the infinite which is his main point. This is certainly a graphic and suggestive description, but I find it unsatisfactory from the standpoint of "understanding sociology" (*verstehende Soziologie*), the more so since he describes in an almost mythical, poetic way, how this spirit accomplishes its work. Fundamentally, this spirit of capitalism, connected at its root to the spirit of the modern state, is only the material embodiment of a social, psychological process by means of which that capitalist economic system was brought about.

This process consisted of individual private entrepreneurs, moved by the desire for profits, taking their risks on the market and producing in competition with each other, without a common plan, goods destined to satisfy the demands for them on an extended economic market. These goods were produced in plants organized by the entrepreneur by means of his own capital and employing free but non-propertied wage labor. If he succeeded, the considerable profit he made inspired emulation, until this procedure became general and pushed the older economic systems into the background. An essential factor, then, was the extent of the original success that inspired emulation. This depends primarily on the existence of an urgent social need to be satisfied, but it depends also on a series of objective cultural requirements that cannot be fulfilled without the aid of state power.

The first and most important of these requirements is the guarantee of some measure of safety and legal protection without which capitalist calculations would be impossible. This guarantee covers the development of lines of communication, of roads, railways, shipping lines, post, and telegraph. None of these may be carried out without the aid of the public authorities. The possibilities offered by communications and the guarantee of safety and legal protection are the basis for the establishment and functioning of what we call the market. The expansion and organization of the market is decisive for the rise of capitalism. Just as handicrafts suit the local market, capitalistic enterprise suits the wider market. Without the help of the state, however, the wider market does not emerge. The wider market is an accompanying phenomenon of the progress of nation-building. Here we find a fundamental connection between the modern state and capitalism, which asserts itself at every stage of their development. Sombart does see this, but it seems to me that he does not appreciate it enough, a point to which I shall presently return.

But this is not the only connection between capitalism and the modern state. The social process that gave rise to capitalism has an internal sociological relation to the process that brought about the political system of the new world of states, whether that system consisted of an establishment of new states such as in the territorial states and city-states of Germany and Italy, or whether it consisted of a remodeling of long-established states like in France and England.

This process, of modern nation-building, can also be regarded as an entrepreneurial undertaking, a political enterprise complementing the economic one. It shared with its economic counterpart the fact that it emanated from the individual initiative of single leading figures, operating from different centers, without a common plan, in constant political competition and rivalry with one another. Whereas the leading figures in the economic process—the regular entrepreneurs—were motivated and guided immediately in their activities by the desire for profit and wealth, the political entrepreneurs—the princes or statesmen—were motivated by the desire for dominion and power. But here, too, such a desire could be successful in the long haul only insofar as it succeeded in satisfying certain needs essential to the life of the people as a whole, and therefore in simultaneously serving social goals. Economic entrepreneurship concerned itself with the production or distribution of goods to meet the current pressing social need for certain commodities. Political entrepreneurship concerned itself with the creation and provision of means of power for the guaranteeing of safety and legal protection. At work in both cases was a peculiar heterogony of purposes, such as is generally characteristic of the sociological structure of modern civilization.

While the leading figures in economic and political life had only their own interests in mind—whether the acquisition of money or power—they also furthered general interests. To be specific, they supplied necessary commodities and guaranteed the security and legal protection without which economic life cannot survive. In the long run money can be made only if at the same time a pressing social need is satisfied; and power can be acquired and maintained only if security and legal protection are guaranteed also. The converse is also true: the social need for necessary commodities can be satisfied only by the competing productive activity of many individual private entrepreneurs; and the guarantee of security and legal protection on the scale required by modern civilization can be obtained only if political life is organized around many individual rival centers of power. The opposites of these would be the planned economy and the universal state, both of which are alien to modern life. And yet these opposites must be borne in mind if the peculiar character of modern civilization and the sociological interrelation of politics and capitalism are to be understood.

In both these spheres of social activity we are dealing with a phenomenon that demonstrates that in the structure of social life an interdependence exists between the accomplishments of individual leaders and the social utility of their accomplishments. In the one case we deal with the desire for profit or power as the direct impulse for the individual accomplishments of leaders in economics and in the state. In the other case, we are dealing with the meeting of social needs and the guaranteeing of security and legal protection as the social utilitarian yield of these accomplishments. In this peculiar relation we can perceive the basic sociological feature of Western civilization, which is more a product of the common history of the West than of any inborn racial element of its peoples. It is the individual initiative and the leadership of many single individuals that has transformed Western society from its foundations. The individual activity and responsibility of numerous leading figures taught them how to give rational organization to the operations of the state and the economy, and to strengthen it intensively.

In contrast, in Oriental cultures, as in China with its kinship system, and in India with its caste system and all the magical or sacral restrictions and limitations that go with it, the extensive growth of the people was not accompanied by any corresponding intensification or rationalization of social life, since no individualist, active, reforming leadership succeeded in having any far-reaching effect. The received, traditional economic and social forms held their own much more easily under the mantle of the kinship system and the sacral caste system. In the West, in the area of Mediterranean civilization, the ancient city-state fused the tribes and their sacral law with the corporative law of the citizen community. Subsequently, in the inland regions, during the Middle Ages, the great cultural force of the Christian Church (in particular, the Roman Catholic) brought about a radical change in social structure. In alliance with the great monarchies, the Church demolished the tribal system of all the peoples in the West—or at least relegated it to the status of a refuge of heathenism, of magic and sacral customs and superstitions. Everything magical or sacral was absorbed by the Church, which in rational or ethical forms amalgamated parts of it into its own worship. Thus the secular life of the Western peoples was freed to a large extent of all the magical or sacral restrictions and limitations that stood in the way of the rationalization and intensification of economic and social activity in the East. The Church itself assumed the leading role in the great social transformation that was introduced. At the end of the Middle Ages, after the reforming Councils had failed, the hierarchical organization increasingly fell apart, and finally the unity of the Roman Catholic Church disappeared. But this educational process produced the individual activity that emerged in its place—the drive to intensify, to rationalize, all aspects of life—that was the characteristic feature of the Renaissance and the Reformation.

This is how I regard the spirit that underlies both the modern state and capitalism. It seems to me that Sombart does not quite put his finger on this spirit when he characterizes it as the "Faustian drive to the infinite." Since this "spirit" is connected with his characterization of the modern state, I have particular reasons to contest what he says. For him the modern state, as opposed to the medieval state, is simply the absolutist princely state representing power externally, and police regulation internally, without any intrinsic bond of community among the governed. Its essence, according to Sombart, is the unending drive for power, for boundless expansion: it wants to conquer, it wants to rule. This is naturally an ideal type, which is supposed to emphasize only the essential features, but even as such it is not apt. The ideal type should not become a caricature.

Sombart clings too exclusively to the model of the tyrant states of the Italian Renaissance. Despite the authority of Burckhardt, the true features of the modern state can be studied better in larger states like France and England. These states offer an essentially different picture: among other points of contrast, we find Estates, Parliaments, and local associations. Admittedly Sombart later (in Volume III) extended this characterization, which mainly concerns the period from the sixteenth to the eighteenth century, into the nineteenth. He does this with the thesis that in this latest epoch the state carries an inner contradiction as a result of liberal ideas, which by definition are in opposition to the absolute state. This, however, overlooks the most salient fact of all—namely, the progress toward the formation of national states which went together with liberal ideas, and thus counteracts disintegration by this inner contradiction.

Nor has Sombart anything new to say on the character of international relations in this context; and even here some objection must be raised to his characterization. The characteristic feature of modern international relations is not the states' drive toward unlimited expansion of their power, but is rather their drive to round off their territory in a more favorable way and to consolidate more firmly. There were certain powers—first Spain, then France—that were of course accused of an imperialist policy of striving toward universal monarchy. But what was characteristic was that they did not succeed in this. Political life as a whole had more an intensive, rational bent than a bent toward adventurous expansion. Even warfare from the sixteenth century to the eighteenth had a methodical, cautious character. It is not, as Sombart suggests, that there are no limits to increase in modern armies—they are a carefully honed instrument of war.

Politics and warfare since Napoleon have had a greater range of action, and the energy devoted to them has been markedly increased, since power politics and imperialism are now carried on by nations and no longer by dynasties. But, broadly speaking, this has not altered the essential character of modern political life. It may be true that power in itself incessantly aspires to expansion, that it cannot limit itself by itself but can be limited only by some other power. The very structure of European political life, however, implies the rapid curbing of any nation trying to expand. There arose in Europe, instead of the universal monarchy of ancient times, a system of great powers which, despite all perturbations, always gravitated eventually toward a balance of power. A society of states arose with a latent feeling of joint responsibility that has always reasserted itself eventually, despite all rivalries and conflicts.

This sense of joint responsibility clearly stemmed from the thousand-year-old community of belief and culture of the Christian Church, especially of the Roman Catholic Church in the West. This feeling became the most important foundation of modern international law, which appears to some extent as a secularized remodeling of that community of belief and culture. But since each power was speedily pushed back into its boundaries, each was compelled to direct its strength internally, to develop the state machinery rationally and intensively, and to content itself with rounding off and consolidating its own territory. This is the true character of modern political life. Within it a constant rivalry reigns between individual states, and this has led to repeated wars but not as a rule to the permanent subjection of one people to another nor to the hegemony of one power alone. In consequence the rivalry itself became a permanent and habitual condition, evoking the greatest possible energy from all the peoples of the West. This was the source of the compulsion toward a further heightening of the rationality and intensity of state machinery, and also, generated at the same time, a degree of security and legal protection never before available, and basic to the rise of modern capitalism.

Similar basic conditions characterize the economic life of Western peoples. Even the drive toward profit did not have a free, unlimited hand. It was restricted by custom and law, even after the breakdown of traditional economic morality suitable to the medieval Christian society, as expounded by St. Thomas Aquinas. We find of course a drive toward monopoly, just as in the political sphere we find a drive toward hegemony. Nonetheless, in the long run monopoly could not prevail in the economic life of the West. The permanent condition remained, rather a restless, more or less keen competition that did eliminate incapable competitors but always left sufficient competitors to forestall the danger of monopoly.

This constant competition also exerted a pressure toward progressive rationalization and intensification of operations, a process that Sombart has penetratingly and convincingly shown to embrace virtually the whole internal history of capitalism. This is, in fact, the distinguishing feature of modern capitalism as opposed to what we refer to as the capitalism of Antiquity. Sombart has not entered upon this theme, but Max Weber has demonstrated the peculiar tie between the capitalism of Antiquity and the political life of the ancient world. He shows how capitalism lived off the private exploitation of political power in provincial administration, tax-farming and leasing of public lands, and how the unlimited economic exploitation of slave labor on plantations and in mines corresponded to the merciless political oppression of conquered peoples. Victory in the wars of the Greek city-states and the Roman Republic regularly led to a plundering of men and land, thus giving slave capitalism constant new nourishment while dangerous opponents and competitors were violently disposed of by the destruction of their cities, such as Carthage and Corinth. The process ended with the suppression of this monopoly capitalism at the hands of universalist monarchy—through the bureaucratization of state operations and the imposition of exorbitant state taxes. This contrast with ancient times must be borne in mind in order to understand the peculiar nature of the new political and economic life from which modern capitalism arose.

Sombart distinguished three epochs in the history of modern capitalism. The first is that of *early capitalism,* from the close of the Middle Ages to the second half of the eighteenth century, the epoch we used to call (though not quite suitably) the era of mercantilism; the second is that of *high capitalism,* covering the century and a half from the end of the eighteenth century to the Great War in the twentieth century—and this we used to call simply the era of capitalism; the third is that of *late capitalism,* upon which the world entered after the Great War. This is a division that is obviously taken from art history and could be applied to other areas of historical study. It rests, it seems to me, on the application of the method of ideal types. The epoch of high capitalism is that in which the ideal type of capitalism (what Sombart calls "the spirit of capitalism") was fully realized.

Early capitalism is ascribed to the age when progressive advances toward this end were made, through the transformation of the medieval craft system with its principle of common subsistence. Late capitalism marks the age when developments move away again from the ideal type and toward some new, unknown goal. Understood in this way, this division has some validity. I think it marks a significant advance in scholarship. But it commits itself to the biological analogy of stages of life, and this has connotations that invariably lead to error. Early capitalism is pictured as youth, high capitalism as the stage of maturity and full power, and late capitalism as the stage of approaching old age and decay. The analogy has something very persuasive about it, but it should be rejected, however natural it may seem and however often it is used in other historical contexts. With regard to our own immediate question, what we want to know is how much this division of epochs tells us about the relation between the state and economics. Sombart tried as far as possible to exclude such a relation from his argument. His purpose, in fact, was to release economic history from the bonds of political history, to set it up on its own, and consequently to determine the epochs of capitalism from its own intrinsic development and not from a historical-political point of view. It seems to me, however, that one does not exclude the other, but rather that both further each other reciprocally and are indissolubly connected.

Of course, in describing the various epochs, Sombart gives attention—next to technology—to the state as one of the foundations of capitalism. But in this connection he always conceives the state as being only a closed and isolated system of institutions. He never thinks in terms of a society of states or of a system of states as a whole, with conflicts of interest and wars of rivalry— that is, with what we can call power politics or imperialism. He considers only the static aspects, rather than the dynamic. But this very dynamic of imperialism has played an important role in the development of capitalism.

Sombart has in fact tied the rise of capitalism to the great and general cultural process, which turned the medieval world into the modern one. This process worked itself out against the background of the disintegration of what we can call the hierocratic imperialism of the Middle Ages and of the transition to the imperialism of modern states, the first form of which was dynastic imperialism. Furthermore, Sombart dates the beginning of the epoch of late capitalism from the Great War of 1914. Thus even this last stage is ushered in by political changes of a catastrophic nature, the consequences of which cannot yet be clearly determined. I personally would call it the transition from a nationalist to a federalist age of imperialism. Can we not then say that an epoch-making political change of this kind played a role in the transition from early to high capitalism? This seems to me in fact to have been the case, and, in my opinion, this transition was historically tied to the transition from the era of dynastic imperialism to the era of nationalist imperialism.

The boundary between the two epochs of capitalism is naturally fluid. Sombart places it between the end of the eighteenth century and the middle of the nineteenth, thus giving it a span of almost one hundred years. This was the time when liberal ideas, the exponents of the English, American, and French revolutions, burst into political and economic life. But Sombart regards their influence on capitalism as inconsequential. He therefore emphasizes all the more strongly the technical inventions that ushered in the machine age. In particular he emphasizes the invention of the cloth-printing process, which created an object of mass production for the English cotton industry and thus opened the way for large-scale operations. He also emphasizes the new coke process, which greatly furthered the output of ironworks and thus made possible for the first time the construction of machines on a large scale. Both of these were invented in the second half of the eighteenth century.

Against this, however, it could be asserted that all these advances in technology could not have had their full effect without the great changes that simultaneously took place in the formation of states, legislation, and politics. It is similar to the significance of the invention of gunpowder for the transformation of warfare: the invention could not achieve its historical significance until the creation of disciplined tactical bodies of infantry. Yet all the political and social changes which gave the new technology its historic significance were more or less directly tied up with the revolutions in England, America, and France, so that the convulsions that occurred in the hundred-year epoch of revolutions have their significance for capitalism. This is of course a view that Sombart would hotly contend. One of his most emphatic claims is that revolutions produced nothing to further capitalism, that they have nothing to do with fixing a boundary between the epochs of early and high capitalism.

The extremity of this claim is partly explained by his battle against what he calls Marx's legend of revolution—against the theory that the origin of all revolutions is to be found in class struggle. This theory is in fact one-sided and to that extent must be rejected. But we should not ignore the fact that during revolutions great and epoch-making upheavals in the social order have been consummated that are not at all insignificant for economic life. In England, revolution resulted in veritable class rule by wealthy rural and urban landowners—the gentry; in France, in the transformation of the feudal social order into that of the legal equality of citizens, which first created the real arena for the class conflict of modern times; in America, in an individualistic social system based on legal equality but also based on property which did not, at the outset, exclude slavery.

The most obvious effect of the revolutionary era was the introduction of freedom of trade, combined with freedom of movement and settlement. In England this did not happen in one stroke as a result of the revolution, but insinuated itself steadily and irresistibly in the course of the eighteenth century as a result of the changes in social and political life brought about by the revolution. In France it came about with the Revolution itself, and on the Continent as a whole it was related at least loosely to the model of the Revolution in France. Free trade has been regarded, traditionally, as the borderline of the restricted, supervised mercantilist system. Even Sombart cannot help but recognize its significance. He regards it as important of course, only insofar as it cleared away obstacles standing in the way of the entrepreneurial spirit of capitalism. But there are other connections between economics and politics in the age of revolution.

When we consider these revolutions, we must think not merely of internal processes in the states in question. The revolutions concerning us here were tied to movements and changes in international affairs, changes of the greatest significance for economic life and capitalism. The English Revolution of 1689, which brought Louis XIV's chief opponent, William III of Orange, to the throne of England, marked also the beginning of the great hundred-year struggle with France, during which "the expansion of England"—the foundation of England's naval and colonial predominance in the eighteenth century—was carried out. The American Revolution of 1776 entailed war for independence from England. It arose not simply from the colonists' feelings that their rights had been violated, but also from indignation at England's colonial policy, which did not countenance the development of any native American industry or merchant marine. It was a struggle not only for political freedom but for the future of American capitalism as well.

But connected to the French Revolution was the great epoch of war to which Napoleon lent his name and which transformed forever the whole political system of contemporary Europe, orienting it toward the formation of national states. At the same time the war with England resulted in a powerful extension of the British Empire. The importance of this fact for the development of world trade is self-evident. Without it the advance toward high capitalism would have been scarcely feasible.

The revolutions in England, America, and France were also of decisive importance for the development and consolidation of great national markets, an important precondition for the transition to the large-scale enterprises of high capitalism. In England, it is true, the usual teaching is that the national economy and industry have been developing since Richard II's time. But what is meant in this context by "national"? It is the area of England proper during the Middle Ages, excluding even Wales until Henry VIII's reign, not to mention Scotland and Ireland, which counted as foreign countries, politically and economically and ecclesiastically until the Puritan Revolution. Only during this revolution did Cromwell combine them into the Commonwealth of England, Sotland, and Ireland. After the restoration of 1660 this union—which even the Stuarts themselves had striven to create—fell apart once more. The three countries formed regional markets of their own, and the Navigation Acts of England were applied to Scotland and Ireland with the same rigor as to Holland and France. Only with the Revolution of 1689, under the aegis of Parliament, which had now taken control of government, was a lasting union with Scotland set up. The capitalist classes on both sides came to an understanding, and Scotland henceforth shared the beneficial effects of the Navigation Acts. Thus Great Britain for the first time became a united market; and in 1801, during the war with France, Ireland too was drawn into this union for political and economic reasons. Now the whole English-speaking island realm formed a unity in commercial and economic affairs, a great protected market for home industry. The Crown had striven in vain for such a union. It belonged first to the revolution, and the rule of Parliament that came with it, to make this union possible and overcome resistance to it.

For a long time this enlarged market remained protected, as elsewhere, by high import duties. The mercantilist controls of industrial policy had been dismantled much earlier than the mercantilist tariff protection that entirely served the interests of the capitalist classes. Even colonial policy served these interests, which were strongly influential in Parliament, for a long time. Had it not been for the brute force with which competition from the highly developed East Indian textile industry was suppressed, it would scarcely have been possible for the English cotton industry to conquer the world market.

In France the large national market was rather obviously and directly a product of the Revolution. Here too, despite Colbert's reforms, the *Ancien régime* could never get beyond a conglomeration of territorial markets. Only the *cinq grosses fermes* had had a unified customs system, and even here industry could not get along for long without protective tariffs.

In America it was the second revolution of 1787 and the new Constitution that created a unified American market for the first time. The general persuasion of American constitutional historians today is that the new idea of an American nation, over and above the sovereignty of the thirteen individual states, was an event of revolutionary proportions. The men of Annapolis and Philadelphia who carried out this second revolution, however, were guided also by political and economic—particularly capitalist—motives. They were concerned not only to make the state secure; they also wished to secure property and its free use. They wanted not only political union—out of considerations of political necessity—but also free commerce in the entire area in place of the constant trade war that then prevailed among the individual states, inhibited intercourse particularly on the rivers, and hindered the advance of a capitalist economy. Among them were typical representatives of the capitalist spirit—above all Franklin, but also Madison and even Washington, who was one of the greatest landowners of the Union and who had a personal interest in free shipping along the Potomac and the tributaries of the Ohio, since he had invested a good part of his fortune in the Northwest Territory.

The new Constitution left it to the single states to regulate trade within their borders, but interstate trade was put under the jurisdiction of the Congress of the Union. It is very interesting to see how politics and technology combined to help the principle of unity to victory. The technology of transportation is no less important for capitalism than is industrial machinery. Even in the days of the Philadelphia Convention, on August 22, 1787, the watchmaker and mechanic John Fitch demonstrated his newly invented steamship on the Delaware to the members of the Convention; and Madison, greatly impressed by the invention, expressed to the assembly his hope that the principle of unity in commercial affairs and communications would eventually prevail completely. In all subsequent litigation on the issue, the Supreme Court consistently decided in favor of the principle of unity. Thus, in this second revolution, the basis was created for the vast American home market, which made possible an enormous advance of capitalism.

Even in Germany, where there was no great revolution, the advance of capitalism in the nineteenth century was nevertheless tied to the general revolutionary era. The Customs Union (*Zollverein*), which fulfilled the most vital precondition for this upsurge, would have been impossible without the tendency toward

national unification unleashed by the French Revolution and
without the shake-up of the Napoleonic era of wars, together
with the subsequent territorial reconstruction of the German
states—particularly Prussia—and the establishment of German
Federation.

In sum: the rise of the great national markets and their weav-
ing into a world market were brought about not only by economic developments but also by political actions intimately tied
to the great revolutions in England, America, and France. This
is a fundamental fact for any assessment of the historical connection between state and economy, between politics and
capitalism.

I should like, however, to show in still greater detail how profoundly the development of capitalism was influenced by the
revolutions in England and France. I say "influenced," not "promoted," for the framing of the question indicated by Sombart's
choice of words—i.e., whether the revolutions promoted capitalism—is too restricted. We are dealing with a complicated set
of relations, in which expediting and inhibiting influences were
bound together.

Of England we can speak rather directly of a furthering of
capitalism by the Revolution. I should like to give a few indications of the basis of this claim, since Sombart expressly maintains the opposite. We are dealing primarily with commercial
and agrarian capitalism, and to a lesser extent also with industrial capitalism. In England the revolutions took place in the
midst of the mercantilist epoch, but pre-revolutionary mercantilism had a wholly different appearance from that of post-
revolutionary mercantilism. The mercantilism of the Tudors and
the Stuarts was fiscal and monopolistic, and encumbered with
certain authoritarian Christian-social traits as represented especially by Archbishop Laud. In contrast, the mercantilism of Par-
liment after 1689 was that desired by the classes whose interests
were capitalistic. The main principle before the Revolution had
been the hoarding of precious metals for political purposes—

hence the prohibition of silver export. Of course, before the Revolution this prohibition had been waived in favor of the East India Company, the hope being that the goods bought abroad with the exported silver could be sold in foreign countries at a much higher price. But this was an exception to the rule, which remained in force. This changed only after the Revolution of 1689, as a result of the capitalist classes' confidence in the new state leadership, which had fallen to Parliament since the revolutionary convulsion. With the establishment in 1694 of the Bank of England, resting on this confidence, and with it the new system of National Credit, which placed the country's wealth at all times at the disposal of the government, there was a final breach with the principle of hoarding, and for the first time the principle of balance of trade became the measure of national prosperity.

A vast rise in overseas trade dates from this time. The great Whig families, who were the chief representatives of the financial interests among the aristocracy, now took part in overseas enterprises. It was under the parliamentary government of Walpole and Pitt that the great colonial expansion of England took place, whose background was formed by the war with France that had raged since 1689. The effect on rural conditions was still more striking. Immediately after the Revolution of 1689, the Corn Bounty Act was passed. This gave a premium for export of grain, in the interests of the landowners; it also made for stability of prices, and remained in force so long as England exported grain on any scale—that is, until the 1770s. The price of grain rose and remained tolerably stable. This stimulated an interest in increased cultivation of grain and set the process of "enclosure" once more into motion: common lands were split up and plots of land put together.

Enclosure proceeded apace after 1707, particularly in the latter half of the eighteenth century, from 1760 onward, when the Tories were in power. They represented the landed interest more than did the Whigs, who represented the financial interest. Local agreements were made, and also numerous private Members' Bills were passed in Parliament, providing for enclosure of common lands and joining of plots, wholly in accordance with the interests of the large landowners and at the expense of the small farmers who received no adequate substitute for the disappearance of grazing rights that had always been the basis of their economic existence. The yeomen farmers could not hold out against the great landowners, who were moving toward intensive and rational operations. They were bought out, and went to the colonies, particularly to Canada, or into industry. *Latifundia* grew up, rationally farmed in large leaseholds. Thus agrarian capitalism developed in England as a consequence of the capitalistic class's acquisition of political power.

There was no question any longer of protecting the peasants, as had still been done under the Tudors when, as a result of the highly tempting wool prices, enclosures of land for sheep-raising threatened to take the upper hand. This difference in development was an obvious effect of the Revolution. It extended its influence to industrial capitalism, for there now began in England the flight from the land by the non-propertied "little men," and the movement to the towns and the industrial areas. The justices of the peace ceased to determine wages periodically, as they were charged to do. Originally these wage schedules had been intended to set a maximum wage. Now it would have been timely to transform the system to fix a minimum wage, given the ready supply of labor and the high price of staples. But this did not happen, because the justices of the peace belonged to the landowning class and had an interest in keeping wages low. When, during the war with France, corn prices rose higher and higher and wages sank lower and lower, recourse was had, from 1795 onward, to paying poor relief to the rural laborers. This system remained in practice for decades. But industry could work with fairer wages, being free of the previous limitations on freedom of movement and change of occupation. The cotton industry could exploit the new machines, and beat Indian competition from the field. It was at this time that the cotton industry conquered the world market.

The effect of the Revolution on France was quite different. Economic conditions during the Revolution have long remained obscure. Only since 1908 has there been a special large-scale publication of documents to shed light on the matter.[3] It is still incomplete; the most important for our purposes of what is available is Volume III, by Georges Bourgin, on the Law of 1793, concerning the partition of common lands. The volume contains only the preparation of this law, not the manner in which it was put into effect. But what is otherwise known about this shows quite clearly that the Revolution in France stifled at its outset the agrarian capitalism that had begun to emerge in France, just as in England. Despite the idea of the *grande culture* championed by the physiocrats and realized in England, in France the small peasantry was purposely protected and preserved. Henri Sée[4] has shown that the peasantry was still as numerous as it was because the feudal system, which was maintained until the Revolution, had preserved the peasantry despite all oppressions. And the Revolution, as we have said, protected the peasants from absorption by agrarian capitalism. This is the great difference in social structure between England and France—and also between France and Germany, particularly Prussia, even if to a lesser extent, for a great part of the small farming class was sacrificed in Prussia with the rural regulations made after 1816.

There was no counterpart in France to the flight from the land that took place in England, no flood of cheap labor into industry. The peasant remained squatting on his turf, and industry developed only slowly. The new laws of the Revolution on freedom of movement and trade, and the larger national market naturally worked in favor of industry; but they were not followed by the same rapid development as in England. The balance between agriculture and industry was not disturbed in France, and this is still, even today, a vital element of political strength for France. The old legend that the Revolution created the numerous peasant class in France has in fact some truth in it: it did not create that class, but it did preserve it and free it from feudal burdens. The Revolution thwarted agrarian capitalism at the outset. This had an important influence on capitalism as a whole, though it inhibited capitalism more than it advanced it.

Even the peculiar inclination to develop a politically oriented and speculative finance-capitalism in France intensified as a consequence of the Revolution. The *assignat* economy ruined the currency and produced general confusion in monetary affairs. The Napoleonic Wars, and the contributions these entailed, cured this malady. Financial affairs, which were linked to the contribution and to military supply, gave capitalism a peculiar orientation during the long war years. The Bank and the Bourse stepped into the limelight. Speculation operated over a wide field. This idiosyncrasy became permanent in French capitalism, and it found characteristic expression in the preparations dictated at Versailles. It also pervades the entire colonial system of France. Here capitalism is much more closely related to power politics, much more politically oriented than in England, Germany, or America. This too, is an effect of the Revolution.

The outcome of these considerations is that in all three epochs of capitalism there is a very close relation between the state and the economy, but a relation that has its own special shape in each of the epochs. The first epoch, that of early capitalism, is in the main identical with what used to be called the age of mercantilism. One only has to say the term in order to indicate the special contours of the connections between the state and the economy, of politics and capitalism in this epoch: we are not dealing with the creation of a capitalistic form of economy by the state, but with laying a foundation upon which it could develop, and with its explicit encouragement and exploitation by the state.

The development of capitalism was furthered in the interests of the state as an indispensable means to political power. The army and the hoarding of precious metals were central to this. Sombart has presented this aspect of the story impressively. But this is not merely a matter of furthering the growth of capitalism by calculated political measures, but also of fulfilling a condition without which capitalism could never have developed: the creation of a larger market, first of all in the territorial states. The geographic size of the market is not without significance for the internal substance of capitalism. The widening of local markets to cover an entire territorial state, like old England, signals a transition from the handcraft operations to capitalist enterprise. The really large operations, however, could develop only at a higher stage of a comprehensive national market, such as Great Britain and Ireland together. Hence the transitional character of this epoch, expressed in the regulation of competition and the protection of capitalist enterprises. It is the age of the protective tariff and the regulation of trade. The influence of capitalist entrepreneurs on the state is very small at this time, the influence of government on them all the greater. The relation between the state and the economy in this epoch may be called the political protection of capital. The nursing of capital and of capitalist interests is a central concern.

In the second epoch the relation was almost reversed. The new reinforced capitalism, now equipped with a large national market and aspiring to large-scale operations, swept away the obstacles imposed by the state. It did not in any way relinquish protective tariffs, and free trade among nations remained merely an episode from 1860 to 1876, emanating from England alone and based on a special set of circumstances. But capitalism liberated itself from the many forms of state intervention and gained with commercial freedom greater independence. It began to exert an increasing influence on legislation, administration, and politics. The relation between the state and capitalism at this time is best illustrated in terms of the close link with the national principle, which assumed a clear-cut economic meaning. The national state became a community of economic interests. This is the real epoch of "national economy." In the same way as absolutism had been the prevailing form of political life in the previous epoch, so now parliamentarism prevailed, and Parliamentarism was the tool of capitalism for the political advancement of its interests. Insofar as these interests involved the expansion of the state's sphere of power, we call it "imperialism."

Imperialism is on the one hand the extension of the old "poli-

tics of colonialism," which already played an important role in
the epoch of early capitalism, concurrent with the development
of the home market. On the other hand, imperialism is also an
extension of the old power politics of the Great Powers, only now
widened to world politics to correspond to the interlacing of national markets into a world market embracing the whole of the
globe. The model for this was the development of the British
colonial possessions into a world empire bound together by naval
supremacy (which in no way, naturally, has the meaning "universal empire"). It is unquestionably true that capitalist interests
have had great influence on the development of such colonial
empires. Sombart did not devote any special interest to this question. He contented himself with establishing that imperialism is
not simply a function of capitalism, as the Marxists maintain. I
am also of this opinion. But still I should like to emphasize that
capitalism has influenced imperialism in two ways: first, through
the interests of industrial capitalism, which wanted secure and
reserved areas from which it could take its raw materials and
to which it could sell manufactured products; secondly, and still
more importantly, through finance capitalism, which undertook
large investments in exotic lands for the establishment of factories, plantations, mines, places of trade and harbors with regular traffic, and for the building of railways, and telegraph and other
electrical installations. For this, however, it was necessary to
have a certain measure of security and legal protection, which,
as a rule, was beyond the means of the governments in exotic
lands. While recognizing this influence of capitalist interests,
however, it must always be remembered that imperialism did not
owe its existence only to these influences; that, like the colonial
politics from which it stemmed, it had an essentially political
origin. This becomes quite clear if we consider the imperialism
of countries like Russia and France, a type not primarily evoked
by economic interests. But even British imperialism predates the
capitalistic expansion, and the same is true of American imperialism, whose precursor was the Monroe Doctrine.

The concept of imperialism as it is currently fashionably used and as Sombart also uses it requires critical examination and essential alteration if it is to be really useful. It is customarily understood to mean, as Sombart defines it, the extension of a state's sphere of power beyond the borders of the mother country. But that is the definition of a colonial empire, not of imperialism. If this definition fitted, then the Netherlands, Belgium, and Portugal would be classic examples of imperialism. In these countries, after all, the sphere of power extends far beyond the borders of the mother country. We need only cite such cases to see what they lack relative to what we understand by imperialism. It is the position and the policy of a great Power in the modern mold—that is to say, of a world power. The usual view— also adopted by Sombart—adheres too closely to the static tangible image of a colonial empire; one might even say that it sticks too closely to the image of the map. This must be replaced by a dynamic, functional image—namely, that of Great Power politics of modern cut, of world-power politics. Imperialism is nothing other than the extension of the old Great Power politics as it obtained for many years in the European system of states, and is now brought into play in the larger dimension of the modern global system of states. An overseas colonial empire is not absolutely necessary, as the examples of Russia and America prove.

Formulated in this way the concept of imperialism gains for the first time its proper world-historical perspective. The name itself points to this. It is connected with the old Roman *Imperium*, the fourth and last of the great world monarchies of ancient times. It is endemic in the structure of modern political life that there should be no universal state embracing the entire civilized world, but rather several competing and rival world empires. What we call imperialism today is therefore only the latest and up till now the highest stage of modern international power politics, intimately connected to modern capitalism but not simply a function of it. The story of this term is the same as that of "capitalism." "Capitalism" was used for the latest phase of capitalistic development after Marx had made the brilliant discovery of a capitalistic economic system, at the very moment when that system was really beginning to bloom. What was simply called "capitalism" then, Sombart calls "high capitalism." Just as he constructed an "early capitalism" to complement his "high capitalism," so we must likewise add an earlier complement to the full-fledged imperialism of the present day. This complement is the so-called "politics of the Great Powers," which we have every right to call "early imperialism."

This early imperialism was produced by the great dynasties of Europe, who founded the system of the balance of power. Even as early as Henry VIII's reign there was talk in England of scales in which the rival weights of the houses of France and the Habsburgs teetered; England was supposed to be the pointer in the scales. Later, it was France and England that fought for pre-eminence, and the system of Great Powers was broadened with the accession of Prussia and Russia into a pentarchy. This was the age of dynastic imperialism, which was closely tied to early capitalism. It was followed by an age of nationalist imperialism, where the nations, both long established and newly founded (like Germany and Italy), became the bearers of imperialist aspirations. This age began with the great colonial expansion of England in the eighteenth century and came to full blossom with Napoleon. It dominated Europe through the nineteenth century and is intimately connected with the epoch of high capitalism. The entry of extra-European nations like America and Japan broadened the old European theater to the modern setting of global politics, and since then it has been customary to speak of imperialism. But this is merely the last and highest phase of a long development. The rivalry of the world powers, and not simply their capitalist competition, led to the crisis of the Great War, which by virtue of the close relations between economics and politics, ushered in a new phase of imperialism and capitalism. We could call this late imperialism, corresponding to Sombart's late capitalism. I prefer to call it the era of federal imperialism.

Just as, earlier, it was the dynasties and the nations, so nowadays it is great federal formations embracing several nations, like the British Empire, a "Pan-America" that is at least emerging, and Soviet Russia which are the bearers of imperialism. Particularly in the British Empire we can see the federal character of the great political formations of today. English imperialists were still striving at the beginning of the twentieth century for a firmer economic and political consolidation of the Empire into a unified federal state. But developments have taken a different course since the war and are leading toward a federalist structure that is more like a federation of states than a federalist state. It would be very wrong to interpret this as a sign of dissolution; it is more a sign of the general direction taken by world powers in the present age.

Pan-American aspirations and the federation of the Russian Soviet republics tend in the same direction. Even the European problem must be viewed in this light. For the moment the so-called League of Nations serves the victorious European powers —at least England and France—as a means of keeping the defeated powers and the neutrals in check. Thus it is really an instrument of federal imperialism. But inside this wider framework the system of so-called regional treaties clearly shows the desire of France and Italy to create a federative bloc of states under their own leadership. Even the present confusion in China will have to be regarded as the birth pangs of such a federalist great state that has not yet reached this goal for the very reason that the capitalist great powers have had an interest in interfering with this process, for it could leave them with a fearsome new competitor.

In this most recent epoch, relations between the state and capitalism show a noticeable shift in balance back to the influence of the political factor. The years of the arms race before the Great War strengthened the influence of the state. The growing proletarian movement and the dangers of class war, which generated everywhere new social legislation, have worked in the same direction. Among the things named by Sombart as indicating a transformation of the capitalist spirit, those derived from considerations of social policy take up a great deal of space. They have not arisen from the capitalist spirit itself but depend in good measure on the influence of state power. Moreover, the subordination of the economy to the requirements of government during the Great War, the vast annihilation of capital, and the subsequent weakening of buying power in most markets have greatly restricted the earlier activity and the independence of capitalism. A social-political cast marks the relation between the economy and the state still more than before the war. The beginnings of international cartels follow the federalist character of the states. All in all, the war years and the decade that has elapsed since then offer no evidence of an autonomous economic development of capitalism, wholly detached from the state and politics. They show rather that the affairs of the state and of capitalism are inextricably interrelated, that they are only two sides, or aspects, of one and the same historical development.

GLOSSARY

Akzise (excise)   A tax on foodstuffs and other goods to which the inhabitants of towns were subjected and which was originally raised at the town gates.

Allgemeines Landrecht   The Prussian law code which Frederick the Great had ordered to be compiled and which became the basic law in the Prussian states in 1794. The law was to be simplified, freed of legal subtleties, and comprehensible for the layman; it was to provide a synthesis of the old German, Roman, and natural law. By providing a single code of law for the scattered provinces of Brandenburg, Prussia, it was a significant step toward the creation of a unified state.

Bund der Landwirte (Landowners' League)   An association founded in 1894 for the protection of agriculture against tendencies toward free trade; it was dominated by the owners of the large estates east of the Elbe and exerted a strong reactionary influence on German politics.

Elector   English word for the German *Kurfürst*, used by Hintze when he means the Elector of Brandenburg; there were six other Electors (*Kurfürsten*) in Germany.

Electoral Prince   Translation of *Kurprinz*, i.e., heir presumptive to the Elector.

Generaldirektorium (General Directory)   Abbreviated name for the *General-Ober-Finanz-Kriegs- und Domänen Direktorium*, the central authority for the *Kriegs- und Domänen-Kammern* in the provinces (see *Kammer*). The General Directory developed into the highest bureaucratic authority in Prussia.

Grundherrschaft   The system of agriculture that was characteristic of the southern and western portions of Germany. Its chief feature was that the landlord did not himself farm the estate but lived off the payments of cash and kind that he received from his peasant tenants. Because they were less under the economic control of their lord, peasants under this system of production enjoyed a greater degree of freedom than those under the system of *Gutsherrschaft*.

Gutsherrschaft   The system of agriculture that came to be characteristic of the region of Germany east of the Elbe. Its chief feature was that the landlord himself farmed the estate, living off the revenues gained by selling its produce in distant markets, and using the services of the serfs, who were therefore bound to the soil. The estate formed a legal administrative unit (*Gutsbezirk*), and the landlord held police and judiciary powers over the peasants. As a result, the peasants were forced deeper into serfdom.

Herrenhuter   A group of the Moravian sect, so called because *Herrenhut* was the name of the settlement on the estates of Count Zinzendorf, where they had found protection from persecution.

Hufe   Originally designated a peasant's farm, and later a fixed amount of land, so that the term served as a land measurement.

Indigenatsrecht   Statute limiting officeholding to those born in the country with which the work of the office is concerned. In the case of Brandenburg this meant that offices bearing on the affairs of the Old Mark, a part of Brandenburg west of the Elbe, with its own estates and estate administration, were limited to men from the Old Mark, and this meant, in practice, the nobility of this area.

Junkerparlament   Name given by Liberals to the meeting of the landowners held in September 1848 in Berlin to protest the abolition of the tax-exempt status of knights' estates.

Kammer has a number of different meanings, so that it has to be translated in various ways. Sometimes the word "chamber" will be appropriate, though the most frequent occurrence in the context of Prussian history is *Kriegs- und Domänen-Kammer* (sometimes referred to merely as *Kammern*), a collegiate administrative board which administered in the various provinces the princely domains and collected the tax levied on the rural population for military purposes, the so-called *Kontribution*. Briefly, the Kriegs- und Domänen-Kammer (probably best called "Boards of War and Domains") had chiefly financial tasks, but they exercised also some judicial functions (*Kammerjustiz*). The officials on the Boards of War and Domains were *Kammerräte*, which might be translated as "Chamber councilors." *Kammergericht* (Chamber Court) has nothing to do with the judicial authorities of the Board of War and Domains, but was the highest court of appeals in Brandenburg.

Kantonist   A conscript soldier whose service with his regiment was limited to two months a year, so that he could carry out his regular work during the remaining months. In practice only younger sons of peasants (not the eldest son) and journeymen were subjected to this regulation. For purposes of carrying out this law, the country was divided in *Kantone;* its administration was in the hands of the most prominent landowner of the single *Kanton*. Since he was frequently an officer, his regiment was composed of peasant sons working on his estate or living around it.

Konkordienformel (Formula of Concord, 1577)   A religious statement accepted, among others, by Brandenburg, Saxony, and the Palatinate, which tried to bridge differences between Lutheranism and Calvinism.

Kontribution   A tax levied on peasants for the purpose of maintaining the army.

Landrat   The official at the head of the administration of a county. The Prussian *Landrat* was originally the representative of the Estates, but became the chief executive of the central government on the local level.

Landwehr   A Prussian military institution divided into two groups. The first comprised those up to 32 years of age who had completed their active

military service and had returned to civilian life but were still obligated—
from time to time—to brief military exercises; in case of war, this group
would be integrated in the *Linie*. The second group comprised those between 32 and 39 years of age who had done their military service; in case
of war they were employed for purposes of occupation or in territorial
defense.

Leibeigene Bauern, erbuntertänige Bauern   Refer to serfs bound to the soil.
Although there was no qualitative difference between the two categories
of servitude, *Leibeigenschaft* was considered a humiliating and inferior
status, and Frederick the Great endeavored to abolish it. *Erbuntertänigkeit*
(hereditary bondage), however, remained until the Emancipation Edict of
October 1807.

Linie   The regular, active, army of peacetime which comprised professional
soldiers and conscripts preforming their military service.

Magdeburger Stift   The Archbishop of Magdeburg (by then a Protestant
Prince or administrator); in contrast to the town of Magdeburg (which
had its own government), ruled over extended territories around Magdeburg in which some families of the landed nobility enjoyed particular privileges which made them almost independent.

Mark   Actually means the Mark Brandenburg, i.e., the Electorate of Brandenburg. It comprised different territories with their own administration and
their own Estates, particularly the Old Mark (Altmark) west of the Elbe,
and the New Mark (Neumark) east of the Oder.

Oberhauptmann   Officer; the rank of general did not yet exist, and the prefix *ober-* or *oberst-* indicates an officer of the rank of general.

Oberkriegs Kollegium   Created only at the end of the eighteenth century as
the central authority for military affairs. "Supreme Military Council" seems
appropriate, so long as it is understood that this agency was concerned
with administration, not military strategy.

Oberstburggraf   Officer at the head of the many fortified castles which the
order of the Teutonic Knights had built in Prussia; consequently the
Oberstburggraf was in reality the commander of the military forces in
Prussia.

Osiander Affair   Andreas Osiander was a Lutheran theologian whose views
on the doctrine of the justification through faith involved him in bitter
fights with other Lutherans and with the Calvinists.

Palatine Elector   Kurfürst of the Pfalz, residing in Heidelburg; Count Palatine
was the ruler of Pfalz-Neuburg.

Quadriga   Frederick II the Great stated in his Political Testament that a ruler
must direct military affairs, administration, foreign policy, and finances in
the same unified manner in which the driver of a *quadriga* guides his
four horses.

Reformed   As used by Hintze, synonymous with Calvinist.

Regierungen (governments)   Governmental organizations which the Estates had established for the administration of a territorial unit. With the rise of absolutism they became gradually superseded by the Central Government.

Retablissement   Resettlement of peasants for better use of the land.

Rezesse   Written agreements between Prince and Estates, which established the results of a meeting of the Estates.

Union   League of Protestant princes and seventeen Imperial towns concluded in 1608 in order to strengthen the Protestant position in the German Empire.

NOTES

The Hohenzollern and the Nobility
(pages 33–63)

1. F. Priebatsch, "Die Hohenzollern und der Adel der Mark," in *Historische Zeitschrift*, vol. 88 (1902).
2. Thus Walter Schotte, *Fürstentum und Stände der Mark Brandenburg unter der Regierung Joachims I* (Leipzig, 1911), in *Veröffentlichungen des Vereins für die Geschichte der Mark Brandenburg*, argues against Kurt Treusch von Buttlar, *Der Kampf Joachims I von Brandenburg gegen den Adel seines Landes* (Dresden, 1889).
3. *Kurmärkische Ständeakten aus der Regierungszeit Kurfürst Joachims II*, ed. Walter Friedensburg, in *Veröffentlichungen des Vereins . . .* (Munich and Leipzig, 1913), 1:192 et seq. Cf. G. Winter in *Zeitschrift für preussische Geschichte und Landeskunde*, vol. 20.
4. Martin Hass, *Die landständische Verfassung und Verwaltung in der Kurmark Brandenburg während der Regierung des Kurfürsten Johann Georg (1571–1598)*, Berlin diss., and, by the same author, *Die Kurmärkischen Stände im letzten Drittel des 16 Jahrhunderts*, in *Veröffentlichungen des Vereins . . .* (Munich and Leipzig, 1913).
5. J. Paczkowski, "Der Grosse Kurfürst und Christian Ludwig von Kalckstein," in *Forschungen zur brandenburgischen und preussischen Geschichte*, vols. 2 and 3 (1889/90).
6. *Urkunden und Aktenstücke zur Geschichte des Kurfürsten Friedrich Wilhelm von Brandenburg*, 16:1058. In general the series of Estates proceedings, vols. 5, 10, 15, and 16, are relevant in the present context. See also Hugo Rachel, "Der Grosse Kurfürst und die ostpreussischen Stände 1640–1688," in Schmoller's *Staats- u. sozialwissenschaftliche Forschungen*, No. 3.
7. *Kurmärkischer Landtagsrezess vom 26. Juli 1653*, in Mylius, *Corpus constitutionum marchicarum* 6.1:427f.
8. The historical sections of Friedrich Casper Schimmelpfenning's earlier work, *Die preussischen direkten Steuern* (4th ed.; Berlin, 1859) have been superseded, particularly as regards the East Prussian *Generalhufenschoss*, by C. A. Zakrczewski, "Die wichtigeren preussischen Reformen der direkten ländlichen Steuern im 18. Jahrhundert," in Schmoller's *Forschungen*, vol. 2 (1887). Also of importance are the lectures on taxes and finance given by J. R. Roden (president of the *Oberrechenkammer*) at the command of Frederick the Great to the Prince of Prussia in 1774–75; these are reprinted in Joachim David Preuss, *Friedrich der Grosse* (Berlin, 1834), vol. 4, App. 2.

9. *Acta Borussica. Behördenorganisation und allgemeine Staatsverwaltung*, 3:441ff.

10. V. Loewe, "Die Allodifikation der Lehen unter Friedrich Wilhelm I," in *Forschungen zur brandenburgischen und preussischen Geschichte*, vol. 2 (1898).

11. Gustav Schmoller, "Die Entstehung des preussischen Heeres 1640–1740," in *Umrisse und Untersuchungen zur Verfassungs- Verwaltungs- und Wirtschaftsgeschichte* (1898), p. 282.

12. *Acta Borussica. Behördenorganisation*, 9:327ff.

13. Marginalia of the King on the Instructions for the General Directory in *Acta Borussica. Behördenorganisation*, 7:563.

14. On Frederick the Great's economic policy, see a lecture of mine, reprinted in the supplements to the *Militärwochenblatt* (1911), No. 12.

15. Among others I should like to cite in this respect Elizabeth Schwenke, *Friedrich der Grosse und der Adel*, Berlin diss., 1911.

16. On Marwitz, cf. the latest edition of his memoirs, by Dr. Fritz Meusel (1908–13). Here Marwitz, leader of the knights and the Estates of the Mark, appears wholly different than in the earlier picture gathered from the publication of his papers in 1852, which was made to bear out the opinions of the Conservative party.

17. Erich Jordan, *Friedrich Wilhelm IV. und der preussische Adel bei Umwandlung der ersten Kammer in das Herrenhaus 1850–1854* (Berlin, 1909).

18. Gerhard Ritter, *Die preussischen Konservativen und Bismarcks Politik 1858–1876*, in *Heidelberger Abhandlungen*, No. 43 (1913).

Prussian Reform Movements Before 1806
(pages 64–87)

1. Namely, the documents of the lately reorganized *Kabinetsregistratur* of Frederick William III (1797–1806), in the Geheime Staatsarchiv, to which *Archivist* Dr. Meinecke has been kind enough to call my attention.

2. Adolph Friedrich Riedel, *Brandenburgisch-preussischer Staatshaushalt*, (Berlin, 1866), pp. 200f., mentions this commission but does not go into what it did. I reserve for another place further information regarding the composition, agenda, and functioning of the Financial Commission; here I mention only the names of its members: the ministers Hoym, Heinitz, Schulenburg, and Struensee; the Privy Councilors Beyer (the senior), Ernsthausen, Grothe, Gerhardt, Borgstede, Schultz, Weiher, Labaye. Schulenburg took scarcely any part in the workings of the Commission: Ernsthausen was relieved of his post on October 13, 1798; and Schultz was replaced on September 25, 1798, by Privy Financial Councilor von Knobloch. Thus the older, more conservative elements of the bureaucracy prevailed in the Commission. The minutes were kept by Friedrich Gentz, then military councilor (*Kriegsrat*).

3. Max Lehmann, *Scharnhorst* (Leipzig, 1887), 2:8.

4. Paul Bailleu, *Preussen und Frankreich von 1795–1807* (Leipzig, 1881), 1:505: Otto to Talleyrand, August 13, 1799.

5. Adolf Stoelzel, *Suarez* (Berlin, 1888), p. 304.

6. The great Instruction for the Financial Commission of February 19, 1798, exists only in the final form and in various copies. The accompanying Cabinet Order to Hoym of the same date was, however, drafted by Mencken. It is of course well known that Mencken was considered to be a *Jacobin*. The establishment of the Commission was the King's own idea, as is evident from the characteristic letter to Köckritz of November 16, 1797 (in Friedrich Eylert, *Charakterzüge und historische Fragmente aus dem Leben des Königs von Preussen, Friedrich Wilhelm III* [Magdeburg, 1843], 1: 107ff.). Ruechel, Köckritz, or Mencken was intended to deputize to some extent for the King in the deliberations of the Commission. The place of Mencken was taken by Beyme in December 1799.

7. For reasons of illness: from 1800 onward he was highly consumptive, and retired to his country estate.

8. In February 1798, just when the Financial Commission was constituted.

9. This, and much else, emerges from a (still unpublished) Memorandum of July 23, 1798, which was the basis of the Cabinet Order of July 25.

10. Only in the hotly contested question of treasury bills did he oppose Stein.

11. Georg Friedrich Knapp, *Bauernberfeiung und der Ursprung der Landarbeiter in den älteren Teilen Preussens* (Leipzig, 1887), 1:96ff. In its very scope this reforming measure was highly important: on Knapp's calculations it turned 50,000 peasants of the Old Provinces (excluding Silesia) into free property owners, whereas in the later Regulation only 45,000 were involved.

12. The effective originator of this plan was Beyme, in a memorandum for the King on July 23, 1798. The basic idea was the same as in the Edict of Emancipation of October 19, 1807: suspension of hereditary serfdom without regard to service, improvement of possession rights. Against these principles of abstract natural law the senior men involved (for example, Schroetter) took the view that economic regulation must precede proclamation of personal freedom.

13. Rudolph Stadelmann, *Preussens Könige in ihrer Tätigkeit für die Landeskultur*, in *Publikationen aus den Preussischen Staatsarchiven* (Berlin, 1887), 4:45f. The rejecting vote of the General Directory (signed by Hardenberg and Schroetter among others) does not by a long way have the meaning of a simple act of hostility to reform, in the feudal interest, as Jacques Godefroy Cavaignac suggests (*Formation de la Prusse contemporaine* [Paris, 1891], 1:164). The positive proposal for reform is nevertheless worthy of attention over and above the emphasis placed on the practical difficulties—difficulties that this plan, like the Edict of 1807, did not solve but merely skirted—such, e.g., as the question of compensating serf owners, which came up again during the regulation of the whole question, and the irreconcilability of the plan with the so-called

"peasant protection." The vote came from Goldbeck's pen, or one of his councilors.

14. The Chancellor, Count Finckenstein—until then, and (as later appeared) in the future also, an inveterate opponent of reform—took charge of the negotiations of the deputies in Königsberg. One deputy was taken from each of the twelve rural districts; then the matter was to be debated in the district assemblies (*Kommissorium* for Finckenstein, October 11, 1802). Schroetter, who had clearly been mistaken about Finckenstein, was full of confidence as regards these negotiations; whereas Beyme from the first disliked the great machinery of deputies and assemblies, which he feared would thwart the plan.

15. The deputies were inclined to throw out the whole thing so as not to prejudice their class equals. They united finally on a few proposals to be presented to the district assemblies, but since these were a very long way short of the provincial government's requirements, the government did not even trouble to convoke the district assemblies. The deputies wished, for instance, to concede that all children born after the promulgation of the law should be free but that they should be obliged to do *corvée* duty until their twentieth year. The other serfs were to be freed progressively over forty years, as selected by their lord, but only after paying sums of money. By contrast, the government proposals were as follows: 1. No free man may return to serfdom (conceded by the deputies); 2. All children born after the day of homage are to be free; 3. All soldiers are free after twenty years' service. (These points recurred in the draft decree of February 6, 1803.)

16. There are no indications in the documents as to the King's motives. Possibly the failure of the plan had something to do with the appearance of a pamphlet, "On the Abolition of Serfdom in Prussia," which was passed by the censors in Königsberg on January 1, 1803, but shortly afterward forbidden. It obviously provoked the anti-reform members of the nobility, at the head of whom was Chancellor Finckenstein. On February 9 the Königsberg publisher approached the royal Cabinet with a request for lifting of the prohibition. The pamphlet went yet farther in its demands even than the draft before the King. It was obviously inspired by Oberpräsident von Auerswald, a fervent champion of the cause of reform in East Prussia: at least, a memorandum he gave to Beyme on the same subject, of August 12, 1802, was largely reproduced in this pamphlet. Among the rural population of East Prussia the rumor gained ground, as in 1798, that the King wished to abolish all serfdom but was being opposed by the civil authorities and the landowners. On occasion there were riots in the summer of 1803; and the press, too, got hold of the affair (*Gothaer Nationalzeitung*, as Schroetter told Beyme on August 24, 1803).

17. Knapp, 2:97.
18. *Ibid.*, p. 101.
19. *Ibid.*, 1:137, 184.

20. On Frederick the Great's attitude toward the acquisition of manors by non-nobles see Johann David Erdmann Preuss, *Friedrich der Grosse* (Berlin, 1834), 3:78ff. The King's policies had taken this direction since 1749. The Edict of February 18, 1775, which deprived the non-noble manor owners of certain honorary seignorial privileges, in fact reveals that earlier the King had permitted non-nobles to own and to purchase these manors where this was beneficial to the former owner. This practice was retained. Again, the withdrawal of seignorial privileges—which was given statutory basis afterward by a special Declaration (*Novum Corpus Constitutionum Prussico-Brandenburgensium 1775*, no. 3, p. 65)—concerned only those non-noble landowners who had bought a manor subsequent to the Edict of February 18, 1775. In East Prussia the Estates desired the suspension of this prescription, which had been inserted in the Prussian Legal Code (Part 2, par. 9, sec. 59) and in the final version of the provincial Code: as the Estates declared, "it would secure a minor aim at the expense of a major one and create injurious tension." The Great Chancellor was then instructed in this sense (Cabinet Order of October 20, 1798, to the General Directory). The Cabinet Order of June 14, 1785, which simply forbade non-nobles to acquire manors (*Nov. Corp. Const. Marchicarum*, vol. 7, no. 39, p. 3145), did not remain in effect after the King's death.

21. Ewald Friedrich von Hertzberg, *Historische Nachricht von dem ersten Regierungsjahre Friedrich Wilhelm III*, p. 9; and Friedrich August von der Marwitz, *Nachlass* (Berlin, 1852), 2:257. These accounts are largely confirmed by the documents: as early as November 24, 1786, Frederick William II issued a Cabinet Order to permit a non-noble to buy a manor, and declared therein that he was by no means disinclined to permit this sort of thing in the future, except that "proper relations" between nobles and non-nobles must be upheld. For this purpose the General Directory was to cooperate with the Department of Justice in ascertaining how many estates were in noble hands, how many in non-noble. Whether this happened I am unable to discover. The King later found the requests too numerous, and in a Cabinet Order of February 27, 1787, charged the fief department with examining these requests; they were to be passed on for royal approval only in such cases as seemed likely to meet with it. Purchase was to be sanctioned whenever it was required to preserve the noble and his family—which was of course the case in a large majority of the transactions (Edict of July 30, 1787). Frederick William III largely accepted the principle of non-noble purchase, except for tenants who were lessees of parts of the royal domain (Cabinet Order to Schroetter of January 26, 1801, and many later ones), and merchants trading in the towns, such as Stettin. The degree to which non-nobles acquired estates in the two reigns can be seen through tables in the Stettin *Staatsarchiv* (St. A. P.1. Tit. 77, no. 624). According to these tables, 61 manors were owned by non-nobles in Lower Pomerania in

1790; in 1804 the figure was 106. In the district of Züllichau, in the New Mark, even in 1781 non-noble estate owners accounted for a third of the whole (*Geh. St. A. Generaldir. Neumark, Landräte*).

22. I have been unable as yet to find out whether freedom of occupations was discussed in the various preliminary studies for the Code of Laws.

23. By the Privy Financial Councilor, von Knobloch.

24. In Potsdam in 1802 a Grenadier-Guard still with the colors had a metal button factory of his own, with a number of assistants. On a complaint about this, Struensee described it as illegal, since the owner bore no civil burdens. Nonetheless, he passed the matter on for decision by the King. The King decided that the Grenadier should keep his enterprise but should in future be bound to carry the usual civic burdens.

25. It had at first been estimated at 850,000 taler; the Commission's report of November 24, 1798, put the figure at 550,000 taler.

26. Cf. his proposals in Colmar von der Goltz, *Rossbach und Jena* (Berlin, 1883), pp. 88f. The officers with whom the King personally discussed this were Courbière and L'Estocq.

27. For this reason official researches were unsuccessful.

28. *Hamburger Neue Zeitung*, October 23, 1798.

29. Letter to the King from the knights of the Crossen district, December 28, 1798; of the Lebus district, January 27, 1799 (among signatories was Count von Finckenstein); of the Oberbarnim district February 5, 1799; of the Uckermarck and Stolpirisch districts February 28, 1799. Von Heyden, Councilor for Affairs of the Nobility (Camnitz bei Konitz) proposed a luxury tax, in a letter to the King of November 16, 1798; and the same was recommended also by certain members of the Financial Commission.

30. Minutes of Conference November 7, 1798.

31. Commission Report November 24, 1798.

32. The following dispositions were made: 1. suspension of all formerly existing exemptions from Excise (of the Court, nobility, and so on); 2. suspension of exemptions from river tolls, licensing and lock dues, grain exports (for the domain administration, monasteries, manors, noble estates); 3. raising of consumption duties on foreign wines; 4. raising of the supplementary Excise, though not as regards basic necessities. Noble manor owners were exempted from the Excise not only on their estates, for farming and consumption there, but also in the towns, if they lived there. This privilege was based, in the Electoral Mark, on the 1653 Rescript and on an Edict of Frederick William I of December 29, 1736 (Mylius, *Corp. Const. March.* IV, 3, 2, no. 84), the prescriptions of which were largely reproduced in the Excise Regulation of May 3, 1787, 11, sec. 2. Exceptions were made, for reasons of trade policy, as regards "highly taxed" goods (Edict of June 24, 1734). A difference was made in this sense between "tax" and "consumption excise"—the "tax" was to be paid by the nobility as well. In some respects, however, this was not

strictly carried out: the nobility had no Excise to pay, particularly on foreign wines and coffee (Rescript of December 20, 1764, *Geh. St. A.*, Declaration of June 19, 1778, *Novum Corpus Constitutionum*, 1778).

33. Letter to the King from the Lebus Estates, January 27, 1799, rejected by Cabinet resolution of February 11. There was a further letter of March 23:

The knights know that from their number is taken the corps of officers, this first and most important part of the army. How can they fail to feel deeply injured when they hear it alleged that it is the army and not the knights that hazard life and limb in the defense of the fatherland? This the nobles still do at all times, and still deserve the privileges they inherited from their ancestors.

Estates of the Niederbarnim district of March 9, 1799; the Oberbarnim district of March 31, 1799; the Halberstadt Estates of April 6, 1799; the County Mark Estates, April 26, 1799; the Estates of Minden, May 9, 1799 (*Geh. St. A.* 89).

34. Cabinet Resolution March 23, 1799.

35. Commission Report December 20, 1799 (Salt: Heinitz against Struensee); December 17, 1799 (Excise, inland tolls); December 14, 1799 (balance of payments).

36. "12. This I desire abolition of these 'land tolls,' which are as onerous as they are futile. They cut off one province from another, hamper trade, lay burdens on it, and bring in little revenue." The Financial Commission agreed that this was possible. The financial loss was estimated at about 100,000 taler. Struensee's oft-quoted remark on the difficulties of reform as communicated in Held's character sketch (e.g., Ernst von Meier, *Die Reform der Verwaltungsorganisation unter Stein und Hardenberg* [Leipzig, 1881], p. 132) was made in the context of this relatively simple affair.

37. By the prohibition on import of foreign manufactures to the Frankfurt Fair of 1800, which turned this fair definitively from an international to a Continental market—naturally a measure wholly justified by the massive, cheap English competition.

38. Report of December 17, 1799 (with appendices); Memorandum by Hoym of December 9, 1799; Memorandum by Heinitz, July 10, 1798, and others. From Borgstede's opinion we may take an interesting calculation of the cost of administration of the Excise, which shows that the high costs were not to be laid on the Excise system itself. By this account, these costs were 8⅝ per cent before 1766, 16½ per cent between 1766 and 1786, and 20 per cent in 1798.

39. Cf., for example, the Cabinet Order of August 21, 1802, in Magnus Friedrich von Bassewitz, *Die Kurmark Brandenburg* (Leipzig, 1860), 1:490.

40. *Geh. St. A.*, R. 89.

41. Minute Collection of the *Geheime Staatsarchiv*, 1805.

42. Reprinted in Georg Heinrich Pertz, *Das Leben des Ministers Freiherrn*

vom Stein (Berlin, 1849), 1:310ff. Pertz doubted whether Stein was the author. Thus also John Robert Seeley, *Stein, sein Leben und seine Zeit,* 1:207. A few parts seem to me nonetheless to come from Stein. The copy I have studied is from R. 80 of the *Geheime Staatsarchiv* and is a version prepared in the Chancellery.

43. This is, to my mind, the essential point in the Instruction, a new principle indicating the transfer to a ministerial system. The originator of the "provisional Instruction" was obviously Heinitz.

44. August Heinrich von Borgstede, of non-noble origin, and ennobled only later, was a Privy Councilor in the Department of New East Prussia, and one of Schroetter's most esteemed councilors. Shortly after the setting up of the Franconian department he was, by agreement between Hardenberg and Schroetter, attached to this department; he was merely to help its chief without any special task. From 1800 he was section chief in Voss's department. After Struensee's death in 1804 he was considered as successor to him; at the time he competed with Stein. They were obviously at odds with each other: for Borgstede, Stein was above all an Imperial Knight of aristocratic bent, while Stein and his friends—for example, the minister Angern—regarded Borgstede as no more than an ambitious and obedient bureaucrat. Borgstede later became a member of the Academy of Sciences, dying in 1824 and leaving an impressive library. His works include *Juristisch-ökonomische Grundsätze von Generalpachtung der Domänen in den preussischen Staaten* (Berlin, 1785), and *Statistisch-topographische Beschreibung der Kurmark Brandenburg* (Berlin, 1788).

45. Separate Opinion in the Financial Commission Report of December 30, 1799.

46. Memorandum of June 10, 1800.

47. The *Generalkontrolleur,* Count Schulenburg-Kehnert, whose relations with the royal Cabinet were close, was also a member of the General Directory without portfolio. He had so far had nothing to do with financial administration as such. His main task was to work out the annual financial *tableau* for the King (Secret Instruction of February 19, 1798, in Hertel, *Die Preussische Oberrechnungskammer, ihre Geschichte, Einrichtung, und Befugnisse,* Suppl. vol., pp. 3f.).

48. Likewise dated June 10, 1800.

49. Then chief of the important department covering southern Prussia, the Marks, and Pomerania, a later opponent of the reformers, the head "of the Junker Party in the Mark," as Schoen said.

50. This was, as in 1807, according to the Cabinet Order of April 26. Voss gave the King on March 10, 1807, a remarkable proposal for setting up a ministry of state with five functional ministers communicating with the King directly. (Leopold von Ranke, *Denkwürdigkeiten des Staatskanzler Fürsten von Hardenberg* (Berlin, 1877), 5:468.

51. This went together with the plan of leaving a chairman to deal with the ordinary business of the department, reserving matters of importance to

the Minister. This plan was drafted by Borgstede, perhaps on the model
of his position in the Franconian department.

52. Memorandum of June 28, 1800, with notes by Schulenburg, who was in
essential agreement.

53. Report to the King, with appendices by the Domain administration of
Clossow, July 6, 1800.

54. "Norm for Conduct of Affairs in the Electoral Mark, New Mark, Pomeranian and southern Prussian Department of the Royal General Directory,"
July 25, 1800 (Borgstede became chairman of this department). Also, "Rescript to the Pomeranian, Electoral Mark, and New Mark *Kammern*,"
August 25, 1800.

55. Report for the King of September 2, 1807.

56. Report for the King of November 4, 1801, April 20, 1802, January 16,
1804. The way in which affairs were conducted in Schroetter's department was somewhat different from that in Voss's, particularly with regard to the chairmanship.

57. Report to the King February 24, 1802. The new arrangements within
the department itself were not at issue here.

58. Rescript to the *Kammern* of the Old Prussian department.

59. Rescript to the *Kammern* of Mark, Cleves, and Minden, February
24, 1802.

60. The idea of combining the Excise administration with the *Kammern* occurs in the Instruction for the organization of New East Prussia (1796),
but it was not put into effect, for Schroetter could not come to any
agreed basis with Struensee on the method of combining. Schroetter
wanted a complete fusion, two sections being instituted (one concerned
with police, forests, domains, the other with taxation, direct and indirect), while Struensee wanted the Excise included under the affairs
of the *Kammern* as an integral part, but wished also to maintain
their existing relations with his own department. Voss raised the matter
again, with southern Prussia primarily in mind, in 1797, and accepted
Struensee's conditions. They submitted a joint plan in a report to the
King of March 5, 1800, proposing that the plan should be tried out in
Kalisch. The King accepted this on March 10; at his desire a second
trial was made in Stettin (Cabinet Order of April 12). The new arrangement did not turn out well in Kalisch, though in Stettin it did—except
that Heydebreck, the Stettin *Kammerpräsident*, wanted a complete
fusion, a plan Voss recommended to the King on March 12, 1802, and
was approved by him. This was in fact realized in the Compensation
provinces, where a decree of April 19, 1803 prescribed a fusion of the
Excise administration and the *Kammern*. With regard to this, Voss proposed to Struensee on February 2, 1804, a similar regulation for Kalisch
and Stettin, but Struensee replied negatively on March 17, alleging that
its usefulness was utterly problematical. After Struensee's death Stein
took up the matter once more, and entered into communication with

Voss and Schroetter. On November 3, 1805, he requested immediate fusion in southern and New East Prussia, and the King approved on November 12. On April 18, 1806, Voss, Schroetter, and Stein sent a joint report to the King containing draft instructions for the new combined provincial authorities for his approval; it was obviously drafted in the opinion that this fusion should gradually be extended to all the provinces. Stein therefore reserved it to himself to make the necessary proposals to the King. After a few trivial changes in the Instructions had been made at the King's desire, they were given the King's signature with the date May 5, 1806. Execution began on June 1. Unfortunately I have been unable to find a copy of the Instructions.

61. Cf. Ernst von Meier, *op. cit.*, pp. 47ff., and E. Loening in *Verwaltungsarchiv* 2:437ff.

62. That Church, school, and pauper affairs should be transferred to the administrative agencies was accepted in principle, though as yet it did not take place. Even then the description *Landesobergerichte* was being considered as a possible future name for the old *Regierungen* (provincial governments). (Goldbeck).

63. The essential features of this reform can hardly be more briefly and relevantly summed up than in Schroetter's words, in a letter to Beyer on September 2, 1800, when discussing his task of drafting a decree for the administrative reforms:

> The new organization comes largely from the intention not only of uniting all branches of financial and police administration in the *Kammern* but also of giving them greater freedom of action with regard to the conduct of their own affairs, and full responsibility in a wider frame of competence, as they themselves see fit, and without forcing them to refer to a higher authority. This will give greater unity, speed, and effectiveness to public administration.

This was exactly the idea that had underlain the reforms proposed by Borgstede and Voss. Otherwise we may add that the most important change in the organization of the lower branches of the civil service, apart from new arrangements in the towns, was the extension of districts of the Landräte to town and country, which happened even before 1806 in New East Prussia, the Franconian lands and the Compensation provinces; also, Schroetter had proposed on March 5, 1806, that this should be done in the whole of the Old Prussian department (Meier, p. 380). The establishment of a *gendarmerie* on the French model had also been proposed before 1806 (Meier, p. 388).

Calvinism and Raison d'Etat . . .
(pages 88–154)

1. *Acta Brandenburgica. Brandenburgische Regierungsakten seit der Begründung des Geheimen Rates,* vol. 1 (1604–5), ed. Melle Klinkenborg (Berlin, 1927).

2. "Oberlehrer am Altstädtischen Gymnasium zu Königsberg," *Hohenzollern-Jahrbuch,* 8 (1904): 92–142, 214–30.

3. For the history of this family in general, see the wealth of material in the privately printed *Aufzeichnungen über die Vergangenheit der Familie Dohna,* ed. Count Siegmar Dohna, 4 vols. (Berlin, 1877, et seq.)

4. Anton Chroust, *Abraham von Dohna* (Munich, 1896).

5. This view is not necessarily contradicted by the adverse remark made by Abraham Dohna in his Diary of the Diet of Regensburg on October 1, 1613, on the defective management of the Berlin court, in Chroust, *Abraham von Dohna,* p. 95. Moriz Ritter, in his *Deutsche Geschichte im Zeitalter der Gegenreformation, 1555–1648* (1889), 2:369, interpreted this passage erroneously and has been convincingly corrected by Chroust. It has been called to my attention by Germanic philologists that the proverbial expression "Man breaks jugs, woman breaks bowls" was used in carnival plays in the sixteenth century. Nevertheless John Sigismund was not a good household manager. But I should like to mention Chroust's remark that the dislike for overindulgence that distinguished the brothers Dohna was also praised in Johann Sigismund (as in Christian of Anhalt). The occasional drunkenness—as at the Königsberg meeting with the Palatine Count Wolfgang Wilhelm in 1613—ought not to lead to extravagant conclusions. In any case it was not so much Calvinism as the more refined French manners that militated against the then excessive drinking at the German courts, although the two are obviously related.

6. Max Posner, in *Miscellaneen zur Geschichte Friedrichs des Grossen,* (1878).

7. Carl Wilhelm Cosmar and C. A. L. Klaproth, *Der Königlich preussische und Kurfürstlich brandenburgische Geheime Staatsrat* (Berlin, 1805), p. 113; A. Stoelzel, *Brandenburg-Preussens Rechtsverwaltung und Rechtsverfassung* (Berlin, 1888), 1:312ff.

8. Apart from the above-mentioned interesting work by Chroust on Abraham von Dohna, a further fundamental book is D. W. Hering, *Historische Nachricht von dem ersten Anfang der evangelisch-reformierten Kirche in Brandenburg und Preussen* (Halle, 1778). This is also documentary evidence of the pious veneration given to the "God-loving" Johann Sigismund, and such veneration was still alive in Reformed circles in Prussia in the eighteenth century.

9. The Instruction was on December 17, the declaration on Communion on December 18, 1613, Old Style.

10. Melle Klinkenborg, "Die Entstehung der Geheimer Ratsordnung vom 13, Dezember 1904," in *Forschungen zur brandenburgischen und preussischen Geschichte,* 39 (1927):215ff.

11. Hassel, in the *Zeitschrift für preussische Geschichte und Landeskunde* 5 (1868):533.

12. *Acta Brandenburgica,* 1:26, no. 5.

13. Cosmar and Klaproth, *op. cit.*, p. 305.

14. Ibid., p. 305.

15. Klinkenborg's argument that the Elector had objected to the use of the term "steadfast" (*Standhaft*) in maintaining Hohenzollern rights in the Jülich succession is not very persuasive and is based on a misunderstanding of the word. *Standhaft erhalten* here means little more than *aufrecht-erhalten* (maintain) and is not an expression of any particular obstinacy in the policy to be pursued.

16. Klinkenborg contents himself with a reference to Moriz Ritter.

17. See my essay "Origins of the Modern Ministerial System" [See pp. 216–66 in the present volume.—*Editor*].

18. In Nicolas Viton de Saint Allais, *De l'ancienne France* (Paris, 1834), 2:149ff. (May 1588). Cf. also Paul Viollet, *Le roi et ses ministres* (Paris, 1912), pp. 247ff.

19. Noël Valois, introduction to the *Inventaire des arrêts du conseil sous le règne de Henri IV* (documents inédits), 2 vols. (Paris, 1886–92).

20. Hübner went first to the Danish Court but returned to the service of Brandenburg in 1613 after Löben's dismissal and was again employed in Prussian affairs.

21. Walter Koch, "Eine Denkschrift aus der Zeit des Kurfürsten Johann Sigismund," in *Forschungen zur brandenburgischen und preussischen Geschichte*, 26 (1913):65ff.

The Formation of States and Constitutional Development
(pages 157–77)

1. I shall go into this concept of *world empire* at a later stage, but I should make clear at this stage that I use the term in its older, historical sense: modern use of the word is different from this in one essential particular. By "world empire" I mean those states of ancient times and of non-European civilization which established a universal authority in an area they regarded as the known and inhabited world, and which recognized no other states as equal. In the European system of states and the world-state system in general, which is now being formed according to the European model, a world empire in this sense is not possible, since it would have to destroy the sovereignty of all other states. Today, although England has a world empire, it does not correspond to a world empire in the old sense. Today the word is used to describe states that have gone beyond their European basis by vastly extending their land, colonial possessions, and overseas interests—as has happened with England and Russia, and also with non-European Great Powers such as the United States. I should make it clear that these empires are different from the structures that I call "world empires" (*Weltreich*).

2. Friedrich Ratzel, *Politische Geographie* (München, 1897), p. 195.

3. Georg Jellinek, *Allgemeine Staatslehre* (1900), pp. 399ff.

4. Otto von Gierke, *Das deutsche Genossenschaftsrecht* (Berlin, 1881), vol. 3.

5. A view expressed time and again by Gneist in his various works.

6. Carl Rathgen, "Japans Volkswirtschaft und Staatshaushalt" (1891), in Schmoller's *Staats- und sozialwissenschaftliche Forschungen*, 10.4:13ff.

7. Leopold von Ranke, *Sämtliche Werke*, vols, 35–36.

8. Rathgen, "Die Entstehung des modernen Japan" (lecture), p. 5.

9. Rathgen himself has especially stressed this.

10. On the effects of this notion, see Ratzel's remarks, *op. cit.*, pp. 319ff.

11. I have in mind particularly the researches of Georg von Below, lately summarized in *Territorium und Stadt* (1900), in *Historische Bibliothek herausgegebe von der Redaktion der Historischen Zeitschrift*, 11:163ff.

12. The old cantons of the Swiss Confederation were political formations of a much older type than were the territorial states of the fourteenth and fifteenth centuries. They corresponded to the formation generally known elsewhere in German areas as *Land* (for instance, the numerous Frisian lands like Harlingerland, Brokmerland, the *Land* Stargard in Mecklenburg, and the *Land* Lebus in Brandenburg). These lands often possessed their own system of Estates and in many cases larger territorial states grew out of several such *Länder;* one might perhaps describe them as tribal states (*Gaustaaten*). Their French counterpart was the *pays*, which came from the old *pagi* (Pierre Adolphe Chéruel, *Dictionnaire historique*, art. "Pays").

13. Even the German Confederation belongs under this head; it was created on the model of the Confederacy of the Rhine, which had lost its monarchical head with Napoleon.

14. Jellinek, *op. cit.*, pp. 366ff.

15. Schmoller, in his *Jahrbuch*, 8:15ff.

The Origins of the Modern Ministerial System
(pages 216–66)

1. For the Royal Council in England, see the monograph by Albert Dicey, *The Privy Council* (London, 1887), based chiefly on minutes published by Nicolas. The earlier sections of Aucoc's famous work on the French Council of State have been rendered out of date by Noel Valois' brilliant introduction to the *Inventaire des Arrêts du Conseil, règne de Henri IV* (Paris, 1886), Book I.

2. This has been more closely examined in my study of court and provincial administration in Brandenburg under Joachim II, in the *Hohenzollern-Jahrbuch* of 1906.

3. This particular development doubtless occurred through the influence of the Polish example, for here the great court officials of the Crown had much the same position as Imperial Ministers. Moreover, the Swedish state officials present a similar type around 1600; cf. Nils Edén, *Den svenska centralregeringens utveckling till kollegial organisation 1602–*

1634 (Uppsala, 1902), pp. 2f. Of the same character are the Bohemian land officials, who, after the Battle at the White Mountain, developed into a Bohemian government authority, or the Prussian councilors who in the seventeenth and eighteenth centuries became a "Prussian government."

4. By Sir Harris Nicolas, in *Proceedings and Ordinances of the Privy Council of England*, vol. 7.

5. Cf. Harry Bresslau, *Handbuch der Urkundenlehre* (Leipzig, 1889), 1: 243f.

6. Nicolas, *Proceedings* . . . , 6:cxix ff., contains a full documentary account of the earlier Secretaries of State in England.

7. *A Collection of Ordinances and Regulations for the Government of the Royal Household* (quarto, London, 1790). An ordinance of Edward III's in 1347 gave the King's secretary in London a rank well below that of the great officials of the court, even below that of the royal doctor, equal with that of the royal surgeon and the kitchen-manager. According to an ordinance of Henry VI (1454), he has two clerics; they are ranked behind the knights but before the esquires. An ordinance of Henry VIII in 1526 gave him a rank among the Privy Councilors and the great officials of the court, placing at his disposal eight horses and three beds for his servants; in 1544 he acquired his own room in the palace, and was given a grant for his maintenance, in place of meals. Under Elizabeth his salary was one hundred pounds, excluding table money; at the end of the seventeenth century, when both were reckoned together, he was paid seven hundred and thirty pounds annually. At first, and until well on in the sixteenth century, these secretaries were priests. In the fifteenth century, as a mark of long service, they became bishops and were made keepers of the Privy Seal. It shows how the social position of the office was rising that Dr. Routhale under Henry VIII kept the office for many years even after being made bishop. Thomas Cromwell, First Privy Councilor and then in 1534 first Secretary, later became Keeper of the Privy Seal and peer of the realm; Sir William Cecil, who occupied the office under Elizabeth, became in 1571 Lord Treasurer and Peer of the Realm. Even so, at this time the office was in reality no more than a stage toward the great ministerial posts; only in the eighteenth century do Secretaries of State emerge in the role of ministers.

8. The work of the Comte de Luçay (*ancien maître des requêtes au conseil d'état*), *Les secrétaires d'état* (Paris, 1881), offers brilliant insight into the subject and is based on documentary research.

9. Claude Bernard Petitot, *Collection universelle des mémoires relatifs à l'histoire de France*, 1st series, 44:102ff.

10. Reprinted in Arthur Guillard, *Histoire des Conseils du Roi*, and in Nicolas V. de Saint Allais, *L'Ancienne France* (Paris, 1834), 2:149–60.

11. 1:1, 26f., 80.

12. In eighteenth-century France the business of Cabinet secretaries was

taken over by new *secrétaires des commandements*, who were entitled
to sit with the councilors at all councils but did not themselves become
ministers. In England it was not until George III's time that a special
Cabinet secretary again emerged, in 1812.

13. Gilbert Burnet, *History of the Reformation of the Church of England*
    (London, 1683), fol. vol. 2 (Coll. of Records), pp. 84f.

14. Reprinted in Julius Hatschek, *Englisches Staatsrecht,* in *Handbuch der
    öffentlichen Rechts,* 2: 108f.; *ibid.,* pp. 68f. for some remarks on the un-
    printed agenda of October 31, 1625.

15. Cf. Ernest Lavisse, *Histoire de France* (Paris, 1905), 7:139ff.; and Jean
    de Boislisle, *Mémoriaux du conseil de 1661* (Paris, 1905), vol. 1. For
    the later period the *Almanac royal* is also important.

16. *Politisches Testament* of 1752, in *Acta Borussica. Behördenorganisation,*
    9:369.

17. *Protokolle und Relationen des brandenburgischen Geheimen Rates aus
    der Zeit des Kurfürsten Friedrich Wilhelm,* ed. O. Meinardus, Publica-
    tionen aus der Preussischen Staatsarchiven, vols. 41 et seq.

18. Reprinted in Leopold von Ranke, *Sämtliche Werke,* 25/26:499ff.

19. *Acta Borussica. Behördenorganisation,* 9:370ff.

20. I might mention here the Handbooks of Austrian Imperial History—par-
    ticularly those of Luschin von Ebengreuth and Huber—and as well my
    own essay on the Austrian Council of State in the *Zeitschrift der Savigny-
    Stiftung für Rechtsgeschichte,* 8:137f.; also my comparative study of the
    Austrian and Prussian civil service in the seventeenth and eighteenth
    centuries, in *Historische Zeitschrift,* 86:402ff.

21. Von Hock-Bidermann, *Der oesterreichische Staatsrat 1760–1848.*

22. Torrens, *History of Cabinets,* 2 vols. (1894); Alpheus Todd, *Parliamen-
    tary Government in England,* 2 vols. (London, 1867); cf. also Hatschek,
    Englisches Staatsrecht, and Felix Salomon, *Pitt der Jüngere* (Leipzig,
    1901), vol. 1.

23. A few further notes will be relevant here, the more so as Count Luçay's
    book does not go beyond 1775 and as other works on the pre-history of
    the revolution scarcely consider this aspect of the matter (see R. Stourm,
    Les finances de l'ancien régime et de la Révolution, 2 vols. [Paris, 1885],
    and Adalbert Wahl, *Vorgeschichte der französischen Revolution,* 2 vols.
    [Tübingen, 1905–7], hardly touch upon this issue). The reforms were
    concerned mainly with the financial department. By an Edict of June
    1777 (François André Isambert: *Recueil général des anciennes lois
    français* [Paris, 1822], 25:50f.), six of the ten financial *intendances* were
    done away with—they had existed merely to assist the labors of the *Con-
    trôleur général*—so as to simplify organization and save money spent on
    salaries. Instead, a *comité du contentieux* was set up as the highest organ
    of financial administrative jurisdiction, consisting of three or four *Con-
    seillers d'état* under the *Contrôleur général.*

After the American War the Règlement of February 26, 1783

(Isambert, 27:256ff.), set up a smaller *Comité des finances* next to the *Conseil Royal des finances*, obviously intending to make a more systematic approach to the question of debts in general. Apart from the King, this was composed of the Chancellor, the chief of the *Conseil Royal des finances* and the *Ministre des finances*. The last prepared the material and had charge of dispatching and registering the resolutions adopted by the body. Apart from debts, the questions involved were such matters as extraordinary royal gifts, appointments, adjudication of tax farms, and the like. This council thus became to some extent a duplication of the financial council, and was held at least once every week. The *Conseil du commerce* by a Règlement of June 5, 1787 (Isambert, 6:354f.), became combined with the *Conseil du commerce*, a commission of the State Council that also met under royal presidency; the body thus created was termed *conseil royal des finances et du commerce*, and its members were the Chancellor, or *Garde des sceaux*, the *Chef du conseil*, the Ministers of State, the *Contrôleur général*, two *Conseillers d'état*, and as well, in commercial matters, the Secretary of State for Marine. Sessions of this body were held at least once every month. A preparatory committee consisting of the *Chef du conseil*, the *Contrôleur général*, and several councilors met at least once a fortnight. This *Comité des finances* took the place of the *petite direction*. The entire financial department was arranged in five specialist departments, presided over by four financial intendants and an *intendant du commerce*. This arrangement recurred in the subsequent finance ministry (*Almanac* for 1790).

By a Règlement of February 2, 1788, a special *Bureau du commerce* was set up as a preparatory commission and an executive organ for the financial and commercial department, governing all questions of trade and colonial policy, factories and manufactures, markets, fairs, and the like. It conducted correspondence, compiled statistics, took charge of all current administrative business. The members were State councilors, the most senior of whom was President; under him there was one session per week; and every quarter there was a session in the presence of the ministers and members of the *conseil*.

24. *Collection générale des loix, proclamations, instructions et autres actes du pouvoir exécutif, publiés pendant l'Assemblée nationale constituante et législative depuis la convocation des Etats généraux jusqu'au 31 décembre 1791* (quarto) 1:1. The "affaires contentieuses, qui étaient portées par les secrétaires d'Etat au Conseil des dépêches," were in future to be decided in a committee similar to that set up in 1777 for the financial department. See Note 23.

25. P. 222.

26. *Décret relatif à l'organisation du Ministère, 27 avril 1791, sanct. 25 mai 1791*. See *Collection des décrets de l'Assemblée nationale*, 7:265ff. The most important of the other relevant documents are to be found in Hélie's collection, *Les constitutions de la France*.

27. I intend to go farther into the rise of the Prussian ministerial system at another place, but for the moment I should mention Philip Zorn's monograph, *Die staatsrechtliche Stellung des preussischen Gesamtministeriums* (1893). Gneist has opposed his arguments in an essay on the subject that appeared in the *Verwaltungsarchiv*, vol. 3 (1894).

The Commissary and His Significance
(pages 267–301)

1. Cf. Gustave Schmoller, *Acta Borussica. Behördenorganisation*, Introduction to vol. 1; Kurt Breysig, "Die Organisation der brandenburgischen Commissariate," *Forschungen zur brandenburgischen und preussischen Geschichte*, 5:135ff.; Friedrich Freiherr von Schroetter, "Die brandenburgisch-preussische Heeresverfassung unter dem Grossen Kurfürsten," Schmoller's *Staats- und sozialwissenschaftliche Forschungen*, 11 (1892): 5, in particular 79ff.; Prince August Wilhelm of Prussia, *Die Entwicklung der Kommissariatsbehörden in Brandenburg-Preussen*, Strassburg diss. (Berlin, 1908).

2. Ernst Meier, *Die Reform der Verwaltungsorganisation unter Stein und Hardenberg* (Leipzig, 1881), pp. 197ff.

3. Gabriel Hanotaux, *Origine de l'institution des Intendants des Provinces d'après les documents inédits;* with a selection of these documents, pp. 179–369 (Paris, 1884).

4. Before beginning their work as ordinary officials, Sully and his assistants traveled around the country as commissaries. The *superintendants* who appear here and there in earlier history seem to have received commissary appointments only. We might note a parallel phenomenon in Austria under Maximilian I, although this does have a special feature of its own: the five superintendents of the financial administration, which the *Hofkammerordnung* of February 13, 1498, envisaged as itinerant control commissioners (art. 5, reprinted in Sigmund Adler, *Organisation der Zentralverwaltung unter Maximilian I* [Leipzig, 1886], and recently also in T. Fellner and H. Kretschmayr, *Die Oesterreichische Zentralverwaltung* [Wien, 1907], vol. 2). This information is based on a fragmentary memorandum, mentioned by Adler (pp. 509 f.)—not, as he supposes, of Dutch origin, but clearly the work of an official familiar with conditions in Burgundy and France. There is no evidence that such superintendents existed even in Burgundy before 1493. (See Andreas Walther, *Burgundische Zentralverwaltung*, p. 182.)

5. Cf. Georg Bernard Depping, *Correspondance administrative sous le règne de Louis XIV* (Paris, 1850), vol. 1; Albert Babeau, *La Ville sous l'ancien régime* (Paris, 1880); Schmoller's essays on the reform of municipal administration in *Zeitschrift für preussische Geschichte und Landeskunde*, vols. 10–12.

6. George Desdevises du Dézert, *L'Espagne de l'ancien Régime* (Paris, 1897), p. 134.

7. *Danmarks Riges Historie*, 4:628 (Fridericia).

8. Henrik Hildebrand, *Svenska Statsförfattningens historiska utveckling* (Stockholm, 1896), pp. 412f.

9. Cf. Max Jähns, *Geschichte der Kriegswissenschaften* (Munich, 1864), 2:1061: "Für die Verhältnisse der Verwaltung und Verpflegung wurden vornehmlich die Erlasse der französischen Krone vorbildlich, welche unter den europäischen Grossstaaten zuerst eine systematische Administration durchzuführen vermochte."

10. Fr. Ludovico Melzo (a Knight of Malta born in Milan), says in his *Regole militari sopra il governo e servitio particolare della cavalleria* that the office of General Commissary was created under Charles V by Ferdinand Gonzaga and retained by Alba and Parma: it was a combination of the duties of a General Quarter Master and General Auditor, and its occupant was also the representative of the Lieutenant-General. See Jähns, *op. cit.*, p. 1050.

11. In Andreas Walther, *Die burgundische Zentralbehörden unter Maximilian I und Karl V* (Leipzig, 1908), I have found a quotation from a documentary source, according to which a Burgundian fiscal official, Guillaume Normand, was used in 1507 as *"commissaire des monstres et revues de la gendarmerie de par deça"* (p. 81). The Burgundian ordnance companies were an imitation of the French; may we not also presume that recruiting officers also existed there? I have been unable to find further information on this. *Commissaires de guerre* appear frequently in the later *Almanacs royaux* of the eighteenth century, and are clearly in subordinate positions.

12. *Acta Borussica*, 2:383ff.

13. *Les six livres de la République de J. Bodin*, Angevin (Paris, 1577), fol. pp. 306ff. [The following quotations are from the English translation by M. J. Tooley, *Six Books of the Commonwealth* (New York, 1967)—Ed.]

14. The *pièces justificatives* printed by Hanotaux show that this practice was still common in the seventeenth century. For in the only two of the many documents listed that mention sealing, we are told that they are sealed with yellow wax. Thus, No. 17 (p. 256): "Pouvoir donné à M. Le Cogneux sur la justice et sur les finances en l'armée commandée par Monsieur" (August 29, 1627)—*"scellé sur simple queue de cire jaune"*; and No. 24 (pp. 279ff.): "Commission aux sieurs de Chasteauneuf, Conseiller d'Estat, de la Thuillerie et d'Estampes, Maistres des requestes, pour avoir l'administration e l'intendance de la justice et police, direction des hospitaux en l'armée de debvant la Rochelle de laquelle M. le Cardinal de Richelieu est lieutenant-général" (February 9, 1628)—*"scellé du grand sceau sur simple queue de cire jaune."* These documents were, moreover, not in the form of *lettres patentes* but were sent only to the officials concerned; there were, however, but a few earlier cases where intendants were given their commissions in the form of *lettres patentes:* cf. No. 1, pp. 179ff.

15. Toward the end of this chapter Bodin returns to the question of the dissolution of offices, and gives examples from Parliament registers he studied, showing that large numbers of official positions were more often created all of a sudden by a single edict. This occurred for sixty *sergents,* whose posts were created through an edict made public in Parliament in April 1544, and for the new criminal judges, whose office throughout the land came into being through an edict of 1527. Even the office of *langayeur des pourceaux* (examiner of pigs' tongues) was *érigé en tiltre d'office* by a special edict, approved and registered by Parliament in July 1544 (Bodin quotes the registers of the Parliament of 1544 particularly frequently: clearly this was a year of which he made a systematic study). The formal edict sealed with green wax was necessary only for the creation of the office itself; appointment of successors in an already existing office did not require this formality.

16. This happened in 1356–57; cf. Marcel Viollet, *Histoire des institutions politiques et administratives de la France* (Paris, 1890–1912), 3:211f., and the sources quoted.

17. The *commissaires du Châtelet de Paris* are clearly meant here. They later appeared as *commissaires des quartiers,* the familiar Paris police commissaires of the *Ancien régime,* copied by Frederick the Great in Berlin. They are fully dealt with in Delamare, *Traité de la police* (2nd ed., 1729), 1:170ff. On the title page he describes himself as *Conseiller-commissaire du Roy au Châtelet de Paris,* and is obviously anxious to raise the dignity and prestige of this office by alleging it to be age-old. The earlier title of these officials was *commissaires enquêteurs et examinateurs;* they were sixteen in number, corresponding to the sixteen districts of Paris. Francis I doubled the number, and gave them the simple title of *commissaires* in 1521; Henry III increased their number in 1586 to forty, retaining this title. They must originally have been assistants of the *Prévôt de Paris,* who could also refer judicial matters to them for decision through a *committitur.* Delamare would seem to be attacking Bodin, without naming him, when he states that these officials had always been *officiers* (apparently to enhance their importance), though he offers no proof of this.

18. Ord. du 21 octobre 1467, Isambert 17:25f.; cf. Viollet, *op. cit.,* 3:324ff.

19. Bodin (p. 315) quotes Celsus against Innocent III (*1.17 De officio praesidis, D.1, 18*): "Si forte praeses provinciae manumiserit vel tutorem dederit priusquam cognoverit successorem advenisse, erunt haec rata." The references given in the context of Innocent III's observations do not in fact seem to have much bearing on the point. In the *cap. qualiter de accus. ext.* (Decretals of Gregory IX, V, tit. 1, De accusationibus cap. 24 qualiter et quando) I can find nothing relevant to the matter, nor in 2 X, De restitut. spoliat, XIII, nor in 2 X, De probat. XIX, 3. Moreover, in both these latter, it is not Innocent III but Lucius III who is cited. At all events, it is important that "the strict law" seems based on canoni-

cal sources, while the common-sense consideration for equity was based on the analogy of Roman law.

20. The royal power according to the formula he did not have to mention: *le Roi ne meurt pas.* He bases himself on the declaration of the Paris Parliament of April 19, 1498, that the King exerts his sovereignty immediately on his predecessor's death, and even before the anointing.

21. Cf. nevertheless Mommsen, *Römisches Staatsrecht,* 2:613ff., and *Abriss des römischen Staatsrechts,* pp. 186ff., on "extraordinary magistrates."

22. For this aspect, see chiefly Schmoller's introduction to vol. 1 of *Acta Borussica. Behördenorganisation,* pp. 15–46; also Hermann Rehm, "Die rechtliche Natur des Staatsdienstes," in Georg Hirth's *Annalen des Deutschen Reiches,* 17:572.

23. History and sources of Canon Law in Holtzendorff's *Enzyklopädie der Rechtswissenschaft* (5th ed., 1890), pp. 205, 321; cf. Paul Hinschius, *Kirchenrecht der Katholiken und Protestanten in Deutschland* (Berlin, 1869–97), 2:364ff.

24. Andreas Walther, *Die burgundische Zentralbehörden,* shows this clearly.

25. I. 5 and 6 De iurisdictione, D. II, 1, 5: "More maiorum ita comparatum est, ut is demum iurisdictionem mandare possit, qui eam suo iure, non alieno beneficio habet"; 6: Lapsing of the mandate for jurisdiction with the death of the mandator, presuming *res integra.* I. 5C. III, 1 De iudiciis: "A iudice delegatus iudicis dandi non habet potestatem, cum ipse iudiciario munere fungatur, nisi a principe iudex datus fuerit."

26. Hinschius, *op. cit.,* 1:171ff.

27. I.32 sec. 3 Cod. Iust. VII, 62 De appellationibus; I.16 Theod. XI. 30 De appellationibus. It is noteworthy that in both places *delegare* appears as a *terminus technicus,* while in the Digests *mandare* is used. *Delegare* is also the canonical term.

28. Cf. also Moritz August von Bethmann-Hollweg, *Der Civilprozess des gemeinen Rechts in geschichtlicher Entwicklung* (Bonn, 1864–74), 6: 86f.: "Für die höchste und allgemeine Gerichtsbarkeit des Papstes bot abermals (unter Alexander III und seinen Nachfolgern) das römische Recht der Kaiserzeit die erwünschten Formen in der Appellation, der willkürlichen Annahme von Rechtssachen in erster Instanz, den Reskripten auf Anfragen von Beamten und der Ernennung ausserordentlicher Kommissarien (*iudices delegati*), durch welche er in die ordentliche Diözesangewalt der fernsten europäischen Länder entschiedend eingreifen konnte. Cf. *ibid.,* 2:112; 3:181.

29. Julius Ficker, *Forschungen zur Reichs- und Rechtsgeschichte Italiens* (Innsbruck, 1868), 1:300ff., 307, 343, 345f.

30. Otto Franklin, *Das Reichshofgericht im Mittelalter* (Weimar, 1869), 2: 49–61.

31. Ducange fails us here, remarking only, "Commissarius generatim is est, cui negotium quoddam curandum creditur v.g. causa disceptanda, lis dirimenda, tuenda in provinciis Regis auctoritas . . . ," and pointing to

the French *commissaire*. The old French dictionaries lead no farther. Godefroy denotes *commissier* as the older form; Delamare's claim (*Traité de la police*, 1:177)—that *commissarius* first appears in an ordinance of Louis IX in 1254—I cannot verify, since no reference is given for the statement. His own hypothesis, that *commissarius* was related to *missus*, and meant "co-envoy" (*committere = simul mittere s. simul iungere*) since plenipotentiaries were always sent in groups of two or more, will hardly stand. The basis is of course *committere* in the sense of *mandare, delegare* (cf. also *Vocabularium iurisprudentiae romanae*, s.h.v.) and the noun derived from it, *commissio*, meaning the task and the powers of the *commissarius*. In England the word took the form *commissionarius* ("commissioner"), as e.g., in the example cited by Ducange from the time of Queen Elizabeth (in Rymer, *Foedera*, 15: 505, col. 1): "Assignavimus vos commissionarios nostros ad tractandum, communicandum et componendum cum omnibus et singulis subditis nostris . . . ." The feudal designation *commissio, commissum*, meaning punishment by confiscation of the fief, has a different origin.

32. Stölzel, *Die Entwicklung des gelehrten Richtertums in deutschen Territorien*, 2 vols. (Stuttgart, 1892); cf. *Brandenburg-Preussens Rechtsverwaltung und Rechtsverfassung* (Berlin, 1888), 1:30f.

33. Eberhard Gothein, *Der gemeine Pfennig auf dem Reichstage zu Worms* (Breslau, 1875), pp. 32, 35.

34. Fellner and Kretschmayer, *op. cit.*, 2:22, no. 1.

35. Viollet, *op. cit.*, 3:254ff.

36. Ibid., 3:261ff.

37. Heinrich Brunner, *Deutsche Rechtsgeschichte* (Leipzig, 1887), 2:189ff.; also V. Krause, "Geschichte des Instituts der Missi dominici," in *Mitteilungen des oesterrischen Instituts für Geschichtsforschung*, vol. 9.

38. Cf. Heinrich Rudolf Gneist, *Englische Verfassungsgeschichte* (Berlin, 1882), pp. 224f.; W. Stubbs, *Select Charters*, pp. 22f.; and F. W. Maitland, *Constitutional History of England* (Cambridge, 1908), p. 69.

39. Heinrich Brunner, *Entstehung der Schwurgerichte* (Berlin, 1871), pp. 70ff.

40. Viollet, *op. cit.*, p. 262, and Note 2.

41. Charles Petit-Dutaillis, in Lavisse, *Histoire de France*, (Paris, 1902), 3, ii, 36.

42. On these cf. Hanotaux, *op. cit.*, pp. 4ff.; and de Boislisle, "Les chevauchées d'un maître des requêtes en Provence 1556," in *Revue des sociétés savantes* (1881).

43. Viollet, *op. cit.*, 2:223f., and 3:311, 349; Adhémar Esmein, *Cours élémentaire d'histoire du droit français* (Paris, 1895), p. 441.

44. See above, Note 3; Delamare, *op. cit.*, vol. 1.

45. There are many examples in Gilbert Jacqueton, *Documents relatifs à l'administration financière en France de Charles VII à François I.*, in Collection de Textes pour servir à l'étude de l'histoire (Paris, 1891).

46. *Ibid.*, p. 246, note.
47. *Ibid.*, pp. 25f.
48. *Ibid.*, p. 27.
49. *Ibid.*, p. 87.
50. *Ibid.*, p. 107.
51. *Ibid.*, pp. 61ff.
52. *Ibid.*, pp. 61f.
53. *Ibid.*, pp. 204, 272.
54. *Ibid.*, p. 180.
55. Federigo Sclopis, *Degli stati generali e d'altre istituzioni politiche del Piemonte e della Savoia. Saggio storico corredato di documenti* (Torino, 1851), pp. 79, 125, 131, 137, 164, 168, 173, 181, 214, 223, 233, 250, 261, 299, 317, 328.
56. Ernst von Meier, *Hannöversche Verfassungs- und Verwaltungsgeschichte* (Leipzig, 1898), 2:390ff.
57. *Danmarks Riges Historie*, 4:229; Dietrich Schäfer, *Geschichte Dänemarks*, 5:663f.
58. Viollet, *op. cit.*, 3:504.

The Preconditions of Representative Government
(pages 302–53)

1. Friedrich Tezner, "Technik und Geist des ständisch-monarchischen Staatsrechts," Schmoller's *Staats- und sozialwissenschaftliche Forschungen*, vol. 19 (1901).
2. Otto Hoetzsch, "Adel und Lehnswesen in Russland und Polen . . . ," *Historische Zeitschrift*, 108:541ff.
3. Otto Hintze, "Soziologische und geschichtliche Staatsauffassung," *Zeitschrift für die gesamten Staatswissenschaften*, vol. 86, no. 1.
4. "Wesen und Verbreitung des Feudalismus," Sitzungsberichte, Akademie der Wissenschaften in Berlin (1929), pp. 321–47.
5. Henrik Marczali, *Ungarische Verfassungsgeschichte* (Tübingen, 1910), p. 23. In like manner to the basic ideas of the 1222 "Golden Bull," the tradition of the Hungarian "Original Treaty" of 890, whose remarkable similarity to the lengendary Aragonese *Fuero of Sobrarbe* has already been stressed by Fritz Kern, *Gottesgnadentum und Widerstandsrecht im frühen Mittelalter* (Leipzig, 1914; p. 370), may also have been influenced by the Aragonese model.
6. Konstantin Josef Jirecek, "Staat und Gesellschaft im mittelalterlichen Serbien," in Wiener Akademie, *Denkschriften der philosophisch-historischen Klasse*, vols. 55–56 (1912).
7. Maxim Kovalevsky, *Russian Political Institutions* (Chicago, 1902); cf. Karl Stählin's recent work, *Geschichte Russlands* (Stuttgart, 1923), 1:379ff.
8. Joachim Marquardt, *Römische Staatsverwaltung*, 1:503ff., in *Handbuch der Römischen Altertümer*, vol. 4 (Leipzig, 1873).

9. Conrad Luebeck, *Reichseinteilung und kirchliche Hierarchie des Orients bis zum Ausgange des 4. Jahrhunderts. Ein Beitrag zur Rechts- und Verfassungsgeschichte der Kirche* (Münster, 1901), in *Kirchengeschichtliche Studien*, vol. 5, no. 4.

10. Tertullian, *De ieiunio* 13: "Aguntur per Graecias illa certis in locis concilia ex universis ecclesiis, per quae et altiora quaeque in commune tractantur et ipsa *repraesentatio totius nominis Christiani* magna veneratione celebratur" (*Hintze's italics*).

11. *Concordantia catholica*, Book 3.

12. Georg von Below, *Der deutsche Staat des Mittelalters* (Leipzig, 1914), pp. 243ff.

13. See *op. cit.*, "Wesen und Verbreitung des Feudalismus."

14. Cf. my essay, "Typologie der ständischen Verfassungen," in *Historische Zeitschrift*, 141:229–48.

15. *Esprit des lois, livre 11*, chap. 6.

16. Erwin Hölzle, *Die Idee einer altgermanischen Freiheit vor Montesquieu*, (München, 1925), in *Historische Zeitschrift*, Suppl. 5.

17. P. 1.

18. *Reallexicon der indogermanischen Altertumskunde* (Strasbourg, 1901).

19. Jacob Spieth, *Die Ewestämme* (Berlin, 1906), pp. 102ff. (quoted in Wilhelm Wundt, *Völkerpsychologie*, 8:298); cf. also Richard Thurnwald, "Social Systems of Africa," in *Africa; Journal of the International Institute of African Languages and Civilization*, 2:204f., under "Touareg Tribes."

20. In the Teubner collective work, *Die Kultur der Gegenwart*, in the section *Allgemeine Verfassungs- und Verwaltungsgeschichte*, pp. 3ff.

21. See *op. cit.*, Kern, *Gottesgnadentum* . . . .

22. Kurt Wolzendorff, *Staatsrecht und Naturrecht in der Lehre vom Widerstandsrecht des Volkes*, in *Untersuchungen zur Deutschen Staats- und Rechtsgeschichte*, vol. 126 (1916).

23. *Capitularia I., Concilium Vernense*, c. 4.

24. Heinrich Brunner, *Deutsche Rechtsgeschichte* (1st ed., Leipzig, 1887; 2nd ed., Leipzig, 1906), 2 (i): 231–2 (ii): 178.

25. *Teoria de las Cortes o grandes Juntas nacionales de los Reinos de Leon y Castilla*, 3 vols. (Madrid, 1813). There is unfortunately nothing about this in Eduardo de Hinojosa, *Documentos para la historia de las instituciones de Leon y de Castilla* (*siglo X–XIV;* Madrid, 1919); nor in Ernst Mayer's *Historia de las Instituciones sociales y politicas de España y Portugal* (Madrid, 1925). On Aragon, where the relation was the same: De la Fuente, *Estudios criticos sobre la historia y el derecho de Aragon*, 3 vols. (Madrid, 1884-86), 3:42f., 63; and Tourtoulon, *Jaime I le Conquérant roi d'Aragon* (Montpellier, 1867), 2:175.

26. Felix Liebermann, *Die Gesetze der Angelsachsen* (Halle, 1916), subject index, under "Bischöfe."

27. Julius Hatschek, *Englische Verfassungsgeschichte* (München, 1913), pp.

308ff. Cf. Pollard, *The Evolution of Parliament* (2nd ed., London, 1926).

28. George Walter Prothero (against Riess), in *English Historical Review*, 5:148ff.

29. Hatschek, *op. cit.*, pp. 192 and 314ff.

30. William Stubbs, *Select Charters* (Oxford, 1913), pp. 512f.

31. Hatschek, *op. cit.*, p. 315.

32. *Ibid.*, pp. 209ff.

33. Georg von Below, *Territorium und Stadt* (München, 1900), pp. 163ff.; 2nd ed. (1923), pp. 53ff.

34. Vol. 2, i; cf. Gottfried Friedrich Hermann Rehm, *Geschichte der Staatsrechtswissenschaft* (1896), p. 179.

35. *Concordantia catholica*, I, III, c. 18; I, 48–122 on ephors.

36. Cf., in particular, Althusius, pp. 29ff.

37. Akos Timon, *Ungarische Verfassungs- und Rechtsgeschichte*, German ed. (Berlin, 1909).

38. George Walter Prothero, *Select Statutes and Other Constitutional Documents Illustrative of the Reigns of Elizabeth and James I* (Oxford, 1913), p. 178 (from Thomas Smith, *Commonwealth of England*). Cf. also Introduction, cxxiv.

39. Pischel and Lüders, art. "Kasten," in *Handwörterbuch der Staatswissenschaft*, 3rd ed., 5:798ff.

40. W. Stieda, in *Handwörterbuch der Staatswissenschaft*, 3rd ed., 2:196ff.

41. *Wirtschaft und Gesellschaft*, in *Grundriss der Sozialökonomie*, 3.2:543ff.

42. If we are to regard the Polish *jus militare* as something like feudalism, then we should have to see it as feudalism without either benefice or vassalage. In reality it represented a ministerial service relation, and even then existed only for a short period of time, for it was speedily absorbed into the more general privileges during the thirteenth and fourteenth centuries.

43. Kutrzeba, *Grundriss der polnischen Verfassungsgeschichte*, German ed. (1912), p. 31.

44. K. Asakawa, *The Documents of Iriki; Illustrative of the Development of the Feudal Institutions of Japan* (New Haven, 1929), particularly pp. 37–79.

45. *Ibid.*: index, "Han."

46. Karl Rathgen, "Japans Volkswirtschaft und Staatshaushalt," in Schmoller's *Staats- v. Sozialwissenschaftliche Forschungen*, vol. 10 (1891).

47. Tokuzo Fukuda, *Die gesellschaftliche und wirtschaftliche Entwicklung in Japan* (Stuttgart, 1900), in *Münchener Volkswirtschaftliche Studien*, vol. 42.

48. P. O. von Tischendorf, *Über das System der Lehen in den moslemischen Staaten, besonders im osmanischen Staate* (Leipzig, 1871). Further, Carl Heinrich Becker, *Islamstudien*, 1 (Leipzig, 1924), particularly No. 9, *Steuerpacht und Lehnswesen*, pp. 234ff.

49. *Ibid.*, pp. 528ff.

50. This is borne out by the importance of heraldry and of war cries, and the emergence of the *banderye rodowe*. Kutrzeba, *op. cit.*, pp. 31ff., 144.

51. Cf. my essay "Typologie der Ständischen Verfassungen."

52. Max Weber, *op. cit.*, pp. 528ff.

53. Emil Hildebrand, *Svenska Statsförfattningens historiska utveckling*, (Stockholm, 1896), pp. 162ff.

54. Kutrzeba, *op. cit.*, pp. 26ff.

55. Timon, *op. cit.*, pp. 154, 227ff.

56. Marczali, *op. cit.*, pp. 35ff.

57. Milyukov, *Skizzen russischer Kulturgeschichte*, German ed., 2 vols. (Leipzig, 1898–1901).

58. Kovalesky, *op. cit.*, pp. 65ff.

59. See my remarks on feudalism.

60. Léon Cadier, *Essai sur l'administration du royaume de Sicile sous Charles I et Charles II d'Anjou* (Paris, 1891). I should also point out that in Aragon the great General Privilege of Saragossa of October 3, 1283, which gave a firm basis to the Estates' liberties, was a consequence of the union of the Estates against King Pedro III, who had taken over Sicily without asking the Estates' advice and had thus also come into conflict with the Pope—which led to Aragon's being placed under interdict. L. Klüpfel, *Verwaltungsgeschichte des Königreichs Aragon* (Stuttgart, 1915), pp. 192ff.

Troeltsch and the Problems of Historicism
(pages 368–421)

1. *Der Historismus und seine Probleme,* Book I: *Das logische Problem der Geschichtsphilosophie* (Tübingen, 1922). See also *Deutscher Geist und Westeuropa;* Gesammelte kulturphilosophische Aufsätze und Reden, ed. Hans Baron (Tübingen, 1925), and *Der Historismus und seine Überwindung, Fünf Vorträge* (Berlin, 1924).

Economics and Politics in the Age of Modern Capitalism
(pages 422–52)

1. In an essay entitled "Der moderne Kapitalismus als historisches Individuum," in *Historische Zeitschrift,* 139 (1929).

2. In *Economic History Review,* 2.1 (1929).

3. *Collection des documents inédits sur l'histoire économique de la Révolution,* pp. 1908ff.

4. *La France économique et sociale au XVIIIe siècle* (1925), and *La vie économique et les classes sociales en France au XVIIIe siècle* (1924).

INDEX

The index lists persons and subject matter mentioned in the text of Hintze's essays.